THEOLOGY AND CHURCH

THEOLOGY
AND CHURCH

SHORTER WRITINGS 1920-1928

✦

KARL BARTH

Translated by
LOUISE PETTIBONE SMITH

With an Introduction (1962) by
T. F. TORRANCE
*Professor of Christian Dogmatics
in the University of Edinburgh*

HARPER & ROW, PUBLISHERS

NEW YORK AND EVANSTON

Translated from the German
Die Theologie und die Kirche (Gesammelte Vorträge 2)
Evangelischer Verlag AG, Zollikon-Zürich
(original edition, Munich 1928)

CONTENTS

INTRODUCTION (1962)
by T. F. Torrance

KARL BARTH is the greatest theological genius that has appeared on
the scene for centuries. He cannot be appreciated except in the context
of the greatest theologians such as Athanasius, Augustine, Anselm,
Aquinas, Luther, Calvin, Schleiermacher, Kierkegaard, nor can his
thinking be adequately measured except in the context of the whole
history of theology and philosophy. Not only does he recapitulate in
himself in the most extraordinary way the development of all modern
theology since the Reformation, but he towers above it in such a way
that he has created a situation in the Church, comparable only to the
Reformation, in which massive clarification through debate with the
theology of the Roman Church can go on. Karl Barth has, in fact, so
changed the whole landscape of theology, Evangelical and Roman alike,
that the other great theologians of modern times appear in comparison
rather like jobbing gardeners.

Who is he?

Karl Barth is a native of Switzerland, born and brought up in the
home of a Swiss pastor who when Karl was but two years old became
a Professor of Church History in the University of Bern. It was in
Bern that Karl Barth grew up and went up to University to study
philosophy and theology, and from there he went on to the Universities
of Berlin, Tübingen, and Marburg. After spending some twelve years
in the pastorate, mostly in the Alpine village of Safenwil in Aargau, he
was called to be Professor of Reformed Theology in Göttingen. Then
after more than a decade of teaching and debating in the Universities
of Münster and Bonn, in which he was the living centre of a volcanic
disturbance in the whole field of theological thinking, and the great
mind behind the German Church's struggle for survival against
National-Socialism, he was ejected from Germany, and found refuge
in Basel, the city of his birth, where he was appointed to the chair of
Dogmatics, which for centuries had been occupied by some of the
greatest thinkers of the Reformed Church.

What is he like?

Perhaps more than any other theologian of modern times Barth
resembles Luther in his sheer *Menschlichkeit*. That is to say, he has an
overflowing love for all things *human*, whether they are the simplicities

of natural life or the great achievements of the human spirit, in the midst of which he manifests a frankness, and childlikeness, and sincerity toward other human beings, which can be both gentle and rough, but always with compassion. His whole attitude to life, and even to theology, is expressed in his passionate love for the care-free, light-hearted music of Mozart, in which the profoundest questions are put to the eternal and the creaturely alike without the dogmatic presumption to any final answer or last word, and it is to the accompaniment of Mozart's music that his engagement in the hard work of dogmatics becomes sheer enjoyment of the majesty and beauty of God.

In the depth of this humanity Karl Barth has a fundamentally *scientific cast of mind*—the mind of eternal inquiry, relentlessly probing into everything he finds, not in order to master it or to show off his own powers over it, but to listen to it, to learn from it, to let it declare itself to him, to teach him how to articulate understanding of it sincerely and faithfully in accordance with its own inner nature and necessity and beauty. That is the humility of the scientist who will not impose theory arbitrarily upon what he investigates, but is always ready to reconstruct what he already thinks he has learned in order to make it possible to learn really new things. It is the eye of the artist who has the faculty of seeing what is actually there and can pick out its deepest and most characteristic forms with which to depict it and communicate it so that his own creative art is allowed to be the instrument of the reality of his subject. All Barth's theology is characterized by relentless, irresistible questioning that uncovers the artificiality that constantly prevents us from attaining objectivity, and therefore has the most disturbing, critical effect in shaking the foundations, but only in order that the fundamental realities may be revealed and that genuine theological thinking may be built up on the concrete actuality of God's revelation in Word and Act.

The basic concern of Barth is, however, not critical but *positive*. In spite of the fact that he is the great enemy of all attempts at constructing rational systems, that is, at imposing systematically upon the subject-matter of theology a rational schematism of our own devising, his is the most constructive and systematic of minds, but it is a mind that finds the co-ordinating principle of its thinking not in its own dialectic but in the forms of rationality inhering in the object or in the material content of theological knowledge. It is in order to uncover this objective depth of rationality that he employs such ruthless, tireless questioning in which he goes round and round the point he seeks to elucidate, interrogating it at every possible angle and every possible level, refusing to break it up into parts in order to master it, so that at last it can stand out in all its own objective and independent nature and form. Behind all this lies a passionate will to sympathy for what he investigates, whether it be the text of Holy Scripture, the concrete matter of some doctrine, or the mind of another theologian, and throughout the readiness to let himself be criticized by what he learns: that is to say, an openness or readiness of mind both for God and for man; and a determination to let God be God, man be man, and nature be nature.

Another aspect of Barth's *Menschlichkeit* or humanity is his irrepressible *humour*. What we are concerned with here is the theological significance of this, for Barth's humour plays a fundamentally critical role in his thinking. He is able to laugh at himself, and therefore to criticize himself, and hence also to direct his ruthless critique at others in such a way that he can appreciate their intention and respect their persons and their sincerity. Here he stands out in marked contrast to the seriousness with which nineteenth-century man took himself, and indeed to those today who make such heavy, boring play with what they call 'modern man'. But above all Barth's humour has critical significance for the nature and form of his own theological construction, for it means that he is ever open to the question as to the adequacy of his own thought-forms to their proper object, and that he will never let himself be a prisoner of his own formulations.

One can perhaps describe the critical significance of humour for Barth's theology by recalling a Rembrandt painting, with its terrific concentration of illuminated significance in the centre, its contrast of darkness and light, and objective depth, but with the humour of a cherub peeping over at it from a corner of the canvas, unable to suppress a smile. In other words, Barth engages in his gigantic task of dogmatics with the consciousness that the angels are looking over his shoulder, reminding him that all theology is human thinking, and that even when we have done our utmost in faithfulness to what is given to us, all we can do is to point beyond and above to the transcendent truth and beauty of God, thereby acknowledging the inadequacy of our thought in response to God's Word, but engaging in it joyfully, in gratitude to God who is pleased to let himself be served in this way by human thinking and to bless it in his grace.

One more aspect of Barth's humanity we must note is its *genius*. That is to say, it is a humanity that is full of surprises. Here, although no doubt he would resent it, we may compare his theological thinking

to the music of Beethoven with its breath-taking turns rather than to
the predestined texture of Mozart's inimitable compositions. Mozart
may well be the greater genius, but when he has announced his theme
and swept you into the skies like a lark, he creates in you the power of
anticipation and you can hear the music from a long way off, and
Barth certainly has that quality, too; but again and again Beethoven's
music suddenly breaks in upon your ear with astonishing novelty that
startles you, and you protest that he has shattered the logic of his
composition, but before you can recover your breath you find that he
has worked the whole symphony into such a rich and complex movement that the new element actually contributes to its unity. That also
is the genius of Karl Barth.

Again and again his contemporaries have spoken of a 'new Barth', and
have described him as a bird on the wing, darting like a swallow into
quite new directions, and yet they have not taken the measure of the
depth and complexity of this man's thought, or of the immense fertility
of his fundamental simplicities which enable him to hold within a profound unity elements which in other lesser minds fall apart into contradictions or hopeless antinomies. The reason for this is the incredible
intensity with which Barth holds all his thinking in obedience to its
object—the Lord God, the infinite and eternal, who has stooped to
reveal himself in Jesus Christ and in him has taken us up to share with
him his own divine life.

How did it all begin?

It took its rise in the struggle of the young minister with the Word
of God in an Alpine community composed largely of agricultural and
industrial workers. Sunday by Sunday Barth was faced with the problem of bringing the Word of God to a waiting congregation expecting
to hear, not the minister's views or those of the Church, but God's own
Word.

The problem was twofold. How could he preach a genuine Word of
God, and not just his own word? How could the congregation hear it
as Word of God and not confound it with something they wanted to tell
themselves? The problem was made more difficult for the minister by
the fact that he knew he must be a man whose heart is steeped in his
own times, who is sensitive to the needs of his own times, who shares
with his contemporaries their life, their problems, their hopes, who is,
in fact, identified with them. But the extent of that identity made it
difficult for him to remain free enough for the Word of God, to come

under its mastery, to be a pliant instrument in its hands, and so to be
the voice of its proclamation to the people.

How could he distinguish an independent Word of God from his
own ideas and wishes, and distinguish the objective reality of divine
revelation from his own subjective states and conditions? How could
he communicate it and really be heard in a Church in which Christianity is already so deeply assimilated to a way of life that the message
proclaimed from the pulpit is inevitably heard only as an expression of
that way of life? If something really new and different is actually proclaimed, will not the people just blink and turn away, like a cow staring
at a new gate, as Luther said so long ago?

The preacher was confronted by an immense difficulty, within him
and within the congregation, a problem created by the fact that Christianity had become so assimilated to the bourgeois culture of modern
man that everywhere it appeared as a manifestation of that culture. No
doubt the world of the nineteenth- and early twentieth-century Europe
had been profoundly influenced by Christianity, and yet Christianity
had become little more than an aspect of the historical life of European
civilization; the Church had become so much world that it was no
longer able really to stand over against it and bring a genuine message
to the world. What it had to say and do fitted in only too well with what
people wanted and desired: like people, like priest; like nation, like
Church; like culture, like theology.

Faced with this problem, Barth did two things. He spent a good
part of his week wrestling with the Scriptures, notably with Ephesians,
Corinthians, and Romans, struggling to grasp the Word within the
words, and letting it attack and criticize himself. But he threw himself
into the activities of the social democrat party at work in his parish,
in order to identify himself with his people, to gain an understanding
of their political and social problems, to become one of the proletariat
with a sympathetic understanding for them. On the one hand, he sought
to identify himself with the Word of God, and on the other hand, he
sought to identify himself with his people.

Two discoveries followed. Barth's wrestling with the New Testament and especially with the Epistle to the Romans opened up for him
what he called the strange new world within the Bible—and what did
that for him most of all was the mighty voice of St Paul to which he had
hitherto been largely a stranger. This was the discovery of the supernatural nature of the Kingdom of God, of the Word of God as the
mighty living act of God himself that came breaking into the midst of

man's life, setting it into crisis, shaking its false foundations, and bringing to bear upon it the very Godness of God. This Word came to Barth with such force, as divine Event, that it refused to be integrated with anything he knew before, objected to being assimilated to the culture in which he was so profoundly steeped, but rather called it into question. It was a Word that interrupted his thoughts, and forced him into dialogue with God; it was a Word that attacked the secularization of Christianity, and uprooted his convictions, re-creating them and giving them an orientation from a centre in God rather than in man. Here was the sharpest clash between the Word of the transcendent Creator God, and the word of man which he seeks to project into God out of the depths of his own self-consciousness. It is the Word of God directed to man that brings a message that is utterly new, and at the same time reveals the nature of man as the creature directly addressed by God and summoned within his historical existence to live his life not out of himself but out of God.

The other discovery was the infinite love and compassion of God, who in spite of his infinite transcendence and distance, condescends to man in order to share his deepest agony and hurt, and to heal and reconcile him and restore him to the Father. The Word of God is certainly the Word of judgement, that searches us out to the roots of our being, and pierces through all artificiality, and thwarts every attempt on man's part to make himself out to be divine or to deck himself out in divine clothing. But it is above all a Word of reconciliation—and a mighty victorious Word at that, the Word of the all-conquering love of God that will not be put off, but that insists on achieving its end. For that very reason it is a Word with a total claim upon the whole of man's existence, and one that will not allow any part of it to elude God's creative and redeeming purpose. Far from being an abstract Word, it is *the* Word that strikes into the depths of human existence, that encounters man in the midst of his actuality, and approaches him as the concrete act of God in human history.

Barth took both these two poles of his discovery with deep seriousness, and bent all his energies and talents to bring the Word as he heard it to bear directly upon the life and thought of his people as he understood them. It inevitably meant a clash with the idealistic conceptions of the social democrats—not that he was any the less concerned with their social passion, but that he could not go with them in identifying the Kingdom of Christ with the social order of life for which they struggled. This very alliance of his revealed all the more intensely the

deep malaise of the Church, its assimilation of the Gospel to the bourgeois culture of the nineteenth and twentieth centuries, and showed
him that the message of the Gospel could only be brought to bear upon
man in that condition when a hiatus was torn between the Gospel and
culture, when God could be heard in his divine Word in such a way
that it did not imperceptibly become accommodated to a word that
man had already heard and could just as easily tell to himself.

Out of this pastorate at Safenwil came Barth's notorious *Commentary
on the Epistle to the Romans*, in two editions, one following hard on the
heels of the other. It was designed to bring the Word of God heard
through the mighty voice of St Paul home to the Church in such a way
that it was allowed to storm its way through the barriers and ramparts
built up against it by the self-assertion of man clothed in the garb of
historic Christianity. It was an attempt to wrestle with the Gospel of
the New Testament in such a way that the walls of history that separated
its writing from the present became transparent and the Gospel shone
through directly in its uninhibited and apocalyptic force upon Church
and world, and above all upon civilized, cultured, religious man.

The first edition aroused such attention that it brought—to his utter
surprise—the call to the chair of Reformed theology in Göttingen,
which he could not avoid, much as he would have liked, but meantime
he had been rewriting his Commentary, which he completed just as he
left for Göttingen. It was with the publication of this second edition
that the storm broke, for the commentary was an all-out assault upon
Neo-Protestant Christianity and Theology.

It succeeded far beyond Barth's expectations, for it created, or rather
was the means of creating in God's hands, the seismic disturbance that
changed the whole course of modern theology, and made it face as
never before since the Reformation the basic message of the Bible.
From beginning to end it challenged theology to consider the sheer
Godness of God and the downright humanity of man. Therefore it
penetrated down to the foundations of modern religion and theology,
laid bare its accommodation to the pantheistic and monistic background
of romantic-idealistic philosophy and culture, and sought to cut the
strings of that connexion wherever it found it in every shape and form,
in order to make it possible to think cleanly and soberly of God in a
way appropriate to God, and of man in a way appropriate to his nature
as man and child of God. It had to assert, therefore, the infinite qualitative distance between God and man, the sheer transcendence of the
Word of God addressed to man plumb down from above, the absolute

newness of grace, and therefore the judgement and crisis that it brought
to all human religion.

The Commentary created upheaval for Barth as well as for his contemporaries—and that was necessary, for he, too, needed still to be
uprooted radically and replanted by the Word of God. Much of the
criticism he let loose bounced back upon him, and he was not slow to
see its relevance to his own position, for he did not flinch to wield the
same sword against himself. But in the midst of the upheaval and fer-
ment, he was able to see the way ahead, and to start out upon the work
of clearing the ground that occupied the next ten years, of ploughing
and sowing, and reaping and ploughing again. And all the time the
academic debate was being matched by engagement with the developing crisis in Germany, in the struggle of a resurgent naturalism, em-
powered by natural theology, against the Gospel which flung the
Church up against the wall, where it had to learn again the meaning
of the majesty and uniqueness of God: 'I am the Lord thy God, thou
shalt have no other gods before me', and also the majesty and uniqueness of Jesus Christ, the Son of God: 'I am the way, the truth, and the
life; no man cometh unto the Father but by me.'

It was during these ten years that the essays and lectures published
in this volume, *Theology and Church*, were written and delivered. In
them we can see how Barth's mind moved as he set out from the
second edition of the *Romans* to travel the road toward his life-work,
the construction of the *Church Dogmatics*, in which evangelical and
reformed theology of the Word is given its most massive and formidable
expression, not only over against the Church of Rome, but within the
context of the growth and development of all theology in ancient and
modern times, in the East as well as in the West. Whether or not contemporary theology agrees with Barth, it cannot avoid the questions he
has raised, or avoid dealing with the situation he has created. If advance
is to be made, it will not be by going round him, but only by going
through him and beyond—and yet since Barth's theology is so deeply
integrated with the whole history of dogma, any attempt to go through
and beyond him must ask whether it may not be trying to leave the Christian Church behind. It may well be that Barth's ultimate influence upon
the whole Church will be comparable with that of Athanasius.

The purpose of this introduction is not to expound the positive
content of Barth's mature theology, but to reveal the context in which
it is to be understood, to show the direction in which it has moved,
and to indicate the great concerns in connexion with which it has been

elaborated. In order to do that we shall have to consider the movement of his thought through the period covered by this volume up to the point where, in 1931, he made his final orientation before settling down to the writing of his *Church Dogmatics*. But to map out the road he has travelled and to make clear the difficulties he had to overcome, as well as to show the relevance of his theology for the whole of modern life and thought, we shall consider his theology in relation to Culture, to the positive task of the Church in proclaiming the Word of God, and then the relation, as Barth sees it, between theology and philosophy, and between theology and science.

1. Theology and Culture

Barth was nurtured in the positive evangelical theology of the Reformed Church, and from end to end his thought continues to reveal the masterful influence of Calvin upon him, and from behind Calvin, the influence of Augustine, the two greatest 'idealist' theologians, as he has called them, in the history of the Church. And yet, as we shall see, Barth's own theology is basically realist.

Early in his University training Barth came under the spell of Kant and Schleiermacher, and began to find congenial the theological movements which in the first decades of this century fell within the orbit of their influence. But in Germany Barth had to come to terms with the teaching and influence of Luther and Aquinas—with Luther because of the great revival of Luther studies and the dominating influence of the Lutheran Church; and with Aquinas because he had to think his way through the theology of the Reformation over against Roman and Thomist theology. There can be no doubt that Kant, Schleiermacher, Luther, and Aquinas—with a strong dash of Kierkegaard—constantly came into his reckoning, not only because of their exposition of ethics and doctrine, but because of the European culture which they have so effectively influenced.

No one has appreciated more than Barth the colossal task of the Christian Church during the last three hundred years in giving intelligent and intelligible expression to the Christian faith in the midst of the greatest advances in the history of civilization. An effort on the part of the Church that could measure up to the astonishing developments in the sciences and arts was required, an achievement of the human spirit within the realm of religion comparable to the achievement of the human spirit in its triumph over nature. That was the task undertaken by Schleiermacher early in the nineteenth century, undertaken with a genius that matched the brilliant culture in the midst of which he lived, and indeed widely regarded as the finest expression of that culture. Schleiermacher's work affected the whole of the rest of the century, for generations of theologians, whether they followed Neo-Kantian or Neo-Hegelian tendencies, or broke out into more psychological interpretations of the Christian faith, built upon what he did, and even Roman theology absorbed not a little from him. In this development Christianity was set forth as the most sensitive quality of modern civilization, and the religious consciousness it mediated was looked upon as the holy flame in the innermost shrine of culture. Intellectually, the Christian faith was looked upon as a necessary and essential element in the development of the human mind, and its doctrines as rational determinations of social and ethical structure. Hence there grew up that profound assimilation of Christianity to culture and culture to Christianity that poured over from the nineteenth into the twentieth century.

According to Barth, there was a fundamentally right intention in this development, for the Christian Gospel must be articulated within the understanding of men, and must be communicated to the age in such a way that it is addressed to it in the midst of its spiritual and mental growth, and its literary and artistic creations. But what a task the Church had to face in addressing itself to the age of Kant and Hegel, of Goethe and Schiller, and many others, not to speak of the world of music and art! The theology of the nineteenth century manifested a responsibility for modernity which, Barth declares, we can hardly respect enough—but in making it its supreme task to speak to the age, it so accommodated its teaching to the masterful developments of the age, above all in romantic-idealist philosophy and in the natural sciences, that it came near to betraying itself altogether. Indeed, in the steady resolve not to interpret Christianity in such a way that it would conflict with the methods and principles of historical and scientific research or philosophical reflection, it lost a grip upon its own essence as theology and became basically anthropocentric, and so was unable to serve the advance of culture as it desired, for it had no positive word to say to culture which that culture did not already know and had not already said to itself in ways more congenial to it. That is the sickness unto death that lies behind so many of the troubles of Europe—the fatal collapse in ethics manifested in the first world war and later, the atheistic insistence that theology is nothing but anthropology, and that God is but the projection of man's own ego or the objectification of his own dreams or desires, the materialism of the Marxist recoil from idealistic religion, the strange terrible lapse back into baalistic nature-mysticism and nature-religion with its arbitrarily deified principalities and powers and dominations. It is the naturalization of the Church and the divinization of nature that follows upon the confusion of God with nature or the confusion of God with reason. Behind it all Barth sees the corrupting influence of 'natural theology'.

In order to throw the problem into clear relief we may note three (among other) elements in this assimilation of Christianity to culture and its romantic-idealist background which Barth sought to expose.

(*a*) In seeking to conquer the consciousness of the age on its own ground theology undertook a radical reinterpretation of Christianity in terms of *inwardness*. This took two forms. On the one hand, a sharp dichotomy was posited between what Schleiermacher called the *sensuous* and the *spiritual*, while Christianity was interpreted in terms of a developing ascendency of spirit over nature. Hence what needed to be carried out in the nineteenth century was a basic re-editing of those sensuous elements in the Christian tradition which appeared to belong to a more primitive stage of development, and a reinterpretation of them in terms of spirit and pure consciousness. On the other hand, spirit came to be regarded rather as the *insideness of things*, and therefore as the *other side* of material objectivity and as correlated to nature. In either way there came about a direct identity between the Holy Spirit of God and the spirit of man or such a mutual reciprocity between the two that it amounted to identification in practical and theoretical elaboration. Hence the development of Neo-Protestant thinking from the Enlightenment and Pietism into the combination of rationalism and subjectivity, so characteristic of idealism, was looked upon as the emergence of the real essence of the Reformation, that is, through a discarding of the objective elements in the teaching of the Reformers and a denigration of them as survivals of Catholicism. But what this really meant was that Christianity was interpreted only as the inner side of the developing culture of the nineteenth century, and was treated as of only aesthetic and symbolic significance. It was thus inevitable that Christianity should come to be regarded as a harmless musical overtone in the mighty symphony of science or as an anachronistic survival of the past that could only hinder scientific progress in the present and future.

(*b*) But if Christianity was to play any part in this developing culture it had to take its due part within the field of scientific study. It was in the realm of history that the overlap of theology and science was to be found, so that a scientific theology was pursued as the critical reflection and interpretation of historical religious self-consciousness, that is, as Troeltsch expressed it, the self-interpretation of the spirit so far as it is a matter of its own productions of itself in history. God himself is not objectifiable, for he does not give himself as such to our experience, but what is given to us is an awareness of him in the experience of the individual and of the community in the form of determinations of historical consciousness. It will be the task of theology to reflect upon that, to dig out and sift out the ideas embedded in that history and reinterpret them as living co-determinants of the human spirit in the present. Thus scientific theology will be concerned with historicism, with the investigation of the objective events of history and with an interpretation of historical ideas.

That may be carried out through an attempt to examine the whole history of the Christian Church and of its doctrine and to penetrate into some fundamental *essence* of Christianity as the kernel of it all, as Harnack sought to do, or it may take the way of interpreting the Christian Religion in the context of and in the light of universal religion with a view to eliciting the basic religious a-priori which enables us to understand and interpret this inner side of the development of the human spirit. It may take a speculative form in which the crude realistic narrative form of the Christian faith as it has been handed down from early times is to be stripped away like a garment grown too tight in order that the timeless essence or the ideas embodied in it may be allowed to emerge into the open. Or it may take a more existentialist form in which the outward events and their realist interpretation in terms of the acts of God in space and time are looked upon as mythological expressions of a deeply significant way of life, and therefore they are not to be stripped away but either reinterpreted in modern scientific myths as more adequate vehicles of meaning or employed as occasions and challenges to attain the same kind of authentic existence that the creative spirituality of the early Church revealed when it threw up these significant mythological forms traditionally called doctrines.

What is all this in the end but to subject Christianity entirely to history on the one hand and so to subordinate it to its relativities and transiencies, and on the other hand to co-ordinate it, not rationally, but by some 'existential leap of faith' with another realm of 'meaning' which is neither susceptible of conceptual articulation in its own right, nor amenable to rational criticism and investigation? And what else can this lead to but to the identification of Christianity with the basic *Weltanschauung* or attitude to existence that already lurks in the prior understanding of 'historical man'? And what has this to do with the Gospel, that is, with genuine *news* communicated to man, for is it not, after all, something that natural man can hear from himself through existentialist analysis, something that is inseparable from a secularized culture?

(c) But there is another line of development that must be noted, not one concerned so much with history considered as the product of man's creative spirituality or with the existentialist fear of rational criticism, but with a psychological analysis and interpretation of the religious self-consciousness that is deliberately pursued as an extension of the Cartesian line of thought—what Wobbermin called 'religio-psychological existential thought'. This is a line of thought which takes seriously the inter-relation between man's knowledge of God and his self-knowledge, and between his self-knowledge and knowledge of God, that is, the correlation between God and man, but it is one which thinks away the free ground of that correlation in God, takes its starting-point in man's immediate self-consciousness, and makes its ultimate criterion man's certainty of himself. Even if that means starting from a religious I-consciousness and returning to it as the criterion of certainty it involves a religio-psychological circle which is fundamentally 'vicious', for it has no objective ground independent of its subjective movement, and no point where its circular movement comes to an end, since the 'God' at the opposite pole is only the correlate of man's consciousness, and so points back to man for its testing and truth.

In all these different movements there is, insists Barth, a basic homogeneity of method from Schleiermacher to Bultmann, in which theological thinking takes its rise from a basic determination in the being of man, so that the only truth it is concerned with or can be concerned with is truth for man, truth which can be validated only by reference to his self-explication controlled by historical analysis of human existence. Two fundamental propositions are involved in this whole line of thought: *a*. Man's meeting with God is a human experience historically and psychologically fixable; and *b*. this is the realization of a religious potentiality in man generally demonstrable. These fundamental propositions remain essentially the same even if the idiom is changed to that of existentialism. It is this line of thought which throws up a theology in which the Church and faith are regarded as but part of a larger context of being and in which dogmatics is only part of a more comprehensive scientific pursuit which provides the general structural laws that determine its procedure, and so are the test of its scientific character. This means that theology can be pursued only within the prior understanding, and by submission to a criterion of truth, derived from a general self-interpretation of man's existence; so that theological activity is merely the servant of man's advancing culture, and the tool of a preliminary understanding which, as Bultmann has said, is reached 'prior to faith'.

The point where this line of thinking creates the most acute difficulty, Barth says, is in its interpretation of Jesus Christ, as we can see already in the theology of Schleiermacher, where it is evident that in spite of its Christo-centrism, Jesus Christ fits rather badly into the system. We can indicate this problem from another point of view, by noting the influence of French impressionism upon interpretation or the science of hermeneutics. Normally when one reads an author one understands what he says by looking *with* him *at* the 'object' to which he points or which he describes, but early in the nineteenth century there grew up the tendency to study the text of an author in its correlation with the 'subject' or the author himself rather than in its correlation with the objective reality he intended, and so to read it as an expression of his individuality or genius. It was largely under the influence of Schleiermacher, followed by Lücke and Dilthey, that theological interpretation made this fundamental change in direction, but it was an essential by-product of the romantic movement of the nineteenth century as a whole, and derived ultimately from the Renaissance.

Applied to the New Testament, however, this meant that the focus of attention was not so much upon Jesus Christ himself in his ontological reality as Son of God become man, or even as objective historical Figure, but upon the creative spirituality of the early Church which produced the interpretation of Jesus we have mediated to us through the New Testament, and only upon Jesus as the occasion or co-determinant of this religious consciousness. Hence the real function of the New Testament was held not to be the communication of divine truth and revelation, but to be the means of provoking us to discover and take up a similar way of life to that manifested by the first generation of Christians. The fact that their way of life was expressed in what must appear to us (it is said) crude mythological forms can only be a challenge to us to probe behind it all to the essential meaning that it enshrined. Looked at in this way, it becomes apparent that there is basically little difference between Schweitzer's insistence that we must use the apocalyptic portrait of Jesus in the Gospels like a painting of Van Gogh to help us 'tune in' to the *Weltanschauung* behind it all, and Bultmann's insistence that we must use the whole 'mythological framework' of the New Testament Kerygma as the occasion for an 'existential decision' through which we can reach *authentic existence*.

Barth's contention is that, apart from the questionable quasi-scientific character of this procedure, far from revealing the essential nature of the Gospel, it reduces it once more to an expression of transient human culture by correlating it to an independent and general anthropology. Schweitzer has shown so clearly, and Bultmann knows very well, that 'the historical Jesus' constructed by the scholars of the nineteenth century was a 'Jesus' dressed up in the thoughts and ideas of the nineteenth century and tailored to fit into the satisfactions of modern man, but because the Jesus reached in that way is always a construction of our own, that does not allow us to by-pass the objective reality of the historical Jesus Christ in order to focus our attention upon something fundamentally different—whatever we may call it, 'the anonymous spirit of Jesus', or 'authentic existence', or anything else— for in so doing we are projecting our own self-understanding in his place, substituting man's creative spirituality for the Word of God, and engaging in a new mythology. Does not all this mean that we have renounced rational knowledge of God, and are seeking to impose forms of our own upon 'faith' which we have drawn from the structures of historical existence and society as we have found them? Does all this carry us one step beyond Schleiermacher? Is it not rather a more dangerous and menacing subjectivism, if only because it thinks it is free from it? Thus Barth's historical studies will not allow him to think of the existentialist exegesis and existentialist theology as something apart, for it does not matter whether it derives its anthropology from Schleiermacher and his school or from Heidegger and his school—the fact that it subjects Christianity to a prior understanding of human existence reachable apart from revelation and faith, and so interprets the Word of God not out of its own objective rationality, but out of some special potentiality or knowledge alleged to belong to man as such, means that this theology is only a manifestation of secular human culture, and that what is essentially and distinctively Christian has been allowed to slip away like sand through the fingers.

It was especially in the second edition of the *Commentary on Romans*, as we have seen, that Barth launched his attack upon the false assimilation of Christianity to culture, and upon the immanentism and pantheism which that involved. What he sought to do was to create what he called a *diastasis*, a radical separation between theology and culture, which he felt to be eminently necessary if we were to think clearly again about God, and about man, and of their reconciliation in Jesus Christ. It was part of the intention of the *Romans* to free man's understanding of Jesus Christ from the prior understanding of culture which dragged him down into historical existence as interpreted by man himself, and to insist that a proper theological procedure involved an approach to him which let our previous understanding and naturalistic *Weltanschauungen* be called into question. It was an attempt to let God himself in all his justifying grace call the bluff of civilized European man, in order to induce him to think soberly, that is, in such a way that he learns to distinguish the objective realities from his own subjective states and conditions.

The intention of the *Romans* was by no means an attack on culture as such, but rather the opposite, upon a bogus mystification of culture which required to be disenchanted of its secret divinity before it really could be human culture. Thus the thinking of Barth at that stage was dynamically dialectical, for he sought to bring both the *No* of God against all man's attempt to make himself as God, and yet to bring the *Yes* of God's victorious love and mercy to bear upon man in his agony and despair in order that he might find healing, not in reconciling principles of his own devising, but in the reconciling grace of God alone. Already there is apparent in the *Romans* that immense emphasis upon *humanity*, as that to which God has directed his saving love, and to which we also in obedience to God must direct our attention in the humanity of our fellow men, but in the polemic to achieve a proper distance or diastasis the negative emphasis appeared, perhaps inevitably, greater than the positive.

Barth tells us in one of the prefaces to the *Romans* that the strangest episode that had befallen his commentary was its friendly reception by Bultmann and its equally friendly rejection by Schlatter! But that helped to open Barth's eyes to his own theological position, for he discovered how deeply he himself was engulfed in the very notions he had been attacking, in the idea, for example, that God and man are posited together in a sort of coexistence which did not allow man to think of God except in a reciprocal relation to himself, so that man's hearing of God and understanding of God itself belonged to the reality of the Word of God. Thus the ten years that followed the publication of the second edition of *Romans* were years of critical self-examination for Barth as he engaged in the many debates with Lutherans and Romans, orthodox confessionalists and liberal Protestants alike. Meantime the form of existentialism which he had himself advocated in the *Romans*, with its attendant notions such as of a timeless eschatology of pure event, had its measure of influence upon men like Bultmann and Gogarten, but while they moved on in the same direction, Barth moved out and beyond to make the centre and ground of his thinking the concrete act of God in Jesus Christ, not in any semi-pelagian correlation of God and man, but in the grace of God alone, which is the creative source and preservation of true humanity. It was on that ground that Barth set out eventually to build up a constructive theology, which laid the foundation for a genuine theological culture, without the confounding of God and man that is destructive both of good theology and good culture.

2. *Theology and the Church*

As we have seen, Karl Barth was concerned from the very start of his ministry with the problem of how to speak of God seriously to his congregation, and so to speak that in and through his speaking it was God's own Word that was being heard. He was convinced that such speaking is not an art that can be learned and mastered like some technique, for even when a pastor does his utmost to speak within the realm of revelation and faith, he knows that nothing he can do can make his very human speech to be speech of God. He is faced, therefore, with the perplexing situation in which he ought to speak God's Word and yet cannot speak God's Word, for he cannot speak it as God speaks it. Therefore if God himself is to be heard when man speaks in his Name that can only be a miracle—because it is not something that falls within human possibility, it is a possibility that is thinkable only at the point where man's possibilities come to an end. But that belongs to the minister's essential mission, to know that he cannot of himself speak God's Word, and therefore in his endeavour to speak what he has heard from God, he points away from himself to God in order to let God speak and God be heard not only in and through his attempts to proclaim God's Word but in spite of his attempts. Because it is God who has commanded him to speak in his Name, God will himself fulfil what he commanded, and in his grace employ human preaching in obedience to his Word as his own very Word to men.

Theology cannot be pursued on any other ground than that: the theologian's task is undertaken at the same command and in reliance upon the same grace in which God promises to make himself heard. But theology also has a critical task to perform. Just because God's grace abounds in the midst of human speaking about God, that does not allow us to sin or to err in order that grace may abound. Rather does God's grace lay such total claim upon us that we are summoned to responsible self-critical service of his Word, as those who have to give an account of their stewardship to God. Theology may thus be described as the critical activity serving the ministry of the Word of God in the midst of the Church. The Church must put its own preaching to the test to see whether it is really preaching of God's Word or simply a form of self-expression. Theology is the critical task that refers preaching back to its source in the Word of God, to make sure that it is really what is heard from God that is preached and not something that is thought out by man and thrust into the mouth of God.

All this meant that Barth had to clarify for himself the meaning of *revelation*. Early in his theological career he came to hold that in revelation God is actively engaged revealing himself and that the only God we know is this God who reveals himself, God-in-his-revelation, God-in-his-Word who comes to us, acts upon us, and summons us into responsible relation to himself. Concretely that means that God reveals himself in Jesus Christ, the Word made flesh, and that this revelation creates out of the world a community of those who hear and respond and who by the impact of that revelation become the realm within which God continues to reveal himself through his Word to the world. This is the line of positive thinking that Barth found himself building up throughout the polemical years from the beginning of his professorship at Göttingen to the end of that at Bonn. There are several important elements here that we may look at one by one.

In the first place, Barth held with increasing vigour that revelation is *act* of God, dynamic event impinging upon us. This was held in conscious contrast to the view of Schleiermacher that God is to be thought of from the side of man's feeling of utter dependence, rather than from the side of any active intervention on God's part—hence doctrines have their ground in the emotions of religious self-consciousness, and not in any direct communication of truth. Admittedly Schleiermacher's insistence that we must think of God as the co-determinant of this feeling of absolute dependence was intended by him to be an expression of the objectivity of God, that is, the unobjectifiable otherness or transcendence of God, but in point of fact, it yielded fruit of an opposite kind. Just because God-consciousness and self-consciousness are inextricably woven together in our experience, theology represents the projection into the mouth of a mute God the reflections of man upon his own feelings, or, to put it the other way round, it means the dragging of knowledge of God down within the circle of our own subjectivity.

As against the development of that line of thought going out from Schleiermacher Barth insists on the activity of God as the mark of his transcendence and freedom and independent objectivity. It is just because God actively reveals himself, because his revelation is and ever remains pure act which will never resolve itself into some effective receptivity or subjective condition of mine, that I continue to encounter it as genuine revelation, as Word of God addressed to me, which I cannot and must not mistake for a word of my own or convert into a word I can tell myself. God's Word is unlike our words, for it is creative Word, Word that is also Act, and so Word that resists our attempts to domesticate or subdue it to forms of our own understanding, Word that acts creatively upon us, thereby calling us in question and summoning us to conform ourselves to it. Indeed God's Word is an act of aggression on his part, for it is grace that contradicts us in our self-will, and so confronts us with a decision in which we have to act against ourselves in self-renunciation and repentance. It is through the objection of God's active revelation that we are able to distinguish it from our own subjectivities and know it to be really objective reality independent of us, real Word of *God*, as distinct from mere word of man.

In the second place, Barth became convinced that one of the great decisive issues in the history of the Church, and therefore of theology, was the relation of revelation to the *Being* and *Person* of God himself—Revelation, as Calvin had taught, is God speaking in Person. In other words, Revelation is God-in-his-revelation, God-in-his-Word. As Barth read his Church history he saw that this was the supreme importance of the struggle of the Church in the early centuries for a true and faithful Christology. What the Church insisted on guarding at all costs in the Nicene Christology is that God communicates *himself* in his revelation—not just something of himself, not just something about himself, but very God himself. That is the meaning of the Trinity, that in Jesus Christ and in the Holy Spirit it is God in his Godness who confronts us. Hence in believing in his revelation we believe in

God himself, and we believe in God by believing in his revelation.

The Reformation represents a new struggle within the Church for the same truth expressed in the Council of Nicaea, by its insistence that Jesus Christ is very God and very man, and that the Holy Spirit is the Lord, the Giver of Life. In other words, it is the truth that God's gift is identical with himself the Giver. The point of battle was doubtless the conception of *grace*, and the objectivity of divine grace was clarified in a struggle over justification by grace alone, but in and throughout it all it was the same truth, that in Jesus Christ and in the Holy Spirit God comes to us in Person and gives us himself. God himself is the content of his revelation, and himself the content of his saving grace— grace does not pass over into some subjective state of ours, or into some transferable quality of the soul, and revelation is not something that inheres in the Church, but God actively confronting us with his own Person, and revealing his own Being in that action.

Is it not precisely the same battle that needs to be fought all over again in the twentieth century, but one which combines the forms which the battle took both in the fourth and in the sixteenth century: God and no other is the content of his revelation, and God is himself really the content of it? When we speak of 'Christ' is it really God himself in his revelation we mean? And when we speak of the Holy Spirit, is it really God himself in his freedom to be present with us, or is it just our spirit that we mean? Is it not the Godness of God in his revelation that has been lost, and is that not the cause of the secularization of the Church and the secularization of modern man? Has revelation not somehow just become identified with change and improvement in the life of man? Has not knowledge of God come to mean something that goes on in the depths of the human soul? Hence is it not high time to take seriously again the ancient cause of the Church, renewed with such vigour at the Reformation, that God's revelation is the revelation of God himself, of God-in-his-revelation, and that he is to be known only out of himself, for the God whom we know in revelation is God who remains Subject even when making himself the object of our knowledge? Hence Barth insists that theology is concerned with a knowledge of God that takes its rise from the sovereign act of his self-revelation and which is actualized only by way of recognition and acknowledgement of the truth of God as the one reality that is grounded in itself and therefore to be understood, derived, substantiated only out of itself. It is the knowledge of the one Truth of God who is of and through himself alone, and therefore a knowledge that is in accordance with the nature of that which is known; it is the knowledge of the ultimate Truth which by its very nature cannot be measured by any standard outside of it or higher than it, for there is no such standard—rather does every other truth take its origin from this Truth and point away to it as its goal.

In the third place, Barth insists that revelation is rational event, for in revelation God communicates to us his Word, and conveys to us his Truth, requiring of us a rational response in accordance with the rational nature of his Word, and a self-critical relation to his Truth as it calls us in question. Not only is revelation God's Act and his Being in that Act, but *Logos*, the source and fountain of all rationality, and therefore knowledge of God in his revelation is rational in its own right, rational on the ground of the supreme and self-sufficient rationality of its object, God-in-his-Word. Thus in revelation theology is concerned with a depth in objective rationality that transcends that of any other kind of knowledge and of every other kind of science. Barth will have nothing to do, therefore, with some kind of faith-knowledge that is basically romantic and non-conceptual and which needs rationalizing through borrowed forms from ethics and philosophy. Knowledge of revelation is *ab initio* rational, for it is engagement in a divinely rational communication.

That does not mean that Revelation is the communication of propositional ideas or concepts already blocked out in propositional form, for what is communicated is God himself, God as Truth, Truth as the Being of God in his revelation. This is Truth not first in noetic form, but truth as ontic Reality, Truth in itself, and only on that ground is it noetic truth for us and in our knowing of it. This noetic truth which belongs to our theological statements is only truth as it derives from and rests in the ontic truth of God's self-objectification for us, and self-giving to us in the revelation of himself—it is truth that has an ontological depth of objectivity in the very Being and Nature of God-in-his-Word. This is the aspect of Barth's teaching which was so strongly affected by his studies of Anselm as well as Calvin.

If we look back at these three aspects of Barth's understanding of the self-revelation of God through his Word, and ask what he means by *theology*, we must say that for him theology is a thinking from a centre in God, deriving from his active communication of himself in the form of personal Being and Truth, and pointing back to him as the goal of all true human thinking and knowing. While theology necessarily involves two poles of thought, God and man, for it is man who thinks and man who knows, it is not a thinking and knowing from a centre in man himself but from a centre in God. It is *man*'s objective thinking of a Truth that is independent of him and is yet communicated to him. Theology is correct and true thinking when its movement corresponds to the movement of the Truth itself, and is a thinking in accordance with it, a thinking that follows its activity, thinking that is obedient to its proper object, the Lord God.

We may say, then, that *theo-logy* is *logos* of God in a threefold sense of *logos*. Primarily we are concerned here with the *Logos* of God that is his own eternal Word and Son, the ground and source of all our human thinking and knowing. But this Logos has become flesh in Jesus Christ, for in him God has revealed and communicated himself to us within the objectivities of our existence in time and space, in creaturely and historical being, and hence in Jesus Christ God has objectified himself for us and given himself to our knowing and understanding. Yet Logos, in this second sense as the object of our knowing, remains the Lord, indissolubly Subject, who encounters us as Truth to be known only in so far as he encounters us as the very Being of God in Person; who meets us within the objectivities of our world which he has assumed for his self-revealing in Jesus Christ, in such a way that he remains the Lord, transcendent to all these objectivities, so objective that we can never master him in his objectivity and subdue him to some form of our own subjectivity in knowing or understanding him, but can only know him as we serve him and are obedient to the Truth. But theology includes a third sense of logos, in which it refers to our way of knowing and understanding the Truth of God in accordance with the way in which he has objectified himself for us in Jesus Christ. Thus theology is an activity of our reason in accordance with the nature of its proper object, God-in-his-Word, or God-in-his-revelation, in Jesus Christ. Theology is critical and positive activity in which we build up our knowledge of God from his Word which he gives as the object of our knowledge, and in which we test our knowing to make sure, as far as we can, that our noetic logos corresponds to the ontic logos in that Word. Thus theology operates with a mode of rationality that is required of us from the side of the object, and proceeds positively and critically in accordance with the way that the Word has taken in his self-communication to us.

We speak of that concretely when we speak of Jesus Christ as the Way, the Truth, and the Life, for he is the concrete act of God in his revelation, and therefore the peculiar object of our knowing that distinguishes theology from every other knowledge or science. He is the One who encounters as the very Being of God come to man within the actualities of man's own existence and life and gives him knowledge and understanding of God.

As such Jesus Christ is the *Way*, as well as the Truth and the Life, who will be known according to the way God has taken with us in him, the way of revelation and reconciliation within humanity and history. Theological thought, therefore, cannot take a way of its own choosing or wander arbitrarily across country, but must keep to the way of the Truth, for that is the Way of Life. Theological thinking is historical thinking, not thinking about any kind of history or about history in general, but thinking that is a thinking out of this concrete centre in all history, Jesus Christ. It is through faithfulness to this Truth become historical event, to this historical event backed up by all the objective reality of the Being of God, that theology is theology.

Jesus Christ is the *Truth* as well as the Way and the Life, and therefore we encounter him in such a way that our thought is critically differentiated from other thought, from thought about other objects. Theological thinking is thinking that learns to distinguish truth from falsehood, because it operates with criteria and basic forms of rationality that it derives from the nature of its object. In so far as it is obedient to the nature of this Truth, it allows itself to be questioned by it, and allows all else that it may have claimed to know or may have claimed to be true, all its prior understanding, to be called into question, sifted and brought into conformity with the Truth as it is in Jesus Christ. There can be no neutrality here, for in obedience to the Truth of God in Jesus Christ theology is concerned with concrete and positive truth that must be articulated correctly, and therefore humbly in accordance with the nature of the Truth himself.

Jesus Christ is the *Life*, as well as the Way and the Truth, for this Truth is Truth in the form of personal Being, and to know this Truth is to know it in a corresponding form of personal being, in a following of Christ, in discipleship, in a renunciation of ourselves and taking up of his Cross, and in union with him. Theological thinking is thus part of man's actual salvation, for it is thinking of the Life that is the actual salvation and liberty of the man who knows and believes. Theological thinking is therefore a practical type of thinking, in which our being and action are involved and not just our minds or our thought. Theology can never be pursued in contemplative abstraction from the concrete acts of God in Jesus Christ for our salvation. It is thinking in responsibility, thinking in which we have to give an account to God for our lives and beings and actions.

Thus theological thinking that involves the two poles of thought, God and man, and is yet a thinking from a centre in God, that is thinking from out of a centre in the concrete action of God in Jesus Christ, as the Way, the Truth, and the Life, is essentially thinking within the *Church*. The Church is the realm created in the midst of human existence and history by the self-revelation of God, the area in the midst of all our other knowledge where God is known in accordance with his revealing and saving acts, where God is known as Subject, and is therefore worshipped and loved and obeyed as the Lord of all our human ways and works and thoughts. The Church is not the society of individuals who band themselves voluntarily together through a common interest in Jesus Christ, but it is a divine institution, the creation of the divine decision and election, of the divine love to give himself to men and to share with them his own divine life and love, and so to share with them knowledge of himself. Because the Church is a divine institution it is not governed by an ideology, some self-interpretation, a controlled and systematically worked out truth of its own historical existence and actuality: rather is it governed by the Word of God, and through obedient conformity to that Word. Theology is thus an essential part of the Church's life, in which it questions its own obedience and tests its conformity and seeks unceasingly to live not out of itself, but out of God in his revelation; not out of what it can think out for itself, but out of what it can hear from God and think into its life and being in history. Theology is part of the Church's humble worship of God, worshipping with its mind as well as with its body, an act of repentant humility, an act of thankful enjoyment of God, an act of the glorification of God.

Theology has two sides to it. On the one hand, it is an act of repentance, in which it puts to itself critical questions, to test its preaching of God's Word, to sift its understanding of the Truth, to see whether it is in harmony with what God reveals of himself through his Word, and so to distinguish what is genuinely heard from what is an artificial product of man's own. That is the scientific task of dogmatics. On the other hand, it is an act of worship, in which it seeks understanding of God, in which it not only travels the road which the Word of God has taken from God to man, but travels the road from man back to God, in order to find in God the goal of all human thinking as well as its source. Theology is a lifting up of the heart unto the Lord, a worshipping of

God with the mind, in which we seek understanding of God in the midst of our faith that we may enjoy him and serve him in his Truth. That is the doxological task of dogmatics.

3. Theology and Secular Knowledge

Theology that takes its task seriously as rational thinking cannot escape encounter with philosophy and natural science, for theology does not operate in a realm all of its own, but in the same realm of human thinking where philosophy and all the positive sciences are at work. Just because it is human thinking concerned with the subject-object relationship, like every other form of human thinking, theology necessarily shares with every other form of human thinking certain important problems and questions which it must not avoid. That does not mean that theology must give up its own peculiar nature, for it can no more do that than give up its own proper object—it would be just as foolish to ask physics or biology to move into some general realm of thought and to detach its thinking from its own proper object or field of investigation. But it does mean that theology must operate with human thought and speech as its instruments, and must take seriously the laws and possibilities and limits of human thought and speech within which every science operates and which it is the business of philosophy to clarify as it seeks to fulfil its own task in developing its understanding of the world of being and idea. On the other hand, because theology has problems that overlap with philosophy and other sciences, it must subject itself to rigorous control and the discipline of self-critical revision in order to ensure that it is really being good theology, and not some debased brand of theology that confuses its task and its subject-matter with those of philosophy or some science of nature. Thus, while recognizing its own peculiar nature, and pursuing it with unceasing vigilance and exacting criticism, it must think out its connexion with philosophy and natural science and make clear its distinction from them.

This was one of the main questions Barth found he had to answer, particularly when he began to move from his earlier dialectical thinking into more positive thinking in the construction of a dogmatics. It became even more acute when he had completed his first attempt at what he called *Christian Dogmatics* and studied it in the light of the criticism it met from his colleagues and opponents and the even stronger criticism it met from himself when he read it again in print. That is the period that follows closely upon the republication of these essays on

Theology and Church in 1928. He set himself therefore to clarify his understanding of the essential nature and method of theological activity in the light of its own proper object and in distinction from knowledge beyond the limits imposed on theology by its object. As Barth saw it, this involved for theology a philosophical problem and a scientific problem.

(a) The philosophical problem

Both theology and philosophy are concerned with the subject-object relationship, but whereas theological thinking is bound to a concrete object and moves in a direction chosen for it by the activity of its object, God-in-his-Word, philosophy is not so bound to a concrete object, and is in a position to move more freely in any direction that its own reflection upon man's existence and actuality may lead it. It is incumbent upon theology to clarify the way in which its thinking overlaps with that of philosophy, and the way in which its thinking is distinct from that of philosophy. An examination of the history of philosophy shows its fundamental dialectic to be concerned with a constant tension between realism and idealism. But that is also the dialectic in which theology engages in its movement between the given object and thought about the object, and therefore it must be in this dialectic that the relevance of philosophical thinking for theology is to be found.

In the first place, then, theology must face the critical questions posed by philosophy as to objectivity, givenness, or reality—that is the problem of *realism*. Classical realism holds that all our knowledge arises out of actual experience of a given reality, but it also admits that this involves an outward and an inward experience, an objective and a subjective givenness. How, then, are we to distinguish the independent objective reality from our experience of it, especially from our inward subjective experience of it? That is the question that a realist theology must face. It takes as its fundamental proposition that *God is*, and so affirms that God has reality independently of our knowledge of him. As Anselm expressed it, it is one thing to say that something exists in the understanding, and another thing to understand that it exists. But how in point of fact are we to distinguish the two? How do we know that the God whom we know in our minds has existence apart from our mental knowledge of him, that 'God' is anything more than an empty 'idea' in our minds?

That problem is made all the more acute when we remember that the God we claim to know is not some God in himself, but God who is known in his Word, the God who reveals himself within the concrete objectivities and actualities of our human and historical existence; that is, within the Church of Jesus Christ on earth. How are we to distinguish God from the outward experience of these concrete objectivities in the I-Thou encounter we have with other people, or in the concrete objectivities of history? Theological realism insists that God is given to me in the actualities of my experience in the form of a likeness to himself, in the realm of being which I have in nature and history, and that he meets me in my neighbour and within the subject-subject encounter of person to person in the Christian Church. But how am I to distinguish God himself from these external objectivities through which he reveals himself to me? And if I hold that God is the source of all Being, and that all other being derives from him and participates in him, and if therefore I think that in virtue of the fact that I exist or have being I am necessarily in encounter with the Being of God, how can I distinguish him from the actualities with which my existence is necessarily bound up? How can I distinguish *God* from necessity or from fate or from nature, or from the concrete historical existence which I share and from which I cannot escape? How can I distinguish a genuine theological realism from a philosophical realism, or reflection about the living God from reflection upon being in general?

These questions are sufficient to show that realism is a very serious issue for theology, but theology has its counter-questions to ask, says Barth. The most fundamental of them is whether theological realism takes into consideration the fact that the grace of God contradicts us. It is on this ground, that grace opposes sinful man, and objects to his sin, on the ground of a contradiction between the revelation of God and the activity of man, that we can distinguish the objectively given reality of God-in-his-Word from our own subjective states, but also from the other objectivities we encounter in our experience of the world around us. Classical theological realism operates with a basic, naïve conviction that we are able to read knowledge of God off what is given to us in our experience because we stand in relation to him by virtue of the fact that we exist. But when we actually know God through his Word a very different conviction arises, for here a light shines into our darkness, and something quite new is revealed to us which does not just reinforce what we already know, but rather calls it in question. This new knowledge comes as grace that forgives and judges us, and which we cannot just assimilate into our existence, for it lays claim upon us and summons us to encounter the independent objective reality of the living God, the Creator and Redeemer.

Concretely this is what happens when we meet God in Jesus Christ and know him as Lord by the power of the Spirit. It is in that encounter that we learn that the objective act of God upon us in the freedom of his Spirit is to be distinguished from our inward subjective conditions, and that the God who meets us face to face in Jesus Christ is not just nature, or history, or the actuality of our existence with which we are bound up and from which we cannot escape, but a living God who really comes to us and acts upon us in the midst of all the other actualities and objectivities of our historical and natural existence. In other words, here we are faced with a deeper and more fundamental objectivity, with the ultimate objectivity of the Lord God, and therefore it is here that theology is both basically realist and yet to be distinguished from every form of philosophical realism.

In the second place, however, theology must face the critical question posed by philosophy as to the adequacy of its thought to its proper object—that is the question of truth, which gives rise to the problem of *idealism*. This is the question that seeks to penetrate behind the given, the finite, the objectifiable, and behind all actuality to its ultimate validation or presupposition. Idealist thinking, says Barth, has a negative critical side, and a positive speculative side. On the one hand, it questions the basic assumption of realism, inquires into the reliability of the correlation between subject and object, and reveals the limits within which realist thinking can operate. It refracts or breaks the movement of realist thinking, and so makes it point beyond itself to its object. This critical operation both reminds us of the inadequacy of our human thought-forms and calls for a greater and more exacting adequacy. But idealist thinking has another speculative side, in which it poses as the criterion of reality and exalts itself over against pure being. Idealism of this sort is the self-reflection of man's spirit over against nature, the discovery of the creative reason as the source of the correlation between subject and object.

Idealist thinking, at least in its critical form, is a necessary element in theological thinking, for whenever there is serious thinking about God, a distinction must be drawn between the givenness of God and the givenness of all other being. That is the relevance of mysticism or of the *via negativa* even for the classical realism of the Middle Ages, for a realist theology requires a powerful element of idealism in order to be genuinely realist. Is the idealist distinction between 'the given' and 'the

not-given' not necessary for a proper understanding of the difference
between divine revelation and all other knowledge that claims to be
knowledge of God? And just because in theology we are engaged in
human thinking about God, and with the articulation of knowledge of
God in human thought-forms, must we not ask the question as to the
adequacy of these thought-forms to God? Does not idealist thinking
teach us that the best of our thought-forms can only point beyond to
the ultimate reality of God which cannot be captured and formulated
within the four corners of our human concepts and propositions? That
is why idealism is the necessary antidote to all thorough-going realism,
for it prevents realist thinking from confounding God with the actualities of our existence, with nature, or history, or necessity.

But may not idealism itself prove the greater danger, especially when
it refuses to rest content with the humble critical refraction of our
thinking, but insists on making out of the reason itself the criterion of
truth, and so exalting itself above God? Is not the danger of idealist
thinking in theology that it may lead to the substitution of ideology for
genuine theology, a system of self-sufficient truth for an activity of
human thinking that points away from itself to the object of its knowledge as the sole source and ground of truth, and as the Truth of God?
Hence here, too, theology has its counter-questions to ask of idealist
thinking in theology.

The fundamental question we have to ask is directed to the idealist
question posed not from the side of the object but from the side of the
subject. Does the attempt to reach out beyond all the dialectical
antitheses and antinomies of human thought to an ultimate synthesis
ever really get outside the circle of its own subjectivity, ever really get
beyond the human subject from which it started? Does it not, after all,
confound God with the conclusion to its own argument or with the
goal of its own upward movement of thought? Is it not in the end projecting its own thought into the infinite and calling it God?

The fundamental question theology must put to the idealist is
whether he is ready to let God be God, and therefore ready to let knowledge of God be grounded in God's own self-revelation, and the establishment of the truth of that knowledge be God's act and not man's.
In other words, the question which theology must pose over against
idealism is the question directed from justification by the grace of God
alone to every Pelagian or semi-Pelagian attempt on the part of the
human reason to be able to acquire knowledge of God or at least to be
able to test and establish the truth of revelation on its own ground. If

God is really God, then knowledge of him must be by way of humble obedience, by way of listening to him and serving his Word, and yielding our minds to the direction of his Truth. God is *God*, and not our *idea* of God, and therefore all our ideas of him have to be called in question by the very critical question from which idealist thinking takes its rise. And yet here, theology must beware lest it is after all engaging not in theological thinking, but in some form of philosophical idealism itself, for the critical question theology directs does not arise out of any independent rational movement of its own, but is forced upon it by the object of its knowledge, and by the nature of the objectivity of the object, the nature of God who gives himself to us in sheer grace and remains sovereignly free in his transcendent Lordship over all our thoughts of him and over all our formulations of the understanding he gives us of himself in his Word.

The problems posed by philosophical *realism* and *idealism* must be taken seriously by theology, but they are questions that theology must learn to raise in its own way and in the closest relation to its own proper object. But the discussion with philosophy shows theology that it must take seriously both poles of its thinking, truth and actuality, thought and being, the knowing subject and the object known. Theology learns that there can be a one-sided realist theology which is tempted to confound God with nature, and there can be a one-sided idealist theology which is tempted to confound God with the reason. Inevitably, therefore, the dialectic between these two counter-movements will throw up the correctives from either side which the other side needs. In such a situation it is possible that a theology may be more realist in orientation and still be theology and another may be more idealist in orientation and still be theology—rather than some species of philosophy or ideology.

But a good theology cannot rest content with that sort of dialectic; rather has it to think more concretely out of the depths of its own concern, and engage in a more material mode of thinking of the tensions between the knowing subject and its given object that is governed by the nature of its subject-matter. Theology just because it is theology must learn to distinguish its dialectic from all philosophical forms of the dialectic between subject and object. All philosophy worthy of the name seeks in some way to reach a unitary understanding of the universe, and so to transcend the dialectic between realism and idealism. But whether it is realistically or idealistically slanted, whether it erects a synthesis from the side of being or from the side of the reason, it is fundamentally a movement *from man toward God*, and claims in the last analysis to be able to say an ultimate word or at least to aim at an ultimate word that transcends the antitheses and contradictions revealed within human existence. But theology as a thinking that takes its rise from a centre in God and not from a centre in man, comes from the very point (from God) which philosophy hopes to reach. There is thus an inescapable tension between the essential intention of theological thought and the essential intention of philosophical thought, for they move in opposite directions.

In so far as philosophy is engaged in unitary or synthetic thinking theology has no quarrel with it, but can only learn from it and co-operate with it. But if philosophy insists on going further, in identifying its synthesis with God, in claiming the conclusion of its argument to be the ultimate reality, in confounding its own word projected above the tensions of human existence with the Word of God, that is, in so far as philosophy turns itself into a *theosophy*, then theology cannot but do battle with it. Theology that is interpretation of the Word of God spoken to human existence cannot allow the place and authority of that Word to be usurped by a word of man that derives from his own reflection upon the problems of human existence. But may not the counter-questions theology poses to every philosophy that is tempted to become a theosophy help to keep philosophy pure, help it to become self-critical, and so to be genuine philosophy that is aware of the limits of human thinking, and will not ascribe to itself the ability to transcend itself?

Theology's answer to the problems posed by philosophy is not only one derived from the essential form of theo-logical thinking as distinct from every ideo-logical thinking, but one that must be derived from the basic content of theological knowledge and one that reposes upon the actuality and truth of its own object, God in his revelation. In other words, the answer that theology must give is one that reposes upon God's decision to give himself to man as the object of his knowledge and upon the content of that gift, for they establish the possibility and determine the reality of all theological thinking. Looked at from one aspect this is the epistemological significance of *election*—which stands for the fact that theology does not move in a direction of its own choosing, but only in the way God has chosen for it, and that therefore it has its necessity outside of itself, in God. This means that theology by its very nature must renounce any claim to possess truth in its own theological statements, for those theological statements are only truthful when they point away from themselves to the one Truth of God as their absolute *prius* and ground. Looked at from another aspect this is the epistemological significance of the Incarnation, for Jesus Christ himself is the Way and the Truth and the Life, and theological thinking is thinking grounded in the objectivity of the concrete act of God in him, and is thinking that is wholly determined by its object, God become man, the Word made flesh, full of grace and truth.

Nevertheless, while theology must be concerned with its own proper object, and only within the bounds imposed by that object take up the problems posed by philosophical realism and idealism, it must seek to articulate its knowledge within the same realm of thinking that is occupied by philosophy and every other science. Hence it cannot but make use of the forms of thought and speech which it finds in that realm. Its task will be to maintain throughout its own proper concern and not allow it to be subordinated to ways of thinking that are not appropriate to its proper object, and therefore it must shape the forms of thought and speech which it inherits into tools that will really serve its specifically theological purpose.

This is a problem of which Barth is acutely aware. On the one hand, it has led him to grasp more profoundly the objectivity of the Word and to move over from an idealist into a fundamentally realist theology, but on the other hand, it has helped Barth to find a way of articulating his realist understanding of the Word of God within the essentially dynamic and critico-idealist style of modernity, and yet in such a way that it breaks through the framework of every form of thinking in its determined obedience to follow the way that the Word of God has actually taken in Jesus Christ in revelation and reconciliation. His contribution to the history of theology must be measured by the success of his critique of the one-sidedly realist theology of the Middle Ages, and the one-sidedly idealist theology of modern Protestantism, and by the extent to which he has learned from both in articulating a constructive dogmatics that presses into the objective unity of all Christian theology and radically calls in question the deviations from that unity grounded in the divine self-revelation in Jesus Christ.

(b) *The scientific problem*

The discussion between theology and philosophy serves to drive theology back upon its proper object; otherwise it betrays itself and loses its own basic concern. But if it is driven back upon its object and learns to think out its problems strictly from within the limits and restrictions to thinking laid down by the nature of its object, and develops a rational method in accordance with the nature of its object, then is not theological activity methodologically more like that of an exact science than of philosophy? If that is so, then theology must clarify its own procedure over against the other sciences which operate within the same realm of human thinking as it does, especially where that thinking takes a strictly *a posteriori* form. Our concern here is not to trace out the relations between the doctrines of the Christian faith, as they are given constructive form in Barth's theology, with the results of modern scientific research, but rather to consider the problem of scientific method as it is posed from the side of empirical science, and to discern how theology takes up that problem on its own ground and works it out in its own way in accordance with the requirements of its own object.

There can be no doubt that theology and natural science overlap in so far as the critical reflection of both takes place within space and time, and within the world of concrete objectivity in nature and history, and yet they differ both in regard to the source of their knowledge and the nature of their object. Theology, as we have seen, is essentially a thinking from a centre in God and not from a centre in man, nevertheless it is not thinking of some 'God in himself', but of a God who has revealed himself to man within the same sphere of actuality to which he belongs, and therefore within the world of concrete objectivities in nature and history accessible to man's observation and reflection. That is the actuality which natural science investigates, but it observes it and reflects upon it as purely contingent existence that is to be known only in its phenomenology and not in its ontology. Natural science by its very nature confines itself to the investigation of phenomena. Theology operates within that same area, but it is concerned with the living God who reveals himself in the midst of phenomenal objectivity as the Creator and Lord of it all and as the ground of its being and reality. Theology is not concerned with the phenomena as such, but with the central relation of it all to God, and is a form of thinking that derives from God's Word and follows the movement of God's Word in its creative and redemptive operation— only incidentally, therefore, does it concern itself with the knowledge of phenomena as such, derived from empirical study alone. In the doctrine of man, for example, it is not concerned as theology with what medical science, with what physiology or chemistry, have to say about him, for it is concerned about the central relation of man to God which constitutes his *reality* as man, that is his *being* a child of God; but what it has to say here on the border of what empirical science discovers of 'the phenomena of the human', as Barth speaks of it, does illuminate the world of man within which alone empirical science is pursued. That does not mean that theology can offer any information of the kind that is assimilable to the knowledge acquired by natural science or that is therefore of any use to it in its empirical activity, although it may serve to remind man of the limits and boundaries of his existence and of his knowledge, and help him to restrict his reflections within the limits set by empirical approach to his object, that is, help him to retain strict objectivity as empirical science.

Because theology operates with the Word of God that has become flesh within the world of space and time, it must recognize that there is an aspect of its object that is open to empirical observation and reflection—and to that extent it must reckon on the justice of historico-critical investigation and its relevance to the concern of theology. But theology is concerned with the *Word* become flesh, with the activity of *God* in space and time, and therefore it is concerned with these concrete objectivities that are necessarily open to empirical and critical observation only in their relation to the ultimate objectivity of God who has come to us in their midst to reveal himself to us and reconcile us to himself. It is that fact that differentiates theological science so radically from natural science, for it is concerned with the outward objectivities of space and time as the form in which it encounters the Object of knowledge who is indissolubly Subject, and which it only knows as Object in so far as it knows it as Subject—although, of course, it does not know the Subject except so far as he makes himself Object of human knowledge within the realm of man's nature and existence.

It is this essential and profound polarity of its given object—which Barth calls its primary and secondary objectivity—that distinguishes theological knowledge from every other kind of knowledge or science. This differentiation, however, is a scientific difference, that is, a difference arising out of precise and exact behaviour in accordance with the nature of its proper object. Thus theology differs from natural science both in regard to the direction and source of its knowledge and in regard to the nature of its object, but within that difference it is still true that methodologically theology stands closer to the empirical sciences than to philosophy, and is indeed better described as *theological science* than as sacred philosophy.

The closeness between theological science and natural science becomes apparent when we note the formal points which they have in common, and the scientific way in which theology develops its own peculiar method.

Barth notes three main points which theological and empirical science have in common, over against philosophy.

(a) They do not operate with a world-view or necessarily develop a cosmology. By their very dedication to their object, they renounce all prior understandings of the universe, and refuse to construct a cosmological interpretation which will serve as a guide to further investigation. Natural science confines itself strictly to phenomena, and refuses to mix its studies up with philosophy, although, of course, it may well listen to philosophical questions in so far as they help it to get free from presuppositions and so help it toward purer objectivity. Theology likewise is dedicated to its proper object, and it is precisely its attachment to its object that detaches it from all presuppositions arising from philosophy or tradition or any other source—not, of course, that the theologian, or the natural scientist, is ever without these or can ever ultimately escape them, but that *methodological renunciation* of presuppositions (except the one presupposition of its object) is scientifically demanded of it. It is for that reason that neither theological nor empirical science can properly lead to or result in cosmological constructions, or speculative ontologies of the universe.

(b) Both theological science and empirical science recognize the centrality of man in the cosmos—both recognize that they are human endeavours, aspects of human thinking and research, and cannot transcend the human correlate in that activity. Thus inevitably and practically empirical science describes the cosmos as the cosmos of man, the cosmos of human observation and inference, knowledge of which is limited accordingly. For theology, too, the cosmos has an anthropocentric orientation, not because the starting-point of man's knowledge is from man himself, and not simply because he can engage only in human thinking, but because his thinking takes its rise from and is determined by the Word of God which is addressed to man in the midst of the cosmos. Theology cannot and must not try to, but does not need to, usurp God's standpoint, for God has come to give man knowledge both of God and man himself from within the sphere accessible to and knowable by man, who may thus have knowledge of God without renouncing his human standpoint. Indeed, it is because God addresses his Word to man in the world, and loves the world which he has made, that theology looks in the direction of the address and love of God—toward the world, as well as toward God. Only because it must travel with the Word the road from God to man in the world, does it and may it travel the road from man in the world to God as the goal of all its knowledge.

(c) Theological science and empirical science resemble one another in that both recognize two fundamentally distinct realms, the realm of the observable and objectifiable, and the realm beyond, which is outside the range of human observation and comprehension. Theology calls these heaven and earth, Barth says, but although empirical science uses different language, it no less than theology respects the difference between heaven and earth; that is to say, it respects the limited range of human observation, investigation, and description, and therefore also reckons with the realm of what is inaccessible to man. As exact science it cannot deny that realm, but acknowledges it at least as the frontier of its knowledge, where it calls a halt precisely in order to be exact science. Therefore, as empirical science, it maintains a respectful silence about what lies on the other side of its frontier, and does not seek to extend its method (built up in correlation with the observable and objectifiable) beyond its range and so to corrupt it.

With the exact sciences that maintain strict scientific faithfulness theological science can engage in fruitful discussion, but it is also the responsibility of theology to take cognizance of what these other sciences have to teach especially about the phenomena of the human or the characteristics of man as a creature, and to relate to it its own knowledge of the reality of man derived from the Word of God; for it is precisely to this man, with his scientific endeavours that the Word of God is addressed, and upon the whole of his existence that it lays the claim of the divine grace.

The methodological closeness of theology to empirical science is seen at a deeper level in the essentially scientific way in which it develops its method, for it does not bring to its task a method that it has already thought out or acquired, but elaborates a method only in its actualization of knowledge. Neither theological science nor empirical science knows a method in abstraction from the material content of its actual subject-matter. Thus the questions theology asks are not correlated with the subject but with the object. If it brings questions to its object, it is only in order that they may themselves be called in question by the object and be restated in accordance with the nature of the object. They are questions designed to let the object declare itself, and so are framed as questions that the object by its nature puts to the inquirer. In so far as they are thus correlated with the subject they are acts of self-criticism designed to clear away all artificiality and to open a way for seeing what is actually there and for learning what the objective reality has to disclose to us unhindered and undistorted, as far as possible, by any prior understanding on the part of the subject undertaking the inquiry. The questions that are put are only designed by the theologian or the scientist in order to let himself be told what he cannot tell himself and must genuinely learn. For theology this kind of inquiry is an act of repentant humility.

Of course, in the nature of the case, the kind of inquiry in which theology engages face to face with its object will differ from the kind of inquiry in which natural science engages face to face with its object, for the nature of object in each case demands that difference as a part of its scientific obedience. Natural science is concerned with creaturely objects, and, as a rule, with mute objects, so that although we speak here of letting the object disclose itself and yield to us knowledge of it, that is a way of insisting upon objectivity in investigation. But the kind of question the scientist has to put to these objects to make them 'talk' or yield their secrets are scientific experiments in which he compels them to reveal themselves. Controlled experiment is the kind of inquiry appropriate to inanimate creaturely objects, but the kind of inquiry appropriate to other human beings will pass beyond that to a kind which allows the other actively and willingly to reveal himself as one human person to another. The kind of inquiry that theology directs toward God must, scientifically, be appropriate to the nature of God before whom I am questioned before I begin to ask questions, whom I can know only as I am known by him, and knowledge of whom I can articulate only as he gives himself to me to be known. In other words, the kind of inquiry proper to theological science is *prayer*, inquiry which we address to God as the Truth in order that we may listen to what he tells us of himself, and may understand it only under his illumination of our minds. It is because the object of theological knowledge confronts us always as Subject, and indeed as absolute Subject, as the Lord God, that prayer is the scientifically correct mode of inquiry, for it is the mode of inquiry that corresponds to God's nature as man's Creator and Redeemer.

We may expound this relation between theology and exact science in another way. All scientific activity is one in which the reason acts strictly and precisely in accordance with the nature of its object, and so lets the object prescribe for it both the limits within which it is to be known and the mode of rationality that is to be adopted toward it. But

for that reason it also lets the nature of the object determine the kind
of demonstration appropriate to it. It will not insult the object by trying
to subject it to some kind of demonstration that has been developed
elsewhere in accordance with the nature of a different kind of object,
nor by employing for its investigation external criteria dragged in from
some other realm of knowledge. The kind of verification it must
scientifically employ is the kind that derives from and is in accord with
the actual way in which knowledge has arisen. That is to say, it never
seeks to impose an arbitrarily constructed possibility upon the reality
it is investigating, but will only argue from the reality to its possibility
and within that movement subject its knowledge to critical examination.

This is precisely the way which Barth adopts in scientific dogmatics
—as we can see very clearly in his brilliant interpretation of Anselm's
theological method, and in the way in which he has worked out his own
epistemology in strict obedience to the nature of the concrete object of
theological knowledge, God come to us in Jesus Christ, i.e. in such a
way that in all his thinking he really allows God to be God, and refuses
to think beyond him or above him. The procedure common to theological science and all other genuine science is one in which the mind of the
knower acts in strict conformity to the nature of what is given, and
refuses to take up a standing in regard to it prior to actual knowledge
or in abstraction from actual knowledge. Scientific knowledge is one in
which the reason does not proceed in the light of some inner dialectic
of its own, but one that arises out of determination by the object known
and derives from the rationality and necessity of that object. In theological knowledge the reason lets itself be determined by the nature of
God in his revelation, and adopts a mode of rationality that corresponds
with God's objectifying of himself for man. That is epistemologically
the meaning of faith—faith is not in the slightest degree any irrational
leap, but a sober commitment to the nature of the given reality, a
determination of the reason in accordance with the nature of the
object, an orientation of the mind demanded of it in encounter with its
unique and incomparable object that is and remains Subject, the Lord
God. Faith means that to the self-giving, the self-revealing, and self-
communication of God in his Truth there corresponds in man a receiving, an understanding and an appropriation of the Truth, but in such
a way that the rationale and necessity of faith do not lie primarily in
itself but primarily in the object of faith. Hence theological knowledge
is not a scientific explication of the nature of faith, but in faith an
explication of understanding of the independent reality known. Theolo-

gical activity does not proceed in the light of the theologian's faith, but in the light that comes from the side of that in which he has faith, the self-authenticating and self-revealing reality of God that according to its very nature can be known and understood and substantiated only out of itself.

Barth can speak here of three levels or realms of reality, the realm of actual knowledge, the realm of objectivity that lies behind it and determines it, and the ultimate and primary realm of the Truth of God itself. Scientific theological activity is concerned with all three and with all three together in a compulsive activity. The realm of knowledge is the realm of noetic experience and noetic necessity. Scientific knowledge is concerned with a knowledge that forces itself upon us and to which we cannot but yield in truthful and faithful rational activity, but knowledge is not established so long as we merely remain on the level of noetic necessity, for the necessity in that realm derives from an ontic necessity at its basis in the object. It is only when theological inquiry presses into that deeper level that scientific understanding arises—that is, in a movement of knowledge in which we do not master the object but in which it masters us, in which we reach an ontic rationality in the object of faith and establish as far as we can the necessary relation between that ontic rationality in the object and the noetic rationality in our understanding of it. It is in the critical clarification of that profound objective necessity that theological knowledge claims to be thoroughly and strictly scientific because controlled and determined from the side of what is objectively given.

But scientific theological activity cannot stop there, for the nature of its object will not allow it to do so—it is required to act in conformity to the ultimate objectivity of God that confronts it within the realm of the objectifiable where God has revealed himself to us within space and time, within our existence and history. It is this ultimate objectivity of the Lord God, in which he stands over against all our thinking in the unique manner of the Creator over against the thinking of the creature, that characterizes all genuine theological knowledge and gives it its ultimate differentiation from all other knowledge. Theology would not be scientific, if at this point it drew back, and refused to acknowledge the unique nature of its object, in some false attempt to content itself with an objectivity that is merely like the relative objectivity with which every natural science is concerned, the objectivity of what is given to it in the creaturely world alone. It is this relation of primary objectivity to secondary objectivity that gives theological knowledge its great depth, provides it with its supreme determination, and gives it its great freedom under the sovereign objectivity of the Object that remains the absolute Subject. It is just because theological knowledge is confronted with the Lord God who lays his absolute claims over us that theological thinking can be carried out only in the strictest discipline, in stringent self-criticism and in utter obedience to the object. But because it is the Lord God who confronts us in theological knowledge, he confronts us necessarily as he who is greater than we can conceive, who transcends all our formulations of him, but who nevertheless gives himself to us as the object of our knowledge. Hence, even if our knowing of him is not adequate to his nature, it is not for that reason false, for he has come to us, adapted himself to us, and given himself to us to be known as reality within the actualities of our own being and existence, in Jesus Christ.

This means that the central and pivotal point of all genuine theological knowledge is to be found in Christology, in Jesus Christ in whom God and Man are one Person, in whom the primary objectivity of God meets us within the secondary objectivities of the given. A scientific theology will therefore operate on a Christological basis, for Christology will have critical significance for its inquiry into the understanding of the Truth of God at every point. Because God has once for all revealed himself in Jesus Christ, not in some merely transient fashion, which God leaves behind, and which man then, too, may eventually leave behind, but in such a way that God has for ever bound himself to our humanity in Jesus Christ, and in Jesus Christ bound us in a relation to him that is creative as well as redeeming. If God in Jesus Christ not only gives us to know something of himself, but gives us himself, if in Jesus Christ we are encountered not only by the Act of God but by the very Being of God in the Act, then we can never think of going behind the back of Jesus Christ in order to know God for that would be equivalent to trying to think beyond and above God himself, and to making ourselves as God. It is Christological thinking that teaches us to let God be God: to know God strictly and only in accordance with the steps he has taken to reveal himself to us, and therefore to test our knowledge of God in accordance with the steps in which knowledge of him has actually arisen and actually arises for us.

Now, if scientific theological knowledge refuses to operate merely within the noetic necessity of our thinking and speaking, but presses into the ontic necessity at the basis of those statements, that is into the inner rationality of the object itself, then it will be concerned to elucidate not only the basic noetic forms of rational theological thinking but the basic ontic forms through which everything is determined, for only in so doing can it establish the necessary relation between its thought and the object of its thought in a proper scientific manner. Hence theological thinking must probe into the inner basic forms and norms of its object as they are revealed in the material content of its thought. In other words, it will not employ any criteria in the testing and establishing of its knowledge in abstraction from its actual content, and will not elaborate any epistemology in abstraction from the full substance of theological knowledge—rather will a correct epistemology emerge, and a proper theological method develop, in the actual process of seeking full understanding of the object of faith and constructing a dogmatics in utter obedience to its object. Strictly speaking, it is only at the end of the work of dogmatics that it will be possible to expound properly an adequate epistemology. And yet, just because theological knowledge is confronted with the primary and ultimate objectivity of God, and must in accordance with its nature and freedom 'break' its theological formulations in recognition of their inadequacy and use them in all their noetic and ontic truthfulness in pointing beyond themselves to the one Truth of God, theological knowledge can never come to an end, but is by its very nature, at least for mortals on earth and pilgrims in history, a perpetual inquiry and a perpetual prayer that take place in the interval between the inception of faith and final vision. There will be no possibility therefore of abstracting from the substance of theology some final theological method which can then be wielded magisterially to subdue all doctrines to some rigid pattern, and there will be no possibility of reaching final solutions to theological problems—true prayer to the living God is unceasing, and true theological inquiry is unceasing worship and adoration. But this would, Barth insists, be prayer and worship without faith in the hearing of prayer and without trust in the grace and truth of God if theological thinking in the prosecution of its inquiry were not entirely certain of its object, and therefore ready to pursue its task in reliance upon the creative and normative activity of the object of its knowledge.

Theological certainty is pivoted upon the object, never pivoted upon the subject of the knower but because it looks for justification not at its own hands, nor on the ground of its own activity, but solely at the hands of God and solely on the grounds of his grace, it will be no less but even more ready to venture forth at its own level with absolute confidence and in its unconditional demands for precise doctrinal formulation. Thus when theological activity engages in self-critical questioning and in acknowledgement of the inadequacy of its own formulations of the Truth, that is not because it engages in doubt or because it is sceptical of its function, but on the contrary because its absolute certainty reposing upon the object requires of it humility and repentance. It is this certainty of the object that lets the theologian know that for all the questionableness and inadequacy of his own human employment of human forms of thought and speech, his theological understanding is not for that reason false, for the truth of his thinking stands or falls with its relation to the object, and derives not from the truth of itself but from the truth in the object towards which it points. By claiming truth in itself, it would become false, for it would arrogate to itself an ontic necessity and truth that belong only to the object, and so would betray its theological thinking into some form of ideological interpretation or speculation, or confound its own objective statements with the independent objectivity of the Truth of God. The truth of theological statements is linked with the fact that considered in themselves they have no truth of their own, but bear witness to the one Truth of God which is their sole justification and substantiation.

When we ask what the contribution of Karl Barth is, through a constructive dogmatics built up in this scientific manner, we may answer by drawing parallels between his work and that of Albert Einstein and Nils Bohr in the realm of pure natural science. If Einstein's immense contribution lies in the fact that he has penetrated down into the deep rationality of the universe of nature and laid bare its fundamental simplicities in a logical economy that is profoundly illuminating for the whole world of natural science and immensely fertile in the solving of many of its most difficult problems, and if in doing that Einstein's thinking involves the establishing of the age-old inquiry of science more securely on its proper axis in spite of the revolutionary effects of his theory of relativity, then *mutatis mutandis*, that, it can be said, is also the contribution of Karl Barth in the realm of theological science. For on the one hand he has penetrated into the deep objective rationality of theological knowledge and laid bare its basic simplicities which are proving immensely fertile throughout the whole realm of theological inquiry, and at the same time has through that attainment of a fundamental, theological economy established the catholic faith of the whole Church on a foundation that cuts across the theologies of East and West, Roman and Evangelical thinking, and presses in the most startling way towards a unitary understanding of the historic faith of the Christian Church in its one Lord, Father, Son, and Holy Spirit.

If the contribution of Nils Bohr in the realm of physics can be said to lie in the construction of an interpretation of nuclear activity that calls for a logical reconstruction of classical physics and mechanics, and so opens up in an astonishingly new way the relation of logic to being or rather of being to logic, so it must be said that the work of Karl Barth calls for a radical reconstruction both of Mediaeval and Neo-Protestant thought-forms, for only in breaking through these historic ways of thinking can we carry out the scientific task of theology in seeking to let our minds be utterly obedient and faithful to what is revealed from the side of the objectively given. Here there opens up a way of articulating theology within the essentially *a posteriori* and dynamic mode of modern thinking that is yet basically realist, in the sense that it is wholly devoted to its object, and will have nothing to do with the elaboration either of an existentialist ideology or an independent ontology. It will take generations to measure the significance of Barth's Herculean efforts in positive theology, but it is already clear that the whole of future theological thinking will have to reckon with what he has laid bare in the inner structure of catholic and evangelical doctrine, and with the central and dominant significance for all theological thinking he has uncovered in the grace of the Lord Jesus Christ.

We have examined and traced out the road travelled by Barth in his break-away from the subjective-idealist theology of Neo-Protestantism to positive, catholic, and evangelical dogmatics conceived and elaborated in the scientific manner. It is through looking at Barth's starting-point as well as at the goal of his thinking that we can appreciate the place and significance of the essays collected and published in this volume. They range from an early review-article of 1920 on the relation of Christianity to history to an essay on the critical bearing of Roman Catholicism on the Protestant Church of 1928. In them we see Barth listening to criticism from unusual sources, in an open-hearted readiness to let himself, and evangelical theology in which he stands, be questioned down to the bed rock in order to determine its foundations, but in them, too, we see Barth wrestling with the inheritance of Protestant theology, from the Reformation and from the nineteenth century particularly, and rethinking what he has learned from his own esteemed theological teachers like Wilhelm Herrmann, in order to break a way through their frame of thinking, and to let the positive Word of God speak again in its native force and creative impact. This is essentially the stage of his thought when he engaged in stringent dialectical thinking in order to let the opposite poles of thought have freedom of movement, if only to get away from the way in which all the great distinctive differences between God and man had been so planed down that the line ran from one to the other in a gentle declivity or a gentle ascent, depending on the direction one travelled. The more cleanly that was done, the more deeply he penetrated into the real relations of God and man, the more he was forced to abandon his dialectical thinking, which for all its negatives concealed ambiguous positives, and to work out openly on the basis of the Word of God a positive understanding of the way from God to man and of the corresponding way from man to God. All the way through one can see struggling together his concern for a biblically grounded theology which he inherited from Calvin and his concern to think it out in the wealth of modern thought which he inherited from Schleiermacher—the interest in biblical exegesis and the interest in culture hold him in a tight grasp, and if he finds that culture must be searched to its foundations by biblico-theological criticism it is not that he is in any sense a Philistine or depreciates the developments of history, but rather the reverse, and if he insists on a theological exegesis and manifests his discontent with biblical scholars who will go no further than elucidating the text from historico-critical and grammatical or perhaps from phenomenological standpoints alone, it is not that he is an opponent of careful Old Testament or New Testament scholarship, but that he wants this scholarship to do its proper work in penetrating into the inner logic of the biblical teaching and so laying bare the Word in the words.

This becomes his chief theological concern, to get at the significance of the Word of God, and of a theology of the Word as distinct from a theology that is only a reflection upon faith. Here it is perhaps the essay on the place of the Word in modern theology from Schleiermacher to Ritschl that is most revealing. On the one hand, he wants to distinguish the Word of God from history—that is an interest of the first essay in the volume which reveals the enlightening influence upon Barth of Overbeck's critique of historical Christianity, as the history of the subordination of the supernatural Kingdom of Christ to the history of man's achievements and failures. And yet while Barth insists on sharpening the distinction here it is evident that he will have nothing to do with a Word of God that is not directed to the concrete existence and historical life of man. But the awe for history, which had almost clothed it with the aura of divinity, had to be punctured in order that sober historical reflection might play its part as a servant of the creative Word of God and not the part of its gaoler. On the other hand, Barth wants to distinguish the Word of God from the word that man can speak to himself in the depths of his own religious self-consciousness, for theology can make no real claim to knowledge until it can distinguish what is objectively given from its subjective conditions and states. No solution to that problem is really possible through elaborating a 'scientific' theological pursuit as the historical reflection and philosophical consideration of the history of religious ideas. All this can quickly come under the critique of one as sharp-sighted as Feuerbach, who without much difficulty can point out that it is but a form of man's reflection upon himself and his own achievements, and is in the end a species of anthropology and not what it claims to be, a theology.

Through study of the teaching of the Reformation, and historical Reformed and Lutheran dogmatics, on the one hand, as is evident from the essays on Lutheran and Reformed theology here, and through a serious grappling with the problems raised by Roman theology and directed at evangelical theology, on the other hand, Barth attempts to clear the ground for a new theology of the Word which carries its own inner rationality, and is to be distinguished from every mysticism and every romantic idealism that is ultimately concerned with wordless experience of God and that requires to borrow from philosophy or science rational forms for its coherent articulation.

But a theology of the Word carries Barth's thinking into the doctrine of the Church as the sphere within history where that Word is proclaimed and heard, and the community within which understanding of the Word is demanded and built up. Here the theology of the Word is understood as a necessary function of the life of the people of God and of its mission to proclaim Jesus Christ to the ends of the earth and the ends of the ages. The Church lives by the message it preaches, but its preaching of that message has to be tested, to ensure that it is really preaching the Word of God and not its own ideas or opinions. The relation of the Word of God to the ordering of the life and mission of the Church in the world means that theology cannot escape the questions of ethics, but it does mean that it is essentially a theological ethics that is required for the life of the Church in the world.

Once again this involves for Barth a clarification of his doctrine of the Word and of the Church with that of Rome on the one hand and with the claims and self-understanding of secular culture on the other hand.

The discussion with the Roman Church carries Barth into a surprising measure of formal agreement with it in the doctrine of the Church, and yet into the most radical disagreement going down to the question of the justification of faith, which Luther called 'the article of the standing or falling Church'. But in this discussion Barth has to wrestle with the meaning of doctrine and the problem of authority, that is, the significance of dogma in the history and life of the Church. In these pages Barth's discussion is carried out through a debate with Erik Peterson, a notable Lutheran theologian who became a Roman Catholic and roused considerable debate. For Barth dogmatics arises out of the critical questions that must be put to the task of interpreting the biblical witnesses and thinking their thoughts after them, in order to press it into theological understanding. At the same time dogmatics must engage in a critical examination of the Church's teaching, and in a testing of old and new formulations of basic ideas and ways of thinking related to the interpretation of the Scriptures. Behind all this it is the function of dogmatics to inquire into the coherence of the historic formulations of the Church, into its decisions, definitions, and dogmas, and to test their basic correspondence with the Word of God, and so to inquire into fundamental 'dogma' interpreted as the basic and determining unity of the Church's faith. This involves Barth in a searching examination of the basic principles which Roman theology employs in the articulation and systematization of its doctrine, and the binding of it to the mind of the historical Church as it is given magisterial definition through the teaching office. Barth's thinking and writing in this connexion gave rise to the notorious debates that followed upon this period of Barth's development with leading theologians in the Roman Church.

The discussion with modern culture, particularly with German culture, was no less acute because of the social and political movements that arose out of it as well as because of the masterful ideology to which it gave rise. It involved for Barth a rethinking of his attitude to the social implications of the Gospel and of the whole problem of Church and State, and his concern to direct the challenge of the Gospel to the very roots of the social and political structures of modern man, where cultural developments were going so obviously astray, as could be seen by the rise of the National-Socialist movement on the one hand and the march of Marxist socialism on the other hand. Barth finds that he must move beyond a dialectical understanding of these questions to a more positive appreciation of the basic intention lying behind European culture, and yet the developing conflict with the Church which he early diagnosed made it even more necessary for the Church to take its stand securely on her one foundation on the Word of God if it was really to be able to declare both the judgements and reconciling grace of God to culture and state. Hence this aspect of Barth's thinking had yet to reach the really decisive point where the way ahead could be seen as clearly as he saw it in 1933. But there can be no doubt that in these essays that bear here on this question, we can see that Barth has and will not give up his deep appreciation for the responsibility for culture that had been so bravely assumed by nineteenth-century Protestant theology in spite of his radical disagreement with the disastrous line that it actually took.

It was in 1927 that Barth published his first attempt at dogmatics, which he called *Christian Dogmatics*. That work was to prove the beginning of a few years of even greater self-criticism and clarification. The lecture which he delivered to a conference of ministers in Düsseldorf on 'Roman Catholicism as Question to the Protestant Church' lets us see to some extent how his mind is moving, to an even more positive conception of the Word and the Church, and to a critical revision of historical Protestant notions which may help it to recover an understanding of the very ground of its existence in the Word of God. It is not surprising therefore that the revised edition of his dogmatics should bear the title of *Church Dogmatics*, although before he could rewrite it considerable further thinking had to be done in disentangling his own theology from the remnants of existentialism and in working out the scientific method of dogmatics over against the claims of philosophy and exact science which we have already discussed.

This volume on *Theology and Church* should be read together with Barth's account of nineteenth-century theology published in English under the title, *From Rousseau to Ritschl* (in USA *Protestant Thought From . . .*). In that work we can see how patient and sympathetic Barth is with his great predecessors in the history of modern theology, how eager he is to learn from every one of them, even when he must disagree and even when that disagreement is sharp and severe, and how dedicated he is to the task of understanding, with all the previous course of Christian thinking and teaching before him, the positive message of the Gospel, and of aiding his contemporaries in their search for secure foundations upon which to fulfil the task of the Church in preaching and teaching the Word of God. It has led him to speak of God the Creator in such a way that man is not allowed to vanish into nothingness or to be treated as a pawn in the fulfilment of God's eternal purposes, but is called to stand before the heavenly Father as his dear child, and to live in such a way that his relationship with God is made visible in his daily existence. It has led him to speak of God the Saviour in such a way as to recognize the sovereign freedom of God's grace in all his ways and works, and yet to recognize in that divine freedom the ground and source of man's true freedom in which he is called to live as a child of the heavenly Father who in Jesus Christ has come to share his humanity and bids him in obedience to the divine love to share in the humanity of his fellows. It has led Barth to speak of God's wisdom and patience with men, of his compassion for the world, and of the creative and regenerative work of God's Word and Spirit for man and all mankind, of his accompanying providence that overrules all the confusion of men, and of the will of God that at last the peoples and nations of the world shall bring of their glory into the new creation, and share together in the glory of the Lord whom they are created and redeemed to serve.

I

UNSETTLED QUESTIONS FOR
THEOLOGY TODAY (1920)

Christentum und Kultur. Thoughts and observations on modern theology by Franz Overbeck, formerly Doctor of Theology and Professor of Church History at the University of Basel. Edited from his papers by Carl Albrecht Bernoulli. Basel, Benno Schwabe & Co., 1919.

How was it possible that the early protagonists of the theology that is today dominant could ignore a colleague like Franz Overbeck and remain so indifferent and so untroubled by the questions which he put to them? How could they possibly have been content to admire his historical scholarship and then deem it sufficient to congratulate themselves on the futility of his 'purely negative approach' and shake their heads in astonishment and disapproval at the fact that he was and remained a professor of theology in spite of himself and the world's opinion?

Some of us have long puzzled over how it happened that at that time (I mean thirty years ago) theologians managed to pay no attention at all to the older and younger Blumhardt and their friends. There would have been something significant to learn—as later developments prove—from the books of Friedrich Zündel, for example. Theology would have been spared all sorts of round-about ways and false paths if we had let ourselves hear it. Were Blumhardt and Zündel too monolithic for us, too pietistic, too unscientific and technically inaccurate? That refusal to listen must be confessed, hard as it is for us to put ourselves back into the lofty academic atmosphere so characteristic of that time, which obviously closed many otherwise attentive ears to sounds from that direction.

But—we must ask today—why then did no one listen to Overbeck? If theologians were unwilling to give further consideration to the rather too murky performances at Möttlingen because the stumbling-block was much too great for the spirit of the time, why did they not turn to consider all the more carefully the equally promising and the closer stumbling-block offered them by the *Christlichkeit der heutigen Theologie* (The Christian-ness of Present Day Theology)?

Actually, Blumhardt and Overbeck stand close together; back to back, if you like, and very different in disposition, in terminology, in their mental worlds, in their experience, but essentially together. Blumhardt stood as a forward-looking and hopeful Overbeck; Overbeck as a backward-looking, critical Blumhardt. Each was the witness to the mission of the other.

Why did no one listen to Overbeck? He was no pietist, no believer in miracles, no obscurantist; he was as acute, as stylishly elegant, as free from all assumptions as could be desired. Was it because we wanted no stumbling-block at all that we did not allow ourselves to hear the call to our real task, even when it was given by a critical Blumhardt, the senior of the Basel Faculty? If we keep before our eyes only this one refusal, can we ever again hold the Lord God responsible for the slow and meandering course of the movement of Christian thought? Can we wonder, when we consider the opportunities missed, that the signs of the time in theology and church today point so definitely to deviation and disintegration? Should not those who today stand secure on the conclusions established by the consummation of the old war against orthodoxy and the like now in all seriousness turn back to the place where so many fruitful possibilities were disregarded? Such were the questions which occupied me as I read C. A. Bernoulli's edition of Overbeck's papers.

The book is a collection of fragments fitted together and given titles by the editor. It is 'part material, part blueprint; half quarry and half foundation', as the editor calls it (p. xxxvi). This is exactly the right form for what Overbeck has to say. The subject itself was too vast and the situation too complicated for him to do more than to make test borings. The well itself will finally be drilled—who knows when and by whom? Overbeck only took some soundings.

But in this prolific period which is so exhaustively exploring the whole meaning of our Hellenistic or pre-Reformation age, we must strain our ears to listen to this man, so that he may teach us to hear him aright, if now finally we have ears. I may add that the origin and form of the book are such that it cannot be read cursorily. It must be read as a whole, read more than once, and be viewed from different angles if it is to have its full effect.

'Christianity and Culture' is the title Bernoulli gives it. He could equally well have called it 'Introduction to Theology', for that is basically its theme. But it is necessary to note that this introduction could easily transform itself into an energetic expulsion of those un-called. I very much wish that our students might gain from this book a real pre-view of what they are about to undertake—or rather will stumble into. But we pastors can still less afford to lose this oppor-tunity for a basic survey of that which is our inheritance, so that we may actually take possession of it.

But be warned! The book is an inconceivably impressive sharpening of the commandment 'Thou shalt not take the name of the Lord thy God in vain'. If it is read and understood, the normal effect would be that ninety-nine per cent of us all will remain caught in its net and will make the discovery that it is impossible for anyone really to be such a thing as a theologian. And the few who escape must leave behind them so much beloved trash, so many dear illusions and practical, all too practical, naïvetés, that they find themselves freezing afterwards and know not where to turn for shelter.

All of us who are at all content with our calling will see the book printed and read with the same discomfort with which a normal physician views Weressajew's *Bekenntnisse eines Arztes* (Confessions of a Physician). For it is a dangerous book, a book filled with the apocalyp-tic air of judgement. It is a balance sheet, a book which calls the com-prehending reader away from the fleshpots of Egypt into the desert, to a place of durance where he can neither lie nor sit nor stand, but must of necessity keep moving, where he can neither gain nor possess, nor feast, nor distribute, but only hunger and thirst, seek, ask, and knock. That place recalls the words of the 'Cherubic Wanderer'. 'The foxes have holes and the fowls of the air their nests, but the Son of Man has not where to lay his head.' All who wish to avoid this place should leave this book unread.

But perhaps the impressions and experiences of the last years have shown us that we have been living until now in a house built on sand; and that theology—if this venture 'Theology' is to continue longer to exist—would do better to clench its teeth and take the road to the desert. In view of the general situation, that would be more fitting than the unchilled confidence with which in many places men con-tinue to assume the possibility of being theologians—as if it were nothing extraordinary.

Some of us are not wholly surprised by Overbeck's revelations. We rejoice at this book. We greet it gladly in the hope that it will raise up comrades for us in our loneliness. For it will not be easy for some men of integrity to kick against these pricks. To all of us without exception, the book has some serious words to say.

I

The editor leaves it to the reader to decide whether on the basis of the material before him he will choose to regard Overbeck as a sceptic or as an inspired critic. Actually Overbeck stands just on the boundary between the two. And one side of his nature (if one can speak of two sides) will be comprehensible only through the other.

If one understands him, as his contemporaries did and as Bernoulli prefers, as a sceptic, one must at least call him as Bernoulli does 'a happy, loving, doubter' (p. xix). If he is understood, as I myself think is more rewarding, as standing guard 'at the threshold of metaphysical possibilities' (p. xxxvi), then his position must be labelled that of an 'inspired critic'. In either case the reader must be able to separate sharply the irreconcilable antitheses of death and life, the world and the kingdom of heaven, and then again to see them both as one, before he can evaluate the concealed power of this unique spirit. For 'this was a man and to be a man means to be a fighter'.

Decisive for any insight into Overbeck's fundamental position are the sections 'Concerning the Investigation of Super-History' (*Urgeschichte*) (pp. 20–8) and 'Of Myself and of Death' (pp. 287–300). In the light of what is said here must be judged what is said (pp. 1–77) about the Bible and original Christianity (*Urchristentum*). All else in the book is application and illustration.

Two points, which are at once gateways and ends, determine and characterize, according to Overbeck, the being of man and of humanity. With the term 'Super-History' (*Urgeschichte*) or 'creation-history', he designates the one; with the term 'death', the other. Out of the supra-temporal, unknowable, inconceivable super-history which is composed wholly of beginnings, in which the boundaries dividing the individual from the whole are still fluid, we have come. To the single, inconceivably important moment of death in which our life enters the sphere of the unknown where, throughout our life-time, exists all which is beyond the world known to us, we go (pp. 20–1, 297). We have perhaps looked too deeply into the cause of things, *we know too much* about all things, even about those most hidden and unattainable, about the things of which we can actually know *nothing at all, the last things*.

'*We cannot escape this knowledge and we must live with it*' (pp. 293, 300).

What lies *between* these two ends, these 'last things', is the world, our world, the comprehensible world which has been given us. Whatever is or can be 'historical' is by its very nature (*eo ipso*) part of *this world*. For 'historical' means 'subject to time' (p. 242). And whatever is subject to time is limited, is relative, and is made manifest as world by the 'last things' of which we are now cognizant, whether we will or not. 'It is in no way possible to concede to the Pharisees a kingdom of God already appearing among them, wholly on this side of the end' (on Luke 17.20–1, p. 47). Frankly, in order to comprehend this world, so far as *that* is our aim, we do better not to step out of it; we should avoid even 'the slightest breath of theology' (p. 5), and as successors of the Rationalists, remain, with the resolute prudence of the true realist (p. xxviii), within its boundaries, the boundaries of humanity (p. 241).

If we cannot defend the things of this world and if none of the relationships in which we walk the earth can withstand the criticism which reduces the whole to relativity, we can still love them and we need take the criticism no more seriously than it deserves (pp. 29, 248). But this (fractured!) love for the things of this world does not originate in religion; it rests, even the smallest fraction of it, on our own action. Its 'natural basis can of course be designated by the term *God* by anyone who knows what he is talking about' (p. 249). The 'capacity for ecstasy' is by no means disregarded as 'the source of the power of culture' (p. xxviii) by the Rationalists with whom Oberbeck liked to align himself, as a sort of anonymous upstart, beside Kant, Goethe, and Lichtenberg (p. 136).

If the concept of death marks the limit of human knowledge, so it must also signify its transcendental origin. It can 'serve us as an irresistible broom for sweeping out all the lies and shams that plague our earthly life'. If the command to remember death (*memento mori*) when rightly understood affects our life for good (p. 297), then we must ascribe to it a peculiarly creative and fruitful meaning. 'Death creates life as well as destroying it' (p. 247). Without a 'tiny drop of ecstasy' (p. 182), rationalism would not be the living, all-embracing principle that Overbeck understands it to be. For it happens that just this 'tiny drop' is the source of the stream. The two great unknowns, super-history and death, are exactly the hinges on which the 'sceptical' world-view hangs! 'We men really go forward only when we launch ourselves from time to time into the air and we live our lives under conditions which do not permit us to shirk that experience' (p. 77).

'The man who actually and resolutely depends upon himself in this world, must have the courage to depend upon nothing' (p. 286).

But such a man must reckon seriously with this 'nothing', and the tiny drop of ecstasy must be *genuine*; it must not be confused with mysticism, romanticism, and pietism—although 'Pietism is for me the only form of Christianity under which a personal relation to Christianity would be possible for me' (p. 179). For 'a human individual can never expect to discover in himself a substitute for God. . . . Self-surrender is no sure road to God, but the (mystic-romantic-pietistic!) idea of man's ever finding God in himself is still more hopeless' (p. 286).

'The essential quality in Overbeck was not intellectual but elemental. He was constantly "out of bounds"; and this was not a matter of stepping across a line in some small area; it was an impressive and genuine advance, a violent *invasion*. In his criticism, the jagged ledges of bared thought leave free the vista of the hidden valley below, green in the springtime.' So Bernoulli says felicitously (p. xix); but unfortunately he somewhat obscures this important insight by the psychological trappings with which he decorates it as a sort of ideological antidote.

I myself would understand Overbeck's fundamental doctrine of super-history and death with the deep sense of the dialectic of creation and redemption which is there expressed (e.g. pp. 29–31, 248 f.), as a transcendence of all 'ideology'; and I would count the writer, with Socrates and Plato, among those 'heathen proclaimers of the resurrection' of whom it is said, 'I have not found such faith, no not in Israel.'

From the unbelievably narrow *and solid* basis of this critical foundation are to be understood the three polemic discussions which in their manifold convolutions constitute the major content of the book. The first deals with the existence of Christianity in history; the second with the nature of modern Christianity; the third with the Christian-ness of all theology, especially of the theology of the present day. Overbeck's unanswered question unfolds into several questions.

II

On the position of Christianity in history and its various aspects much has been said in the last decades. If I am not mistaken, Troeltsch's thesis of the temporary social significance of the church and his dismal picture of the coming ice ages in which this social significance would be ended, constituted the last important stage which this discussion reached before the war. I listened to him, in Aarau in 1910, with the dark foreboding that it had become impossible to advance any farther in the dead-end street where we were strolling in relative comfort. But wholly different from the questions which evoked such answers is the question of whether there can possibly be any talk at all of a position of the church in history or of its historical aspects.

Does Christianity *have* the possibility of an historical development? That is, can it undergo the continuance, the becoming and perishing, the youth and old age, the degeneration and progress which are temporal characteristics? Does it in itself give evidence of a will to become an historical entity? Is it possible for a historian as such to do justice to Christianity? Or, to put the question from the world's standpoint, can Christianity claim real significance as an historical entity? Is it possible for a historian to treat Christianity apart from culture?

Overbeck denies such a possibility categorically. Inflexibly he confronts us with the choice: If Christianity, then not history; if history, then not Christianity. 'Historic Christianity—that is Christianity subjected to time—is an absurdity' (p. 242). History is precisely the basis on which Christianity can *not* be established; for 'neither Christ himself nor the faith which he found among his disciples has ever had any historical existence at all under the name of Christianity' (pp. 9–10). 'The first Christians are no proper subject for human historical writing' (p. xxi). 'History is an abyss into which Christianity has been thrown wholly against its will' (p. 7). 'From the a-priori of our concept of time, it follows that Christianity as a phenomenon of history has become indefensible' (p. 244).

'The best school for learning to doubt the existence of God as ruler of the world is church history, if it be granted that that is the history of the religion, Christianity, which was established by God in the world and if it be assumed that God has guided its history. Obviously he has done nothing of the kind. There is nothing miraculous in church history. To judge from it, Christianity seems as completely abandoned to the world as anything else which exists there' (pp. 265–66). 'Church history teaches that Christianity has been incapable of extricating itself from the effect of a single human weakness—just as has the supposed divine guidance of its destiny. Not *one* horror of history, not one horror among all the horrible experiences which history includes, is lacking in the experiences of church history' (p. 19). 'So far as Christianity in the area of its historical life has not been spared the corruptions and confusions to which other things are subject, church history possesses no advantage—least of all a special protecting power governing the church. On the evidence of the history of the church, the existence of God can be maintained only on the assumption that he withdrew his hand from Christianity in its historical existence. Such an assumption need not damage at all the honour due to God or to what men call God' (p. 266).

'To include Christianity under the concept of the historical, means to admit that it is *of this* world, and like all life has lived in the world in order to die' (p. 7). 'From purely historical considerations, the only possible conclusion is that Christianity is worn out and has grown senile' (p. 71). 'The idea of judging Christianity simply as history only heralds the dawn of the age when Christianity will come to an end and vanish' (p. 9).

The only possible abode of Christianity lies, so far as the past is concerned, not in history, but in the history before history, the super-history (*Urgeschichte*). And only non-historical concepts, standards, and possibilities of observation could put us in the position to under-stand, to talk about—in fact, to represent in any way—this Christianity which is not Christianity in any historical sense. 'Christianity means nothing else than Christ and the faith of his followers in him; it is something above time; in the life-time of Jesus, it had as yet no exis-tence at all' (p. 28). 'Pursuit of the problems of super-history is per-mitted only to investigators who can see in that light—therefore to investigators with cats' eyes who can manage in the dark' (p. 20).

The beloved historical division between events and that which calls them into existence is impossible in relation to Christianity. For ex-ample, to take a New Testament book seriously means to know nothing of its author except for the book itself, and nothing of the 'history of the times'. Direct conversation with the author makes the book as such superfluous and deprives it of its historical existence. Author and book coalesce into one (pp. 21–3). For another example, original Christianity in relation to the world had *Socialism* within itself; while our present-day combination of Christianity and Socialism, whether subsequent or anticipatory, only betrays our lack of the inclusive and conclusive possibilities of the super-historical (pp. 26–8). Hastily formulated his-torical hypotheses on the relation of beginnings to their continuations become impossible. 'Can *one human figure as passive as Jesus* be thought of historically as the founder of anything in the world? Is not Christian-ity an historical edifice to the dimensions of which the figure of Jesus is wholly irrelevant?' (p. 39). 'The faith of Paul, springing to life after the death of Jesus, is no less of a miracle than the faith of Jesus in him-self' (p. 62).

The usual historical-psychological value judgements become impossible. For example, the dissimilarities between Jesus and Francis of Assisi are much more significant than the renowned likenesses (*conformitates*). On the one hand, 'Francis exemplifies in himself the peace which Christianity proclaims even more completely than Jesus himself. Jesus required faith in himself, a demand which in itself excludes all peacefulness and presupposes the possession and use of power. Francis merely displays faith and shows a trait of amiability which Christ wholly lacks.' On the other side, 'to follow Christ, as St Francis understood it, was to follow him in the way which most exalts Christianity to the heights and glorifies it, and not to follow him where Christ himself stands, outside the ideal of Christianity' (p. 39). Our Neo-Franciscan friends should ponder on that a little.

Most impossible of all becomes the all-too-hasty adaptation and application of supposedly historical concepts in general to suprahistorical phenomena. Who, for instance, could dare to claim to understand Jesus unless he finds in *himself* the place where he *feels himself to be simply one with God*? And who could dare assert that oneness of himself? Who can fail to see that Jesus was ruled by the conviction that what is impossible in the actual world could be basic reality *in another world*? It is precisely in the demands which are based on this conviction that Jesus seems least of all to be a vague dreamer without experience of the world. But in this conviction, which alone would make him comprehensible, who dares to follow him with real earnestness and consistency (pp. 47–9)?

'The contradiction between the original Christian eschatology and the contemporary hope for the future is fundamental' (p. 66). 'It is of no use to make profession of Christianity and to march in the opposite direction' (p. 67). 'The demand of Matt. 18.3 by itself either removes the possibility of Christianity in the world or takes the church off its worldly hinges' (p. 64). Whoever recognizes all these ordinary impossibilities as such and yet finds a road to the super-history, to Jesus —let him walk that road, but not too quickly nor with too much assurance.

At the instant when things lose their immediate connexion with the *last* things, when the plain tie between the other side and this side ceases to bind, when any view other than the absolutely critical becomes possible for us, at that moment, which is all too similar to death, there begins the history of degeneration, church history. Overbeck even agrees with Zündel in his significant judgement that Paul already belongs in this second period; although it may be true that no one has really understood Paul who thinks today that he can share Paul's opinions (p. 54), and equally true that Paul does not wholly lack important marks of the super-history (pp. 55–63).

But church history 'stands actually between life and death, and to see it overweighted on the one side or the other depends solely on the situation and the arbitrary choice of the observer. History also continues life, even as it prepares death, (p. 21). But in any case, after the expectation of the Parousia had lost its reality, Christianity lost its youth and itself. It has become something wholly different; it has become a religion, an 'ideological antidote', as we must admit with Bernoulli. And 'religion certainly shares with the world its origin from the human world' (p. 74).

But Christianity *will not* be a religion, will not be in any sense an antidote—quite apart from the fact that such an antidote is of no use whatever to man. Man lives and must live from his certainty of the 'last things'. And that is something very different.

III

Overbeck, unlike Kierkegaard, does not make his complaint against modern Christianity as himself an advocate of a true Christianity in opposition to a false (p. 279). He cannot assert forcibly enough that he is *without* any relation to Christianity of any kind. He claims for himself no religious mission. He holds so little of Christian belief that he never once counts himself among its believers! (p. 255). He will speak only of what he knows. And he expects (even apart from himself) no reform but only 'a gentle fading away' of Christianity (p. 68). He was early conditioned to regard even the religious struggles of the Reformation as pathological, even 'without the stimulus of a serious hatred for Christianity and religion' (p. 289).

But on our side, we know from his own words the significance it had for him when he thus placed himself 'in the air'. Actually a more positive position does not exist than the mountain path he walks between the two chasms. His controlled, restrained pathos, as he steps forward, with the utmost knowledge of his subject, to give warning against the fictitious relationship between Christianity and the modern world, his far from 'sceptical' insight and reverence, and the urgency with which he speaks of those matters which merit it, the hopeless conflict of his whole life which was never fully resolved just because of his complete respect for reality, all these in the last analysis can be understood only as 'Christian', as a fragment of 'super-history'. There hovers above this wholly critical book something of the peace of God that is higher than all reason—and perhaps this is all the more felt because its author did not at all so intend.

Yet it can even be debated whether Overbeck was more anxious to protect Christianity against the modern world or the modern world against Christianity. Bernoulli seems desirous of emphasizing the latter. Of course, Overbeck does both. But if his position is accurately portrayed at the end of the preface, where Bernoulli makes him stand guard on 'the threshold of metaphysical possibilities' (p. xxxvi), with the humanist culture in front of him and behind him Christianity, 'the problem which puts all history in jeopardy, the problem whose nature is fundamentally enigmatic' (p. 7)—it is a picture which inevitably reminds us of the Faustian 'May the sun remain behind me'—then we may well be tempted to a different emphasis from Bernoulli's.

It is not from humanist culture and it is not from Christianity that this theologian who does not wish to be a theologian comes. He comes rather from the elemental, the primary, the transcendental, the immediate expectation of the Parousia in the world, which stands behind Christianity (p. 291). From his words we catch a note of Jeremiah, however sternly it may be suppressed; under all the repression there is a sense of compulsion to act and to participate, which is *not of this world*. But we can be content with the sober statement that he was the guard of the boundary between here and there (the original), and not a mere observer.

The nature of 'modern' Christianity (it has always been determined to be 'modern') is therefore denatured, because in it the tension of contradiction is transformed into a normal relationship which must result in the corruption of both parts—humanity and Christianity (p. 68). Christianity has become such a problematical entity because it has lost the 'force of the offensive thrust' which it once wielded against the world, and therefore has also lost its victory over the world (pp. 65–6). But it has kept its impossible claim to advise man and direct him beyond himself. That claim, which has lost all validity since it is removed from the super-historical era with its unique possibilities, can only act as the wisdom which brings death (pp. 69, 279).

True Christianity and the world, since the loss of the immediate bond created by the expectation of the Parousia, can no longer understand each other nor be mutually understood. There is nothing which true Christianity rejects more firmly than a history in the world. Such Christianity never even thought of 'the effect of Jesus on history'. His was the Spirit—and by that term Christianity meant something quite different (p. 68).

But nothing lies farther from the mind of the present day than belief in an imminent end of the world. The Christianity of today 'has so little room left for the whole conception of the Return of Christ that it cannot even conceive it historically as belonging to the original Christianity; at the most it may admit its presence as a negligible factor (*quantité négligeable*)' (p. 68). 'A modern hat! Very good. That can conform to the fashion; but modern Christianity? Is not that quite different? . . . We who so judge are content with this truth; but the modern world around us is not and it speaks of modern and historical Christianity as realities to be taken seriously' (p. 245). *Historical Christianity* ('the religious community which developed into the Christian church out of the gospel as its pre-historic embryo' p. 63) is in itself a contradiction.

'Has Christianity brought a new era? Is the Christian form of dating, *anno domini*, based on actuality? Certainly not; for originally Christianity spoke of a new age only under a presupposition which has not been met, namely that the existing world was to perish and make room for a new world. For a moment that was a genuine expectation, and it has re-emerged now and again as such; but it has never become the historically established fact which alone could offer a real basis for a complete new calendar supposed to conform to facts. It is the world which has asserted itself—not the Christian expectation for the world; and therefore the alleged "Christian era" in it has always remained a figment of the imagination' (p. 72). 'The Christianity of all periods has always shown itself incapable of giving a universal message to the human world. It has helped only individuals and it has helped in no other way. In the community at all times a mediocre Christianity rules' (p. 268).

'A façade can lack an interior . . . on the other hand it is unendurable that an interior should present a false façade; and that is the case with present-day Christianity. But you cannot summon its interior as a witness *against* its exterior as though it could be found without it. And anyhow, no one has to listen to it. . . . Those representatives of Christianity who currently appeal to its "inner life" are its worst traitors' (p. 71). For 'the innermost and the real *need* of Christianity at the present time is the practice of it in life (*Praxis*). What Christianity lacks most in order to be able to assert itself in the world is evidence of its practical applicability in life' (p. 274). 'But our life is obviously not ruled by Christianity. In view of that, it is of little interest to proclaim how far it may rule the thoughts which are presented in writing. Modern Christianity itself performs only a grave-digger's job, as by the sweat of its brow it widens the gulf between theory and practice.

'Christian dogmas are polished carefully and fitted to modern thought. But the process merely erases the last traces which true Christianity still has left in life. What is accomplished serves wholly for the greater glory of the modern (*ad majorem gloriam moderni*) and to the detriment of Christianity (*ad detrimentum Christianismi*)' (p. 67).

'It is no wonder that the modern world so thirsts for orthodoxy and has so little use for Pietism, or that a dogmatic system like Ritschl's won such a following while Rothe's suffered so tragic a shipwreck. . . . The modern world is ready to do everything to make it possible to remain within the *illusion* of Christianity; and for that purpose, as it is easy to see, orthodoxy is more usable than Pietism' (p. 274). 'In modern life, Christianity is thirsting for life and in so far for Pietism. In modern Christianity, the modernity thirsts for orthodoxy since it has already drunk its fill of life; and so in modern Christianity, Christianity gets nothing to drink. For its thirst is of a wholly different nature from that of modernity. . . . Can this tragicomedy really have a prospect of playing before the world much longer?' (p. 275).

And so it is that 'the most significant fact about Christianity is its powerlessness, the fact that it *cannot* rule the world' (p. 279). Think of its relation to Socialism (pp. 26–8). Or consider how shaky a bulwark it has shown itself against the danger of nationalism (p. 257). Look at the air of solemnity which Ritschleanism habitually wears when it handles in a cursory way the concept of vocation (pp. 278, 288). Consider (and in dealing with this evidence Overbeck for his part puts on a certain 'solemn' attentiveness) the religion of Bismarck (pp. 148–59), which provides the most magnificent example of the way the world pleases itself and wins the applause of the representatives of religion. Therefore Bismarck is the best-known advocate of the indispensability of religion for all earthly effectiveness. He had religion simply in order to keep his hands free for secular work. For the enigma which religion wills to solve, he had no time. All he wanted was something to free him from anxiety. His religion was erected on the basis of his self-esteem. Moreover, it was something which he had reduced to the size of a personal plaything and which he could lay aside at any time.

But the fact that he could play with it and occasionally had a Christian notion was sufficient in the eyes of the modern advocates of Christianity to make him a Christian, even a model Christian. He could even be hung in the gallery of 'the classics of our religion' next to Jesus, Francis, and Luther—to amplify with a more recent illustration. Thus Christianity has now been handed over to every holder of power. So cheap is today's canonization in the Christian heaven. But none the less, it is this Bismarck who has done more for the historical existence of modern theology that Ritschl and Harnack. And what can be expected for this Christianity except 'a gentle fading away' ?

Again we are reminded of the attack on Christianity which the men of Möttlingen and Bad Boll once made from the same central standpoint, the expectation of the Second Coming; of their inquiry concerning the real power of the Kingdom of God, and the overcoming of religious subjectivity. But the friends of historico-psychological realism and the alleged Overbeck specialists in Basel need not be troubled. Against the greater keenness of observation and thought on the side of Overbeck is to be set the greater love, the enthusiasm and the joy in witnessing on the side of Blumhardt.

Yet Overbeck also was not without the holy fire, and Blumhardt was not without knowledge. In its essential nature—and that alone is important—the attack made is the same here and there. And with this double attack, theology has not yet really grappled.

IV

Overbeck's third protest is directed against theology specifically, against the theology which today in Germany and Switzerland (and where not?) presides over the pulpit and the professor's desk, the theology of a positive or liberal shade. One and all, those in authority today are 'modern'.

I confess that I am not wholly of one mind about this attack, about which I feel strongly. I feel a glow of approval hard to restrain for the strong polemical food which is there offered. And yet there is the other feeling that it would have been better for the sake of the essential point to have held back some of these priceless apothegms on men and events. The 'chest stuffed full of alphabetic notes' left by Overbeck (as the preface states, p. xx) must, according to reliable reports, have included also some wholly different comments.

Bernoulli will be able to say in his own justification that he was forced to practise restraint in dealing with such a mass of material. But I recall what Overbeck himself said (pp. 3 f.) about the inaccuracy, in fact the impossibility, of all writing of contemporary history. I think of the emphatic words: 'Men are not called to give final judgement on one another' (p. 250). Now if what we read (pp. 159–80) under the heading 'Albrecht Ritschl as Head of a School of Theology', for example, or (pp. 198–241) under the heading 'Adolf Harnack, a Lexicon' is not a 'final judgement', then I have no idea what would deserve the name. Diana of the Ephesians will be overthrown only from within and below. Arguments *ad hominem* such as these, in which the other side still has the advantage of us, offer to our psychological age such easy opportunities for counterattack that any instruction which can be so turned aside will never penetrate. After this observation on tactics, we can now turn to the matter itself.

What is theology? 'The Satan of religion' (p. 12), 'Christianity become worldly-wise' (p. 124), Overbeck answers. It is 'the attempt to impose Christianity on the world under the explicitly hallowed garb of modern culture, by concealing, even by denying its basically ascetic character' (p. 125). It is 'a desperate wrestling match, fought on behalf of religion against certain primary truths which show us too ruthlessly the final problems of our existence, the difficulties and the limitations under which men live' (p. 13). Its typical representative is the Abbé in the French salon of the eighteenth century (pp. 125, 198). Its fiercest opponent is Blaise Pascal, who had no fear of using caricature, 'the knight of truth, who undertook the impossible' (pp. 126–34). Accordingly its nature is Jesuitry, the classic witness to the dire state of the church (p. 122).

The worst error of the Jesuits was not that they questioned morality, the most questionable of all the assumptions which exist among men. It was rather that they sublimated and refined and accommodated Christianity—an enterprise in which Protestant Jesuitry in the form of modern theology has far surpassed the Catholic (pp. 123–5). By this activity, the theologians have become 'the most outstanding traitors to their cause' (p. 236).

'Do the modern theologians think that they can put us off much longer with their absurd delusion that Christianity's best defence to insure its continued existence is its unlimited capacity for change?' (p. 138). 'Moses, Christ, Paul, and Luther are still given a place by these modern theologians as a part of their understanding of world history, but only as a kind of ornamentation which is recommended for display in public exhibitions. So far even modern theologians remain orthodox. But at the bottom of their hearts, they are the best of "believers in new things" and their master is Bismarck' (p. 155).

'Basically they have little to do with Christianity, but just for that reason they have a particular itch to start something with it' (p. 278). 'The Zeus on the Olympus of their priestly company they call "the present". Their gaze is directed unwaveringly to the *modern man*' (p. 218). 'Theologians are never simply Christians, never men whose relation to Christianity is simple and unambiguous' (p. 273). They expect indeed 'to put God daily into their bag' (p. 268). They allow themselves 'to play [with God and the human soul] like children with their dolls, and they have the same assurance of ownership and the right of disposal'. They live in the naïve confidence that 'men may do all things with God and in his name'; that 'with God man finds himself in complete adjustment with the world; with him, man succeeds best' (p. 267).

But the very existence of these servants of Christianity has as its prerequisite the existence of a world beside and outside of Christianity. 'They are, under the most favourable conditions, middlemen between Christianity and this world; and therefore no one really trusts their counsel. . . . There always remains the sense that they are middlemen—a kind of men against whom there is a well-founded prejudice. And then besides, Christianity itself rejects middlemen. It recognizes no world beside itself, for it is absolute in its claims.' And so theologians must undergo the painful experience of finding that the service they intend to offer is accepted with the most polite thanks, 'but with no overlooking of the basic defect that those who offer the service come themselves from the same corner of merely *relative* evaluation of Christianity in which men in general commonly stand and out of which they would gladly be rescued. And when it is realized that this service is done for us by someone who merely shares with us our common need, it understandably elicits a very faint acknowledgement. . . .' The theologians might be called 'the Figaros of Christianity. In any case, these modern representatives of theology are the most available and usable, but also the most unreliable of its factotums. And as such, all honourable Pietists consider them, in the bottom of their hearts' (pp. 273–4).

Their position is equally doubtful when considered from the standpoint of culture. 'The Philistines of culture are men who are enthusiastic advocates of culture but have no aptitude for it; men who would like to be cultured but who apply themselves only half-heartedly and "part-time", only for the sake of appearing as its representatives. Therefore theologians are the born Philistines of culture in all ages—not just at the present time. They always drag along with them the Christianity into which they were born or which was taught them and it weighs down all their cultural aspirations. Their culture therefore is culture with a bad conscience' (pp. 270-1). We need only read over the descriptions of the Pharisees in Zündel's book on Jesus to be convinced of the parallel here.

How radically Overbeck questions the possibility of the theology dominant today (and for him that meant questioning its *Christian-ness*) and with what earnestness he renounced it, will have become plain from the preceding excerpts. (I have for my part 'practised restraint' here.) Theology still owes the answer to the inquiry made to it in 1873.

In conclusion we naturally ask whether Overbeck believed a different, a better theology to be possible. His editor's answer will be roundly 'No'; and he can support his verdict by the fact that Overbeck himself, at least so far as it concerned him personally, repudiated this possibility. 'I have no intention of reforming theology. I admit its nullity in and of itself and I am not merely attacking its temporary decay and its present basis' (p. 291). An end to Christianity! (*Finis christianismi!*) rings his prophetic imprecation—still more an end to theology!

But the man who spoke so profoundly of death must somehow have combined with this *finis* a fruitful, living concept originating in the beginning. On the other side from the direct final question must be an answer; on the other side from the nothingness a new beginning; beyond the desert into which we are led must be a promised land. At least the fact about which his watching contemporaries talked so much and for which (at least in this book) neither Overbeck nor his editor is able to give a credible explanation—the banal fact that Overbeck himself was never anything but a *theologian*, cannot be without significance, in spite of his resolute repudiation. To call Overbeck, in his own despite, 'a theologian learned in the ways of the kingdom of heaven and in the ways of earth', as one of his secular colleagues said beside his grave, ought to be from the historico-psychologial viewpoint at least a portent; and from the point of view of reality it is perhaps not such a bad portent. The last can still sometimes be first. A theologian who is determined *not* to be a theologian might perhaps—if the impossible is to become possible—be a very good theologian.

Overbeck himself wrote, a few lines after his repudiation: 'Theology, like everything else which exists, will be or has been good for something. Why not, for example, for establishing the limits of humanity, for our final, radical rescue from all demonic superstition and from all transcendental other-worldliness ?' (p. 292.) Now this comment, when examined word by word, makes an important assertion concerning matters which are fundamental and are not yet decided. (In considering it, we might even be permitted to overlook the *has been*.)

There are a few more statements which escaped the author almost against his will and which deal with at least the possibility of a theology of greater insight and more caution. They should not be omitted in this connexion. 'Religious problems must eventually be based in a wholly new area [in contrast to the antagonism between Catholicism and Protestantism] at the expense of what has until now been called religion' (p. 270). 'Theology cannot be re-established except with audacity' (p. 16). 'The first, fresh Christianity is a Christianity without the experience of growing old and it cannot be saved by any theology which does not renounce all its pretensions, historical, scientific, *and* theological' (p. 8). 'Only a *heroic Christianity which takes its position without regard to any era and establishes itself on itself alone* can escape the fate of Jesuitizing' (p. 126). 'He who is to represent Christianity is not thereby called to represent "the truth", although he may be convinced and show himself convinced that both are identical' (p. 268). No presentation which attempts to 'establish Christianity historically will ever be possible; only that composed *from the heart of the matter itself*, the non-historical Christianity' (pp. 9–10).

Would it not be worth the effort to consider the spiteful assertion that 'theologians are the fools of human society' more seriously than Ritschl did ? 'Perhaps it might be concluded that *the foolishness asserted is not such an unmitigated misfortune*, and that just because of it theologians may be a necessary ballast and consequently be prized as necessary in human society' (p. 173). 'The eternal permanence of Christianity can be claimed only from the eternal viewpoint (*sub specie aeterni*), that is, from a standpoint which knows nothing of time and of the contrast of youth and age existing only in time' (p. 71). 'Religion does not so much bring us information about God (where do we have such information ?) as assure us that God knows *us*. Furthermore, knowledge about God in itself could not help us where we feel in need of help; but everything which concerns us depends on his knowledge of us' (p. 266).

The man who could express such thoughts, even if he himself developed them no further, as a theologian certainly wanted more than 'to provide culture with information about theology' as the editor asserts (p. x).

But we must urgently warn all those who desire positive results and directions that they should not rush too quickly towards the standpoint which Overbeck indicated, but did not himself employ. Still less should they suppose that the promised land will be reached tomorrow—perhaps even today! Our next task is to begin the desert wandering. Otherwise a new misfortune and a new disappointment could come. The matters dealt with in this audacious undertaking are too large for the theologian to be able to pass all the way through the narrow door of Overbeck's negation—even if we think we know something of Blumhardt's *Yes*, which is the other side of Overbeck's *No*.

There were good reasons for Overbeck himself to refrain from the attempt to pass all the way through—and we are grateful to him for so refraining. A theology which would dare that passage—dare to become eschatology—would not only be a new theology but also a new Christianity; it would be a new being, itself already a piece of the 'last things', towering above the Reformation and all 'religious' movements. Whoever would dare to build on that tower would truly do well to sit down first and count the cost.

The next work for all of us, and the best we can do the more we feel ourselves forced under the pressure of present events to make decisions, to break through our limits, is to remain standing before that narrow door in fear and reverence, and without clamouring for positive proposals; to understand what is at stake and to realize that only the impossible can save us from the impossible.

We have the question of the practical significance of the 'last things', the question of the insights and possibilities which none can assume for himself unless they were given him from above. We have the question of pre-suppositions. To have thrown these questions at us, and, as was proper, only to have hinted at the answers—that is the service of Overbeck, for which presumably there is great appreciation in heaven.

Let us be content with the mighty STOP! which the dead has here given us. Let us not undertake to believe in the impossible, since we see, with Overbeck, that this STOP will *not* be the last word 'on the threshold of metaphysical possibilities'. 'It is sown in corruption; it is raised in incorruption; it is sown in dishonour; it is raised in glory; it is sown in weakness; it is raised in power.'

Σπείρεται ἐν φθορᾷ, ἐγείρεται ἐν ἀφθαρσίᾳ· σπείρεται ἐν ἀτιμίᾳ, ἐγείρεται ἐν δόξῃ· σπείρεται ἐν ἀσθενείᾳ, ἐγείρεται ἐν δυνάμει.

I Cor. 15.42-3.

II

LUTHER'S DOCTRINE OF THE
EUCHARIST: ITS BASIS AND PURPOSE
(1923)

I

'A CHRISTIAN must know that there is no reliquary on earth more holy than the Word of God, for the sacrament itself *is created* and blessed and hallowed through God's Word.' [1] In the context in which Luther wrote these words, the statement has primarily a *critical significance*. There are similar statements also in his earlier writings. The sacrament is what it is only through the Word of God *and not otherwise*.

Luther defended the validity of this truth on two fronts. First, by repudiating the equation of sacrament with sacrifice. It was not man's act for God which established the sacrament as such; it was the act of God in joining his Word to a sign. 'In the sacrament thy God, Christ himself, acts, speaks, works with thee through the priest; and what happens there is no human work or word. There God himself tells thee plainly all the things which have been said by Christ.' [2] 'When a man is to undertake a work together with God and is to receive something from him, it necessarily follows that the man does not begin and lay the first stone. God alone, without any solicitation or demand from men, must come forward and give men direction and promise. The same Word of God comes first, and the Word is the foundation, the rock on which every work, word, thought of men is built. This Word a man must thankfully accept and he must truly believe the divine promise. And he must not doubt that as God promises, so it happens.' [3]

The Mass is nothing other than 'a testament and sacrament, in which God makes a promise to us and gives us grace and mercy. So it will not do for us to make out of it a good work, an act of service to God. For a testament gives a benefit; it does not receive one (*beneficium datum* not *acceptum*). It is not the acceptance of any benefit from us,

---

[1] 22/38 (1522). References are to the first Erlangen edition. For the German the volume numbers are given in Arabic figures, for the Latin in Roman notation. The sentence divisions, etc., are mine.
[2] 21/266 (1519).   [3] 27/144 (1520).

but is the gift of a benefit to us.' How can the acceptance of a bequest be a good work? 'Only if one were to call it a good work for a man to stand still and let himself be benefited, be given food and drink, be clothed and healed, be helped and set free.' Therefore 'there is here not duty (*officium*) but benefit (*beneficium*), not work or service, but only enjoyment and profit'.[1] It is 'not my work but *God's*; with it I merely let myself be helped and benefited. Therefore, as far apart as are God's work and my work, so far separated also are conceiving this sacrament to be God's work and conceiving it to be our work.' [2]

Certainly at times Luther made the attempt to re-interpret the idea of sacrifice instead of discarding it. We are to 'offer' to God 'an empty and hungry heart',[3] or 'ourselves and all that we have, with constant prayer', to offer 'praise and thanksgiving'. But in the continuation of the last passage, it becomes clear that reinterpretation become rejection. For we are not ourselves to present this sacrifice before the eyes of God; we are to lay it upon Christ and let him present it. He 'prays for us in heaven, receives our prayer and offering, and through himself as a good priest makes them acceptable before God.' Therefore, 'we do not offer Christ, but Christ offers us'.[4] The fact that blessing and thanksgiving are included in the Mass, according to the example of Christ, 'bears witness that men are receiving or have received something from God and are not offering something to God'.[5]

Luther also repudiated, validating this position again by the Word of God, the identification of sacrament and the *sacramental elements*. The sacrament as such did not depend on the sacramental character of an element, but on the Word joined to the element. 'If you cannot accept . . . the Word, then you do not accept the sacrament, for if the elements are without the Word, they are not sacraments.' [6] 'If the Word of God were not with the bread and wine, there would be no spiritual food, and there would be no exercise of faith. Therefore, food and drink *on which God has set his Word and sign* are equally spiritual food everywhere, however external and material they may be. And if God tells me to hold up a straw, then there would be spiritual food and drink in the straw—not because of the nature of the straw, but because of the Word and sign of God's truth[7] and presence.' Again, '*if God's Word and sign is not there or is not recognized, then it is no help if God*

---

[1] Ibid., p. 156 and cf. V/46–47 (1520).   [2] 11/181 (1523).
[3] II/314 = 17/56 (1518).   [4] 27/160–1 (1520).
[5] VI/154 = 28/72 (1521/22).   [6] III/428 = 11/161 (1524 ?).
[7] This can be paraphrased to clarify the meaning: because it is through the Word a sign of divine truth.

himself be there; even as Christ said of himself (John 6.63) "the flesh profiteth nothing", because they did not heed the words which he spoke in his flesh, the words which make his body the true food. . . . Therefore we must not attend merely to God's works, signs and wonders as blind reason does, but to the Word of God in them as faith does.' Without the Word, 'the signs and works of God' are not there; 'or if they are there and are seen without the Word, only by the eyes; then men only gaze at them open-mouthed and are momentarily astonished at them as at all other new things which require no faith'.[1]

Occasionally Luther can also put it conversely. Christ, who is truly this bread, is not to be enjoyed until 'God speaks the Word thereby, so that you can hear him and recognize him. For what help is it to you if Christ sits in heaven or is under the form of bread? He must be imparted and served and come to words through (!) the inner and the external Word'.[2] Even in this converse form, the *Word* makes the sacrament, that is makes it with spoken words a real sacrament. 'A thousand times more depends on the words than on the "forms" of the sacrament, and without the words it is a mockery of God',[3] 'idle gesture and pointing',[4] 'a body without soul, a cask without wine, a strong-box without money, a form without substance, a sheath without dagger'.[5] 'The words belong in the ears, the signs in the mouth.'[6] Or, 'the words are his divine pledge, promise and testament. The signs are his sacrament, that is, holy signs.'[7] And the conclusion in the last two passages runs: 'much more' depends 'on the words than on the signs'; 'where the preaching was not required, the Mass would never have been instituted'.[8] And he continues further: 'The signs indeed might not exist and man might still have the words and accordingly still be *blessed without sacrament, but not without testament.'*[9]

Consistently with this judgement that more depends on the Word than on the sign, Luther showed a certain indifference [10] towards the

---

[1] 8/94, 96 (1523). [2] 21/206 (1518). [3] 28/305 (1522).
[4] 28/374 (1522). [5] 27/153-4 (1520). [6] 22/39 (1522).
[7] 27/153 (1520). Luther at this time seemed tending towards substituting for the concept 'sacrament' that of 'testament' (equals 'Mass', which equals 'Word plus sign') or towards understanding 'sacrament' as only the holy sign in itself. The latter was according to his earlier and later use of the term definitely *not* sacrament. [8] Ibid., p. 167.
[9] Ibid., p. 153. 'Man can have the Word or testament and use it apart from sign or testament' V/43 (1520). 'The sign we can do without, but the Word is indispensable' 22/39 (1522).
[10] 'Truly it is not very important', 'not that I want to make a commotion about it', 27/168; cf. V/29 (1520). This point, which for Luther was such a nonessential, would be according to K. Goetz (*Die Abendmahlsfrage*, 1904, p. 44) 'the most certain advance' of his doctrine over the scholastic.

question of the *cup for the laity*, which so exercised his contemporaries. The Hussites 'are not right when they think it *must* be given'. One can equally well take only one element of the sacrament, or none at all 'as actually the patriarchs did in the desert'.[1] Even in his first tract on the Lord's Supper, directed against the 'signifiers', Luther repeated that 'the most important and the main part of the sacrament is the Word of Christ', that 'far more depends on these words than on the sacrament itself', that it is 'most necessary' 'in the sacrament to lead the people again to the Word.' [2]

But it would be a serious error if, because of this crucial importance of the concept of the Word, we should try to picture Luther on the way to supporting a mystical, spiritualistic concept of the sacrament. Criticism and negation are the same only for theological dilettanti. Luther meant negatively neither the distinction between sacrament and Word, nor that between the sacrament and the sacramental sign. Such distinction is much too meaningful not to be full of hidden implications. Parallel to the contrast between Word of God and sacramental act and sign runs the other contrast between Word of God and *work of God*, between promise and *being and event*, between promising and *giving*, between conferring benefit and *receiving benefit*,[3] between the 'blade of straw' which God could tell us to hold up and that which it then would be by the power of this Word as sign of 'God's truth and presence'.[4]

This second contrast points clearly to its own transcending. Must not the first contrast between (the same!) Word and the sacramental act and sign (which indeed presents and proclaims the second contrast) share in the prospect of that transcending? Was not the 'and is made' (*et fit*) in the Augustinian canon, 'the Word is joined to the element and it is made sacrament', to be more true and more important for Luther than the critical 'is added' (*accedit*)? A further group of passages shows us that Luther's thinking on the Word in the Lord's Supper did of necessity proceed in this direction.

It is at once evident that in many of the passages already cited, Luther speaks, not of 'the Word' but of 'the words'. However, these 'words' (no proof is needed) are the instituting words of Christ at the

---

[1] 27/73, 72 (1520).   [2] 28/390-1 (1523).   [3] Cf. above pp. 74², ³, 75¹, ².
[4] Cf. above pp. 75⁷, 76¹. Luther will make use of this figure later. If he holds out only a blade of straw and speaks such words, I must believe it,' 29/341 (1526). And at the castle in Marburg in 1529 the figure is even more sharply pointed: 'If the Lord points out a crab-apple to me and tells me to eat it, *I ought not to ask why*' (Zwingli, *Werke* ed. Schuler and Schulthess, II, 3, 48).

Last Supper, according to the Synoptics and Paul. These recorded words of God make the Lord's Supper a *mighty Word*, the *Word* and *Work of God*, the *real* sacrament.[1] We come now to a plain statement of the position from which alone the interpretation of the development postulated above is to be understood. 'But I set against the decisions of all the Fathers, against the wisdom and word of all angels, men or devils, the Scripture and the Gospel. Therein it is plainly stated that the Mass is a Word and Work of God, in which God promises and manifests his grace. Here I stand, here I challenge, here I walk proudly and say, God's Word is for me above all. God's majesty stands beside me, therefore I yield not a hair's breadth, though a thousand Augustines and a thousand separate churches were against me. I am certain that the true Church holds to God's Word with me; let the so-called churches depend on men's words.'[2] Even in *these* recorded words of God there is a limitation. In them God 'bears witness that remission of sins is given to all who believe; Christ's body is given and his blood is shed for them'.[3] The words contain the promise (*promissio*) in which Luther recognizes the *Word* of God. Because of the specific content of this promise, Luther explains the whole Christian message as nothing but an exposition of the words of the Lord's Supper. 'The preaching should be nothing but the explanation of the words of Christ when he said, This is my body. . . . What is the whole Gospel except an explanation of this testament?'[4] 'For this would be teaching faith and truly building the Church.'[5]

What then can the Mass, the sacramental act and sign to which these words of Christ apply, be, other than the testament itself as explained in the preaching, the highest actual fulfilment of those words of promise? And therefore obviously Luther can make the equation: the Mass=the New Testament, as he does in the title of the important treatise of 1520;[6] or he can call the Mass 'the centre of the eternal and new testament' in the title of another writing of 1522.[7]

'These words' are the meaning and content of the Mass. 'As I said, the whole virtue of the Mass consists in the words of Christ.'[8] 'If we wish to hold Mass rightly and to understand it, we must let go of everything which the eyes and all the senses may show us in the service . . .

---

[1] Or according to Luther's temporarily altered usage (cf. p. 76[7]), 'to the revealed and fulfilled *testament*'.

[2] 28/379 (1522).   [3] V/42 (1520).

[4] 27/167. Cf. V/54, 'Assemblies of people are for no other purpose than the exposition of the Mass, that is, for clear statements of the promise, of the testament'; and 20/232 (all 1520). Further, VI/168=28/87 (1520/21).

[5] V/54.   [6] 27/139 f.   [7] 22/38 f.   [8] V/42 (1520).

until we stand before the *Word* of Christ; and we must fully realize that with the Word, he consummates and establishes the Mass and has commanded us to consummate it. For on that Word the Mass wholly depends, with all its nature, work, use and fruit; otherwise nothing of the Mass is received.' [1] 'Therefore if you will worthily receive the sacrament and testament, see that you bring forward these living words of Christ, that you establish yourself upon them with strong faith, and that you crave what Christ has promised you in them. And so it will be yours, if you are worthy and ready.' Thus it is necessary to believe the *words* of Christ and so to allow them to be true. Everything depends on the words 'which one grasps as firmly as gold and jewels, and keeps nothing else more steadily before the eyes of the heart'.[2] Luther makes everything so dependent on the 'words' that he can identify the Lord's Supper with their content. 'You see therefore that the Mass is the promise of the remission of sins made to us by God, and it is such a promise that it was confirmed by the death of the Son of God.' [3] This promise it is which makes the sacraments (of both the Old and New Testaments) to be a sacrament, in distinction from a mere sign. God promises that 'whoever has the sacrament, is to have with it this and that good'.[4]

The concept of 'testament' which was so important to Luther in 1520 was used in a brief formulation in the following way: 'The testator, Christ, is about to die; the words which they now call words of consecration are the words of the testament; the inheritance is the forgiveness of sin promised in the testament. The heirs are all who believe.' These four components 'complete the testament'.[5]

According to this interpretation as given by Luther himself the *words of the testament* are not the whole 'testament'. They point backward, back to the testator, and point forward to the inheritance and the heirs. It therefore will not and cannot be possible to persist in understanding the sacrament as testament which is *only* promise! The

---

[1] 27/144 (1530).

[2] Ibid., pp. 151 and 150. 'In the might of the same Word and in attentiveness to it' a man 'must receive the sacrament and must have no doubt that according to the sound and content of the Word of Christ it will be done unto him' 17/69 (1521). 'Whoever goes to this precious sacrament, let him see to it that he brings this Word with him' 22/40 (1522).

[3] V/37 (1520).

[4] 24/66 (1521). In the basic Latin text of this work in 1520 this sentence was lacking (V/168). But the translation comes from Luther himself and was an intentional improvement; V/155, cf. V/63 (1520).

[5] VI/164=28/83 (1521/22); already further developed 27/145 f. Cf. also V/37 (1520).

emphasis must now be put on the other side. 'These words' are the *meaning* and *content* of the sacrament. They *make* the sacrament. But actually they require (for us!) an *endorsement* of what they say to us. For there, where the promise appears as endorsed, there is the sacrament. The fact that in need, 'in the desert' [1] the implementation must be and is dispensed with, does not change the rule that we need the implementation and nothing can alter at all the *power* of the 'endorsed' promise. The possibility of declaring the sacrament to be something superfluous lies as little within the range of Luther's thought as does doubt that the Word really *makes* the sacrament. On both points, that the Word necessarily establishes the sacrament and that it possesses effectuating power, Luther is consistent throughout. (Even here he is in agreement with Augustine's *visible word*.)

The Word becomes visible as sacrament, is revealed and brought within our sight, so to speak, for a transaction in 'open court' (*publici juris*). It moves outside the sphere of the merely audible and intelligible to the threshold of the world of sight and touch. (Exactly so much and no more, in my judgement, should be said here.) 'Hence it follows that the sacraments, that is the external words of God spoken by a priest, are in truth a great consolation and are perfectly comprehensible signs of God's purpose. On them a man should support himself as on a good staff, like the one with which the patriarch Jacob went through Jordan. Or they should be like a lantern by which a man guides himself, on which he must keep his eyes steadily as he walks the long road of death, sin and hell.' [2]

Luther interpreted the elevation of the host, not as a sacrifice (*oblatio*) to God, but as 'an admonition to us, by which we are summoned to faith in this testament which [the officiating priest] so exhibits and proclaims with the words of Christ, while at the same time he shows the sign of it; and the lifting up of the bread fitly corresponds to the proclamation, "this is my body" '. [3]

But Luther prefers to the figure of the relation of promise and sign that of the *seal*, which he connects with the idea of the testament. 'His words are for us like a letter, and his signs are like a seal or signet.' [4] 'This is what the priest means when he raises the host. He addresses us rather than God, as if he meant to say: Look here, this is the seal and

---

[1] Cf. above p. 77[1].   [2] 21/266(1519).
[3] V/52 (1520); and still more plainly, 17/68 (1521): 'namely that it be explained to the laity that with the priest's elevation of the host and the little bell they are hearing loud and clear the words of Christ which the priest has read secretly'.   [4] 22/40 (1522).

sign of the testament in which Christ assigned to us the forgiveness of sins and eternal life.' [1] Through this seal, the promise is *given* to me, a binding promise, so that the content (although it is not yet in my possession) is my legal property, so that the promise becomes a deed of transfer. 'This is the use of the sacrament: thou art able to say, I have this clear (*apertum*) word (in the German, 'here I clearly have this word'), my sins are forgiven. Also I have received the seal, I have eaten and drunk. This I can certainly prove, for I have done it in the sight of Satan and the world.' [2]

Thus while the figure of the 'testament' is kept, and I am told that I am the heir and the inheritance is mine, the Word which has clearly come to the threshold of sight and touch in order to tell me this, has ceased to be a second component, separate from the sacramental act and sign. The hidden penetration has occurred in power, and the sacrament is made (*et fit sacramentum*). 'Behold, this is then truly God's Word, Christ is the bread. The bread is God's Word, and yet is a thing, a piece of bread. For it is *in the Word*, and the *Word* is *in it*. And believing the same Word means eating the bread; and he to whom God gives it lives eternally.' [3] Divine food and drink *is* now in this 'blade of straw'—in the sign established through the Word of divine truth and the divine presence, not otherwise—but just because of that: *est*, it *is*.

II

'Promise and faith are correlative, so that where there has been no promise, there cannot be faith; and where faith has not been, there is no promise.'[4] 'God prepared here food, table and a meal for our faith, but faith is not fed except by the Word of God alone.' [5]

This, then, is the second pillar of Luther's doctrine of the Lord's Supper, faith nourished by the Word of God. And this also has primarily a critical significance. The sacrament is received *only* through faith and through nothing else. In this context also the two restrictions, not through sacramental act and not through the receiving of the sacramental sign, would be distinct; but the nature of the content results in a continual fusion. Without impairing the clarity of our investigation we can therefore speak of both together.

The sharpest expression of this critical interpretation is found in a

---

[1] 27/149 (1520).   [2] III/433=11/166 (1524?).   [3] 21/206-7 (1518).
[4] VI/153=28/70 (1521/22).   [5] 27/154. Cf. V/42 (1520).

Corpus Christi sermon on John 6.[1] Luther there protests against con-necting this passage of Scripture with the sacrament. The argument runs: 'However true it is that the sacrament is real food, yet it is no help at all to him who does not receive it in his heart by faith. For it makes nobody religious or believing but demands that he be religious and believing beforehand.' [2] On the contrary the eating and drinking of which John 6 speaks is from the beginning 'nothing else but believing on the Lord Christ who has given his flesh and blood in our behalf'. That eating is done 'in the heart and not with the mouth. Eating in the heart does not deceive, but eating with the mouth, that deceives. Eating with the mouth has an end, but the other eating continues forever without ceasing.' [3] What is 'profitable' is not the physical eating of the flesh but 'the believing that this bread is the flesh of God's Son'. [4] In every way the festival preacher is declaring war against the festival of the sacramental object, Corpus Christi, which brought him to the pulpit. There was no other festival to which he was so opposed. He would like to advise that it be wholly abolished, for to him it was the most pernicious festival of the whole year.[5]

These were ideas which Luther expressed without restraint *before* the beginning of the disputes on the Lord's Supper. Here belongs especially the well-known passage from the Corpus Christi sermon of 1519: 'Be careful! You need to be concerned with the spiritual body of Christ rather than with the natural; and faith in the spiritual is more needed than faith in the natural. For the natural without the spiritual is of no use in this sacrament.'[6] Or '*the sacrament in itself without faith does nothing; yea God himself*, who does all things, *does not and cannot do good to any man unless he believes* in him firmly. Still less can the sacrament do anything.' [7] Or 'not the sacraments but faith at the sacra-

---

[1] 15/338 f. (1522). Cf. also the sermon on the same text: Weimar edition, 4/700 f. (1519 or 1520). Zwingli several times used the 1522 sermon against Luther, e.g. *Fründlich Verglimpfung*, II, 2, 12; *That this Word of Jesus Christ*, II, 2, 85; *Marburg Debate*, II, 3, 49. The statement cited in note 2 has been (without mentioning the source) incorporated in a Reformed Creed (*Conf. Sigism.* 1614, K. Müller, p. 839, n. 45). Cf. note 7.

[2] 15/343.   [3] Ibid., p. 341.   [4] Ibid., p. 343.   [5] Ibid., p. 341.   [6] 27/40.

[7] 27/164 (1520). Cf. the passage cited in p. 76[1] from the Septuagesima sermon of 1523, to which Zwingli also refers. Luther later (26/302 [1533]) regretted that one of his sermons ('preached by me before the sacramental faction was heard of, thought of or named') had been printed by his opponents in order to compromise him. This could apply equally to the Septuagesima sermon, to the Corpus Christi sermon of 1522 or to the sermon on the Body of 1519. But which of Luther's earlier writings would not have provided material for that pur-pose? Luther himself had said everything necessary against his own position—long before Zwingli appeared. If he had continued to say this is *also* essential, there could be no doubt on the right and the wrong in the Lord's Supper controversy.

ments makes alive and justifies. Wherefore many take the sacrament and yet do not thereby become alive and truly religious. But he who believes is godly and lives.' [1]

With the word *believe* Luther has also answered the question of the right fitness (*dispositio*) and of the right preparation (*praeparatio*) for partaking of the sacrament, and of the right use (*usus*) of it. It is clear that with this answer, questions arising out of the practice of penance [2] acquire a wholly new character. The problem of man's attitude to the gift is transformed into that of his attitude to the giver. Without faith in God or Christ, the Giver, the gift is *not* given—even though the gift be God himself.[3] 'It does nothing but harm if it is only a "work done" (*opus operatum*); it must be a "work of doing" (*opus operantis*)', which Luther interprets as 'it must be used in faith'.[4] Later he will no longer employ this formulation, for 'faith is not a work, but the teacher (*magister*) and life of works'.[5] But in the same writing in which this sentence occurs Luther also said: 'Let him who is to approach the altar . . . beware lest he appear empty before the Lord God. But he will be empty if does not have faith.' [6]

What that 'work of doing' meant was that faith in the *Giver* asserts a claim on the whole man, predicates a taking possession of the whole man; and this is not denied but affirmed by calling faith 'the life and teacher of works'. In this context, both before and after 1520, we find the very centre of Luther's concept of faith. 'Take heed that thou becomest another person, or do not go' must be said to the communicant. Otherwise 'there is not much difference between giving a man the holy sacrament and shoving it down the throat of a sow. It is a mockery and a dishonouring of the sacrament.' [7]

But what does it mean to believe, not to come empty, to become a different person ? The best beginning for an answer is the genuine, early-Luther definition: 'The best fitness (*dispositio*) is truly that thou art worst fitted; and contrarywise thou art worst fitted when thou art best fitted. But this is to be understood as meaning that when thou feelest thyself most miserable and most in need of grace, even so, by that very fact, thou art capable of receiving grace and art especially fitted for the sacrament. Again, more than thou fearest death and hell, do not imagine thyself fit and worthy as if thou wert to bring to God a

---

[1] 24/61=V/167 (1520/21).
[2] Cf., e.g., II/315 f.=17/56 f. (1518); V/42 (1520); 11/184 f. (1523).
[3] See above pp. 82[7], 76[1].
[4] 27/41 (1519).   [5] V/46 (1520).   [6] Ibid., p. 42.
[7] 11/180 (1523). Cf. also here the parallels in p. 76[4]-[6].

clean heart—that clean heart must be asked for by thee and must be received by thee. The statement of Matthew 9.12 stands firm and inviolable. . . . He is thy God and needs not thy goods; but he is generous with his goods to thee, and he comes to thee with the purpose of giving thee his goods.' [1] And further, 'if the man realizes that he is not offering an empty, hungry and thirsty soul to God, and that he does not go the sacrament with a sufficient faith, and moreover, that he cannot do such a thing rightly (as every man in truth will realize, if he will examine and understand himself), then that man must not be ashamed nor afraid to pray according to Luke 17.5; Mark 9.42'.[2]

The right 'preparation' is therefore just the painful recognition that we lack the right 'fitness'. This recognition, the faith which so to speak leaps into the very gap where there is *no* faith, is the faith which receives the gift, because that faith is directed towards the Giver. If the Devil 'winks' at thee to tell thee that thou art unworthy of the sacrament, 'just cross thyself and cease worrying over worthiness and unworthiness; only take heed that thou believest. . . . Faith makes worthy; doubt makes unworthy.' [3]

'The sacrament is given only to those who need comfort and strength, who have a timid heart, who carry a frightened conscience, who suffer from the assault of sins or have fallen under it. What can it do for the free, confident spirits who neither need nor desire it?' [4] 'This is what Paul also means when he says, let every man examine himself and then eat of this bread. For the man who rightly examines himself, who forgets the wickedness of other men and does not judge them, but who knows concerning himself that he labours and is heavy laden with many sins and transgressions, will then be greedy for the grace and help of Christ. For as St Augustine says, "the food seeks none except a hungry and empty soul; it flees none but the full and proud who judge and condemn one another, as those would do of whom the Apostle wrote these words." For if by these words the apostle had required of us that we should examine ourselves until we were certain that we were without deadly sin, he would have laid upon us an impossible requirement and wholly deprived us of the holy sacrament. Therefore it is enough, if thou dost not know of a deadly sin of a specific, gross kind, or of a certain intention to commit a deadly sin. Leave what may lie in the background to the grace of God and let thy faith be thy cleanness;

---

[1] II/315=17/56–7 (1518).
[2] Ibid., 17/58. The Latin text II/316 is somewhat shorter.
[3] 21/268 (1519).   [4] 27/33–4 (1519).

then thou art sure.' [1] The sacrament will be received by those 'who know their transgression, who feel that they *are not* good and yet would gladly become good. Therefore it all depends on so feeling (on knowing one's self to have sinned), for in truth all of us transgress and are sinners; but not all so confess.' [2]

The 'fitness' (*dispositio*) achieved by such 'preparation' is therefore the 'becoming another man' which must precede the use of the sacrament (not first follow it) in order that the believer may receive in it the 'testament', the effective promise of the forgiveness of sins. This capacity (*capacitas*) can *only* be compared to an empty, outstretched hand. That it shall not be unused is provided for by word and sign. There is needed only the third component, man's concurring affirmation that 'as the words of Christ declare, so it is in truth'. ('For where God speaks and reveals, there man must believe with a wholly firm heart that the truth is as he speaks and reveals; so that we do not hold him to be a liar and a juggler, but to be faithful and true.') [3]

So these three components are interwoven: (1) The 'fitness' of man (negative), the recognition of a lack; (2) the truth of God's promise, offered in Word and sign; (3) the impossibility, recognized by man, that God could lie, the faith, which is counted by God 'as a fundamental, sufficient piety for blessedness', [4] the faith which *receives* the sacrament. The essential one of the three is unquestionably for Luther the second —neither the negative fitness nor the positive effect which are on man's side, but the divine promise. 'For where the Word of God who promises is, there is of necessity the faith of the man who accepts. Therefore it is clear that the beginning of our salvation is faith which depends on the Word of God who promises, who comes to us, in his free and un-deserved mercy, without any effort of ours, and offers the Word of his promise.... The Word of God is first of all; faith follows it and charity follows faith.' [5]

But this does not exclude, on the contrary it includes as corollary that the third point (believing God to be true) involves a most direct and immediate claim upon men. And it is upon that claim that Luther in this connexion will enlarge particularly. Not as if faith were again to become a kind of *work*—a most inward, most refined human act of conscience, penitence, and obedience. Certainly not! 'Be thy remorse

---

[1] 36/154 (1519 ?). [2] III/434=11/166 (1524 ?); 20/231 (1520).
[3] 24/64, 62 = V/66 f. (1520/21). Cf. p. 79⁴. 'He cares nothing for works and needs them not, only that he be held by us to be true in his promises', V/41 (1520).
[4] 24/62. [5] V/38 (1520).

and thy true or false(!) penitence what it will, attend most earnestly to
this, that thou go to the sacrament trusting in the Word of Christ our
Beloved Lord, which is there repeated. For if thou so goest, thou wilt
be illuminated and thy countenance will not fall nor be ashamed. Thou
canst not possibly in any way succeed in making the blessed mother of
God a liar; and she said (Luke 1.53), the Lord has filled the hungry
with good things. . . .' [1] But just this 'therefore so go' (in view of the
questionable character of even our most sincere wanting and desiring)
makes a requirement of men, without which the sacrament, or even
God himself can effect 'nothing at all'. It asserts a claim upon men as
certainly as the promise announced in the sacrament is its prerequisite.

There is also another thing (not really a different thing) which must
be added. 'Christ does not say to us, see, there it *is, there it lies*; but he
says, take, it is to be *thine.* It is therefore not consistent with the nature
of the sacrament that we should *keep* it lying there for we must *use* it.
Now there is no other right use except that thou *believest* that this body
was given for thee and this blood shed for thee. So thou hast it as thou
believest.' [2] And already *before* 1520 he wrote: 'How does it help that
thou picturest to thyself and believest that death, sin, hell are overcome
in Christ for others, if thou dost not also believe that thy death, thy
sin, thy hell are overcome for thee and destroyed and that therefore
thou art redeemed? The sacrament indeed would be worth nothing if
thou dost not believe the very thing which is there revealed, given and
promised to thee.' [3] But even a year earlier Luther had thought it
necessary to counteract this stress on the second person singular and
offer the following assurance: 'If thou art still weak in faith (and that
nullifies all other "preparation"),[4] learn that last remedy of the weak
and allow thyself to be nourished like an infant in the arms and bosom
of *mother Church,* yes on the bed of the paralytic, that the Lord may at
least see their faith when there is none of thine; that *thou mayest
approach in the faith either of the universal Church or of a believing man
known to thee* and mayest say boldly to the Lord Jesus, Behold me,
Lord Jesus Christ; I grieve that I am so weak that I believe not at all,
or so little, in thine inestimable love toward us. Accept me therefore in
the faith of thy Church and of this or that man. For however it be with
me, *it is required,* O Lord, *that I obey thy Church which orders me to come.*
In obedience at least I come, if I bring nothing else. Then believe
firmly that thou dost not come unworthily. There is *no doubt that he will*

---

[1] 17/58=II/316 (1518).   [2] 11/184 (1523).   [3] 21/267 (1519).
[4] What is meant is explicitly described in pp. 84 [1-4], 85 [1-3].

accept obedience given to the Church as to himself. Then it cannot be that the faith of the Church will permit thee to perish any more than the babe who is rightly baptized and saved by the faith of others.' [1]

This last idea, like that cited on the *opus operantis* ('work of doing') [2] was for obvious reasons not offered in this form later. From 1520 on, we find the bluntest antithesis: 'Thou canst not depend on the faith of another when thou approachest the sacrament. *Each one must believe for himself*, as each one is also required to fight for himself against sin, Satan and the world.' [3] The question remains whether this antithesis is *more* than dialectic, whether it is wholly dropped or whether here 'an obvious remnant of the Catholic point of view' [4] is still to be found. In 1519 Luther writes: 'Whether I be worthy or not, I am a member of Christianity.' [5] And against the vehement 'each one for himself' stands all which he said later of the character of the Lord's Supper as 'communion'.[6] Not to the individual as such, but to Christianity, to the Church, the properly instituted sacrament was intrusted. This is for Luther axiomatic.[7]

The requirement of personal faith and the reliance on the faith of the Church are correlatives, not mutually exclusive antitheses. A final undialectic word on true faith is to be found when Luther writes: 'See to it that thou dost not make for thyself a false faith when thou merely believest that Christ is there given thee and is thine. If thy faith is only a human idea which thou hast set up, remain away from this sacrament. For the faith must be a *faith which God creates*; thou must know and feel that God has wrought such a faith in thee that thou therefore holdest it to be indubitably true that this sign is given to thee and thou art therefore become so brave that thou thinkest to thyself thou art willing to die for it. And if thou art still wavering and doubting, then kneel down and pray God that he impart to thee grace to escape from thyself and to come to the true, created faith.' [8]

How deeply in earnest Luther was in this critical interpretation of the concept of sacrament from the standpoint of faith is shown in the practical conclusions which he drew from it (at least in theory). He

---

[1] II/319=17/62 (1518).   [2] Cf. above p. 83⁴.
[3] III/429=11/162-3 (1524). Cf. V/47 (1520); VI/163=28/81 (1521-2).
[4] So Karl Thimme, 'Entwicklung und Bedeutung der Sakramentslehre Luthers', *N.Kirchl.Zeitsch.*, 1901, p. 753.
[5] 21/269.   [6] Cf. below p. 96⁴.
[7] Without this presupposition, the doctrine of the eating of the unworthy, as developed in the conflict over the Lord's Supper, would not be understandable.
[8] 11/185 (1523).

opposed strongly a general, required, conventional attendance of the Lord's Supper. 'A Christian on compulsion is a very cheerful, pleasant guest in the kingdom of heaven; God has a particular pleasure in such and will put him at once below the angels where hell is deepest.' [1] The man who does not come 'from his own conscience and from the hunger of his soul' Luther earnestly advises to stay away, even with the risk that in future 'scarcely one will go where now many hundreds go'.[2]

In addition, after 1523, he develops the proposal of testing the communicants. 'On this account, it should henceforth be arranged that no one is allowed to go to the sacrament unless he be questioned beforehand and it be ascertained how *his heart stands*, whether he *knows* what the sacrament is and why he comes to it'; whether he is 'such a vessel that he can contain it and whether he knows how to witness to his faith.' Luther would like to bring it about that 'in the church service, the true believers could be given a separate place together and so be distinguished from the others. I would gladly have done it long ago, but it would not have been allowed since it has not yet been preached and urged sufficiently.' There is necessarily a difference between preaching and the distribution of the sacrament. 'When I preach the Gospel, I do not know who is reached by it; but I ought to be sure that it has reached him who comes to the sacrament. Therefore I must not act at random, but be certain that he to whom I give the sacrament has received the Gospel.' [3] And in the *Rule of Mass and Communion for the Church of Wittenberg* there was actually included a requirement that the communicants had to present themselves once a year to the *episcopus*. They were to report (1) on their knowledge of the nature and use of the Lord's Supper; (2) on their purpose in their previous participation in it; but also (3), because Satan could also answer these two questions, on their life and morals (*vita et mores*) in relation to their faith. According to the result, the *episcopus* is then to admit them or to keep them back on account of their ignorance or their unrepented unworthiness.[4]

So strongly critical had the concept of faith become that Luther had almost—become Calvin. That he did not, but remained Luther, must chiefly be explained on other grounds than the merely 'historical'.

Only believe means receive, have, enjoy what is given in 'Word and sign'. But this statement, like the one quoted above, 'only the Word

---

[1] 23/165–6 (1530).   [2] 22/41 (1522). Cf. 17/66–7 (1521); 23/169 (1530).
[3] 11, 180–1, 185–6 (1523).   [4] VII/12 f. (1523). Cf. below pp. 91⁵, 92¹.

makes the sacrament', can be given a more positive expression, 'Faith means receive, have . . .', and it is in such positive expression that Luther's meaning and intention become clear. But it is more difficult to understand how far he is certain of faith's receiving than how far he is certain of an act of the Word. If we turn to consider the subjective side of the problem, we find presented a veritable plethora of obviously preliminary observations, which show indeed the direction in which Luther was *searching*, but have nothing to do with the actual answer which he *found*.

In what does that which man through faith receives in the sacrament really consist? That is the question. During those years, Luther plainly laboured to distinguish what was so received by giving it a *special* character within faith in general. If this effort was not wholly fruitless, then the preliminary assumption must be made that the effect on us resulting from the Lord's Supper is not merely a repetition of the general gift of God tendered to us in Christ but something specific within this general experience, either a specific object or a specific receiving or both at once and combined.

The matter of particularity was already present in the concept of the Word.[1] It lay close to Luther's assumptions entirely to repudiate such a particularity. But there is no such repudiation. 'Believe, says Augustine, and you have eaten. But what is to be believed there except the "Word" of promise? So I can daily, hourly have Mass, while as often as I wish I can set before myself the words of Christ and nourish and strengthen my faith on them; that is truly to eat and drink spiritually.'[2] It might be, as Luther in the same year conceded, that everyone could, when *on the march*, have such a *faith* in Christ, consigning to him at need prayer and praise that he may carry them to God in heaven, and that in so doing a man may think upon the sacrament and the testament and sincerely desire, and may therefore partake of it spiritually. . . . *What, then, is the need of having Mass in the Church?* Answer: It is true that such faith is enough and truly suffices wholly, but . . .[3] This *but* is essential to complete the answer. And such statements serve only to stress the critical (that is the fundamental) significance of 'faith'. Their quintessence is compressed in the sentence: 'Without the physical partaking of the sacraments (*provided they are not despised*) one can become godly through faith; but without faith, no sacrament

---

[1] Cf. above pp. 76[9, 10], 77[1, 2].
[2] V/43 (1520). Cf. the saying about the patriarchs in p. 77[1].
[3] 27/165–6 (1520).

helps; rather it is of all things most deadly and destructive.' [1] But here
the parenthesis already makes it plain that eating and drinking with the
mouth is the rule which is merely established by the exception and
remains no less essential.

There are six arguments, if I judge rightly, which Luther offered
in support of the particular significance of the external and actual
celebration of the Lord's Supper.

1. He pointed to the divine institution of the rite, the honouring of
which would be in itself alone sufficient reason for holding the 'material
Mass'.[2]

2. He asked how, without the material act, such a faith as is truly
effective can be attained; whether we are at all capable of ruling ourselves in spirit; whether it is not necessary for us to come together and
be mutually enkindled to such a faith by physically seeing and receiving
the testament.[3]

3. 'Nor ought that to be omitted; but rather great care must be taken
so that the memorial of Christ's passion be not omitted. For the Lord
gave direction that this ceremony is to be celebrated only in memory
of him. Therefore it can be omitted only if you wish to give up the
memory of him.' [4] Luther can on occasion paraphrase the words of
institution: '[I] leave you this sacrament forever, for a sure and true
sign that you *do not forget* me but use it daily and remind yourselves of
what I have done and do for you.' [5] He could even compare the institution of the Lord's Supper with the Catholic custom of binding the
heirs in a will to hold celebrations and requiems for the benefit of the
dead testator. 'So therefore Christ has established a celebration of himself in this testament, not because he had need of it, but because it is
necessary and profitable for us to so think of him and be thereby
strengthened in faith.' [6] In this sense the Lord's Supper can at times be
called 'the memorial sign of the promise'.[7] And in the homiletic exposition of this point of view, Luther could go so far as to say: 'If thou
wilst now become a God-maker, come hither, listen. He will teach thee
the way . . . not that thou art to make his divine nature, for that is and
remains ever the same and uncreated; but that thou canst make him
God for thyself, that he become true God to thee, to thee, to thee, as

---

[1] 24/82 (1521); omitted in the Latin text V/167.
[2] 27/166 (1520); 23/169 f. (1530).
[3] 27/166. 'We poor men, because we live in our five senses, must have at
least some external sign', ibid., p. 148.
[4] II/320 = 17/63 (1518).   [5] 27/33 (1519).
[6] 27/147; 20/230 (1520).   [7] V/43 (1520).

he is to himself true God. But the way is this . . . *"This do in remembrance of me".* [1]

4. This brings us to the fourth argument. 'Christ in commanding that this be done by us in memory of him plainly desires nothing else than that the promise with his pledge be constantly repeated for the nourishing and strengthening of faith which can never be strengthened enough.' Through constant renewal of the memory of God's sweet and rich promise, the spirit becomes so to speak more 'sturdy' and 'well nourished' (*saginatur!*) in faith.[2]

What Luther understands by such strengthening of faith he has once stated in highly Platonic terms, but in noteworthy tension with his second argument. It is necessary that the love, communion, and presence of Christ be *hidden, invisible,* and *spiritual* while the sign only is material, visible, external. Otherwise we would not rise to faith. It is necessary that 'all temporal and sensible things fall away and that we be wholly weaned from them if we are to come to God. To that end the sacrament serves. [It is for us] a ford, a bridge, a door, a boat and a litter in which and by means of which we journey from this world into eternal life. Therefore all depends on faith. For he who does not believe is like the man who must cross water and is so fearful that he does not trust the boat and must therefore remain where he is, and can never more be blessed because he does not embark and cross. For the man who relies on his senses and fails to exercise his faith, the result is that the crossing of the Jordan of death will be bitter.' [3]

5. Christ instituted the Lord's Supper with the purpose 'that it be like a badge or label by which Christians are distinguished from others; therefore as an opportunity to confess Christ'. Luther stresses the need to know who and where the Christians are 'in whom the Gospel now brings forth its fruits'.[4] The communion of the Lord's Supper is 'a part of the confession of faith in which they confess before God, angels and men'. The communicants have to take special places at the service to identify themselves; they must be what they are openly not secretly (*furtim!*).[5]

6. Unlike preaching, but like confession, the sacrament has the

---

[1] 23/174 (1530).   [2] VI/153=28/71 (1521/22).
[3] 27/43-4 (1519). Calvin could have used this interpretation of the Lord's Supper in support of his own teaching (which was strictly dialectic in contrast to Luther's and Zwingli's). Cf. the conclusion of his *Petit Traicté de la Saincte Cène* of 1541 (*Op. Calv.,* V/460); and the close of his liturgy for the Lord's Supper of 1542 (ibid., VI/200).
[4] III/428-9=11/162 (1524 ?).
[5] VII/14 (1522). Cf. also above pp. 88[4], 89[1].

advantage 'that the Word is directed *to thee personally*. For in the sermon the Word is sent forth to the community and even though it touches thee, yet thou art not so certain of it. But here it can touch no one but thyself alone. Must thou not be sincerely glad, if thou knowest a place where God wishes to speak with thee thyself?' [1]

Certainly the homiletical, apologetic, and practical value of all these arguments for the Church and their content for its own sake are not to be lightly valued. Just because they are not definitive for the intent and purpose of Luther's doctrine of the Lord's Supper, but are supplementary embellishments, they afford an expressive witness to the vigour and richness of his spirit as it reaches after every conceivable possibility. Luther himself at a later time made an independent and coherent use of these same ideas when he was preparing for the use of the Church an explicit defence and recommendation of celebrations of the Lord's Supper.[2] But his answer to the question of the particular character of the sacrament itself ought never to be sought in them. As a whole, they are (at least methodologically!) identical with the positive core of the Lord's Supper doctrine of—Zwingli! And in Calvin they have come into their correct systematic position in dialectical relation to Luther's real answer to that question.[3]

In Luther's own thinking, however, these considerations if they do not really act as a foreign body, are yet certainly in the nature of incidental experiments. No one of these arguments, nor all of them taken together afford an answer to the question of the how and the what received by faith in the sacrament. What they offer are psychological descriptions of faith so far as faith is a human act or experience; of faith as it sees itself in relation to God's binding *ordinance*, that is, in relation to a physical, reciprocal, and hence beneficial act by which the *memorial* of Christ is celebrated in a way effectual for salvation, in which faith is openly confessed and in which the Word of God is directed to each *individual for himself*. But all that says nothing about the divine *gift* itself; it tells only of the reactions of men which are the result of the gift. All these points are therefore informative only if the answer

---

[1] III/124=11/158; cf. above p. 88[4].

[2] In the frequently-cited work, *Exhortation to the Sacrament of the Body and Blood of our Lord:* 23/162 f. (1530).

[3] If these points had been important to Luther, he would have had to take towards Zwingli the same position which Calvin took. He could have argued with him and won dialectically. Most of all he must have understood Zwingli's own concern in the matter. But as we know, Luther treated Zwingli as if he were dealing with a heathen. How secondary then the 'Zwinglian' elements in his own doctrine must have been to him!

which they ostensibly intend to give has already been given elsewhere. From this cul-de-sac there is no exit *except* by going resolutely backwards from the faith to its correlative (*correlativum*), the promise.[1]

By *that* method Luther did actually make clear what the receiving and possession of the sacrament meant for him. The truly unique character of the sacrament and therefore the only possible defence for it consists in its 'fruits' and these fruits come from the Word—from faith only so far as faith affirms the Word: 'Be it therefore as the sacrament orders and obligates.' [2] This affirmation is the prerequisite, then follows (and this is the distinctive constituent) the gift of the sacrament in power, the inevitable concomitant (as it was designated earlier at the end of the first section), the step from Word to work, from the affirmation to the actual existence and eventuation, from pledge to fulfilment, from promising to giving. This is 'having the Word', which becomes a reality with the acceptance of the visible sign.

What Luther has to say of the 'fruits' of the sacrament leads us directly to an insight into the *dynamic* character of his concept of Word. The sacrament is a divine sign; 'therein Christ is *promised, given and received,* and all the saints with all their works, suffering, service, grace and good deeds'.[3] In the uninhibited way in which Luther (from the beginning and throughout) combines these three very different acts (promise, give, receive) as if the combination were axiomatic, centres in my opinion the greatness and the difficulty of his doctrine of the Lord's Supper—and perhaps not only of the Lord's Supper. The 'thou must become another man' [4] now suddenly appears no longer as preparation for [5] the sacrament but as the result of partaking of it. And it has, in fact, a wholly new content. A few lines before that command we read: 'The sacrament ought therefore to go along with us, to

---

[1] From this cul-de-sac, Zwingli never emerged after he had once entered it. It is at this point, at a time when he had still not reached a clear position on the Real Presence of the Body and the Blood in the elements, that his difference with Luther first seems to become clear. Cf. *Uslegen und gründ der Schlussreden,* 1523. 'Therefore I eat this food; for years I have called it a memorial of the suffering of Christ and not a sacrifice. But for some time Martin Luther called this food a testament, a name which I will gladly borrow, for he has named it according to its nature and character. I have named it according to the breaking of the bread and the procedure; and there is no contradiction in the two names' (Zwingli's Works I/249). Certainly not! That is the only possible comment if both names are actually given their true significance. It cannot be said that Zwingli so gave it. But there is also an opposite cul-de-sac and in that Luther —not the Luther whom we are here discussing, but the Luther of the dispute over the Lord's Supper—was himself caught.

[2] 21/270 (1519).   [3] 27/38 (1519).
[4] III/442 = 11/173 (1524 ?).   [5] Cf. above p. 83'.

transform us and make us into different people; for the words and works of God cannot lie idle but must accomplish some great result.' (The Latin reads: 'The works of God are not wont to be ineffective [otiosa] but are the beginnings and sources of the greatest things.' [1])

What does Luther mean when, in obvious parody of the official mediaeval doctine of the transubstantiating power of the sacrament, he speaks of 'the high, rich change' [2] which is there effected on and in the believers? 'The significance of the work (!) of this sacrament is the *communion of all saints.*' Synaxis or communion is comparable to the solidarity generally recognized in good and bad fortune, in rights and duties, into which a man enters when he receives citizenship rights in a city.[3] Or still more briefly put: 'The name is communion, the act is unity of heart.' [4]

But this unity is consistently from the very beginning a double unity. 'So the communion, the unity is of two kinds: first, that we partake of Christ and all the saints; second, that we let all Christian men partake of us.' [5] Or, from the end of the period we are considering, 'You have two fruits from the holy sacrament: one is that it makes us brothers and fellow heirs of the Lord Christ, therefore that from him and from us is made one body; the other is that we also become united with one another and are one with all who believe wherever they are on earth, that we are also one body.' [6] 'The unity therefore consists first in that in this sacrament there is given to us the immeasurable grace and mercy of God so that we may put away from us all our grief and temptation, laying it upon the Christian community and especially upon Christ.' God says to thee 'that thy sins trouble not thee alone but . . . Christ and all his saints in heaven and on earth. Therefore be bold and comforted, thou dost not fight alone, great help and support is all around thee.' [7]

Because faith 'honours God by believing him and affirming him to be true, God shows himself as a gracious God to him who honours him and confesses him and deems him true . . . so follows then the Holy Spirit, who is given to him on account of the same faith'.[8] *If I believe that his body and blood is mine, then I possess the Lord Christ wholly and*

[1] III/441=11/172.   [2] 15/344 (1522).   [3] 27/29–30 (1519).
[4] II/313 (1518). F. Graebke (*Die Konstruktion der Abendmahlslehre Luthers,* Gött. Diss., 1907, p. 16) labels the translation (in 17/55) of res by act as false. But did not the translator really have a more correct understanding of this point in Luther's thinking? To Luther the res sacramenti is not a thing but an act.
[5] 27/44–5 (1519).   [6] 11/186 (1523).   [7] 27/32, 31; 21/270 (1519).
[8] 27/144–5 (1520).

also everything which he can do, so that my heart becomes gay and confident so long as I do rely not on my own goodness but on the innocent blood and the pure body which I receive there. Now what does our Lord Jesus Christ have and what can he do? His body and blood are without sin, full of grace, are truly the material dwelling place of the divine Majesty. In brief, all which the Lord God has is Christ's; here these goods become altogether mine. . . . Therefore his wisdom, truth and goodness take away and destroy all my sins; his eternal life devours death for me; through his strength and power, I overcome the devil.' But still more 'so long as thou hast his flesh and blood, *thou hast all the power which God himself has;* that is we become one body with the Lord Christ, we hold a community of goods with him and he takes common property in our misfortunes. For here are pressed together his goodness and my sinfulness, my weakness and his strength; and all becomes property held in common. What is mine is his and what is his I also possess.' Therefore, 'what more canst thou want? *Thou hast all and more than thy heart desires and thou sittest now in Paradise.*' As I eat the sacrament, 'so it in turn eats me . . . so Christ takes me and consumes me and eats me and my sin, and I partake of his righteousness. Therefore his goodness and his riches swallow up my sin and misery so that I thereafter have real righteousness. . . . Is it not magnificent that the high majesty of God meets me and gives itself to me to possess?' [1]

In the second place, this sacrament is a 'sacrament of love'; and it is true that 'as love and support come to me, I show in return love and support to Christ and to his needy ones. For now thou must feel the pain of all the dishonouring of Christ in his holy Word, of all the miseries of Christendom; all the undeserved suffering of the innocent, of which there is overwhelmingly too much in all parts of the world, must give thee pain. Now thou must defend them, act and pray, and where thou canst do no more thou must sincerely pity.' Mutual burden-bearing, joint possession of all things in and with Christ, 'upholding of the truth, seeking the betterment of the Church and of all Christians with person, property and honour' will here take root.[2] From the eating and drinking of the body and blood of Christ follows the result that we 'in turn allow ourselves to be eaten and drunk by others; that is, we devote all our actions, all our life to furthering the advantage of our neighbour', that we say to our neighbour, 'take me, eat me, drink me! not in jest but in earnest', for 'I have enough and plenty when I have

[1] 11/187-90 (1523).   [2] 27/32-5 (1519).

Christ. Do thou therefore enjoy those things which I also have, for all mine is equally thine.'

God's own witness and that of the angels and of all good men convinces us that here is forgiveness of sin. But our own witness must be added to theirs and our witness must be that of the shining light of the 'duties of religion' (*officia pietatis*).[1] 'For where love does not grow daily and so change a man that he becomes one with all men, there this sacrament has no fruit and no significance.'[2] It is not as though a manifest lack of love ought to subject anyone to the judgement that 'he is not a Christian'! It is just because of such a lack that Christ has instituted the sacrament, 'as a kind of exercise by which we seek to obtain that which we know we lack'. This life is nothing but a life of faith, of love and of the holy cross. But these three never come to completion in us while we live on earth. In relation to Christ we are always like burning straw in relation to the sun. But if nothing at all is to be found of our own witness to the forgiveness of sin, 'then thou hast cause to take a different course, for that is not a good sign'. Our life remains a going forward 'from faith to faith, from love to love, from endurance to endurance, from cross to cross, not *justice* but *justification*, not *purity* but *purification*'. ('We have not yet come where we longed to be, but we are all on the journey and on the road', some farther along and some not so far; 'God is content to find us at work and holding to the purpose'.) Thus the eating of the Lord through faith in the Word which the soul takes to itself and 'my letting myself be eaten' in turn by my neighbour remain indivisible.[3]

Luther states explicitly what this second side of the 'unity' involves and he is explicit also on the mutual coming of Christians *before* God in behalf of one another. 'If it so happens that I am a sinner and thou by God's grace art virtuous, then do thou take the lead and share thy virtue with me; pray for me before God and take my sin upon thyself before God, as if thou wert thyself a sinner. So with thy virtue thou dost absorb my sin, *as Christ has done. Therefore eat me, as I in return eat thee.*' While Christ stands there 'and says the sinner is mine, on him I will lay my holy finger, who will raise an objection against it? . . . *So we Christians do the same for one another.*'[4] And in immediate connexion with the foregoing stands the significant practical demand: Those in whom the 'fruits of the sacrament' will definitely fail to appear 'ought to be excluded from the community. Then it might again come

---

[1] III/435 = 11/167 (1524 ?).   [2] 27/136 (1519).
[3] III/436 f. = 11/168 f. (1524 ?).   [4] 11/189–90 (1523).

to the right note and one would know who were true Christians and who were not.' [1]

Such is (obviously on a wholly different plane from the things of which those psychologizing arguments speak!) the divine gift of the Lord's Supper. Therefore the two fruits can not be separated from each other. No forgiveness of sin, no divine mercy; no saving communion with Christ which is not interwoven with forgiveness, mercy, and communion for other men with Christ. But also no morality, no obligation to men, no relationship with men which is not interwoven with the new order of relationship with God through justification. It has no real significance that Luther within this whole concept gives sometimes more emphasis to the one side, the forgiveness of sin, sometimes to the other, the ethical side. In fact, in the earlier writings he stresses the first and in the later writings the second.[2]

What, then, can the divine gift be, for Luther, except Christ himself? At one time he may speak more forcibly of Christ as standing before God in behalf of our weakness and at another time of Christ uniting us with one another in his love. But what is important for establishing the meaning of Luther's doctrine of the Lord's Supper is not the description of the content of the gift, formulated now one way, now another; but the conception which appears in all these descriptions of the way this gift is given to those who believe. Significant therefore are the metaphor of becoming 'one loaf, one body' with Christ and the other more forceful than pretty metaphor of the mutual 'being eaten' of Christ and the believers and among all believers; and the extravagance of the assurance that faith here makes a God gracious to it, that here is received 'all power which God himself has', that a man comes here to a seat in Paradise, that the high Majesty of God here meets him and gives itself to him as his own, that here a transformation befalls him, etc.

We are now able to establish that the two lines designated by the

---

[1] If this idea of Luther's on church discipline had been carried through, the lack of love (in this statement of course, he was not thinking of the first 'fruit' of the sacrament, although he does not exclude it) would be sufficient ground for excommunication. I do not need to say that the Calvinistic church discipline seems lax in comparison.

[2] Compare, for example, on the first, the 'Sermon on preparation for death', 21/253 f. (1519); and on the second, the sermon already quoted, 'Beautiful Sermon on the receiving of the Holy Sacrament', 11/179 f. (1523). Graebke's *Construction* (cf. p. 94[5]) which has plainly found favour with recognized authorities is for me an object of astonishment. I cannot, after full comparison and consideration, find the crucial interpretation which was according to him attained in the year 1520.

concepts 'Word' and 'faith' converge towards the same point. At this point the 'Word' will no longer be Word alone, nor faith be faith alone. As the gift of the divine Word on the one side, so the acceptance by human faith on the other side reaches the limit of the visible and the conceivable. What is left of present actuality where *Christ himself* gives enabling power to his Word? And is Christ himself to be excluded if on the human side there is the receiving of this enabling? Is not the desire understandable to discern clearly at least the receivers (if not actually *what* is received), those 'truly made Christians', who because of what they have received, stand in faith and love (even having special benches in church); just as at least the *sign* of what is given them is clearly seen?

In any case, how can we possibly avoid recognizing that on the point toward which the Word and faith converge in the sacrament, there is nothing else to say?

III

'To *signify* such communion, God has instituted such a *sign* as this sacrament.' [1] 'Signify' and 'sign' mean for Luther in the first place actually and simply what the words say: a symbol for something else towards which it points. 'Signifying' in this plain sense are first *bread* and *wine* as such, because (Luther here takes up an early Christian idea) 'many different grains, losing their individual character, are brought into one loaf of bread; likewise many grapes, also losing their separate identity, are made into one wine'. [2] 'So we also ought to be and are (!), if we rightly use this sacrament. Christ with all his saints, through his love, puts on our nature . . . and thereby we, kindled in love, take on his nature . . . and are therefore, through the communion of his good and our ill, one loaf, one bread, one body, one drink; and all is in common.' [3]

The second 'signifying' is the *eating and drinking*. 'For there is no more inward, deeper, indivisible union than that of food with him who is fed. For the food goes in and its nature is transformed and it becomes one substance with the fed.' This cannot be said of broken things, nailed or glued together; 'and so we are united with Christ in the sacrament'. [4]

But Luther knew also a third 'signifying'. 'Above all that, he has not merely instituted two empty symbols, but he has given *his real*,

---

[1] 27/36 (1519).
[2] II/314=17/55 (1518); 27/36 (1519); III/440=11/171 (1524 ?).
[3] 27/36 (1519).   [4] Ibid., p. 37.

natural flesh in the bread and *his natural, real blood* in the wine, so that he gives a complete sacrament or sign. For at the same time as the bread is transformed into his true natural body and the wine into his natural true blood, we are also transformed into the spiritual body, that is into the communion of Christ and all the saints.' [1] It should be noted that in this statement exactly the same parallelism of sign and signification appears as in the preceding. Only here the 'signifying sign' which he interprets is the *change* of the elements into the body and blood of Christ. The objective givenness of this change Luther states as unconcernedly and assumes to be as obvious as the bread and wine or the eating and drinking!

What is important in this passage is not Luther's acceptance in 1519 of the doctrine of transubstantiation, but the fact that he took as self-evident the identification of the signifying with what is signified, of the sign with the signification. Luther can say the same thing also without the doctrine of transubstantiation. Christ lets 'himself be the last and greatest memorial sign, reminding men of his love for sinners'.[2] Or, 'instead of letter and seal, he has given here *his own body* under the bread and wine'.[3] Or, he has 'confirmed these words by his death and his giving me his *body and blood* for a sign and confirmation of his Word'.[4]

The explanation of the 'sign' can also be given in the form, 'Since there is a difference between what we see and what we believe, *faith* is thereby exercised. For if we hear the Word and receive the sacrament, we have there a very simple word and work. Yet we *grasp therein life and all good things*, and in addition even God himself.' [5] What does that 'difference' mean except that Luther at the climax of his exposition, intentionally drops the concept of the *merely* signifying and in its stead, that is, in the place of the sign (although the sign does not vanish), sets the reality itself? To eat the body of Christ in the bread is not a *mere symbol* of our union with him; it is the experiencing of the union signified by the symbol. The sought becomes the found, the promised becomes possession, the likeness becomes identity.

According to the evidence given in our first two sections, there can be no doubt that what we find here is not a slip in logic, but the purpose which manifests itself with compelling inner necessity in the whole intent of Luther's doctrine of the Lord's Supper. There is no ground for assuming that Luther's intention was something different and that the dispute over the Lord's Supper which began at this point might

[1] Ibid., p. 38. [2] II/319=17/61 (1518). [3] 20/231 (1520).
[4] 22/40 (1522). [5] III/440=11/171 (1524 ?).

have been avoided.[1] No! 'In the development of Luther's doctrine of the Lord's Supper, the unmoving axis is the Real Presence. He never loosened his hold on it.' [2]

This much is surely clear. What Luther said at the height of his teaching stands under the thesis of two parallel lines meeting *at infinity*. No wonder that Luther himself could not carry through his doctrine in unified and unassailable form. He could say with frightful clarity: 'I believe firmly not only that the body of Christ is in the bread, but also that the bread is the body of Christ.' [3] Or in the flow of homiletic affirmation, 'Thou shalt not doubt that Christ is there. Hold simply to this that flesh and blood is there according to the words, for he says, "This is . . ." Hold to that, forbear to imagine how it occurs, how and how much he is there. Let fools be fools. Only believe it; he will do it. Remember now with this bread which is Christ's body to strengthen thy poor, weak and powerless soul.' [4]

But Luther could also say: we must recognize 'the outward with the eyes of the body; the spiritual, the inner, with the eyes of the heart'; [5] or 'outwardly I eat the sacrament, but inwardly and spiritually I take all the good things of Christ and Christ himself also, just as I am eating physically bread which strengthens me inwardly in body'; [6] or 'we receive through faith spiritually and with the mouth physically'.[7] But such easily understandable variations in Luther's statements only point to what he *meant* to say, 'that he whom heaven and earth could not contain was under the bread' [8]; to the assertion of the *concomitant*

---

[1] This assumption was already made by Luther's contemporaries. 'This, brothers, I say honestly, and before God I so believe, that the truly religious must wish that nothing had ever been written against Luther about the Eucharist. *For he had already rested everything on the spiritual eating, and he had spontaneously quite disparaged the material eating and had done away with reliance on the external work. But when Carlstadt stirred up the mud,* Luther, as if he had convinced himself that Carlstadt wished to remove entirely the external Word and sacrament, was wholly carried away as if there were nothing but vehemence in him. The result was that we ourselves and our Zwingli and Oecolampadius thought that he was giving the power of justification again to externals, which he never thought of doing' (Bucer to Boniface Wolfhardt and the Augsburgers, 1537; cited from Gieseler, *Kirchengeschichte*, III, p. 190.)

[2] Walther Koehler, *Zwingli und Luther*, I, 1924, p. 177.   [3] V/34 (1520).

[4] Weimar edition, 9/648 (1521). Luther's opponents could cite such passages if they wished to prove that Luther actually taught, as they charged him, a God made into bread (*deus impanatus*).

[5] 27/148 (1520).   [6] 11/188 (1523).

[7] 28/374 (1522). Luther could therefore even answer the question of what the communicant took into his mouth by, on one occasion, 'Mum, mum', 'the pap rolls around in the mouth'. 'Fish in troubled waters' 'go pilfering in the dark', he later taunted his opponents (26/299 [1533]). Those who want still stronger words may be referred to 30/350 (1528).

[8] Weimar edition, 4/701 (1519 or 1520).

presence of God, of *the actuality of the fulfilment* of his revelation. 'He added the *memorial sign* of so great a promise, *his own body* and *his own blood* in bread and wine.' [1]

One must certainly admit the 'vehemence' with which one concept is identified with the other,[2] with which the 'have' and the 'signify' are fused together; but the emphasis is always on the 'have'.[3] The following passage is enlightening for the road Luther takes. 'So that this divine promise may be to us the most certain of all and render our faith most secure, he set upon it the token and seal which is the most trustworthy and precious of all, as he himself was the price of the promise, his own body and blood under the bread and the wine. By this he guarantees that the riches of the promise are given to us; and this requires our acceptance of the promise.' [4] The last sentence is definitive. In order to make the promise 'most sure' (*certissima*) and the faith 'most secure' (*tutissima*) the inheritor of the promised riches must become at the same instant, simultaneously the acceptor of the promise. But then is he merely the acceptor of the promise? The answer to this question is in Luther's mind indubitably negative. With the presence of the giver the gift is presented; there is not merely the repetition of the promise. The 'promise' therefore becomes the gift; 'faith' becomes possession. Just because for Luther all depends on this presence, 'there is nothing here which is not imperative (*vehemens*).' Therefore for him the presence of the giver is absolutely requisite. 'He who gives and what is given should be the same and whoever would partake, would partake of him. Here untrustworthy human reason ceases and leaves to God what is his—his omnipotence to do what he wills without our understanding it.' [5]

It is possible to understand the step which Luther took here as the act of pure Christian faith in revelation, or as an act manifesting truly demonic force. His position in the Lord's Supper controversy, with which we are not here concerned, shows that actually it was both. One can say confidently that he would not have been Luther if he had not taken this step; but with equal confidence that 'controversy', or should

[1] V/43 (1520).
[2] But the vehement emphasis lay elsewhere than where Bucer (p. 100[2]) sought it.
[3] E.g. 27/148 (1520).
[4] VI/159=28/77 (1521/22). Seeberg (*Dogmengeschichte*, IV, p. 226) sees in this passage a 'step forward', in that the presence of the body is based on the truth that through the body of Christ forgiveness was earned and made possible. But Luther had already in 1520 (see p. 79[5]) established the inseparability of the testament from the testator and the inheritance. (Cf. also the passage cited in note 5).
[5] Weimar edition, 4/701 (1519 or 1520).

we say *debate* (which the controversy necessarily had to be), upon this step was unavoidable.

There are still two points to be examined in our consideration of this final culmination of Luther's doctrine. First, his relation to the church doctrine, official since 1215, of the transubstantiation of the elements into the body and blood of the Lord. We have already presented the *allegorical* use which Luther made of this doctrine.[1] Beyond that, he was concerned with it because the indirect identity of bread and body, wine and blood, which was important to him, was expressed positively in it.[2]

There is nothing further to be said. His attitude to this doctrine was unimportant to himself at the time when he still affirmed it and equally unimportant later when he repudiated it. Very early he warned against 'the art and subtlety' which inquired where the bread stays when it is turned into the flesh of Christ. 'It is enough to know that it is a divine sign, for the flesh and blood of Christ is truly therein. The how and the where may be left to him.'[3] Or even more sharply, 'leave off those trumperies of the scholastics who worry much over how the body of Christ can be present, especially in such a miserable substance as bread. Do not scrutinize that miracle, but cling simply to the Word and let it be thine only care how thou canst receive the fruit of this sacrament, the remission of sins.'[4]

When he realized that the indirect identity of bread and body could equally well be expressed in a form different from the doctrine of the Roman Church, he discarded that form with as little sentiment as one expends on discarding an old coat. 'The third error [the first is the interpretation of 'is' (*est*) by 'symbolizes' (*significat*); the second is the substitution for 'body' (*corpus*) of the 'communion of the spiritual body' (*communio corporis spiritualis*)] is that in the sacrament no bread remains, but only the form of bread. But not much is involved in this error if only Christ, body and blood, remains there with the Word.'[5] So he wrote after he had for three years publicly presented the new doctrine.

He had clearly already reached this point when he said, looking back to his Sermon on the Eucharist,[6] that he had then been travelling the accustomed road and had not troubled about the right or wrong of the Pope in the matter.[7] But even in 1520 he was fighting only for Christian freedom in this matter. The presence of Christ in the Lord's Supper

---

[1] Cf. p. 94[1], [2].   [2] Cf. p. 99[1].   [3] 27/38 (1519).
[4] III/432 = 11/165 (1524 ?).   [5] 28/402 (1523).
[6] The sermon on the Body (1519) is meant. (Cf. p. 99[1].)
[7] V/22 (1520).

can be thought this way or that; 'and so I allow anyone to hold either opinion as he wishes. This only I require in order to remove scruples of conscience.' A man is not a heretic if he calls bread bread and wine wine. The doctrine of transubstantiation cannot claim to be 'a necessity of faith' (*necessitas fidei*).[1]

Luther himself declared for the theory of the late scholastic, Peter von Ailli, whom he names specifically. According to this theory, not only the accidents but also the substance of the elements remain preserved in the Lord's Supper, *but* the 'body of Christ' (*corpus Christi*) is present 'within the substance of the bread' (*intra substantiam panis*).[2] Luther declares that 'the body can truly be there while the bread still remains'.[3] He likes to describe this under the simile used long before by John of Damascus (*Ekdosis* 4.13) of the presence together of iron and fire. Why would it not be still simpler for the 'glorious body' of Christ (without denial of the presence of the substance of either the body or the bread) to be in every particle, its substance together with the substance of the bread? [4] Therefore the real bread is the real body and the real wine is the real blood of Christ.

But all such precise formulation is for Luther a scholastic question in which he has no interest. He will contend sharply neither against the doctrine of transubstantiation nor for the so-called consubstantiation doctrine; but only *against* those who make out of the former 'a necessary article of faith and law'; [5] and *for* the real presence of the body in the bread. Without noticing it, he occasionally slips back towards transubstantiation.[6] And fully eight years after he had reached his own view, he states explicitly how little importance he attached to it.[7]

---

[1] Ibid., p. 30.

[2] Ibid. pp. 29, 30. Cf. on this Mücke, 'Luthers Abendmahlslehre bis 1522', *Stud. und Krit.*, 1873, especially pp. 450–79.   [3] 28/367 (1522).

[4] Ibid., p. 368. Cf. V/32 (1520). A similar indirect identity of bread and body was taught (without disputing the transubstantiation doctrine) by Ratramnus and Rabanus Maurus. The rejection of any narrower definition of the relation of the two substances (so important to Luther, cf. pp. 100[4], 102[3], [4]) is found also in Peter Lombard. The interpretation of 'this is' (*hoc est*) by 'is contained under' (*contentum sub hoc est*) is in Durandus of St Pourçain (d. 1334). Co-existence in opposition to the official dogma is also in Rupert of Deutz (d. 1135), William of Occam, Gabriel Biel, and the already mentioned Pierre d'Ailli.

[5] Ibid., p. 366.

[6] 'He takes the bread and by the word which he speaks, *this is* . . . the bread changes into his body', VI/150=28/67 (1521/22). Cf. also the passages cited for the allegorical use (15/344 and III/441=11/172) which come from the year 1522 and, if the dating of the last sermon is correct, from 1524.

[7] 'Now I have formerly taught and I still teach that such fighting (over the doctrine of transubstantiation!) is unnecessary, *and not much depends on whether or not the bread remains*. Although I agree with Wyclif that the bread remains, still I also agree with the Sophists that the body of Christ is there', 30/292 (1528).

However pleasant it would be to expand on the theme of how far the Lutheran doctrine is superior to the Roman in paradoxical depth of meaning—Luther himself never felt its superiority strongly enough to offer any important presentation of that aspect. His advance beyond the view of 1519 really consisted only in establishing the thesis that the bodily presence of the Lord, which was to him all-important, was not tied to the assumption of the vanishing of the substance of the bread, with its 'superfluous miracle'.[1] 'For Luther the true presence of the real body and blood of Christ in the Lord's Supper is independent of that idea.' [2]

The second point is much more important and with its consideration this investigation can properly close. It is the question of whether or of how far the possibility existed that Luther might have retreated even from this culmination of his doctrine by going over to the view which later won historical significance as the *Reformed Doctrine*.

The starting-point here is given in the oft-cited words of the letter to the Strassburgers, 15th December 1524. 'This I admit, if Dr Carlstadt or anyone else five years ago had convinced me that in the sacrament there was nothing but bread and wine, he would have done me the greatest service. I have undergone such severe temptations, because I saw very plainly that I could thereby have given the hardest blow to the Papacy, and I have so struggled and writhed under them that I should very gladly have escaped free.' [3]

It is necessary to consider first the context in which these words and their well-known continuation stand. Both before and after them, Luther makes the charge against Carlstadt that he acted 'as if the whole strength of essential Christianity lay in destroying images, upsetting the sacrament and delaying baptism', while he evaded the question of 'what makes a man a Christian'. This attitude, this outrage against 'the Christian freedom' (which Luther here uses as synonymous with the *reality* of Christianity) is what he 'cannot endure in Carlstadt'.

Unless we assume that our passage [4] is without context, then the

---

[1] V/29 (1520).

[2] Mücke, op. cit., p. 470. On the whole one could say that Luther's inner relation to his 'advance' in this matter was even more tepid than to the question of the cup for the laity (cf. p. 76[10]) in favour of which he at least made later a firm decision.

[3] 53/274. Luther admits, too (29/244 [1525]), that he had anguish of heart over this sacrament. He speaks of the 'distress of our conscience' in a letter (Enders, *Briefwechsel*, 5, p. 386 [1526]), and of his being troubled (29/341 [1526]).

[4] From 'This I admit' to 'as is well known'. Notice also the 'therefore' with which Luther continues.

'temptation' which Luther suffered in that specific period (around 1519) must have consisted primarily in the impulse to undertake a decisive attack against the old Church by neglecting the really essential element in Christianity and setting up a doctrine of the Lord's Supper which would reject entirely the presence of the body and blood of Christ in the elements. From this point of view [1] he appears at least to have weighed the possibility of reaching a different conclusion. But (on the assumption that his declaration in the letter to the Strassburgers is not an isolated fabrication) he must have immediately repudiated such an idea with the opposing argument that the difference is not a matter of externals [2] and by going back to his fundamental doctrine of 'Word' and 'faith', from which there was for him, as we have seen, a direct road leading to the doctrine of the Real Presence.

But apart from the advantage in the war against the Pope, there must have been special inner motives which could at least have suggested such a possibility to him. He had so 'struggled and writhed' that he would 'gladly have escaped free'. Free from what? Clearly not from the temptation to make a tactical move. In the older and fuller preface to the *Syngramma Suevicum*, he speaks for the first time, so far as I know, of the two reasons which I believe his opponents in the question of the sacrament could have urged to their own advantage. 'Therefore I give my decision, however greatly it angers them. Yet I know that it is true. *For I recognize clearly in this matter faith and the devil* (!). There are two grounds for their error. First that to the reason the idea is almost absurd; the other that it is unnecessary for Christ's body and blood to be in the wine. It is an absurdity and it is not a necessity (*absurditas et nulla necessitas*). They have grasped these two weapons and tempted by Satan have carried the matter through.' With these 'coloured glasses' they came 'marching upon the Scriptures' and sought to interpret them in their own sense.[3] Where did Luther find these 'two grounds'? Certainly not in the writings of his opponents. Neither the Bohemian Brethren nor Hoen nor Carlstadt nor Zwingli nor Oecolampadius gave these reasons for their doctrine.

Also to be noted is the parallel passage which states: 'There are still understanding hearts who are troubled by the two weapons I have

---

[1] Cf. with the 'hardest blow to the Papacy' the letter of K. H. Hoen of 1522 (Enders, op. cit. 3, pp. 412 f.), especially p. 419: 'briefly . . . if you would take that away, the whole religion of the Pope will fall'.

[2] Precisely at this point he took 'the Pope' under his protection against attacks like Carlstadt's, 29/269 (1525).

[3] 65/184 (1526). The same charge in greater fullness and with refutation of the two 'grounds' is found 29/332–42 (1526).

mentioned.' *For such* it can be said that they are 'subtle philosophical phantasies' in contrast to 'plain grammatical phantasies'; they distort the words of institution. Among such, Carstadt, Zwingli, and Oecolampadius have plainly shown themselves to belong.[1]

If in the first passage, Luther brought all his opponents—for one a '*tuto*' [τοῦτο], for another a 'symbolizes' (*significat*), for another a 'metaphor' (*figura*)—into clear connexion with these 'two grounds'; he has in the second passage repudiated the connexion and divided the representatives of the two reasons not unflatteringly from the rest of his opponents.

We may then conclude that Luther is not clear on this point. Who are the representatives of the 'two grounds'? This question is related to another obscure 'pair' which refers not to arguments but to men. Indeed, the continuation of the letter to the Strassburgers reads: '*I have also heard from two who wrote to me more wisely* on the matter than Dr Carlstadt and also have not tortured the Word to fit their own thinking.' [2] These two correspondents so favourably judged must have been, if we are not wholly mistaken, the representatives of those 'two grounds', either separately or together—whatever their names may have been.[3] And as Luther so plainly distinguished 'in this matter faith and the devil', it is presumably correct to see if not in the two correspondents, yet certainly in the two arguments he attributed to his opponents (the *absurdity* and the *no necessity*) the best indication of the considerations which had brought Luther himself to some uncertainty. And plainly he felt the second argument to be fundamentally much more serious than the first.[4]

---

[1] 29/342.   [2] 53/274.

[3] On the last point I have no suggestion to make. Enders (op. cit., p. 84, n. 4) states without evidence that the letters of Hoen (Enders, 3, pp. 412 f.) and of the Zwinglian, Franz Kolb (Enders, 4, pp. 374 f.) are meant. But a year earlier Luther had already criticized Hoen's view: 'One must not so trifle with God's Word as to give a word a meaning different from the natural one, without offering a clear passage of Scripture in proof' (28/393 [1523]). Enders himself (3, p. 425) accepts this statement as directed against Hoen and so also does W. Koehler (op. cit., p. 178). And the exceedingly boorish letter of Franz Kolb (which according to the correspondence was contemporary with the Strassburg letter) made no other impression on Luther than that 'this evil creeps far', and brought him to his first angry statements against Zwingli (Enders, 5, pp. 52, 80). Ullman (*Reformers before the Reformation*, II, pp. 511 f.) thought that the other with Hoen was Wessel. That is, Luther was referring to a treatise of this older theologian on the Lord's Supper which was brought to Wittenberg along with Hoen's letter by Rhodius and Sagarus. But M. Goebel ('Luthers Abendmahllehre', *Stud. und Krit.*, 1843, p. 337) had already noted that unless Luther expressed himself very carelessly when he wrote 'who wrote to me', he must have meant friendly contemporaries.

[4] Cf. p. 82[1-5].

The charge of 'absurdity', the question of 'the methods of divine work' (*modi operationis divinae*) became acute for him, I believe, contemporaneously with the abandonment of the doctrine of transubstantiation. Those warnings against useless speculations over the mystery of the sacrament [1] must be connected with it. But the second consideration would have been of much more concern to Luther— the question whether the doctrine of the Real Presence in itself and not merely as formulated by the Roman Church, did not involve 'a superfluous miracle'.[2]

We have seen how from the concept of 'Word' as well as from the concept of 'faith', Luther had come close to a pure symbolic position and how his opponents had recognized this fact.[3] But the idea that these 'two grounds' ever had sufficient weight in Luther's mind to lead him to abandon his own teaching is *not* admissible, as the writings which we actually possess plainly demonstrate. Alongside the occasionally spiritualizing variations in the statements from 1518 and 1519 stand the passages which take the doctrine of transubstantiation for granted and in which the Real Presence is explicitly stated.

Contemporary with the 'advance' beyond this position and the emergence of the question of 'absurdity' is the forceful repudiation of the first interpretation which appeared among those in sympathy with Luther, the Picards of Bohemia, who 'do not believe that Christ's flesh and blood are really there, and have several more heresies. These Bohemians I consider heretics. May God have mercy on them.' [4] And the same Septuagesima sermon in which Zwingli found decisive witness to his own doctrine contains in immediate continuation of the pages he could so use the unambiguous denial of that doctrine. 'There are those who wantonly distort scripture because of their own wickedness. . . . Therefore thou must not allow the words to be taken and distorted for thee . . . but take them directly as they sound: the bread is *really* and *immediately* my body, etc. . . . But when one cannot do that, he is to submit himself to God's Word.' [5]

It is also very significant that Luther, when the dispute was in full swing, was able to propose to his opponents, impromptu, a theory of the Lord's Supper *without* the Real Presence which did not 'torture' the text as he accused them of doing. He offered it as proof that 'if to produce phantasies were an art I could "phantasize" as finely as they'. Christ could literally and really have called bread his body. He is the

---

[1] Cr. pp. 101¹, 103⁵, ¹; also V/33 (1520).   [2] V/29 (1520).
[3] Cf. pp. 76¹ 82¹, ⁷.   [4] 27/74 (1520).   [5] 8/96–8 (1523).

God who gave his body to the Christians in the place of the Mosaic Passover lamb. This means as the thing created and used according to his will; all things are God's and are called God's. And 'this red wine which is the blood of my grapes is now to be my blood with you'.[1]

In the continuation of the passage cited from the Strassburger letter of 1524, Luther admits that he 'still, even today' is 'unfortunately all too much inclined—so much trace of the old Adam is visible' to an interpretation which denies the Real Presence. Therefore Luther's questioning of the culmination of his own teaching, a questioning which continued ineffective and suppressed, must be interpreted negatively so far as those 'two grounds' are concerned, especially the second; but positively in relation to the identity of the body of Christ with the creation of God. Luther would certainly have known that among his opponents, especially Zwingli and Oecolampadius, this solution in its positive aspect could not be accepted, if he had given a moment's serious consideration to *their* position—which he notoriously never did.[2]

With the Reformed objection of the threat to the glory of God involved in the acceptance of a definite given object of contingent revelation, or with the emphasis which the Reformed put on Christ's ascension, this suppressed reformed theory of Luther's had no connexion. Luther so wholly missed the point of the Reformed objection that he could answer 'a good man does not so seek the glory of God that he ignores the blaspheming of Christ'.[3] He could even ridicule it. 'They have in their mouths and at the point of their pens "the glory of God, the glory of God, the glory of God we seek".' [4] Therefore even this suppressed reformed theory could not lead him one step nearer to the real Reformed position. Their considerations were as alien to him as—his to them.

[1] 30/42-6 (1527). It is not prudent to make one's phantasies public, especially when one is Luther—even if they are only fancies. Zwingli would not have lacked an answer to this rash experiment. This impromptu interpretation (Zwingli naturally repudiated it with scorn) only shows in what suspicious relation to *pagan nature mysticism* Luther's doctrine stands, according to his own testimony.

[2] W. Koehler ascribes this attitude to Luther in relation to Carlstadt, of which I know too little to judge. 'He was not capable of a calm judgement of an opponent, still less of any real evaluation of him' (op. cit., p. 127). In my opinion, this statement involves only a very limited condemnation of Luther. In all periods, those who were incapable of really comprehending the thought of others have not made the worst theologians. Luther belonged, I believe, to such wholly independent thinkers. Theological achievement and historical objectivity are perhaps mutually exclusive charismatic gifts. But this is not to say that everyone who lacks the second has the first—on the contrary.

[3] Enders, 5, p. 388 (1526).   [4] 53/363 (1526).

But however that may be, Luther strongly and successfully withstood the temptation to make use of his impromptu theory. He was in truth *determined* not to eliminate the Real Presence but to assert it. 'In my own thinking, I did not adhere to that error however strongly I was tempted.' [1] 'We have never said that either element was not the flesh and blood of Christ and does not bring salvation, but we did say that it must be preached as true food of the soul.' [2] So he later judged his own past; and we have every reason to believe him. Our whole inquiry has supported these statements.

The best-known words of that letter to Strassburg run bluntly: *'But I am bound and cannot get loose; the text is too plain and will not let its meaning be changed by words.'* Here we stand before the sledgehammer with which Luther suppressed his 'reformed' inclinations. At first, in opposition to the advocates of the doctrine of transubstantiation he had established in relation to the words of institution that no violence might be done to the letter of the text, 'but so far as can be done (!) the words must be kept in their simplest meaning. Unless clear fact compels it (!), they are not to be taken contrary to grammar and proper usage, lest an opportunity of evading all scripture be given to our opponents.' [3] 'If I cannot reasonably comprehend how bread is the body of Christ, yet I will make my reason captive in homage to Christ; and holding simply to his words, I firmly believe. . . .' [4]

It does not lie within the scope of this paper to show how with *this* argument Luther beat down rather than refuted the opinions of all who differed with him. Everything else he said in defence of his thesis, partly clarifying it and partly intentionally adding to the difficulty of comprehending it (for example, the consubstantiation doctrine and the 'figure of synechdoche' and the doctrine of the ubiquity of the body of Christ, and the defiant teaching of the 'eating of the unworthy'), is only paraphrase of the 'This is body' (*Hoc est corpus*) which for him settled the whole matter. So it stood written and so it must remain written.

But Luther would have stated the whole doctrine differently from Zwingli, even if he had not found the problematic *est* in the Bible.[5]

---

[1] Enders, 5, p. 104 (1525). [2] Enders, 5, p. 265 (1525).
[3] V/31 (1520). [4] Ibid., p. 34.
[5] Cf. on this point Karl Bauer, *Die Wittenberger Universitäts-Theologie und die Anfänge der deutschen Reformation*, 1928, p. 146. 'For Luther brought his hermeneutics with him, so that his question on the Lord's Supper was not "What did Jesus say to his disciples on the evening before his death?" but "What does he say to me now at the celebration of the Communion?" The answer he gave to this question was then strongly influenced (although not consciously) by his personal religious need and desire which only the real presence and Christ's giving of himself could satisfy. So for him, I Cor. 10.16

The passion with which he nailed himself to these three letters when he wrote them with chalk on the conference table at Marburg had nothing to do with philological fidelity to the text, and nothing at all to do with slavery to the doctrine of verbal inspiration which Luther did not accept. Such a professorial cord would have bound Samson as little as the cords he had already snapped at other points where he had not bound himself.[1] The basis of faith must always be something higher than 'the rules of grammar'. 'If my faith is to stand on Donatus' grammar book, or on the spelling book, it is badly off. How many new articles of faith we should have to set up if we construe the Bible in all places according to the grammatical rules?'[2] So Luther spoke of philological fidelity to the text if it were to be observed.

The significant culmination of his doctrine, logically expressed in what he later called the 'predicate of identity',[3] existed in all its aspects in the beginning of his teaching, long before the little sentence 'This is body' (*hoc est corpus*) gained his professional attention. His dynamic understanding of the concepts 'Word' and 'faith' entailed the conclusion *a priori* ; so that when the question of the meaning of this sentence was propounded, *est* had to mean, not *symbolizes*, but to all eternity *is*. In Luther's interpretation of the words of institution of the Lord's Supper we have to do not with the *source*, but with the supplementary arguments supporting his doctrine.

However, the Reformed doctrine will gladly go along in its own fashion on the whole road which Luther took, both *here* and elsewhere, so that when the *last* word falls, the Lutheran *Yes* may be crossed with the Reformed *But*—not with *No*—to complete and explain it, remem-

---

became "the living medicine of his heart when he was tempted about this sacrament" (*WA*, XVIII/166 f.). For here he found it said that those who take the broken bread, take in it the body of Christ. Whether a historical or grammatical exegesis would establish this as the apostle's meaning was a question which did not exist for Luther's hermeneutics, since for it the "use" (*usus*) was more important than the "history". And so for Luther the question of the Lord's Supper was decided according to the comfort received in the sacrament, not according to scholarly interest.'

[1] K. Holl, who sees in Luther a forerunner, even the trail-blazer of modern exegesis and hermeneutics, interested in historical objectivity as such, cites (*Luther*, 2nd edition, p. 565, n. 1) the following passage from the *Table Talk*, I, 333, 25: 'When we and visionaries of their sort use the Word of God in common and each party prides itself on the correct interpretation, there can appear to be the greatest doubt of what is the proper basis of certainty. The inner witness of the Spirit, the outer agreement of the brethren makes us certain that we must hold to the side of Luther not of Zwingli.'

[2] 29/232 (1525).   [3] 30/291 (1528).

bering that when the *last* word falls, that road is a closed circle. The point *from which Luther* began is again reached; the point where identity again becomes likeness, where the critical question must again arise so that the divine answer may be and may remain the truth. The world of the Old Testament and the world of Humanism which have announced themselves in this recall to the Word, will certainly, at least under this form, not be excluded from the kingdom of heaven.

It was Luther's limitation that he had the freedom to close the door to the castle without the freedom or the power to open it again. Could he have opened it (no word of his would have had to be left unsaid) Zwingli would have been fighting windmills—and he had sense enough to leave such a fight alone.

But it does not become us to fight a supplementary battle with Luther. We can only establish the fact that he believed he could say a *Yes* without a *But*. Such a *Yes* did not lie within the limit of his or of any human ability or obligation; when it was spoken it was not the *divine Yes* which he had meant to establish by his words.

Luther stood in opposition to Zwingli, who himself stood even more questionably on his own undialectical assertion, since his much less popular message was obviously only the *But* without the *Yes*. And perhaps Luther himself in the extreme vulnerability of his historical position, with his awkward stabs, was the embodiment of the question mark which he himself had neglected to note. The name of Calvin, the man who later knew and spoke both *Yes* and *But*, points the tragedy of this historical cul-de-sac—perhaps also the *way out* and *hope*.

III

THE DESIRABILITY AND POSSIBILITY OF A UNIVERSAL REFORMED CREED

An address given at the World Council of the Alliance of Reformed Churches holding the Presbyterian System, held June–July 1925 in Cardiff, Wales; and repeated as a lecture to the General Assembly of the Reformed Association of Germany, in Duisburg-Meiderich, 3rd June 1925.

THE concept 'Reformed Creed', according to my understanding of the history and nature of the meaning of the words in the past, is to be defined as follows:

A Reformed Creed is *the statement, spontaneously and publicly formulated by a Christian community within a geographically limited area, which, until further action, defines its character to outsiders; and which, until further action, gives guidance for its own doctrine and life; it is a formulation of the insight currently given to the whole Christian Church by the revelation of God in Jesus Christ, witnessed to by the Holy Scriptures alone.*

It will perhaps best serve as introduction to the specific problem which today occupies us if I first attempt to explain the separate components of this definition.

1. The Reformed Creed will be the formulation of a specific insight derived from God's revelation in Jesus Christ. This character it has in common with all other Christian creeds. On the finality of definition and the final indefinability of the Reformed Confession, as of the Christian confession to which it witnesses, I will not elaborate further.

2. The addition, the revelation of God 'witnessed to by the Holy Scriptures alone', begins at once to make a distinction. Fundamentally in agreement with Lutheranism, we differentiate ourselves first from the Catholic Church which sets beside the Holy Scriptures as second and third authorities, the apostolic tradition and the tradition of the Church embodied in the doctrinal office of the Pope; and so directly identifies the Church itself with the revelation. Also we differentiate

ourselves from the modern Protestantism and especially from the sects, so far as they give to history or to single significant historical events a character of revelation which is not fundamentally but only quantitatively different from the revelation of the Bible. 'Let us not seek him elsewhere than in his Word, let us think nothing concerning him except with his Word, let us say nothing of him except through his Word.' [1] So Calvin stated this cardinal principle of the making of a Reformed Creed. It will be wise to recognize clearly that a creed or any interpretation of a creed which is not rigid in respect to this 'not elsewhere', and rigid also against the hidden apotheosis of history which is no less characteristic of the new 'positive' Lutheranism than of the liberal, would no longer come under the definition of a Reformed Creed.

3. The Creed is a statement of an 'insight derived' from revelation 'given' to the Church. The Reformed Church knows that insight from the revelation in the Holy Scriptures is possible and real only through the Holy Spirit; in other words, that revelation can only be known through revelation. When the credal statement is recognized as the statement of an insight from God's revelation, it is not regarded as the statement of cherished human opinions, convictions, and so-called 'expressions of faith'. It is regarded as strictly *dogma*; that is, as the entirely human presentation of an insight which is *qualified* by its object and its origin. When Luther writes in his treatise on Councils in 1539: [2] 'The articles of faith cannot grow on earth through Councils out of a heavenly inspiration, but must be plainly given and revealed from heaven through the Holy Spirit', his statement is, except for the abstinence from the word 'revealed' which we like to practise, truly 'Reformed'.

And on the other side the exaggeratedly anthropocentric credal concept of the older and newer Congregationalists with its overemphasis on the human *understanding* of the creed at the expense of its divine content, is in this aspect un-Reformed and sectarian.

4. The Reformed Creed is understood as the statement of an insight which was given by God throughout the whole Christian Church, but which has been perhaps many times, perhaps widely, misunderstood or lost. Accordingly, a consciously non-sectarian emphasis and value is put on agreement with the Church of the first five centuries. In discussions with Lutheranism, the Reformed Church is wholly on the

---

[1] Calvin, *Against Caroli*, Op.7, 311: Non alibi quaeramus ipsum quam in eius verbo, nihil de ipso cogitemus nisi cum eius verbo, de ipso nihil loquamur nisi per eius verbum.

[2] *EA*, 25/267.

defensive against an opponent whose Christianity it does not fundamentally challenge. In its sharp, even in the sharpest, polemic against Catholicism, it does not doubt the presence of the Church of God even in the Church of Anti-Christ. In the strongest thrust of its anti-Roman argument, it actually accepts the theological-ecclesiastical tradition of the Middle Ages on a broader front than does Lutheranism. It calls itself neither Zwinglian nor Calvinistic, but Christian. It will not use nor advocate in its Creed any 'special character' such as one hears at times approved in Germany—not even a 'divinely ordained' special character. The Creed shall be the voice of the One Holy Church (*Una Sancta*). Hence derives both its conciliatory and its unyielding spirit.

5. But all insight into God's revelation given to the Church by God is understood as 'insight given for the moment'. There is a third entity between, on the one hand, the unchangeable Word of God which is spoken in the revelation by the Word who was in the beginning and is authentically witnessed to in the Scriptures alone, which is to be heard through the Church and to which obedience is to be required through the Church; and on the other hand, human religious opinions and convictions. The Church has not only the Spirit and receives not only the Spirit, but also the Church has and receives, through the Scriptures and the Spirit from generation to generation, the truth which as God's truth is whole and unchangeable, but which as received and possessed by men is fragmentary and changeable—but is still none the less truth. According to the Reformed conception, this third entity is *dogma*, 'the true and pure doctrine' (*doctrina vera et pura*), the insight for the time, given by God. But such insight is always to be given again, to be given new, purer and deeper; it must be received by the Church, considered and earnestly pondered; but it needs always to be grasped more completely and better.

Only by emphasizing first one side and then the other, the absolute giving and receiving and then the necessary step forward which must be made where God's goodness is new every morning, can the twofold character of Reformed credal formulation at its highest be understood. There is, on the one hand, the strictly defined dogmatic position which takes no account of consequences, and on the other there is the kind of pious and free relativism with which it regards its own declarations.

6. This brings us to the twice-repeated 'until further' of my definition. 'Until further', the Reformed Creed is to stand as the presentation of the insight which defines for outsiders the character of the confessing

community; and 'until further' as the directive for the community's own doctrine and life. Here we come to an important difference from Lutheranism. The Lutheran *Augustana* (Augsburg Confession) is to be, according to the Formula of Concord [of 1577],[1] the authority for the correct interpretation of Scripture 'for all posterity' (*ad omnem posteritatem*).

> Secure Church, our Church!
> Her wall, her safety and defence
> Is Augsburg's conquering creed,
> A mighty rampart round her.

So wrote a Lutheran eighty years ago. No Reformed Creed could be so hymned. The Reformed Church has never been in that sense 'a secure church'.

From the beginning, the Reformed Church has treated its creeds as open to discussion and improvement, as liable to be superseded. I quote an introductory passage from the official declaration of the Bern synod, as typical of many others:

'But where something is brought before us by our pastors or by others, which brings us closer to Christ, and in accordance with God's Word is more conducive to mutual friendship and Christian love than the interpretation now presented, we will gladly accept it and will not limit the course of the Holy Spirit, which does not go backward towards the flesh but always forward towards the image of Jesus Christ our Lord.' And the Reformed practice has in fact followed this insight, to which Calvin himself explicitly subscribed.[2]

Reformation dogma, taken seriously as such, is in flux. It is dogma, but only in the act of recurring renewal of the statement of faith. This mobility is strikingly demonstrated by the often regrettable disappearance of many excellent old creeds (for example, the Scots Confession) and by the fact that the same revival movement of the nineteenth century which in Lutheranism led to the renovation of the Formula of Concord resulted among the orthodox free churches of the Reformed persuasion in the formulation of so many new creeds.

7. The principal pre-supposition underlying this mobility of Reformed Creeds is that they are (at least in comparison with the Lutheran) not 'Symbolics', but are viewed in their earthly, historical actuality— and are *also* continually reviewed. They are honestly and actually 'Confessions of Faith' (*confessiones fidei*). A confession of faith is, according

---

[1] *Sol. Decl.: De Compend. Doctr.*, forma 16.
[2] *Against Pighius*, Op.6, 250; *Institutes*, IV, 9, 13.

to a definition which Calvin once gave,[1] a 'testimony to the faith inwardly held . . . sought from the pure fonts of Scripture'. I should put it: a declaration of the insight given to the Church from the revelation, a human and therefore fallible declaration! So the Reformed Creed looked back and judged the decisions of the old Church Councils to which it related itself, and then made the same judgement on itself. It distinguished strictly between its own dignity and the immeasurable superiority of its object. Scripture remains Scripture, unique and incomparable, beyond any scale. A creed is always recognized as only action necessary for the time, undertaken and carried through for the sake of the good order and the up-building of the community of God on earth. It is a definite requirement made by Christ, the Ruler of the Church, in the area of human freedom and temptation; as Calvin put it most instructively in his Apology for the Reformed oath imposed on the residents of Geneva in 1537,[2] 'WE, HERE, NOW, confess faith in THIS!' Certainly we are conscious of speaking in the name of the one Holy Church (*Una Sancta*), conscious of speaking the truth—but *we, here, now* speak. So also the Synods understood it, and the governments and princes who supported the later creeds. For them, the haze of the concept, 'symbol', was lacking—as it ought to be. It is to be hoped that no member of the Reformed Church has lapsed into acceptance of the idea that the Heidelberg Catechism or the Dort Confession could be inspired, as Lutherans have taught the inspiration of the Formula of Concord.[3] In so far as the Congregationalists have expressed their particular horror at all 'church power properly so-called',[4] they represent a genuine part of the Reformed concept of creed.

(I prefer to postpone until later the discussion of the confessing subject as 'a geographically limited Christian community', because this is a part of our main theme.)

8. I said that the Reformed Creed must be 'spontaneously' formulated by the community (to be more closely defined later). Behind the Reformed Creed there stands ultimately, if all is rightly done, neither a consistorial nor a royal court, but (at least in theory) the market place or the Town Hall where the citizens of state or country, who are Christian communicants sharing the Lord's Supper, meet together. What did the Lutheran community have to do, even theoretically, with

---

[1] *Against Caroli*, Op.7, 312: conceptae intus fidei testificatio . . . e puris scripturae fontibus petita.
[2] Preface to the Latin Catechism of 1538: Op.5, 317 f.
[3] Hase, *Hutterus Redivivus*, 10th edition, § 51.
[4] Savoy Declaration: K. Müller, *Ref. Bek. Schr.*, p. 656.

the origin of the *Augustana* or of the Formula of Concord? Reformed folk do not walk in leading strings, controlled from above like that. They confess their own faith or none.

Calvin understood fully and exactly what his aim was when he even used force to require the citizens of Geneva in 1537 to take that public oath to the Reformation and the Reformed Creed, after the same oath had been taken in Basel in 1534. At Basel until 1821, that oath was virtually affirmed yearly at the solemn reading of the Confession in the week before Easter.

The oldest Reformed Creeds are entirely the result of discussion and subsequent voting, carried on with wide-open doors. And though the later creeds are as a rule the work of mixed synods, yet the synod (again if all is rightly done) is nothing but the commissioned voice of the Reformed community. Its formal *aristocracy* is only representative Christian *democracy*, the corollary of the *autocracy* of Christ. No office, no clerical group may intervene between the Lord, Christ in Heaven, and the Christian community of the land, sovereign on earth. The competence of the synod to declare dogma is according to Reformed understanding not excluded by this representative character, but legally, in human law (the legally trained Calvin had a sense for this necessary aspect of the matter), depends precisely on this Christian-democratic character of the synod.

On the contrary, what the Margrave Ernst Friedrich of Baden-Durlach did in 1599 and the Elector Johann Sigismund of Brandenburg did in 1614 (along with other similar actions) belong in this aspect outside the concept of a Reformed Creed as a spontaneous act of the community for which it is to be authoritative. It is clear that this aspect of the concept is an outcome and an enforcement of what I have called the 'religious relativism' which the Reformed Creed ascribes to itself.

9. Finally, a further word on the practical significance of the Reformed Creed. It is intended, I have said, as a definition of the community for those outside, and as a directive for its own teaching and life for those within. It addresses itself to the widest possible public, demanding recognition and consideration, not for the individuals who accept it, but for the content of what they confess, which is universal. Typical of this demand are the open letters (even though they are personal in form) to Francis I of France with which Calvin and Zwingli prefaced their main theological works. Something of this herald's trumpet belongs to all the Reformed Creeds, whether the area immediately involved is great or small.

Such creeds were thought of not only and in many cases not primarily as theological ordinances for the Church; they were conceived in the consciousness of the mission of the Church to those outside who were surrounded by a Christianity which had fallen into error. The Christian character of the Community confessing their faith must be made manifest for all who hear the confession, must be recognized and must stir them to reflection. Therefore the Creed is to be also a directive for the Community itself, by which the Community will be guided in doctrine and life. It will not be without value to emphasize 'in doctrine *and* life'. The doctrine, the proclamation of Christian truth among the Reformed, much more unambiguously than in the school of Luther, included the essentials for men's lives in society and in the State. In fact, it sets forth the problem of ethics radically in every line.

It would be incorrect to say that the Creed is the law or norm of doctrine and life. In the Church, the Scripture alone is law and norm; dogma and creed are not. The Creed is a commentary on the law which points out the direction of action. Its obligatory force is lost if the law itself convicts the commentary of falsehood; or if knowledge of the law no longer exists. For, as the dogmatic theologian Franz Turrenti affirms: 'Confessions of faith cannot be binding in the inner court of conscience, except in so far as they are perceived to agree with the Word of God, which alone has the power of binding the conscience.' [1]

No obligation of church law and no internal authority of pastor and community prevents the demise of a creed. Therefore, the 'credal position' of a Reformed Church differs fundamentally from the Lutheran and is to be understood as stable only in relation to the moment of insight given by God from his revelation. Apart from that act between God and man, an act which cannot be legally established, the Reformed position must be called unstable. The Creed offers little externally to the Church, and is certainly not a protection against creeping degeneration. The power which originated it is the power of the Holy Spirit, and that power is also the power of its continuing endurance and effectiveness. It has no other power, but that power it has.

So far, we have presented our definition of the concept of a Reformed Creed, and by it have established the necessary basis for answering and have found a provisional answer to the question pro-

---

[1] Heppe, *Dogm. d. evang. ref. Kirche*, p. 504. Confessiones non possunt obligare in foro interno conscientiae, nisi in quantum deprehenduntur convenire cum verbo Dei, quod solum vim habet conscientiam obligandi.

posed to the General Council. One common Reformed Creed could, in any situation whatever, be declared desirable and possible by the General Council only if it conformed exactly to the requirements laid down in the definition, in its form and content, and also in the purpose for which it was formulated, proclaimed, and introduced. Otherwise there would be a 'contradiction in terms' (*contradictio in adjecto*); it would not be a Reformed Creed. And the Council which presented it would have to be repudiated as in schism.

For instance—this I have already mentioned, but it cannot be over-emphasized—a creed which should allow itself laxity in the matter of the exclusive normative authority of the Holy Scripture, according to the liberal and modern 'positive' trend, would *per se* not be a Reformed Creed, and therefore for us would not be a desirable and possible creed. The same would be equally true of a creed which presented merely a lyrical expression of religious emotion without binding force, which lacked the courage to be dogma and tell us, the Reformed University Professors for example, in blunt, basic words what the Reformed Churches intend to proclaim in the name of God, 'until further'.

This would be equally true of a creed which was intended as merely a documentation of the 'peculiar' character of the Reformed Church, and of one which forgot its own limits and should claim for itself infallibility and finality. Equally true of one at the making of which the churches involved had not spoken by direct and definite representatives. And of one which did not intend to be a real proclamation and a real commentary on Scripture, but merely to make scriptural references, with however great seriousness.

I hardly need to say that the promulgation of a creed, even though it be only the solemn reaffirmation of one of the old creeds, is not a simple matter, if it is really to be done in the sense and in the spirit of what can be called a Reformed Creed, as determined by origin and content.

You will not have failed to notice what a sharp dialectic curve we have described in this summation of the different essential components of the concept of the Reformed Creed. It concerns not conceptions of faith, but dogma; yet fundamentally variable, fluid dogma. Universal Christian truth; yet truth understood now and here in a specific way and expressed by *one* Christian community. A definite and specific Church, sure of its truth, 'a Church of possessors' (*ecclesia possidentium*), but a Church which precisely as possessing is completely 'a school of seekers' (*schola quaerentium*). The eternal revelation of God;

but revelation and eternal only in the moment in which it is known as such through God himself.

One must be already somewhat at home in his Calvin, and still more in his Bible, if he is not to burst out in loud complaint over these impossible contradictions and inconsequences; if he is to recognize calmly that all these components have been required and must be required for a Reformed Creed. Only so will he know that this road between two great gulfs is the road on which our fathers walked with the simplicity of wisdom and with the wisdom of simplicity, but steadily and with entire assurance. It is the road on which, if we are really to undertake to do what they did, we must walk again, if we can.

Truly, 'if we can'? And that is the question which I would offer as my first response to the questioners and would set before this Council. Do you really believe that the Reformed Churches of the present day are individually or collectively in a position to grasp fully the concept of a Reformed Creed and then to walk the only Reformed road, the only desirable and possible road to such a creed? Have we the simplicity and the wisdom to do this thing as it must be done? Does Peter believe that the waves of the sea will bear him? Is it really for Christ's sake that he desires to walk this road?

If the answer is 'Yes', then he will not hesitate for an instant to do it. If not . . . But we had better postpone the 'either-or' which is here visible, until the end of the discussion.

The question to be dealt with in the Council in Cardiff is defined as the desirability and possibility of—not a creed of some sort or other but—a single creed for the Reformed Churches of the *whole world*. We must consider the question further under this specification.

We come back to the part of our definition which was omitted in the previous discussion of our theme. The proclaimer of the Reformed Creed is 'a Christian community, geographically limited'. The specific local or national church makes its Confession of Faith: the Church of Bern, of Basel, of Bremen or Bentheim, of France or of Scotland. Each one looks for his direction first in direct appeal to the Bible. They greet one another, back and forth, as from one island to another, from Basel to Strassburg, from Geneva to Zürich, rejoicing over every possibility of mutual understanding. But every church lives its own life; and with surprising independence, each church, marked off by the accidental boundaries of the authority of the various states, goes its own way, even in the matter of creed-making. So there results that diversity of formulae which led Luther to judge that the doctrine of South Germany was certainly from Satan;[1] that variegated mass of 'small town' Reformed creeds which was taken for granted by the Reformed, but which so mightily astonished the Catholic polemicist, Bossuet. The Reformed were called 'Confessionists', and they accepted the label, as if a hidden but real compulsion held them to their position.

Even Calvin (and this fact deserves consideration) with his international Christian orientation, with his legal instincts, with his innumerable personal connexions in all countries, with his strongly developed concern for the shrewd practical co-operation between individual churches, took so far as I know, no specific concrete steps in the direction of one common Reformed Creed.

Two attempts to deal with the problem were offered for consideration in the sixteenth and seventeenth centuries. It must be said that the Reformed Church as a whole made astonishingly cautious and unenthusiastic use of them. What meaning did the 'universality' of a Christian Creed in the sense of our theme have at that time? Just the ecumenicity of the Church of the Roman Empire, the only surviving portion of mediaeval Christendom (*corpus Christianum*). Under the shadow of this ecumenicity, Lutheranism took shelter in its Creed presented to the Emperor and Empire at Augsburg, and thereby nullified the ban of particularity both theoretically and, what was still more important, legally. It was this quasi-ecumenical character, its quality as a public document, not its inner value, which made the *Augustana* so dear to Lutheranism, and which made adherence to the *Augustana* desirable under certain circumstances also for non-Lutherans.

These circumstances existed in Germany, where up to the threshold of the modern age the idea of corporate Christendom (*corpus Christianum*) had incomparably more significance (even practically) than in Switzerland, the Netherlands, or in the French and Anglo-Scottish West. This accounts for the conspicuous, almost magnetic attraction which the *Augustana* has exercised on the Reformed in spite of its unquestionably different theological orientation, in spite of the unpleasant fictions to which they felt themselves compelled in order to hide the difference, in spite of the understandably slight cordiality with which their efforts were received by the genuine and legitimate adherents of the *Augustana*. At Regensburg in 1540, even Calvin as representative of Strassburg signed the *Augustana Variata*.[2]

[1] Enders, *Luthers Briefwechsel*, 5, p. 294.
[2] Op.9, 19; 16, 430.

But a significant fact must be noted. As soon as he was no longer in the abnormal position of taking part in the politics of the German Reformed Church, he made it plain that he had not at all intended by that signature to recognize the *Augustana* as a universal Reformed Creed, although the Germans repeatedly did so under their political oppression. On the contrary, Calvin explicitly warned the French Church against the step of union with the Germans, not only because he feared the German quarrels over the interpretation of the *Augustana* would be transplanted to the West, but because he judged it to be in content 'poorly supported, lax and obscure' (*maigrement bastie, molle et obscure*).[1]

If we read Calvin's blunt letters to Farel from Regensburg and if we remember the designs against the continuance of the Roman Empire which Calvin then considered, as Zwingli had ten years earlier, it is clear that Calvin, in fact that the whole Reformed movement as such, had preserved no ideal of connexion with the mediaeval 'corporate Christendom' (*corpus Christianum*). Therefore, where political considerations were not present as they were in Germany, the Reformed had no nostalgic desire for an ecumenical Creed; they were not wistfully looking backward. Along with the ideas of Emperor and Empire, of Pope and the Church of the Empire, an ecumenical Creed had become for them an empty abstraction, if not something worse. A very different form of objectivity and universality than that would be needed to correspond with the objectivity and universality of credal content.

The other possibility of breaking through the formal particularity of the individual Reformed Creeds was plainly one which looked forward and which involved fundamentally the same problem which we should meet today. The problem of uniting the evangelicals or rather (since the Lutherans exclude themselves) of the non-Lutheran evangelicals under the sign of an already existing creed or under the common proclamation of a new creed. But significantly, there was surprisingly little effort in this direction to be noted. As is well known, there was no lack of Reformed solidarity in practical activity, nor of sympathetic cooperation among all the leaders on theoretical points. And the lively interchange in basic theoretical activity continued into the eighteenth century. But of an identifiable attempt to move forward to a Reformed world-creed or even to achieve a Reformed World Church able to agree against Rome nothing is known, at least to me, during this classic age of the Reformed Church.

[1] Op.18, 733.

In this kind of action the Reformed were uninterested. They seem to have known of a unity which made agreement on paper (however important in other ways paper may be) superfluous. They met from time to time in brotherly and friendly agreement, with simultaneous mutual concessions, even on points which one would rather not concede. Calvin gave to such compromises the significant label of 'pious conspiracy' (*pia conspiratio*).[1]

Under this heading, so far as I see, there are five possibilities:

1. The union of individual churches in a newly proclaimed common creed; for example, the Swiss churches in 1536 and again in 1566 with the two Helvetic Creeds, thus making a particular creed more inclusive.

2. The declaration of mutual, special recognition of the creed of one church by another, without either giving up its own creed and without the proclamation of a joint third creed, as, for example, was agreed in 1538 between the national Synods of France and the Netherlands.

3. Unofficial recognition of the creed of one church by many others on the ground of its inner value and its especial usefulness. This happened especially with the Heidelberg Catechism.

4. Mutual written or personal counsel in difficult circumstances, such as Geneva asked and received from foreign churches in the cases of Bolsec and Servetus, and the Netherlands at the Synod of Dort.

5. The private decisions of assemblies of the learned; for example, when the *Augustana Variata* had to be agreed to for the sake of the Germans. Similar were the Harmony of Confessions of Salnar 1581 and the *Corpus et Syntagma* of Caspar Laurentius 1612. Salnar, at the same time with the Belgic Confession, gained the approval of the French. Laurentius in 1653, at the re-establishment of the Reformed University of Marburg, was declared the standard for the teaching of the theological Faculty.

These are the only instances of such action that I know of, and I do not think that there is anything further of great importance which relates to the achievement of unity. There is nothing which goes beyond the 'pious conspiracy', and nothing like the concept of a universal creed, like that in today's question.

If the reason for this phenomenon is sought, it can be said that it is the Reformed conception of the Church which at least puts serious limitations in the way of going further towards unity. As defined in Reformed Dogmatics, the Church as the visible Church is 'a company

[1] Op.5, 321.

of those who by external word, use of the sacraments and ecclesiastical discipline have joined themselves into one external body and association'.[1] The points which have decisive force in relation to our question are designated in this definition by the terms 'company', 'external body', 'association', 'join'.

The Church as 'the ecumenical and universal company scattered through the whole world' (*coetus oecumenicus et universalis per totum orbem dispersus*),[2] that is as a church which is visible but whose members are not concretely (*in concreto*) conscious of community of action, is fully capable of believing, loving, hoping. But for concrete church action (and as concrete action the Creed must be understood) the concepts of the definition must not only be logically within the grasp of the separate members; they must also to a certain extent be actually and concretely achieved. The 'joining' of the members together must be at least believably in process. The 'company' (*coetus*) must really exist before the eyes of its members as an 'external body' (*corpus externum*), that is as a community of men which can be seen and known or about which information is available, as obvious an entity as any national group.

A creed proclaimed where this human credibility and visibility of the confessing 'external body' was wholly lacking would violate both the Reformed concept of creed and the Reformed concept of Church. There would then be a concrete action of the Church which would be something different from the concrete action of the 'external body' united through Word, sacrament and discipline. A church would then be only an institution, only an official board—and therefore the Reformed concept of the Church prohibits the proclamation of such a creed.

But it does not follow that a universal creed as such would necessarily be contrary to the Reformed concept of the Church. Theoretically it is possible to think of an extension of the concrete visibility of the Christian company which would finally spread over all lands and seas. But practically (and it is the actual situation which concerns us in relation to a Reformed Creed), such an extension becomes more improbable the more inclusively it is conceived. Are we who are allegedly one in Christ really a single 'company' (*coetus*), a single 'association' (*societas*), one nation, one in Christ and therefore one in our agreement

---

[1] *Leyd. Synopsis* (Heppe, op. cit., p. 481): coetus eorum, qui per verbum externum, sacramentorum, disciplinae ecclesiasticae usum in unum externum corpus ac societatem coalescunt.

[2] Heppe, op. cit., p. 492.

with one another? I can *believe* with the most distant, with the 'ecumenical company' (*coetus oecumenicus*); I can *confess* my faith (with no admixture of un-Reformed ideology) only with my neighbours, that is with those known to me as fellow believers—and that means known above all as fellow sinners and fellow prisoners. I must confess with the 'particular company' (*coetus particularis*) which I know, be it larger or smaller.

The 'particular company' must itself become the 'ecumenical company' before it can agree honestly in an ecumenical creed. Our cohesion in the one 'external body' of the Church must be completed under the rule of the Lord—for example, with the French Reformed—and must be humanly felt and acknowledged by them as well as by us. We must have *found* one another mutually, not just in a sentimental brotherly love but in the *criminality* common to them and to us, and in the pardon for criminals common to them and to us—exactly as pardoned criminals recognize one another. This is essential, not for loving one another as Reformed brethren, as fellow believers in Christian faith (that happens to a certain extent) but—and this is something more—for making together a real Confession of Faith, for proclaiming a real Creed.

Any road to a universal creed which by-passes the concrete actuality of unitedness would not be a Reformed road. So, I think, the reluctance of the old Reformed to take inclusive credal action is to be understood. Their creeds came into existence on the basis of a concrete situation; the creed was an act, an event, a transaction, not only as a response to God in his revelation, but also and simultaneously as a demonstration of real, human-earthly unitedness. Therefore it was undertaken with sober-minded renunciation of the glitter of both the old and the new ecumenicity, behind which it no longer saw reality or did not yet see it. Therefore I think that the restriction 'a Christian community geographically limited' in the definition of the concept 'Reformed Creed' belongs as an indispensable link in this unbreakable chain.

'Geographically' is to be taken 'with a pinch of salt'. The old Reformed individual church was the legitimate proclaimer of the Reformed Creed, not because it was surrounded by a city wall or a national boundary, but because its members came and went together in the same place and shared a concrete community life, out of which could come something as pre-eminently common to all as a Confession of Faith. This 'place' can be extended at will, it can even be a wholly spiritual place, but it must not cease to be a place where human people stand, where men meet one another in human fashion, where they really

weep and rejoice together. There, in this definite place, perhaps—probably—certainly—in sin and under condemnation, in the muck and
misery of this definite earthly place, there the Christian community
lives, there it confesses its Faith. So far as Christian community is
everywhere, we will rejoice in it; but as a community of creed, it must
be present in a definite, concrete sense.

From this point I would direct a second counter-question to those
who posed the question to Cardiff. How do they understand the relation
between the concreteness indispensable to the Reformed concept of
the Church and the universality of the Creed about the desirability
and possibility of which they are asking us? Does this relationship proceed in accordance with the Reformed concept of the Church, the
great, visible, believable, divine existence of the confessors in the dust
and dirt of an earthly place, in opposition to all ideologies?

If the answer is Yes, is it probable that the 'particular company'
(*coetus particularis*) of those bound by it will grow into the 'universal
company' (*coetus universalis*)? It is already pretty difficult to feel ourselves united in this sense with our near neighbours. Will this kind of
union be easier with those afar off? Have the questioners seen the signs
of the times which would warrant such a hope? Are they entirely sure
that the Reformed 'universal company' (*coetus universalis*) of tomorrow
will be a company of the humbled and will not, in fact, resemble that
other 'universal company', the company of the Pope, which lacks precisely this common bond and therefore has not the right to confess a
common faith? Are they entirely certain that the promulgated world
Creed, regardless of whether it be one of the old creeds or one to be
newly formulated, will not be actually a worldly creed, one of those
mixtures of resolutions and exhortations by which in the *world* men summon one another to great matters, which are proclaimed and listened to,
but which are never, now or hereafter, *believed* by anybody? Are they
entirely sure? If they are sure, then why was not the universal creed
immediately, at the dawn of that day of certainty, simultaneously
desirable, possible, necessary *and* actual? If they are not sure . . . but
here again is the 'either-or', the discussion of which we leave to the
conclusion.

Let us assume for the moment, at the beginning of the third and last
consideration, that the first and second questions may be answered
with an unqualified Yes. Accordingly:

(1) The Reformed Churches are in fact in the position to fulfil both

the positive and the negative conceptual prerequisites for proclaiming and establishing a truly Reformed Confession of Faith. And

(2) The especial requirement of the concreteness of the association necessary for the Reformed Creed is not an obstacle to the proclamation and establishment of a universal Reformed Confession of Faith, because this requirement also is in general fulfilled or can be fulfilled.

If we assume that these requirements are met, there would still remain a consideration which we have already noted, but which requires special attention. Namely, if we are really to proceed to the proclamation and establishment of such a universal Reformed World Creed, we should unavoidably be venturing to take a step which our fathers, with Calvin at the head, never took.

But why shouldn't we? Why are we not perhaps required to take it? Our situation may have become so entirely different that it imperatively demands from us different measures from those required of them. It is possible that we are *in the position* to actually carry through these different measures. The stress is on the point: *Are we in the position* to do in relation to the Christian Creed what Calvin did not do? To do something bolder and greater? Even, we must really say, something more Christian than he did? Is this true? If it is true, then what we decide to do must at least stand comparison with what was done. The value, the importance, the Christian-ness of our universal Creed must be fit to be measured fairly against those of the particular creeds of the old Reformed Churches. When the present intends to progress beyond the past, the past poses the question to the present of whether it is really making progress.

The new, universal Reformed Creed which the questioners of Cardiff had in mind does not lie before us, and we do not have to discuss its content. We are asked only about the desirability and the possibility of such a creed. We do not know whether it is a modernized proclamation of an old creed—the Heidelberg Confession or perhaps the Westminster —or (this second possibility would in itself be more in accord with the history of the Reformed Church) the editing of a modern formula, which waved enticingly before the circles where our question originated, as the eventually desirable and possible creed. The requisite comparison between the past and the present cannot therefore deal with content.

But the question of the desirability and possibility of the whole action which is under discussion can be put into the form of a comparison and can be so answered. There are fixed factual conditions for a Christian Confession of Faith which are decisive for the question of whether it is desirable and possible, regardless of what its content may be.[1] These factual conditions have still to be discussed.

I anticipate no objection when I state the first condition. It is simply that to make such a step desirable and possible we must, at least as certainly as our fathers, have the assured consciousness that by it we are obeying the will of God. Behind their particular creeds stands the consciousness of this highest necessity. The same consciousness must equally stand behind our universal creed. There is little to say in clarification, but this much can be said: May God guard us and all men who are faced with this question against all possible conceivable and practical makeshifts, against all undertakings which today in the age of aeroplanes and radio lie technically in the range of possibility, but behind which stands neither Christian need nor Christian compulsion, nor any serious despairing search for and discovery of its inevitability in the will of God.

There are things which one dares do and can do only if he must do them. To these things belongs a Christian Creed. No enthusiasm, no goodwill, no charitable brotherly love, no considerations of church politics can be a substitute for this *must*, this desperate recognition of the inevitability of a Creed. *Credo*, 'I believe', is first to be said after all other possibilities are exhausted. When struck on the mouth, I can say nothing except 'I believe'. A Creed of any other kind is a bit of lazy magic and comes from the Devil—even though verbally it be the

---

[1] Besides my own paper, the Cardiff Council heard papers by Professors Martin (Edinburgh) and Shaw (Halifax). The former answered the question in the negative, arguing, so far as I understood, from the point of view of its practicality for the Church. The latter concluded by laying before the Council the possibility of a modernization of the Westminster Confession and repudiated expressly the proposal for a new creed. The wording may be of interest to the reader.

'We believe on God the Father, Maker of heaven and earth, Whose love is over all, and Who is able to make all things work together for the accomplishment of His purpose of Holy Father-Love with His children.

'We believe on Jesus Christ, His only Son, our Saviour and Lord, through Whose life and death and risen, working through His Spirit, we have forgiveness and eternal life, and are called into the saving fellowship and service of God's Kingdom of love and righteousness and peace, both now and hereafter.

'We believe in (not 'on') the Holy Catholic Church, the Body of Christ throughout all the world, indwelt and possessed by the Holy Spirit through whose working we with all the saints are led into even fuller truth and holiness and power.

'All this we believe, primarily and particularly, through the Divine redemptive revelation recorded and interpreted for us in Holy Scripture, and verified by the testimony of the Holy Spirit in our hearts. And in this faith we commit ourselves unto God the Father and unto His Son Jesus Christ, and unto the power of His Spirit, that we may live not unto ourselves but unto Him Who loved us, and gave Himself for us. Amen.'

Apostles' Creed. The Reformed Church cannot afford to speak that kind of *Credo*. For the Reformed Church knows itself as a church confessing its faith, as the 'communion of the chosen and called' (*communio electorum et vocatorum*), as the fellowship of those chosen out of destruction, of those called out of darkness. It is wholly and entirely the 'church of the desert'. At its furthest boundaries, in the mountains where the Rhine begins and in the Netherlands where it ends, its genuine Confession of Faith was first heard. Also today if the Confession be genuine, it must come from the boundaries. It must be the Creed of those who are forsaken by God and who, as the forsaken, are visited by God; of those who are lost and who, as the lost, are rescued. It must be the Creed of those shipwrecked on the will of God who in the wreck are clinging to his will. If the universal Reformed Creed were to be a Creed like that, like the Creeds of our fathers, how could it fail to be desirable and possible?

This simple condition I would now develop in two ways. First, he who thinks he must *speak* in obedience to the will of God and therefore in the name of God; he who so accepts and performs in the world the office of prophet (and that must be done wherever a Christian Confession of Faith is to be made), must believe—not to elaborate further the prerequisites to be considered here—that he has something true and important to say about the counsels of God and that he has something definite to offer in God's name. There is, to separate topically, both a dogmatic and an ethical content requirement for a creed. On both sides it is necessary that some concrete situation be present which forces the Church 'in the concrete' (*in concreto*) to make a Confession of Faith. There is a witnessing which *will* be declared; a communicating of something to know and something to undertake in which the will of God, the sole reason for credal action, is manifested plainly and intelligibly.

If this more accurate formulation is correct, two corollaries follow.

1. As an indispensable prerequisite for a desirable and possible creed, the Church must have come into possession of certain special insights from the Scriptures; the Church must have fought a hard battle against theological lies and half-truths and have won definite affirmations to present as the truth now available to it, which will endure 'until further'. Also the Church must have become so sure of the rightness and importance of certain cardinal ideas of its preaching that it feels itself constrained to bear witness to them before the world in a formal document and to set them up as an Ebenezer for itself. This witness is then the Confession of Faith.

When and where has there been a true creed which was not the result of a definite phase of the long history of the interrelation of Church and Bible, the conclusion of long, earnest theological discussions, the expression of a definite and specific application of the Christian Gospel? A creed without such a preliminary history, a creed which was proclaimed only for its own sake 'so that something might appear done' (*ut aliquid fieri videatur*), would have no sense. It might serve as a testimony to man's benevolent love of unity; as an expression of a common wish or ideal; as a compromise formula for groups whose differing statements are no longer the expression of living Christian thinking and who can now make a common statement, only because they no longer know what once divided them; as a preamble prefixed to a church constitution, because a church constitution must have a preamble with a sort of credal sound; as a beautiful flag which is left in the barracks when the regiment is on the march.

If it is any of those things or if it is any similar thing, a Confession of Faith is wholly in the air and without foundation. It could not possibly be a genuine Confession of Faith. A creed without a preceding, serious theological history can never be other than horribly dull, unoriginal, second-hand. It says nothing and accomplishes nothing. From a creed without true and individual biblical insights, without the scars from the preceding battle, without a compelling concern; from a creed without dogmatic significance, especially from a creed which deliberately evades such significance, may the Lord our God deliver us!

If the revival of an *old* creed is what the questioners had in mind, this should be said: Never, without a genuine commentary! Repetition without commentary would be both laziness and cowardice.

Now I must confess that *I* at least should be embarrassed if I were asked what events and conformations characterizing the theological history of the present and the recent past can be considered as the history preliminary to the Confession of Faith to be proclaimed as resulting therefrom. Where has anything occurred in theology in our time which the Church can claim as the upholding of a great truth? Or what great heresy has arisen by which the Church feels itself [in 1925] seriously and successfully invaded? Where among us is an Athanasius? A Luther? Not to wait for men who are not only moving and inspiring, but whose thinking is also well grounded and systematically developed, where is an Augustine, a Thomas, a Calvin? What would be the compelling concern upon which the Church must today bear public witness?

Let us not deceive ourselves. We are not living really in a classical period of Protestant theology, the possibilities of which could somehow induce us to open our mouths full width. We stand actually *between* the times, burdened with the unhappy pietistic-rationalistic heritage of the last two centuries, from which it is not so easy to free ourselves as many men not closely involved imagine. And we stand before a future which we, who are armed with only a few very modest new approaches, must meet very cautiously.

The Church should and can *believe*, always, even in times of such theological transition and testing. But for a Confession of Faith, so far as can be determined from German and Swiss theology, there exists today no real possibility. Is the situation different in France, Holland, England, or North America? It could be. But we must be given very strong proofs if we are to be convinced that we are failing to see what is really there to be seen, or ignoring realities in the theology of today which would allow a universal Reformed Creed to appear desirable and possible.

But suppose that the situation were quite different from that which I have just described. Suppose we stood, not *between* the times, but already victoriously at the turning-point; that is, within the historical period precursory to a creed. We should then be again cognizant of what theological exegesis is and of what constitutes a dogmatics worthy of the name. The flood of philosophical, historical, and edifying dilettantism would be subsiding or would have already ebbed. The Bible would be read again as Holy Scripture, not merely investigated for its religious interest, but seen in its true character. The Trinity and predestination, Christology and the sacraments, and other really pertinent topics would be discussed among professors and students, and at ministers' meetings. Then there would no longer be listlessness and tedium, but real excitement would be kindled if a universal Reformed Creed was under consideration, with its prerequisites of serious preliminary decisions on such questions.

Let us suppose, for example, that this Creed should then take the very significant step of naming the great heresy, the heresy of Schleiermacher (it is recognized by present-day liberal and 'positive' Christians alike as orthodox), and should politely but deservedly and specifically repudiate it as impossible for the Church. Fine! But the second condition still remains.

2. Is this second prerequisite fulfilled? The Creed, according to the precedent of biblical prophecy, must also have something positive to

offer, must have ready in its content a 'Thus saith the Lord'; must include not only what is essential for doctrine but also what is essential for living and for living in the immediate situation.

I confess that for myself, personally, the dogmatic preparation lies closest to my heart; but I am very willing to be blamed for this preference. It certainly cannot be assumed necessary.

In this second aspect also the old Reformed Creed was based on the premise that the Church had something to say. Acceptance of dogma among the old Reformed had nothing to do with abstract gnosis. It was wholly ethical. The *whole* man, the whole *city* was requisitioned by the 'parole de Dieu' which was confessed. The Creed did not proclaim the glory of God as one aim of its content among others, as the religious aim; but as *the* aim *above* all others. As Creed, it required obedience, it set forth an absolutely prescribed way of life for sinful people who had received grace. They were not to obey for the sake of reward and certainly not in order to attain any specific goal; they were to obey without any illusionary expectations, simply for the sake of obedience. This obedience was not something which had to be discussed at length; it was a self-evident and necessary corollary. The picture is this: a predestinated man, a baptized man, whose sins are forgiven, is now, not in the abstract but concretely, a member of a contemporary society with rules of conduct which were, according to our ideas, very simple. That is the exact situation. It was, in fact, as an ethical creed that the Reformed Creed decisively influenced the contemporary rise of sociological reconstruction in Europe.

We may take it for granted that this second requirement for a Reformed Creed is also today recognized as indispensable. The Church must have something to say, some pronouncement to make which concerns the concrete life of men. The Church, of course, says it of and says it to its members, not as a piece of secular wisdom, but as its own provisional understanding of the Gospel and law of God—just as is true of everything which the Church says. But the Church sets a light 'not under a bushel but on a lampstand'. The Church is under no delusion; this light is seen. And what kind of light it is, *is* important. Precisely in its ethical stand, the Church declares unmistakably to those outside what it is and what it has. It shows this equally when the lamp is empty. If in its relation to life, the Church is a 'dumb dog' and does not fulfil its watchman's task, then its best dogmatics is useless.

A church which today desired to confess its faith must have the courage to express the insight currently won from Scripture on the

problems of life which *today* beset its members. It cannot wait until its
statement comes thirty years too late, like the Social Manifesto of the
Bielefeld Church Assembly. It must act while the problem is still 'hot',
while the Church can speak its word upon it where the word of the
Church belongs, at the outset of the problem. The Church must have
the courage to speak today (I mention only one specific problem) upon
the fascist, racialist *nationalism* which since the war is appearing in
similar forms in all countries. Does the Church say yes or not to this
nationalism? Does the Church, deliberately and in principle, say Yes
to war, or has it, in spite of all practical considerations, a final, principled
No to set on the lampstand? A *No* which is unqualified and fully
audible, not a pacifist's No, but a specifically Christian *No* against the
war? Does the Church intend to affirm and establish by a creed in all
lands the unambiguously militaristic position which it took in 1914?
Or does it intend rather to confess that it has meanwhile reached a
different judgement?

I am only asking; but the decision for which I ask must be made this
way or that. And I state openly my doubt whether the Church of today
really *wishes* to say anything definite on such burning and dangerous
questions of life, where Christian and other commendable interests are
sharply opposed to one another—and my doubt that it *has* anything to
say.

We see the Church of today in no sure position, wavering between
yes and no, even more in ethics than in dogmatics; now silent where it
ought to speak, now speaking where it ought to be silent; always two
steps behind in its deliberations, behind what the world has done
without it; sulky and self-conscious in its ethical objectives; definite
only where it has nothing to fear for itself. It is full of goodwill towards
all sides; but certainly, very certainly it raises no prophetic voice, no
watchman's cry, above the confusion of other voices. Is it different in
the Reformed West and in America? Really different than in Germany
and in Switzerland, of which again I think first?

I have described the unencouraging picture which I see, only for the
sake of the conclusion to be drawn from it. You can reject my personal
judgement on the ethical lack of direction in the evangelical Church of
today. But you will concede that if my judgement were correct, if this
necessary prerequisite were also lacking, the proclamation of a universal
Reformed Creed could not be deemed desirable and possible. The
herald's summoning trumpet blast, which according to definition such a
Creed must sound, would then in reality be merely a conspicuous

fiasco. If I am right, the Church still can and must believe; even more than ever it must believe. But the unnecessary and unrequired proclamation of a Confession of Faith would then be 'tempting God'.

We have come to the end. To the two conditions for the desirability and possibility of a universal Reformed Creed which were discussed in the first and second sections: (1) our ability to fulfil the Reformed Concept of the Church Creed (*confessio ecclesiastica*) and (2) the possibility of combining the term 'universal' with the Reformed concept of the Church, the third must be added: the present will of God for this undertaking which transcends the action of the past; and God's present will is to be recognized by the presence of definite pre-requisites in preparation for such action.

We stand on a knife-edge. The 'either-or' has been made manifest along the whole line of our thought. I do not stop at this point with the purpose of easing your discussion. How I personally would decide if I had come to Cardiff as a member of the Council has not been concealed from you. But that is not the point. Do not consider my opinion. Consider the material which, as fully as I could, I have laid before you for your decision.

There remains only for me to add explicitly a statement of what the decision in faith, for one side or the other, would mean. If the answer to the proposed question is Yes, then at once desirability, possibility, necessity, actual decision and action must occur simultaneously, done in one stroke, indivisibly *(ἐν ἀτόμῳ)* in the power from above which wipes away all opposing forces, makes good all which to human sight appears to be lacking for such a deed. Why not? Nothing is impossible for God.

If the answer is No, then we must turn at once to radical thinking on what is lacking. Then, instead of commentary and proclamation, what is required of us is a confession of the sins of the modern Reformed Church; instead of the founding of a world Church, each one of us must return modestly to his own 'particular company' in the realization that we are *not* the pentecostal Church of Jerusalem, but must wait in humility for the Holy Spirit. But we shall also take with us the old Reformed knowledge that the grace of God *suffices* and his power is mighty in the *weak*—even in the weak *churches*.

You see, there are divine possibilities which must be given serious consideration on both sides in the decision which we have to make. And how can it remain wholly hidden from us that these possibilities themselves, like parallel lines, converge at infinity; that in the peace which is above all reason these two sets of possibilities are one and the same?

But God is in heaven and we are on earth. We have to test in earthly fashion and decide in human fashion. It is on this secondary level that we have to decide whether we say yes or no on the first level. On the first level, the question is, what is good and well-pleasing to God? What is his perfect will in this matter? If the secondary question proposed to us leads us to the other, the primary question, then our answer however it may be worded is the right answer.[1]

[1] The result of the proceedings in Cardiff was (I cite from a report by Adolf Keller in the *Reformierte Schweitzer Zeitung*) 'that a commission be established which should examine the whole question until the next or the succeeding quadrennial General Assembly' — ! — —

IV

SCHLEIERMACHER'S *CELEBRATION OF CHRISTMAS* (1924)

A GLANCE at the few Christmas sermons and drafts for sermons by Schleiermacher which have survived from the years 1790–1810 shows that so far as is known he preached three times on the text, Galatians 4.4.[1] The content of these three sermons leaves no doubt that what interested him in this text was the clause 'when the fulness of the time was come' *(ὅτε δὲ ἦλθεν τὸ πλήρωμα τοῦ χρόνου)*. There he believed that he found an expression of the truth that the advent of Christ must be understood as the result of the continuous direction of this world by divine Providence, or in other words as an historical necessity.

'The circumstances of the birth of Jesus, both the great and the small': the land, the race, the time, the position of his parents, the shepherds, Simeon, Herod—'all become important to us because they have an effect, directly or indirectly, on Jesus and on his character; because they all had to occur together in order to make him that which he had to be. This insight excites in my soul a great increase of love for Jesus. . . . The more necessary the extraordinary guidance of Providence, the dearer he becomes to us . . . the more freely and deeply we rejoice that he is and that he is exactly what he is.' So we hear in 1790.

Why so? Because the experience is universal, because in the Christmas message, when it is so understood, we have the rule which governs ourselves and our whole lives. In 1795 Schleiermacher declared: for something good to befall us, the time must be fulfilled; everything follows the law of nature; everything is subject to rule. And in 1802 he said with only a slight variation: God's benefits come to men when the time is fulfilled, occurring (here the historical sequence is emphasized instead of the natural) according to the rule of justice and order.

The question naturally arises of how the specific festival theme of Christmas is related to the theme of universal truth which is dominant

---

[1] 1790 at Schlobitten (*Predigten*, VII, pp. 55 f.); Christmas 1795 at Landsberg a.d.W. (J. Bauer, *Ungedruckte Predigten Schleiermachers*, Leipzig, 1904, p. 85); Christmas 1802 at Stolp (ibid., p. 87).

in these sermons. In 1795 the question is answered: 'The agreement of this example [i.e. the Christmas narrative] with experience [i.e. with universal truth] is a fresh proof that the sending of Christ was an act of God.' Here the particular is proved by the general. This logic was reversed in 1802: 'The birth of Christ is the *symbol* of all divine beneficence and of the divine dispensation. The order which was observed here [i.e. in the events of Christmastide] is the same everywhere.' Thus the general is proved by the particular. Either way obviously, the real festival theme has been almost wholly pushed back into the shadow of the universal truth, by which it is to be illustrated or which it is to illustrate, because of the preacher's preponderating interest in the latter.

Schleiermacher himself seems to have recognized this—to judge from the close of the 1790 sermon. Here, somewhat hurriedly and outside the sequence of the sermon, he says that according to this view (i.e. understanding the birth of Christ as the consequence of the direction of Providence) we rejoice doubly, since we see all desires satisfied in him so richly and in accordance with our needs. Man longs for someone of his own kind through whom he can become fully aware how far man and therefore how far he himself can, with the help of God, go towards completeness. And now let us set before us the example of Christ, 'the loftiest triumph of human nature'; and so give ourselves a new and shining proof of the love and mercy of God which by ourselves we fail to grasp.

It is in the light of this thought that Schleiermacher's concept of the specific theme of Christmas can be understood, as a glance at what he preached twenty years later proves.[1] We feel ourselves drawn to the child in the manger with a peculiar devotion for which no outward expression is adequate. We find always something deeper in our hearts which we long to utter, something as yet uncomprehended and incomprehensible lies in this picture. What is it? It is the divine nature and the human person [likeness] (Phil. 2.6 f.) united in Christ; humanity with all its needs on one side, on the other divinity, standing under the law of time, developing only gradually and by definite steps, manifested as the object of 'devoted love, directed towards the higher', the love of Mary, who brought him up differently, more purely and rightly than we are brought up. The original relation between the spiritual and the sensuous which lie in the inmost core of human personality is revealed in the deeply rooted, inviolate serenity of Jesus, in the entire absence

[1] 1810 at the 'Trinity': *Predigten*, VII, pp. 566 f.

of all contradiction and struggle in the heart of Jesus. Here we find the clear outline of the 'complete' man, the vision of whom, as early as 1790, hovered before Schleiermacher, on the margin of his thought, as the real object of the festival.

Within the same period, Schleiermacher preached twice [1] on the passage, Luke 2.15 f. 'Observations on the different images which have been utilized in the description of the nature of a Redeemer' is the theme in 1794. In 1802 he shows his purpose somewhat more clearly by stating the theme: 'the reflections of those who received the first news of the birth of Jesus, applied to our own attitudes'. Their reaction to the news agrees with ours not only in general, but precisely and in detail. The shepherds in the field present the type of 'theoretical belief'. They are interested in the revelation, they investigate the miracle, they are zealous in spreading the belief, they have religious experiences. 'But we do not hear that they became Christians.' Such a belief does not make us true disciples of Jesus; it does not bring us the true fruits of religion. Through it one becomes an observer of rather than an active participant in the kingdom of God.

Those who 'marvelled at the story' are the unbelievers, the doubters or the indifferent. A passage here on the doubters should be noted; it is not without significance for the origin of the *Speeches on Religion*. They doubt 'because the miraculous is forced upon them and moral freedom in religion is therefore disregarded'. 'They will be more inclined toward religion when they learn to know it better and at the same time become better acquainted with the nature of the human soul and the character of human nature on earth.'

Mary, who kept all these words and pondered them in her heart, exemplifies finally the ideal position. 'The miraculous provokes investigation; the moral evokes approval.' And 'the smallest and best class is that in which we must also reckon ourselves; our relation to Christ is Mary's'; so Schleiermacher affirmed in 1794. In 1802 he stated it more precisely: we must be thankful that we have been truly chosen by the introduction of Christianity into our Fatherland and by our present participation in it. We must watch closely for the further developments of Christ's kingdom and must be resolute to fulfil with increased fidelity our duty in its further development.

Schleiermacher also interpreted [2] the angels' song of praise in Luke

---

[1] Christmas 1794 at Landsberg (Bauer, op. cit., p. 83) and Christmas 1802 at Stolp (ibid., p. 86).

[2] Christmas 1794 (Bauer, ibid., p. 82).

2.14 from the same point of view. His theme was the feeling of the Christian as he meditates on the birth of Christ. First, his feeling toward God as he recognizes the universality and wisdom of the redemption which comes in Christ. Second, his 'regulative' feelings: peace with heaven, among Christians as such and as dwellers on earth who are well pleased by the wisdom manifested by the coming of Christ and by his teaching, by the perfect pattern which he is, and by their efforts to imitate him.

In all this we can see that what occupied the mind of the preacher was the variety of human attitudes, from the dialectic of which one position, that of Mary, stands out as normative and desirable. But the object towards which these attitudes are taken, the Christmas message itself, appears like an unknown X in the problem, or is visible only on the margin of thought, labelled 'revelation' or 'redemption'. Even in 1831,[1] when the same triple division is used in a sermon on Luke 2.15, Schleiermacher did not succeed in giving any independent significance to the Christmas message in this context.

In the first sermon of 1794 we find the term *Urbild*, original, perfect image, which is so important for Schleiermacher's theology. Over against Christ, the perfect image, stand the Christians. But there exists, as we have heard, a 'relation' between them and him, the possibility of approaching him in imitation. Here we touch the nerve of Schleiermacher's theology. According to him, the business of Christianity is to make this possible approach actual. To present this 'relation' systematically was Schleiermacher's aim from the very beginning. We are subject to the same law as Christ. We must 'imitate' him.

The second sermon in 1795 puts it: 'God can assure to us *also* the enjoyment of his beneficence in no other way' (except according to the universal laws of his Providence). And in the second sermon of 1802 we find 'so can we *also* . . . so it happens in *all* circumstances . . . Everything by which human well-being is really forwarded must conform to the same conditions.' The second sermon of 1794 ('On the Shepherds', etc.) proceeds from beginning to end on the same plan: in the image . . . in its reflection. In the incompletely preserved conclusion of the sermon of 1790, he had already said: 'But let us not uselessly dissipate this beautiful feeling of joy, the distinctive characteristic of this festival. When we become certain of some good thing in us and for us, then we are joyful, then we are always most inclined to make some contribution which will render this good still more our own, will

[1] *Predigten*, II, p. 329.

make it ours to use. Christ is here and therefore we rejoice; but let us also strive to make him so much as possible here *for us.*'

We have another Christmas sermon of the young Schleiermacher in which from the same starting-point he reached exactly this theme.[1] We make the profitable application of this festival of Christ when we take delight in the sentiment which was for him always dominant and through which he has become everything to us—in the 'exalted emotion of the warmest, most universal human love, of the most inclusive goodwill'. 'Our soul is roused to follow the footprints of him who loved men so deeply. On the day of his birth we may vow to act, at least within our own group, according to the sentiment he most valued.'

Even the first sermon of 1794 turned in this direction, as we see from what was said about the 'regulative' feelings, and also from its conclusion, 'the striving to imitate Christ must always be the corner-stone of all Christian experience'. And the same trend appears also in the sermon of 1810, although it also runs comparatively close to the tradi-tional interpretation of the well-known passage in the letter to the Philippians. There, too, is the triple-arched description of human in-completeness, contrasted with the completeness of Christ in a threefold exhortation. The divine image of Christ offers us a training exercise in purifying and in bringing into existence the human race of the future. His image hovers above us, showing the points at which we must labour to improve ourselves; it impels us to put away every sin that besets us so that we may keep pure the divine in us and may hold fast to his holy image and enable it to grow and increase in us. However, the connexion of this third concern with Christmas is for the preacher very plainly indefinite, accidental, and superimposed.

The correct interpretation of the Christmas preaching of the young Schleiermacher should be clear from the foregoing analysis. What interested the preacher in the event of Christmas was the idea of necessity, of law ruling in history and in life, and the consideration of the best possible way of receiving what comes from God. There was a sharpening of emphasis on the law and on the demand for inner acceptance and imitation. In relation to all these secondary considera-tions, the primary event, Christmas itself, the coming of Christ, stands in the background. Schleiermacher's aim already emerges in 1790 with his phrase 'the highest triumph of human nature'. In 1810 this thought has moved from the edge to the centre, and we see more plainly what it involves.   *   *   *

[1] 1791 at Schlobitten (*Predigten*, VII, pp. 117 f.).

The most important source for the answer to our question is *The Celebration of Christmas*. It appeared first in 1806 and later in the revised edition of 1826.

In 1804 Schleiermacher had become a University Professor at Halle. His lectures on Dogmatics and Pauline exegesis, his plan for a translation of Plato, and in his private life his painful renunciation of Eleanor Grunau are the events which especially affected him toward the end of the year 1805.

The immediate occasion for the book he explains briefly in a letter: 'Most wonderfully the thought came to me, suddenly one evening out of doors, just after we had left Dülon's flute concerto; and less than three weeks after the idea had come to me (I first realized its importance a few days later), the writing was finished.' [1] It should be noted that Schleiermacher had first intended to present his reflections in 'a collection [of comments] on all the festivals and sacraments'. But he 'was greatly attracted by the notion of finishing the book before the Christmas festival' [2] as a surprise for his friends. And 'for their sake' he allowed the publisher Schimmelpfennig to issue it in Halle and Berlin, but without the author's name. [3] So it happened that the project ended with the attempt to provide for himself and others an evaluation of the meaning of Christmas. [4]

To understand the meaning of this work one must not look exclusively or even primarily at the theological discussion in the third part. [5] That would be an overvaluation of abstract theory, which would misread the author's purpose.

Schleiermacher knew what he wanted to accomplish when he expanded almost into a didactic short story the form of the Platonic dialogue which he was using to set forth his solution of the problem of Christmas. In spite of the somewhat irritating artificiality of the presentation, the reader should make the effort really to see and listen to *the cultivated German family* [6] and their friends, who are made the

---

[1] *Briefe*, IV, 112, and compare II 49, 60 (*Briefwechsel mit Gass*, p. 42).

[2] *Br. mit Gass* (*Briefe*, II, 60), p. 42.   [3] Ibid., 63 f., p. 42.

[4] The citations from the *Weihnachtsfeier* are made from the critical edition of Hermann Mulert, Philos. Bibliothek, vol. 117, Leipzig, 1908.

[5] This is what is done in the introduction to Mulert's edition. So far as I see, Dilthey should be credited with having been the first to point out explicitly (in his essay on the *Weihnachtsfeier*, which is printed by Mulert in his second edition, pp. 761 f.) that the book must be considered as a whole if it is to be correctly understood.

[6] Walther Sattler in his edition of *Weihnachtsfeier* (Leipzig, C. F. Amelong, 1923, pp. 75, 82) speaks of a parsonage. The passage (Mulert, p. 17, lines 11 f.) on which he bases this conjecture seems to me to offer too little support for it.

medium of the solution. Their sociability, the play of their conversation, their special 'feeling' on Christmas Eve, the 'atmosphere' of the two sections preceding the didactic speeches, which Schleiermacher has filled with charming miniatures—all this part of the book is not merely preparation or preface, but presents in its way, quite as much as do the lectures, the answer itself. 'The festive joy of this Christian company does not simply provide, as one might suppose, the starting-point of the book. The composition turns back to it again; in a certain sense it is really one presentation of the answer.' [1]

We become acquainted with the elders of the house, Edward and Ernestine; and with their children, especially with their little daughter Sophie, well behaved, clever, musical, already religious and often astonishing to her contemporaries. In addition we meet the engaged pair, Ernest and Frederika, 'at the gate to the pinnacle of life' (Dilthey); also a young wife named Agnes; an unmarried woman, Caroline; and the lawyer, Leonard, who offers himself as 'the devil's advocate' so eagerly that he almost, though not wholly, falls out of the picture. On the last two pages Joseph enters the scene without any definite characterization. Joseph not only speaks the concluding and conclusive sentences of the book; he also expresses some sentiments which are all too plainly connected with Schleiermacher's own situation at the time.[2] As the painter can be recognized in some corner figure of a mediaeval painting, so we may see in Joseph the author's self-portrait.

But Joseph's words serve really as a dialectical foil. There is a second rule for the interpretation of the book. We must not expect to hear from the lips of the other characters anything which is not also Schleiermacher's own thinking—not even from Leonard. In the relation of these people to one another we may learn what Schleiermacher understood by 'community'. As its germ cell, he frequently extolled the *family*: men and women, adults and children, simple and poetic souls, each one retaining the right to be himself, but bearing along with that right a common label, invisibly united into one whole as a *unit* bearing the same name. However much they may differ in character, experience, and ideas, even when they contradict one another, even though each

---

[1] Dilthey, p. 781.

[2] '. . . so today my long, deep, enduring pain is eased as never before. I feel myself at home and new-born in the better world in which pain and lamentation have no meaning and no place. With happy eyes, I look on everything, even on what hurts deeply. As Christ had no bride except the Church, no children except his friends, no house except the temple and the world; and yet his heart was filled with heavenly love and joy; so I seem to myself to have been born to aspire also for the same.'

one sounds his own note, they are yet all the more deeply harmonious in the Christian festival of joy. Each individual characteristic seems in the end to serve only to enrich and strengthen the common unity by its distinctive contribution, and to permit the essential unity to appear more plainly.[1]

Also we must take note of the general structure of the edifice—i.e. of both the accompaniment to and the sequence of the talk—for these also pertain to the subject-matter. First come the familiar preliminaries of the celebration: the entrance into the decorated room, the gifts, the singing, a small lighted model of the Christmas story included among others showing of important events in church history!

In the centre of the group, as is fitting, is the figure of the wonder child, Sophie, with her thoughtful sayings, her delight in the gifts, her piano-playing and her singing, her touches of mysticism. She it is who provides the constantly renewed occasion for the series of remarks by the adults. The talk at first runs aimlessly hither and thither with observations on bringing up children, on religious ecstasy, on the Church and art, on the middle way which is victorious over joy and sorrow, and the like.

Then—here a second section clearly begins—Ernestine, Agnes, and Caroline at the request of the men begin to recount experiences of earlier Christmas Eves, all on the theme of mother and child. Frederika by her music, which accompanies or concludes the accounts, gives to the proceedings the character of a musical drama.

In the third section, the men: Leonard, the critical rationalist; Ernest, the man of calm, inner experience; and Edward, the speculative mystic, take their turn and give in longer expositions their views of the meaning of Christmas or of the Christmas celebration. Which of the three is right? Or defends the right? The question remains open, for while the last of them is still speaking, Joseph appears on the scene and (take notice!) mildly rebukes such discussion, asking instead for 'speechless joy' over the 'unspeakable object'. 'Come along then—and especially the child, if she is not asleep—and let me see your beautiful things. Let us be gay and sing something religious and merry' (p. 56). It must

---

[1] Reminiscences of Herrnhut had a much stronger influence on Schleiermacher's concept of the family than had the direct impression of the happy homes which then surrounded him. In the preface of the 1826 edition he stated that since the purpose of the book was to show 'how', in the face of the many divisions and contradictions, 'the most diverse ways of understanding Christianity co-exist peacefully in an ordinary room, not by ignoring one another but because they have a friendly attitude towards one another as they draw comparisons.' This is a variation on Zinzendorf's programme.

be admitted that this road to the goal is given a good recommendation.

The little book begins 'with a description of the quiet inward Christian life as the true and the highest human life, exemplified in the companionship of superior men, where reflection is elevated and raised to the conscious investigation of the higher life of humanity in Christ, and is then again overwhelmed and submerged in the emotion of this exalted Christian life . . . in the accompanying vision of human existence fulfilled through Christianity', with which the scene began.[1]

But let us look more closely. Was the sympathetic interpreter of Schleiermacher, whom I have just cited, really correct when he identified as the core of the view here presented 'the religiously inspired mood' with 'man's truly exalted, liberated life of thought and emotion', with 'exalted, wholly consecrated humanity as such'? Was he right in his interpretation of 'living emotion . . . in its final depth and breadth, knowing itself grounded in the unconditioned and one with all else, in comparison with which all concepts could only be a "retrogression" or a "game" ' ?[2]

Certainly we must not fail to allow full weight to the first two parts of the 'conversation'. We can see when the curtain rises 'the merry and intelligent Ernestine', feminine, lovable, and busily occupied with arranging the table of gifts. 'And when the company streams into the centre of the hall from which the whole can be seen, all eyes turn to her. So beautiful was the arrangement, and such a complete expression of Ernestine's own feeling, that unconsciously and of necessity feeling and sight were drawn to her. . . . She it was in whom the whole company first delighted. As though all the rest had been already enjoyed and as if she were the giver of all, they gathered around her. The child clung to her knees and gazed at her wide-eyed, not smiling but infinitely loving. Her friends embraced her; Edward kissed her beautiful, downcast eyes. Love and devotion were manifested by all, as was her due.'

And when after the first look at the gifts, the whole company gathered around the miniature representation of the Christmas scene, we are told that little Sophie 'suddenly realized that her mother stood just behind her. She turned to her without leaving her place and said with deep emotion: "O mother! Thou couldst just as well be the happy mother of the Divine Child, and does it not grieve thee that thou art not? And is that the reason that mothers love the boys better? But think only of the holy women who followed Jesus, and of all that thou

---

[1] Dilthey, p. 774.   [2] Ibid., pp. 777, 779.

hast told me of them. Truly, I will be such a mother as thou art." Her mother, much moved, lifted her up and kissed her' (pp. 9 f.).

'Mother love is eternal in us, the basic harmony of our being.' So the thoughtful Agnes (in the name of all women) later formulated the conception which here is plainly moving towards the centre. She states it precisely: 'Do you think that love is directed to what mothers can make their children become? What can *we* make them be? No! It is directed to the beautiful and divine which we believe is already in them, directed to what every mother looks for in every movement, so soon as the child's soul expresses itself.' And Ernestine supports her: 'In this sense, every mother is again a Mary. Each one has an eternal divine child and seeks devoutly for the stirrings of the higher spirit in him' (pp. 23 f.).

This point of view is fully developed in the stories told by the three women. The climax of the first is the meeting which the narrator had in a church with an unknown woman holding a small child in her arms. 'Her expression seemed to me now smiling, now sorrowful; her breath came now with a catch of joy and again burdened with heavy sighs; but the abiding impression throughout was the tenderness, peace, and loving devotion which gleamed gloriously from her great dark eyes as she looked down at the child. . . . Also the child seemed to me unusually lovable; he moved with liveliness, yet quietly, apparently absorbed in a half-unconscious interchange of love and longing with his mother. I had before me a living embodiment of the beautiful pictures of Mary and the Child. . . .' Frederika accompanied the tale softly on the piano. At its close, after a fanciful transition, she broke into a beautiful church melody. Sophie, who recognized it, ran to her to add her voice, and they sang together the exquisite words of Novalis:

> O Mary, I have seen thee
> In a thousand paintings shown
> Yet of them all none paints thee
> Such as my soul has known. (pp. 30 f.)

The culmination of the second narrative is the moment when a baby is baptized by his father, a pastor, on Christmas Eve in the midst of a deeply-moved group of guests. 'When, according to the good old custom in those parts, we all laid our hands on the child, it was as though beams of heavenly love and joy converged on the head and heart of the child as on a new focus. The whole company felt that those beams would kindle there a new life and from it radiate outwards again in all directions.' Leonard interrupted with: 'Just like a negative, a Christ-child

in reverse, towards whom, not from whom, the heavenly light streams.'
'You put it splendidly, dear Leonard,' answered Agnes. 'I could not
have put it so beautifully. Only the mother, whose love sees the whole
man in the child (it is this love which you call "the Annunciation"),
sees also heavenly splendour already streaming from him' (pp. 33 f.).

The third narrative tells of a mother who in great grief had inwardly
accepted the loss of her fatally sick child on Christmas Eve and had
reconciled herself to the renunciation. Then in her absence the healing
crisis occurred and she returned to find the child on the road to recovery.
'I was moved with the sorrow and also with the sweetness,' she says,
'of sending an angel to heaven at the season when we celebrate the
sending of the greatest gift from heaven to earth. Now both gifts come
to me at once direct from God. On the feast of the world's rebirth, my
heart's darling is born to a new life.' To this is added, 'like Mary in
reverse, who in the deepest grief a mother suffers begins with the
Stabat Mater and ends with joy in the divine Child'; and overdoing
the dialectic on the other side, 'or not reversed, for Mary's grief must
have vanished when she realized the divine greatness and splendour
of her Son' (pp. 37 f.).

There is no doubt that in these scenes we can easily recognize the
centre of the celebration of Christmas as Schleiermacher conceived it,
which we might have missed in the earlier sermons. 'The highest
triumph of human nature' which we celebrate at Christmas would be
according to this section the centre of the *family, the relation of mother
and child* in its various phases. First the tender mother herself as seen
from outside, then the child who (like Sophie) recognizes in the mother
her own ideal and her own future, then love to the child as the deep
and eternal quality of a mother, then mother and child seen together as
a group, then the child by himself with his negative and positive 'holy
light', that is with what he receives from the group and gives back to
it—the latter prophetically known to the mother alone. Finally there is
the *mater dolorosa*, whose grief is none the less comforted by the life of
her son which overcomes death. Always Mary, always Christ; and
whether Mary or Christ, always we ourselves, the woman honouring the
divine child in the man, the man honouring the pure mother in the
woman, the concept of the noblest, most elevated humanity uniting
both.

'Therefore', says the third and last of the theological speakers at the
close of his dissertation, 'Therefore, every mother who feels it . . .
who knows it, sees Christ in her child; and it is just this which consti-

tutes the inexpressible mother love which compensates for everything. Also each one of us discerns in the birth of Christ his own higher birth through which nothing lives in him except love and devotion; through which, even in him, the Eternal Son appears. . . . And just this is the glory of the festival which you wanted me to praise' (p. 55).

But if that is for Schleiermacher the centre of the celebration, is not Christmas as the festival of the birth of Christ again pushed into the margin of the picture just as it was in the historical and philosophical, the psychological and ethical considerations of his earlier sermons, and by a far more alien point of view? Does it need to be Mary and Christ whom we celebrate when we are concerned with celebrating Christmas? Could not some other divine mother and divine son take their place? Are Mary and Christ merely a paradigm and symbol for the mother-son relationship? Or in what sense are they more than that? With this question we turn to the theological discussion of the men which constitutes the well-known third section of the little book.

There is today general acceptance of the correct interpretation that no single speaker but in some sense all three speakers represent Schleiermacher's 'real opinion'. So also naturally does Joseph who enters the picture at the end, like Elihu in Job, and 'annuls' all three by directing them back to the women's truer, unintellectual experiencing of the Christmas festival. It is the musician Frederika who proposes, as the evening advances and the waiting for the last expected guest is prolonged, to make the meaning of the festival the topic of discussion for the men. 'It has so many aspects that everyone can praise it as he likes best' (p. 42).

The first speaker, Leonard (pp. 42 f.) is a rather subtle creation, the product of the theological rather than the literary imagination of the author. He declares at the beginning that in the first place he does not want to forestall 'those men' (i.e. the pastors) who have to preach the next morning, and therefore he will keep as far as possible from 'their line'. And in the second place he does not intend to 'praise' the festival, but by setting forth appropriately its perfection and completeness to give it the honour which is its due (to treat it 'phenomenologically', one might say today).

If we assume that the beginning of Christianity is a matter of really great importance, the festival is certainly a more appropriate way of keeping that beginning alive than either the Bible or religious instruction. For proof, consider the Roman Catholic Saints' Days, which give much more persuasive force to the legends than the mere written or spoken tale could do. Not seldom the 'festival' becomes the motive for inventing the corresponding story. So Leonard thinks, 'in the same way, devotion to Christ is preserved more effectively by the festival than by the Scripture'. [*This sentence was omitted from the edition of 1826.*] Christianity may indeed be recognized as a strong and mighty force in the present, but it has little relation to the real person of Christ. [*1826: 'The earthly, personal activity of Christ seems to me far less related to it . . . than is usually supposed.'*] The doctrine of the atonement may be excepted, since because of its supra-temporal nature it has to be considered 'more mythological' [*1826: 'symbolically'*]. Christ as the historical founder of Christianity, on the contrary, has only a limited significance. [*1826: 'To him is to be ascribed only a small part of the present structure of Christianity.'*]

Jesus stands closer to John the Baptist than to Paul; it remains uncertain whether according to his will a separate Church ought to have been established. Also the anxious effort of the early evangelists to bring Jesus into relation with the house of David is not pertinent for the founder of a world religion. [*1826 adds 'the supernatural birth of Jesus although asserted in the oldest tradition, was unknown to many'.*] On the other hand, the message of the resurrection and ascension, the essential basis of the founding of the Church, makes the historical life and death suspect. [*1826 adds 'in a measure'.*] The strife between the old Ebionites and the Docetists (who denied either the true deity or the true humanity of Christ) and the disagreement between the Lutherans and the Reformed over whether the presence of Christ on earth [*at the communion table*] is both bodily and spiritual or is purely spiritual both point in the same direction—to the belief that 'Christ was formerly on earth and lived among his followers in a way which differed not at all from his presence on earth today'.

In short, the historical basis of the feast, considered as an actual experience, is so weak that the glory of our festival is greatly enhanced and its power approximates what was mentioned earlier; from the observance of the customs of the festival originated the history itself (p. 45). This wonderful power to preserve and perhaps also to create history, Christmas owes to its entrance into the home and especially into the world of children. Therefore the traditional form of the festival must not be in any way altered.

As a child is the centre, so it is before all others the children who take up and sustain the festival and through the festival Christianity itself. It is celebrated in the night because night is the historical cradle of Christianity; candles are lighted in imitation of the stars, without which the stable and the child in the dark stable could not have been found 'in the otherwise starless night of history'. Therefore Leonard liked best in the women's stories the negative Christ-child with the holy light streaming not outwards from him but towards him—from his Christian environment. To this evaluation [*1826 adds 'and to an unending continuance of our festival'*] the speaker asks the company to raise and empty their glasses.

Christ therefore is not the *necessary* origin of our festival; but our festival itself is so beautiful and possesses such 'power' that it would even be *possible* to celebrate it as the 'origin' of Christ. Pure humanity and its exaltation in the celebration, which earlier appeared to be an intrusion into the Christmas message, *could* be (in relation to the historical) the primary element of Christmas. The festival has in itself eternal justification and significance.

But one must not overlook the reserve with which Leonard offers his historical scepticism—it is rather an enthusiasm for the present. For here Schleiermacher himself speaks, although naturally from the most extreme dialectical possibility. That he once called Leonard's speech 'essentially frivolous in nature' [1] is no evidence to the contrary. The way he clarified and softened this speech in 1826 and adapted it to his later, more cautious attitude towards history [2] shows too clearly that Leonard's speech was not given in order to be refuted.

The next speaker does not refute him nor does he wish to. 'The unbelieving rogue' (p. 46) must submit to being scolded by the ladies and at the end must listen to the rebuke of the mild harmonizer, Joseph: 'Your evil principle . . . this Leonard, the thinking, reflecting, dialectic, too intellectual man' (p. 55). So far as this condemnation is meant harshly (one must note that the condemner is Joseph, who steam-rollers everybody else also in his praise of the women and Lady Music), it is directed against 'intellectual reflection' as such which is embodied in Leonard; and it is one-sidedly expressed. Leonard's speech is 'frivolous' because it ignores the 'royal road' (*via regia*) which runs on a level above reflection. Precisely because that road is higher, a refutation of Leonard's interpretation on the intellectual level is not possible. Also it is not wanted, since he has affirmed an essential aspect of the festival itself. Even the devil's advocate (*advocatus diaboli*) with his Feuer-bachian inversion *remains* within the company of the religious.

The second theological lecture is delivered by Ernest, the happy

---

[1] *Briefe*, II, 49.   [2] Mulert edition, pp. 67 f.

bridegroom. To accept him on account of his name as the special representative of Schleiermacher's real opinion is obviously impossible, because at that time Schleiermacher would have felt it in bad taste to present himself in the role of a bridegroom. But it is true that Ernest, too, is Schleiermacher and is, in fact, the representative of that form of his Christology which is the most attractive and the easiest to understand.

Leonard's speech had troubled the women a little and Ernest is asked to refute him—a task which he explicitly refuses. However, he will say that he is not quite satisfied with the glorification of the feast as Leonard presented it. He wants to say more about its content than Leonard has said. 'You considered only the fact that every festival is a memorial of something. To me it is important to know of what.' And this 'what?' he now defines as 'that through the representation of which a certain mood and feeling can be roused in men'. The mood of Christmas is joy. Is it 'the peculiar and essential character of the festival in itself' which has this effect, he asks himself; or do men rejoice because of the interchange of gifts? No: even for children, the joy of Christmas is something very different from the joy of a birthday on which there are also gifts. If this joy 'is wholly an inward feeling, bearing witness to our inclusion within a specific relationship', then the joy of Christmas is 'wholly ablaze with the swift movement of an unbounded, universal emotion'.

Through the great part of Christendom at least, it is true that everyone is busy preparing gifts. The consciousness of this is the enchantment by which all are mastered. [*In 1826 this consciousness is only 'a great part' of the enchantment.*] Concrete examples of goodwill are mentioned: the zealous working in preparation for the appointed hour of the festival, the Christmas market, etc. What must we then conclude? 'That which is so universal can never be arbitrarily invented. Some internal cause must underlie it.' 'But this inner cause can be nothing other than the source of all the joy moving hither and thither among men.' [*In 1826, Ernest moves directly to his goal in this sentence. He says: 'This internal cause can be nothing else but the appearance of the Redeemer, which is the source of all other joy in the Christian world; hence nothing else can deserve to be so celebrated.'*]

The postponement of the festival to the New Year is therefore a custom to be regretted, for the New Year can only mean change and contrast in time. But for all who do not live merely in the changes of time, who do not rejoice merely in the renewal of the past, there can be no other principle of joy except the redemption; 'and the starting-point of redemption for us must be the birth of a divine child'. [*1826: 'In the unfolding of this redemption, the birth of the divine Child is the first definite point; after it we do not need to expect anything essentially different, and we need postpone our joy no longer'.*]

What does 'redemption' mean? The annihilation of the contradictions between appearance and being, between time and eternity, as they are annihilated in the life and joy of the original perfect nature, but *not* in our nature. Redemption can proceed only from One who himself does not need it. Now in 'the divine Child', that is in the first germ of the 'new, untroubled' life, we see its most beautiful blossom, its highest completeness. The feeling of Christmas, however little it is consciously understood by many, cannot be explained as anything but 'this microcosmic view of a new world which can be pictured in a thousand ways: as the rising of a returning sun, as the springtime of the spirit, as the king of a better realm, as the truest messenger of the gods, as the beloved prince of peace'.

'And so, Leonard, I come to confute you, although I agree with you.' The festival depends not on the historical evidence, which is weak when looked at critically in a strict sense, but in the necessary *idea* of a Redeemer. [*1826: 'on the necessity of a Redeemer and so on the experience of a spiritual existence which can be related to no other beginning than this.'*] Whoever concedes, as Leonard surely will, that Christianity is a powerful force in the present, must also recognize the 'thread' [*so also in 1826*], however tenuous it be, on which this present power hangs crystallized. 'With this slight improvement', for which he expects to gain Leonard's approval, Ernest ends his contribution and he hopes— or rather he promises—for the 'beautiful festival', what is according to him its real character, 'true joy in the rediscovery of the higher life'.

The 'slight improvement' so achieved in the progress of the discussion moves obviously in the same direction as the earlier Christmas sermons. Leonard's speech stated the problem of the centre of Christmas. Ernest would put at the centre a certain 'mood' or 'emotion'. He emphasizes its 'universality'; he shows that as universal it must be related to 'redemption'; he points out the necessity of redemption through *a* divine [*1826: 'the' divine*] child in whom the dichotomy is overcome.

If we had only the first edition, we should have to assume that by all this Ernest means only the 'necessity of the *idea* of a Redeemer' and by his 'birth' the invisible presence which carries germ-like within it the fulfilment of the truth of redemption guaranteed by this idea—that is, it assures the overcoming of contradiction in us. But the corrections in the 1826 edition occur in Ernest's speech as well as in Leonard's.[1]

These changes set beside the 'idea' the 'experience' of a heightened existence which somehow points back to an historical beginning, to the 'appearance' of the Redeemer in the world, to the first definite point after which we have no need to expect anything essentially different. Therefore the 'germ', the beginning, the centre of the crystallization, is now indubitably the historical Jesus. As the result of a real historical process, the present is the outside layer enclosing this central germ. In 1805 it was not wholly clear how far Leonard's view that the historical in Christianity could be essentially secondary, was refuted; how far the question presented to us in the Christology of the women's stories was answered; whether Christ is more than a paradigm of our own 'elevated humanity'. But the 1826 edition unmistakably gives the primary place to the historic. However, it is only the primary place in a sequence; continuity with all that follows is unbroken. The 'divine child' therefore is nothing and has nothing which differs from what we ourselves basically would possess in our own existence. Christ is the idea or rather the historical beginning (an author who with the stroke of a pen could make *this* alteration should never be named in the same breath with *Kant*) of our own heightened existence, our higher life. It must be admitted that the question of whether the child of Bethlehem is *more* than a pattern is left unanswered.

We now listen to the third speech (pp. 52 f.), given by Edward, the head of the household and the host. Here again Schleiermacher himself, as the obviously dominant position of speaker shows, is speaking—Schleiermacher and not Schelling; of course, Schleiermacher debating with Schelling, but still Schleiermacher.

Edward begins with the statement that he will depend less on the mythical [*1826: 'the more external'*] account of the life of Christ—that is on the Synoptic Gospels—than on the 'mystical' 'in which almost nothing historical appears' [*1826: 'in which very little of the external circumstances appears'*], and which contains no specific Christmas narrative, although an eternal, childlike Christmas joy dominates its spirit. So we are given the spiritual and higher view of our festival!

The prologue of the Gospel of John therefore provides the take-off

---

[1]These are not unrelated to certain points made elsewhere in the first edition. The mistake noted in 1805 (*Briefe*, II, 49) by Schleiermacher himself, that the second speech 'did not exhibit a sufficiently individual character and was too easily confused with the third', also needed to be corrected.

for the following bold flight of speculation. The 'flesh' is unending nature. The 'Word' is thought, understanding. What we celebrate in 'the Word become flesh' is nothing other than our collective selves, or human nature, or whatever you want to name it, seen and understood from the divine 'principle'. Why, then, must we set up *one* person and why *this* particular one person, and 'locate' in his birth the unity of deity and soul? The answer is: man-in-himself, humanity, is world-spirit (*Erdgeist*), is understanding in its eternal being *and* in its ever-changing becoming. An individual man, however, is *only* becoming. This means that he is fallen and corrupt. He must find his redemption in humanity as such. The identity of being and becoming as the world-spirit possesses it, must rise, that is must come into existence and grow, in each man (in the individual man). Consequently he must come to perceive and to love all becoming, including himself, in its eternal being only. He can wish to be nothing else than a thought of the eternal being which is identical with becoming. In humanity, that identity *is* eternal; in the individual man it must *become* as the thought of a living and acting community. The individual must see humanity as a living community, and so build it. In it he must lose and find again his separate existence. Only then does he have within him the higher life and peace with God.

Now this community is the Church. The Church is related to the rest of humanity as the self-consciousness of humanity is related to the lack of that consciousness in the individual. He in whom this con-sciousness of self 'rises', who truly and vitally possesses this knowledge, comes therewith to the Church—at most he can only deny it externally. But women, who do not have the 'knowledge' in themselves, possess that high consciousness of self in their 'emotion'. They are therefore more dependent on the Church.

But though this community is in process of becoming, it is also a community which *has* become. And it becomes a community of indivi-duals by the transmission of the community which *had* already become. So 'we seek a point from which this transmission actually began, since we are certain that it must proceed independently from each individual, that humanity in itself must be born and take form in every indivi-dual'. He who is to be regarded as the point from which the Church began must have been born already as man-in-himself, as humanity (which equals world-spirit); he must have been born as God-man, originally born of God, without need to be born again. But *we* must be born again through the spirit of the Church which proceeds from him, 'the true Son of Man'.

'In Christ therefore we see the world-spirit as it was formed originally for the consciousness of self in the individual.' In him we celebrate not only ourselves but all those who will attain this self-consciousness. Therefore, every mother perceives . . . 'she knows it by a message from heaven, that the spirit of the Church, the Holy Spirit, dwells in her. She sees the Christ in her child; and each one of us sees his own higher birth in the birth of Christ.' 'Therefore the festival dawns like a heavenly light in the night. Therefore there is a universal throb of joy in the whole reborn world, which only those members long sick or maimed do not feel.'

Now where do we stand? The mediating position of Ernest has been taken by assault, and a sharp antithesis against Leonard has been successfully achieved. But is this antithesis irreconcilable? Or do we have here merely a second focus of an ellipse? Certainly the centre of Christmas seems to have been found and securely established as Christ, the One, precisely *this* One, separated absolutely with sharp demarcation from us others. We need rebirth; he is the God-man originally begotten of God. Also the order of rank now seems to be validly established with the primacy of what was in him over what is in us. As we have seen, Schleiermacher in 1826 had to make many serious corrections in the speeches of Leonard and Ernest, but he made scarcely any important and decisive changes in Edward's speech. This should suggest that here we find the advance front of Schleiermacher's thought—not in the speculative sense but in the positive content. Here we have an expression of the thinking of his middle period, which later, at the height of his maturity, he could claim almost without change as still his.

Can the questions with which we have pursued the course of the discussion up to this point find here their final answer? We must consider carefully. Certainly the formalism of Leonard with his 'festival' which appears to have no content at all is left behind. Far behind also is Ernest's still indefinite 'idea of a Redeemer' or the accompanying 'experience'. In their place now stands full completeness, 'man-in-himself', the 'world-spirit', the 'true Son of Man', the 'Word become flesh'. Is that not the central, primary and sufficient content? We shall have to answer, it certainly seems to be.

Obviously we cannot shut our eyes to the not inconsiderable enrichment which the conception as a whole has received through the opening of the problem of the individual and the Church. What possibilities seem revealed here! But at this point we are brought to a halt. How does Edward get from his Church to his Christ? We are to seek for a point from which the transmission starts, or (as we heard it more plainly stated at the beginning) we must *set up* One in whose birth we *locate* the identity of the divine and the earthly. How does this Christ, *sought, set up*, differ in principle from Ernest's 'idea of a Redeemer' and from that historical 'germ' or beginning to which our heightened existence points? If the primacy of Edward's Christ is genuine, how can there be any talk of *seeking* or *setting up* or the like? And what about Leonard's theory that the 'festival'—he could equally well, like Edward, have said the Church—could under certain circumstances have produced Christ? Does it not stand unrefuted and uncontradicted alongside of Edward's doctrine? Cannot the seeking, establishing, etc., be thought that way, too?

Further, how does it happen that in Edward's theory the relation between the individual, Christ, and the individual Christian can be interchanged? That the transmission begun in the founding of the Church must go forth automatically again from every individual? And that man-in-himself, humanity, must be born and given form in every individual? How does every mother come to see Christ in her child? And every one of us come to know 'that also in himself appears the eternal Son of God'? How does man-in-himself, etc., remain One, *this* particular One, as the beginning of the speech stated, if it now becomes clear that we all can be and already are the same?

Can the unique dignity of the revelation, which has apparently been established, be transformed (as here it really must be transformed) into the exact opposite? Into the universal religious dignity of man whose participation in being is guaranteed with his becoming? If 'knowledge' (the awakening of the individual to the self-consciousness of humanity) establishes for men their participation in the Church, and if for somewhat more foolish women 'emotion' achieves the same thing, what remains of the central place of Christ, which for a moment appeared to be a presupposition for setting up the concept of the Church?

Finally, what kind of Christ is this? We can let the term 'worldspirit' applied to Christ stand as a romantic peculiarity. Edward has not failed to predicate the Absolute for this entity. But what remains of this 'Absolute' if Edward can say 'what we celebrate is nothing else than *ourselves* as we are collectively, that is human nature'? What remains even if one notes that the passage continues 'viewed and understood from the divine principle'? Is there anything to 'celebrate' in ourselves and in human nature? Or if this celebration were a possibility, what does the added phrase mean? Is the 'Word become flesh' really anything different from the 'elevation of humanity'?

And so we are brought back to the women's talk, to which Edward explicitly refers, where the mother and child relationship is presented as the real essence of Christmas. And if this is Edward's position, what is left except for us also to remain with a symbolic Christ in his sense? With such a Christ certainly, Leonard's Feuerbachianism may well remain unrefuted and Ernest's vacillation between idea and experience may stand without objection. In the end it matters little whether we say the one or the other.

And now Joseph can step on the stage [1] to speak the final word on the ineffable joy over the ineffable object, and to add the positive judgement: 'The poor women have had to endure a good deal (i.e. the theological discussion). Only think what beautiful melodies they would have sung to you, in which all that is religious in your speeches would have been far more deeply revealed; or how sweetly they would have talked with you from hearts full of love and joy. You would have been helped and refreshed far more than by these elaborate speeches. . . . Now let us be joyful and sing some happy, religious song.'

The significance of this final pronouncement must not be overlooked. Its mild triumphing over all earthly trouble is by no means merely for literary effect; it is decidedly theological. I would venture as its interpretation (somewhat sharply pointed!): the true theological substance of this little masterpiece consists of *music* and '*the divine in woman*', here once more 'praised' and 'celebrated' as the 'royal road' (*via regia*) to the ineffable.

1. Music. Not for nothing was it Dülon's flute concerto which, as we heard, inspired Schleiermacher in 1805 to undertake this writing. Whenever during the conversation there was singing, then at once came 'a few silent moments in which all knew that the heart of each one was turned lovingly towards the others and to something higher still' (p. 10). Little Sophie, with her weightily symbolic name and her disinclination for women's work, shows a marked talent for music, especially for music composed 'in the grand church style' (p. 7). 'Every lovely emotion', says Edward (pp. 21 f.), 'is experienced completely only when we have found the appropriate chord for it—*not* the appropriate words (words can never be more than an approximate expression of it) . . .

[1] Light would be thrown on Schleiermacher's understanding of the Brethren Community if with Sattler (op. cit., pp. 77 f.) there could be seen in the name of this important figure a word play on 'Brother Joseph', the Moravian Bishop August Gottlieb Spangenberg.

but the musical notes, in the real sense.' 'To help' men to reach again a common group expression of religious emotion, song must again be set in a truer relation to the word. 'What the word makes clear, music must make *alive*; as harmony it must be directly transmitted to and grasped by the whole inner nature.' And further, 'Christianity is a single theme presented in endless variations. . . . Also it is an obvious fact . . . that church music could dispense, not with singing, but with definite words. In a Miserere, a Gloria, a Requiem, what do the separate words matter? The music is sufficiently understandable by its own character, and no one will say that he missed something because he did not understand the attached words. Therefore today, the two, Christianity and music, must be joined closely together, since each clarifies and elevates the other.' [*1826 adds 'and a piece of music like Handel's Messiah is for me at the same time an epitomized proclamation of all Christianity'.*] [1] 'Yes, certainly,' said Frederika, 'it is the most religious music which most touches the heart'; 'and,' added Caroline, 'it is the *singing* religion which most gloriously rises closest to heaven.'

We could ask 'why music precisely?' And we should be answered: because words stand opposed to all which Schleiermacher understands as the genuine miracle of Christmas. Words are hostile to it, detrimental, always powerless to justify it. The man who undertakes to celebrate in *words* his own 'elevated humanity' becomes all too easily confusing and incredible to himself. 'All patterns are too stiff for me and all speech too tedious and cold.' How fortunate that when we are disturbed and oppressed by the problem of words we can flee to the realm of music, to Christian music and a musical Christianity! Exactly because of its lack of concepts, music is the true and legitimate bearer of the message of Christmas, the adequate expression for the *highest* and *final* dialectical level, a level attainable by singing, by playing on flute and piano.

2. Woman. It is really much more than a gallant act of homage, when Joseph at the end assumes that the women would have contributed something better than the men's 'elaborate speeches'. It is the women, down to little Sophie, who with their many variations on the mother and child relationship present what in Schleiermacher's judgement is truly pertinent to Christmas; and the men's Christological theories with all their dialectics can only, however unwillingly, point back to it.

---

[1] Schleiermacher was 'until his old age an active member of the Berlin Academy of Singing' (Kattenbusch, *Die Deutsche Evangelische Theologie seit Schleiermacher*, 5th edition, p. 26).

For (pp. 28 f.) if Christianity speaks of a *conversion*, of a change of mind, of a *new* through which the old is to be done away (and the speakers are agreed that this demand is in fact justified by the restless, striving, struggling nature of man); then this conversion is really already superfluous in relation to the quiet, gracious way of women which unites holy seriousness and lovable play. 'Christ himself', Caroline replies, 'was *not* converted; and therefore he has always been the protector of women. And while you have only argued about him, we have loved and honoured him. . . . We remain always children, but you must first be converted in order to become children again.' [1] Therefore the woman already *is* and *has* what we celebrate at Christmas so far as that is 'the immediate union of the divine and the childlike', 'for which there is no need of any further conversion'. As music is beyond logic, so woman is beyond ethical dialectic. Precisely that quality, her unconversion, unconvertibility, and her need of no conversion [2] makes woman with her 'heart full of love and joy', a worthy vessel along with music for the message of Christmas, an instrument for the direct communication of its true content.

It is, then, the possibility, or rather the actuality, of direct communication which is Schleiermacher's concern in his weighty emphasis on music and women. Naturally also he stands by what is here directly mediated. This is the substance of Schleiermacher's Christmas message—'the highest triumph of human nature'. Dilthey is right: the final word for Schleiermacher's ultimate pronouncement upon Christmas is the phrase 'living feeling' (*Lebensgefühl*).

It would be an undertaking of much greater scope to continue with Schleiermacher's later sermons and especially with his *Christian Faith*. But an answer which differed in principle from what has been given here, I could not accept as correct.

[1] With this should be compared the statement in the letters (*Briefe*, I, 417): 'I always find that the nature of women appears more noble and their life happier, and if I ever play with an impossible wish, it is with that of being a woman.'

[2] Because 'the letter kills and only the spirit makes alive', as was said at the end of the preface to the second edition.

V

SCHLEIERMACHER

This attempt at a brief presentation of Schleiermacher's theology is part
of the lectures given in the summer of 1926 at Münster on the history of
modern theology.

The abbreviations used for references are:

R. Reden über die Religion (Otto's ed., page numbers of the 1st ed.);
S Speeches on Religion, trans. John Oman, London, 1893, and in Harper
Torchbooks, 1958.

Gl.L. Der christliche Glaube (known as *Glaubenslehre*), 2nd ed.; *CF
The Christian Faith*, editors H. R. Mackintosh and J. S. Stewart, Edinburgh, 1928.

S.L. Sendschreiben an Lücke (Mulert's edition).

W.F. Weihnachtsfeier (Mulert's edition); cf. *Christmas Eve: a dialogue
on the celebration of Christmas*, trans. of 1826 ed. by W. Hastie, Edinburgh, 1890.

Ph.E. Philosophische Ethik.

K.D. Kurze Darstellung des theologischen Studiums, 2nd edition; cf.
Brief Outline of the Study of Theology, trans. W. Farrer, Edinburgh, 1850.

Pr. Predigten.

1. *The Word and Religion*

THERE is abundant testimony from Schleiermacher's contemporaries
(among whom, W. Dilthey, his most important biographer, has borne
witness) that the scene of his most characteristic theological activity
was not the professor's platform, nor the writing-desk, but the pulpit.
Schleiermacher felt this himself and explicitly affirmed it. Prior to
Christian theology in the strict sense comes the Christian *word* (although
the word is not the primary factor). According to Schleiermacher's
understanding, that word surges up from the direct union of the
preacher with his congregation and gives expression to the life in which
they are united. Theology is dependent on this reaction.

Theology is [1] 'the sum total of those scientific concepts and methods,
without the use of which a uniform direction for the Christian Church,
that is a Christian church order, is impossible.' To Schleiermacher,

[1] *K.D.*, § 5.

who came out of the Reformed tradition, 'church order' means essentially the office of preaching.

But what is 'preaching'? It was not by chance that Schleiermacher gave the title *On Religion* to his *Speeches to its Cultured Despisers*. In the five chapters of this book, by which he first made a name for himself, he described this profession of his as a 'speaker' under the categories of virtuoso, prophet, mediator, priest, and hero. Let us summarize the description of the mediator, the most comprehensive of these concepts. The mediator, sent from the deity, builds the necessary bridge between the 'limited' individual man and 'unlimited' humanity. Gifted with mystic and creative sensitivity, his spirit strives toward the infinite in order to return again to the finite and wrestle with images and words as a poet or a seer, as a speaker or an artist. In accordance with ancient prophecy, these mediators will at some time become superfluous. Ultimately only the placid silence of the holy virgins will be needed to maintain the sacred fire. But for the present every man, with the exception of a few choice souls, needs such a mediator, such a guide, to awaken his religious sense from its first slumber.[1]

Which of these different possibilities of mediation belongs to the 'speaker' in company with poet, seer, and artist is suggested by what is said on the concept of the priest. The priest 'comes forward to make his own insight an object for the contemplation of others, to lead them into the realm of religion where he is at home, and to implant in them his own holy emotions. He expresses the universal; and the community in holy silence follows his inspired word. . . . And when he turns back from his wandering in the universal, his heart and the hearts of all individuals are the common seat of the same emotion.' [2] The individual experience of being called gives rise primarily to the prophetic; perfected capability in speaking is indispensable for the virtuoso; and the possible presence of an extraordinary 'heavenly spark' [3] perhaps induces the heroic.

Speaking about religion proceeds in a circle. Starting from and returning to a particular node of the reality designated as religion (the 'speaker' himself should be such a node), words and images are made audible for the purpose of maintaining the holy fire. For the present they are the indispensable means of maintaining it by reminding the hearers that they share in the same reality. Schleiermacher later formulated exactly the same thought: [4] 'The edifying effectiveness of the

---

[1] *R.*, pp. 9–13, 121; *S*, pp. 6 ff., 91.
[2] *R.*, p. 182; *S*, p. 151.   [3] *R.*, p. 30.   [4] *K.D.*, § 280.

Christian church service rests primarily on the communication of the religious selfconsciousness which is being presented for reflection.' ('Primarily' points to the distinction between religious reflection and religious poetry.) And still later he wrote: [1] 'Christian doctrines are accounts of the Christian religious affections set forth in speech.'

We come directly to a most important characteristic of Schleiermacher's theology, if we select, from the plenitude of questions which have been raised, those which bear on the general relation between the factor finally presented as 'speech' and the reality, that is to say the Christian religious attitude out of which the speech and thought have arisen, and which they 'express'. Schleiermacher has presented this relation as clearly in *The Christian Faith* as in the *Speeches*, in his sermons as clearly as in the *Kurze Darstellung*. He approaches the consideration of religious speaking, the Christian word as such, with most serious reservations. He is convinced, as few men have been, of the inexpressibility of the divine. He foresees a future time when speaking on religion will be replaced by the 'placid silence' of the 'holy virgins'. How rigid this conviction was he has made plain in his *Celebration of Christmas*. He wants the effect of *The Christian Faith* to be 'a continual strengthening of the realization that the dogmatic statements are only derivative; the inner feeling is the original'.[2] Words 'are only the shadows of our insights and feelings'.[3]

In § 15 of *The Christian Faith*, he distinguishes three kinds of speaking: poetic, rhetorical, and didactic. Undoubtedly in his opinion the first of these lies closest to reality, but unfortunately it cannot predominate in the church service and in theology. But more fundamental than all speech whatsoever is the wordless expression which precedes speech, and especially music. 'It is the singing religion which most gloriously rises closest to heaven.' [4] Kattenbusch called Schleiermacher the artist theologian and he was right. 'I have struck up the music of my religion', he once let slip in the *Speeches*.[5] That sentence shows in what direction he searched and from what point of view his sermons should be judged—and not his sermons alone, but also, although perhaps not primarily, his scientific work. Obviously for Schleiermacher, even the most religiously adequate expression and presentation of reality in words is an emptying, a kenosis, if not a profanation, of that reality.

In a sermon of 1831,[6] Schleiermacher permitted himself the assumption that we ought to distinguish two components in the great all-

---

[1] *Gl.L.*, § 15; *CF*, p. 76.   [2] *S.L.*, p. 34.   [3] *R.*, p. 140; *S*, p. 122.
[4] *W.F.*, p. 21.   [5] *R.*, p. 135; *S*, p. 119.   [6] *Pr.*, V, p. 85.

inclusive gift of God: 'the one which has no magnitude and no mass, but is always the same, and a second which is really subject to the law of time, which expands in time, grows more beautiful, unfolds wider, and then again contracts. The first is the consciousness of the restored relation with God in which we stand, the peace in which consciousness of the eternal will abides in our soul, rules it and moves it so that from this germ a wholly new life gradually comes into being.' The second, fragmented and secondary to the first, is naturally the definite external word which intrudes with a claim to truth. Against the overvaluation of this second component, Schleiermacher made the accusation of uncomprehending and loveless reverence for and defence of the dead letter. His pulpit polemic was never more vigorous than when he was bringing this charge.

The final point to be noted about the *word* as such is simply that it is free, changeable, relative and unauthoritative. According to a sermon of 1832,[1] Schleiermacher was certain that the apostles of Christ were 'as far away as possible from any trust in the letter, from any anxious caution in regard to the reflections in which the new teaching took form in their hearts. They regarded only the impression which the teaching made on their hearts and followed that.'

On the truth of Christian doctrines he expressed himself as follows:[2] Christian doctrine was, is, and will be a product of the Christian religious affection of the human heart, accustomed to expressing itself in this way among others. This heart's affection goes through an historical process in the course of which at certain times certain points of doctrine become especially important. Therefore every age has the right and the duty to interpret the state of its own heart's affection as fruit of the earlier and as germ of the future development. As a presentation of the position of the Christian consciousness at the moment and therefore as 'the formulation of the opinions of the Church',[3] dogmatics is a branch of the present knowledge of the Church.

Dogmatics does not deal with final truth, nor with the truth which would be the concern of philosophy, nor with the truth of a revelation which lies basically outside of the religious affection. But in a systematic fashion it gives an historico-empirical description of the actually prevailing Christian doctrine. (Of course the convictions of the dogmatic theologian himself are a part of the requisite subject-matter.) It ex-

---

[1] *Pr.*, III, p. 336.
[2] Here I combine what Schleiermacher developed in §§ 196–231 of *K.D.*
[3] *Gl.L.*, § 19, Postscript; *CF*, p. 92.

presses the feeling of the religiously moved Christian heart in the way possible and necessary at the given time. Its 'validity' lies midway between the two limiting concepts—both as necessary as they are dangerous—of orthodoxy and heterodoxy; between the definiteness given by the current era of the Church (for us by the Reformation) and the free individuality of the particular teacher concerned; between dependence on the Bible and on the Creed, and the contemporary position of philosophy, logic, ethics, and psychology.

A decisive and final yes or no is not to be expected from all these efforts at formulation. They exemplify the laws according to which the process of developing Christian doctrine has gone on through thousands of different experiences until the present time, and will continue to go on in the future. The truth itself is and remains a property of the life which permeates this process; it is therefore a property of the Christian feeling, which in the individual (*in concreto*) unites with the human self-consciousness. The definite individuality of a Christian man is to be distinguished not psychologically but actually from the inner substratum which is without specific quality and is timeless, the feeling of absolute dependence in itself. In the final analysis, truth is ascribed only to the latter. In any case, for Christian dogmatics the formulation is also the confirmation, for 'every proposition in it is permissible only because it is presented as the correct expression of the Christian self-consciousness'.[1]

On this foundation stands the doctrine which is most important for understanding Schleiermacher, more significant than any other for both the spirit and the external pattern of his dogmatics. This is the doctrine of the three forms of dogmatic statements. According to § 30 of *The Christian Faith*, dogmatic propositions can be classified either as descriptions of human states, or as conceptions of divine attributes and modes of action, or as utterances regarding the constitution of the world.

Now if the basic datum, the feeling of absolute dependence, must be united with a newly sentient selfconsciousness in order to become an actual consciousness existing in time, then every formula for the feeling of absolute dependence must be at the same time a formula for a definite state of mind. But if every such lower, intelligible definition of self-consciousness refers back to something which is outside selfconsciousness, then a formula for the feeling of absolute dependence united with it must be at the same time a pronouncement about the world as it

---

[1] *S.L.*, p. 56.

actually shows itself in this specific modification. And if the feeling of absolute dependence is in and for itself a co-existence with God in the selfsame consciousness, then statements about the selfconsciousness become also statements about God.

Put somewhat more simply and summarized: from reflection on the religious *self*consciousness proceed statements about the religious feeling as such; from reflection on the religious self*consciousness* proceed statements about the world; from reflection on the *religious* selfconsciousness proceed statements about God. Schleiermacher calls the type of the first group of statements the basic type in dogmatics, because their content depends necessarily on pure experience, while the statements about the world and about God could in themselves be derived from natural science or metaphysical speculation. They require therefore the guarantee that they are deducible from the statements of the first type. Hence dogmatically their type is a secondary type.

What all this means in relation to statements about God, for example, is clear from § 50, the key sentence of which reads: 'All attributes which we ascribe to God are to be taken as denoting not something special in God (in God there is no multiplicity of functions, no contradiction, no differentiation), but only something special in the manner in which the feeling of absolute dependence (in which in itself there exists no real differentiation) is to be related to God.'

When Schleiermacher was working on the revision of his book he considered (as appears from § 50 and especially from the second letter to Lücke) [1] the possibility of discarding as in a strict sense superfluous, both secondary types in favour of the first type. The book would then be, he said explicitly, dogmatics 'in its proper character' as it had shown itself to him.[2] But he dropped this idea, first to preserve the 'historical approach' and the 'churchly character' for his work, and secondly not to deprive himself of the possibility of criticism for such statements of the second and third types as were intended to be something more than simply statements of the first type, that is more than affirmations of feeling about feeling and nothing else. 'I can at least rejoice', so he ends his account of his reasoning in the letter to Lücke, 'in the conviction that I have seen from afar a freer, more vital way of treating our dogmatics.' [3] In the method he was contemplating, dogmatics would not even appear to deal with anything other than the human state of mind. We must acknowledge that Schleiermacher came very close to this ideal in the way he presented the relation between his three types of statements.

[1] *S.L.*, pp. 47 f.   [2] *S.L.*, p. 49.   [3] *S.L.*, p. 51.

Looking back from that relation, we understand the well-known assertions about God and immortality in the *Speeches on Religion*, that the deity can be nothing other than 'an individual religious way of seeing',[1] that a religion without God can be better than another with God,[2] that faith in God *that* he is and *how* he is, depends on the 'direction of the imagination',[3] that God is not the whole of religion, but Oneness and the Universe is more, and that immortality in religion means 'in the midst of finitude to be one with the Infinite and in every moment to be eternal'.[4] I have quoted these sentences here not for the sake of their content, but to illustrate Schleiermacher's position on the possibility, the meaning and the range of what he called 'speaking', speaking on religion, and also called Christian preaching and teaching.

2. The Principle of the Centre

If we wish to gain a clearer understanding of Schleiermacher and of his work, we must inquire next about the final goal towards which, according to him, the words of the religious speaker ought to be directed. What is the nature of the good, of the salvation which constitutes the true object of Christian preaching?

I start here from an observation which first impressed itself upon me in the study of the sermons from Schleiermacher's last years, 1830–4, the same years in which *The Christian Faith* received its final form and in which he was preparing his *Dialektik* for publication. Death interrupted this last labour.

A concept which plays a very striking role in these writings is the concept of *peace*. When the elderly Schleiermacher became vehement in the pulpit—and this happened more frequently than one would expect, especially in the course of his homilies on Mark, which he delivered at the morning service—this vehemence appeared most often when he was speaking against the 'dead letter' and in that context was denouncing all sharp disagreements and divisions in the Christian Church. He felt it as his especial responsibility to emphasize 'the extraordinary gentleness of the Saviour'.[5] He found the pietists and rationalists of contemporary Berlin unmistakably predicted in the Pharisees and Sadducees of Mark 12.17–27; and the practical application which he drew from this text runs: 'The Saviour sided with neither

---

[1] *R.*, p. 124; cf. *S*, p. 93.   [2] *R.*, p. 126; cf. *S*, p. 95.
[3] *R.*, p. 129; *S*, p. 98.   [4] *R.*, p. 132; cf. *S*, pp. 100 f.   [5] *Pr.*, VI, p. 39.

of the two schools; he stood above them. Christians also should do the same.' [1]

Disagreements must arise and be worked out—but let there be no schism, no intolerance of one another, no dissension. This is not merely a matter of neutrality, or of abstention from quarrelling. 'One and the same strength of the earth produces thousands of different plants. Look at the most beautiful adornment of the flower garden, turn to the most inconspicuous flower in the field. The bees hum above both and thrust themselves into both alike; and out of them all they collect the same precious honey. Let us act towards our brethren like the bees and draw honey from all in whom anything of the spiritual life-force is found.' [2]

Here we have to do not with any incidental attitude, but with a ruling principle of Schleiermacher's *church polity*. It was not by chance that he was *the* great theologian of the Prussian Church Union. The union was of the highest importance to him—so much seemed to him dependent on it. It would not only render innocuous the opposition between Lutheran and Reformed, which in wide areas had already become obsolete. Schleiermacher was much more concerned with ending the disagreement between the orthodox-pietistic and the rationalist parties within the United Church.

It was for the sake of promoting the unity of the latter parties that he dropped a plan which (though it would not have altered the real character of his work) would, if it had been carried out, have given his book in the eyes of ninety per cent of his contemporaries a wholly different and much more churchly aspect. He had, in fact, thought [3] of reversing the order of the two main parts of *The Christian Faith*, putting the Christological-Soteriological part at the beginning, immediately after the introduction, and concluding with the much more controversial section dealing with the universal religious assumptions which the particular Christian religion shares. He dropped the plan because he was unwilling to contribute by it 'to the forcing out of our church community' 'those worthy men who are called rationalists'. But while he decided to leave the position of the first part unchanged, he wished to record his desire to transpose it and so to set himself against the prevailing current of his time, 'out of the natural fear that the little boat, in which we all are sailing, might overturn'. However, the concept of union was important to Schleiermacher not merely for church polity, but also and fundamentally for theology. Or rather, his church polity was rooted in the much deeper theological significance.

[1] *Pr.*, VI, pp. 164 f.   [2] *Pr.*, III, p. 105.   [3] *S.L.*, pp. 31 f.

We now turn back to the sermons to demonstrate that the positive aim of the preacher is consistently directed towards an X—an X which is conceived as a combining of two dichotomies, as an equilibrium of two opposing forces, as a common element in two diversities, as a neutral point between two motions continually moving away from or against each other. As examples of the antitheses, the sermons offer: the great (estimated by its importance for life) and the small, strength and weakness, joy and sorrow, the individual and the whole, youth and old age, petition in prayer and thanksgiving, spiritual and physical well-being, the inner and the outer world, receptivity and activity, the human heart and the Holy Spirit, finally even human sin and divine grace.

The teaching presented always proceeds from the conviction that it is necessary to understand these opposites in their relativity, in their purely quantitative contradictoriness; and to find between them or above them the 'common feeling', or the 'common equalizing note', or the 'one thing needful', the 'complete rest of the soul in God', the 'good' (the mark of the good is unity, while evil is manifold), 'community', 'unity', 'identity', the 'simplicity of the mind of Jesus'. It is necessary to discover, for example, the place where we 'can no longer distinguish between the impulse of our own heart and the inspiration and work of the Holy Spirit'.[1] 'Of necessity the truth that God wills (the realization of the relationship in which his will can be fulfilled) must lie in the centre between the two.'[2] This centre beyond all contradiction, this One which absorbs every two into itself, is the deeper sense of Schleiermacher's concept of union. It is this which he meant when he preached peace.

From here we can understand why Schleiermacher turned his forceful polemics in a third direction, not unrelated to the first. He is an outspoken enemy of all excitement, of everything hasty, sudden, immoderate, in the Christian life. Eschatological texts which he encountered on his way through Mark's Gospel became for him chiefly occasion for earnest warnings against all eschatological enthusiasm. He could see no benefit in penitential sermons which forced men to face the death they would have to suffer, which proclaimed the agony of men's souls over their present situation, which demanded of men a sense of their own impending annihilation. Christ's demand that a man deny himself, and take the cross upon himself, ought to be restricted to that historical period; certainly it should not be universalized.

The separation between heaven and earth was ended in Christ and

[1] *Pr.*, III, p. 332.   [2] *Pr.*, III, p. 410.

ought never to be renewed. But that separation is inherent in the concept of law. From this angle it is easy to understand Schleiermacher's fundamental repudiation of the Old Testament (and of the character of John the Baptist in the New Testament). To this repudiation he committed himself in all possible ways, in his scholarly works as well as in his sermons. 'In the one word *Peace*, the whole is really included', he once proclaimed.[1] Truly in this unity, out of which duality has issued, which waits for duality to return again to itself, he saw, according to his own explicit explanation, the divine spirit itself, or communion with God or the kingdom of God.

We should next turn our attention from the sermons to Schleiermacher's academic teaching as a whole, as he presented it in his *Philosophische Ethik* and in his *Dialektik*. There are some variations; but so far as I see and understand, we find that precisely the same X which he preached in the pulpit as 'Peace' coincides on the whole consistently with the last and highest substantive and formal principle of his philosophical writing. What is called in the sermons the kingdom of God is obviously here the absolute Subject-Object, the highest knowing in its identity with the highest Being.[2] It is the innermost basis and source of our finite knowing and being. It can perhaps also be something more and different in us and for us. But in any case it stands over against our existence in the duality of reason and nature, and is never identical with but is always related to our knowing in the duality of the ideal and the real, of ethics and physics.[3]

And as our existence in reason and nature is further split into spiritual and sensuous being,[4] so also our knowing in ethics and physics is divided into 'reflective', that is thinking, speculative knowing; and 'observing', that is describing, specific, empirical knowing.[5] As speculative disciplines on the ethical side, Schleiermacher included for example, Aesthetics, Political Science, Philosophy of Religion; as empirical, Law, Theology, History. The complete union of finite being, the combination of nature and reason in an all-inclusive organism, is the world.[6] And so the highest unity of finite knowing which is the complete mutual interpenetration of the ethical and physical, and the complete conjoining of intuitive and positive knowledge is World-Wisdom, Philosophy.

Continuing with the same method of division, Schleiermacher then defined the separate disciplines. As we have already heard, he defined

[1] *Pr.*, III, p. 468.
[2] *Ph.E.*, § 290.
[3] *Ph.E.*, §§ 55 f.
[4] *Ph.E.*, § 46.
[5] *Ph.E.*, § 57.
[6] *Ph.E.*, § 54.

the concept of dogmatics as the self-expression of the Christian consciousness, on the one hand, midway between orthodoxy and heterodoxy; on the other hand, midway between the spirit of the Church in the current era and the spirit of the age stamped upon the contemporary philosophy. So he described ethics in the strict sense, the actual science of morals, as teaching on action related to the highest good, on the one hand organizing and symbolizing, on the other hand universal (identical) or individual. Similarly, his theory of hermeneutics sets on one side grammatical or psychological interpretation, on the other side interpretation by divination or by comparison. And so on.

The crossed threads which are used in astronomical telescopes provide an appropriate symbol for this method of contradictions. The ideal position lies always in the centre, where between the two, or rather between the twice two contradictions, peace rules. Peace is the truth.

But here two points must certainly be noted:

1. This centre, and therefore the truth in any area, is actually reached by *no* finite knowing; on the contrary, all finite knowing is actually overweighted on at least two sides and therefore always stands in an incorrect position.[1] Why this is so will appear presently.

2. All of the contradictions mentioned, with the exception of the last, highest one, are not strictly mutually exclusive opposites, but are relative, quantitative, fluid differences. Finite knowing is, for example, always also somehow finite being; nature is always also somehow reason. Philosophy understands all ethical knowing also as physical, all physical also as ethical, all speculative also as empirical and vice versa. And the same holds true similarly with the antithesis of spiritual and material in being.

In a strict sense, all these contradictions of Schleiermacher's cannot present any real problem. One might well wonder why the 'peace' between them should not be actually attainable—except for the one truly problematical point, the nail on which the whole system hangs. There still remains the original antithesis between finite and therefore divided being and knowing, in its totality on the one side; and on the other side infinite and therefore identical being and knowing, the Absolute Subject-Object.

To make this last antithesis relative would mean first to subsume world and world-wisdom, the totality of finite being and knowing, as one in itself, under itself, and then to establish being and knowing in contradiction as identical with being and knowing without contradic-

[1] *Ph.E.*, §§ 37–8, 41.

tion. Schleiermacher was never willing to take this last step, as the philosophical idealists—most radically Hegel—have done. In fact, he both took it and did not take it. He did not take it inasmuch as he continued, in his dialectic, to leave world-wisdom related to the world, and denied to philosophy as such a grasp of the transcendent basis of the world. 'The highest being is not existent for us either as an entity or as an activity, and the highest knowing is not within our understanding either as proposition or as concept.' [1] Our knowledge is and remains only an image of the highest knowing which is set above all contradictions, just as our being remains an image of the highest being set over all contradictions.[2] On the basis of what Schleiermacher understands by philosophy, he is not to be classed as an 'identity' philosopher.

But as a dialectical thinker, he raised himself above that which he calls 'world-wisdom' and asserted that on the one side, beyond the antithesis of finite knowing and being stands the problem of the absolute foundation of being; on the other side, beyond the divided psychological reality of thinking and willing rises the unity of feeling, not disconnected with them, but related to them as the foundation of certainty. (The actual position taken in his *Dialektik* is complicated and its purport is disputed, but I think I can formulate the conclusion which in any case is to be drawn from it.) In this unity of feeling Schleiermacher now found even the antithesis of infinite and finite dissolved. He found 'the original foundation' 'established' even in us 'as things are established in us when we accept them as true' [3]—*not* as knowable. So soon as this original foundation becomes knowledge, what holds of knowing in general holds of it also: only an image of the original foundation can be *known*. But the foundation can be *felt*. (We can now easily understand Schleiermacher's scepticism in relation to the word.)

Inasmuch as Schleiermacher affirmed feeling to be the seat of the presence of God, he had obviously taken the decisive step along with the major identity philosophers, in spite of all his reservations in relation to the knowability of this presence. He knew what he was doing when he preached such a 'peace' in the pulpit. He knew it in so far as he conceived this feeling to be necessarily and truly the most immediately original, the most inclusive component of human selfconsciousness, which as already in itself peace, is the quiet centre above thinking and willing and is also simultaneously nothing less than God's surrogate, the Absolute Subject-Object in men. And Schleiermacher's dialectic is still identity philosophy in so far as at its summit it becomes

---

[1] *Ph.E.*, §§ 32 and 31.   [2] *Ph.E.*, § 36.   [3] *Dialektik*, p. 430.

knowledge of this feeling and of that which is 'established' in the feeling, knowledge of that Other who is the inaccessible source of our being and knowing, but who also can be known as our original foundation within us.

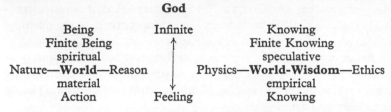

                                    God

        Being   Infinite   Knowing
     Finite Being   ↑   Finite Knowing
       spiritual   speculative
Nature—**World**—Reason   Physics—**World-Wisdom**—Ethics
       material   empirical
       Action   Feeling   Knowing

                  Finite Selfconsciousness

And now we go directly to Schleiermacher's system of theological-scientific principles, beginning with the well-known § 3 of *The Christian Faith*. 'The piety which forms the basis of all ecclesiastical communions is, considered purely in itself, neither a knowing nor a doing, but a modification of feeling, or of the immediate selfconsciousness.' It is that specific modification, according to § 4, by virtue of which man is conscious of himself as absolutely dependent or (what is the same thing) of himself as in relation with God.

The object of Christian preaching and teaching according to Schleiermacher is the specific good of salvation and the object of theology is religion itself, the Christian selfconsciousness or feeling. This follows from two propositions. (1) Feeling understood as religion is in respect to its content neither a knowing nor a doing (however invariably it is accompanied by both), but is a centre transcending both. It is the peaceful third (*tertium*) or rather the One (*Unum*) above every contradiction. For what contradiction could there be that is beyond knowing and action? (2) Just in this centre exists 'absolute dependence' or 'what means the same thing, relation with God'. 'Ye shall see heaven open, and the angels of God ascending and descending upon the Son of Man' (John 1.51). Schleiermacher (in 1832) found this text explicitly verified by the 'most complete and most holy experience of a believing heart', for which there no longer exists any separation between heaven and earth.[1]

Religion not only seeks, hopes for, expects and prays for but actually *is* that *X*, that peace which is higher than all human reason. And when religion preaches wholly and only itself, it preaches the highest which

[1] *Pr.*, III, pp. 167 f.

can possibly be preached at all. Therefore the speaker and the hearer, although unavoidably making use of words, can forgo (if they do not actually disdain) all knowable truth, all truth apart from religion's ineffable reality—that is, of course, they can dispense with the letter. Religion preaches very God, and yet as we have heard, it can simultaneously abandon God, as 'an individual religious concept', to the relativity of everything knowable and still remain none the less true religion.

Before we go farther, we should deal briefly with three aspects of Schleiermacher's life-work (the wide separation between them is only apparent) for which the meaning of this principle of the centre is plainly significant and determinative.

1. I come first to the formulation of the concept of religion in the *Speeches*. This formulation is especially fitted to clarify for us the relation of the two points in Schleiermacher's system which are farthest apart and at the same time closest together: the relation between God and the religious selfconsciousness. In the *Speeches* we read for the first time that religion is neither thinking nor action. But, somewhat confusingly at first glance, when we come to the works of Schleiermacher's maturity, religion is *viewing and feeling* the Universe. We should not let ourselves be confused. This apparent extension of the concept of religion which includes viewing in addition to feeling is only a preliminary stage of an historical development towards what Schleiermacher later learned or preferred to express as the feeling of absolute dependence. 'Viewing' in the *Speeches* is passive; 'feeling' is the spontaneous side of the attitude of consciousness through which man, within the finite, becomes partaker of the infinite, partaker of the 'Universe' as Schleiermacher then called it. 'Viewing' in the *Speeches* stands for what in *The Christian Faith* Schleiermacher will call the sense of being united in the religious selfconsciousness with the source of the feeling of absolute dependence; a sense of being affected; the awareness of the modification of the religious selfconsciousness by this feeling of absolute dependence as such. The vocabulary is different; the content is the same.

'Feeling', in the sense in which the word is used in *The Christian Faith*, is the whole of religion even in the *Speeches*. In the *Speeches*, Schleiermacher already asked his readers [1] to excuse him for lamenting a little that he could not speak of viewing and feeling except as separated. 'The finest spirit of religion is lost in my words.' 'Viewing without feeling is nothing . . . feeling without viewing is also nothing. Both then

[1] *R.*, pp. 72 f.; *S*, pp. 41 f.

are something only when and because they are originally one and un-separated.' Their original and genuine nature is the 'mysterious moment' when both unite.

'If I could and dared express it, or at least give some indication of it without profaning it! It is fleeting and transparent as the first mist which the dew breathes on the awakened flowers, shy and tender as a maiden's kiss, holy and fruitful as a bridal embrace. It is not merely like, it is itself all these. . . . I lie on the breast of the infinite world. In this moment I am its soul; for I feel its powers and its endless life as my own. In this moment it is my body; for I pervade its muscles and limbs as my own, and its innermost nerves are moved according to my mind and my whim as if they were my own!' The slightest shock, and the holy embrace dissolves; now 'viewing' stands before me as a separate experience. I measure it and it is reflected in the open soul . . . like the 'figure of the vanishing mistress lost to the eyes of her lover' and feeling rushes up and 'spreads like the blush of shame' on his cheeks. This moment is the highest flower of religion. 'If I could create it for you, I should be a god—may holy destiny pardon me that I have had to disclose more than Eleusinian mysteries. It is the birth hour of every-thing living in religion.'

Consideration of this passage as a whole is rewarding in more ways than one. Rudolf Otto has called it the key to Schleiermacher's con-ception of the experience of the Eternal. One conclusion must certainly be drawn from it. There exists above the antithesis of religiously affect-ing and being religiously affected a Schleiermacherian Unity, a peace in relation to which this contradiction is relative and evanescent. The goal of religious speaking is therefore the surmounting of this contradiction, the good of salvation is to be sought not in a *relation* between God and man but in their *undifferentiatedness*. And when we remember a sermon of the elderly Schleiermacher on the ultimate inability to distinguish between the impulse of his own heart and the work of the Holy Spirit, we realize again that the speaker in 1799, however different the words he used, remained throughout true to himself.

2. I have already mentioned the fact that the principle of the centre becomes significant also in Schleiermacher's doctrine of *sin and grace*. It is well known that it is this antithesis which Schleiermacher chose for the theme and principle of arrangement in the second part of *The Christian Faith*. The title reads 'Explication of the Facts of the Religious Selfconsciousness as they are determined by the Antithesis of Sin and Grace'. Then follows the 'First Aspect of the Antithesis: Explication of

the Consciousness of Sin' and 'Second Aspect of the Antithesis: Explication of the Consciousness of Grace'.

How are these antithetic aspects to be related? Schleiermacher himself explains it: [1] Within the one inclusive bracket, redemption (redemption, as Schleiermacher explicitly asserts, means a transition not a re-creation), are enclosed both the consciousness of sin (that is, the constriction of the higher life-consciousness, the lack of the facility of emergence of a religious moment of life, the absence of the predominance of the feeling of absolute dependence) and the consciousness of grace (that is, 'the facility with which we are able to graft the God-consciousness on the various sensuous excitations of our selfconsciousness' [2]). Therefore the consciousness of sin is at the same time the consciousness of impartation of the divine. There is no real Christian consciousness in which these two are not in the relation of 'more and less' 'in a fluctuating difference'.[3]

Schleiermacher indeed held as conceivable an absolute relation to God without antithesis in a negative or positive sense—it is obvious that he had in mind certain possibilities of the pietistic psychology—but he cannot treat of the actuality of an absolute relation, for 'clearly our religious consciousness is not such that more and less do not apply to it; on the contrary it oscillates between these two, sharing as it does the variations of our temporal life' (e.g. of development and limitation, of desire and apathy).[4] 'Every Christian is conscious both of sin and of grace as always combined and associated with each other' . . . and 'only the exposition requires a separation' so as to treat first of the one and then of the other.[5] The reality of which the Christian is conscious lies always in the *and* and the *also*. So Schleiermacher can even say once in a sermon, 'our consciousness cannot be really complete until sin enters it as an actuality'.[6]

3. The third point which must be considered in this connexion is, surprisingly enough, Schleiermacher's theory of marriage as he developed or outlined it in the *Monologen* (*Soliloquies*), in the *Vertrauten Briefe über Fr. Schlegel's Lucinde* (1800), and in the well-known *Hausstandspredigten* of 1818 in which he continued the same theme, and finally in the pertinent sections of his philosophical and theological ethics. This teaching is important from more than one point of view for understanding Schleiermacher. First of all because sexual love is for

---

[1] Especially in sections 11, 62, 63 and 64 of *The Christian Faith*, to which parallels enough can be found in the sermons.
[2] *CF*, p. 263.   [3] *CF*, p. 259.   [4] *CF*, p. 259.
[5] *Gl.L.*, § 64; *CF*, p. 265.   [6] *Pr.*, III, pp. 7 f.

him so exceedingly closely related to religion that a comprehensive description of the one experience at its height is necessarily reminiscent to the point of identity with the typical description of the other. We have seen already (from the *Speeches*) that Schleiermacher had no objection to portraying the 'mysterious moment' of the coincidence of viewing and feeling by a fairly detailed description of a love scene. He was here following a way of religious expression much travelled both before and since Bernard of Clairvaux. Many witnesses can be called to justify it, from the oriental religious lyrics or even from the biblical example of the Song of Songs.

But Schleiermacher moves on a line peculiar to himself when he reverses the comparison and gives to love or to the ideal marriage a content which he explicitly calls religious. Not only does he glorify love and marriage as mystical or as mystery, as the holiest worship of humanity and the Universe; but also, even after he has learnedly analysed marriage into its separate elements, he feels constrained to claim it as the most important paradigm for the content of the religious experience.

His analysis of marriage is carried on by the same method of over-coming antitheses by the principle of the centre. Here also that which is consummated in an instant of undifferentiatedness involves many elements. First of all, naturally, the human individual meeting the pre-destined individual of the other sex, then the separate wishes and aims of the man and the wife, which in this close relationship should not be suppressed or balanced, but should cease to have separate existence. Such is the ideal of earthly love. Beyond that, in heavenly love, according to the sermons on the family (*Hausstandspredigten*), the married pair become one with Christ as the third in the union. And so again, heavenly and earthly love (in his early period, Schleiermacher said spiritual and sensuous love) ought in themselves to be not two but one. According to the *Soliloquies*, Schleiermacher believed in a kind of pre-destination of two individuals for each other, or according to the *Hausstandspredigten*, he believed that the complete marriage is con-summated in heaven. But he preached 'absolute unity' as 'the ideal of married love'.[1] He opposed most firmly (at least in theory) the pos-sibility of divorce and he pronounced the remarriage of the widowed to be really illegitimate on Christian principles.

According to the *Speeches*,[2] he saw in marriage the fusion of two persons through which they became the instrument of the creating

[1] *Ph.E.*, § 260.   [2] *R.*, p. 215; *S*, pp. 169-70.

Universe. And in his old age, he founded upon the development of the
ethics of love and marriage his highest expectations and hopes for the
future of the progressively Christianized human race. 'God must be in
those who love; their embrace is truly his embracing — — —. I admit
no delight in love without this spiritualization and without the mystical
character which proceeds from it.' These words from the Lucinde
letters [1] may serve to indicate Schleiermacher's centre, in this area of
his thought.

3. Religion as Life

We know from the preceding that the X, the reality to which the
religious word bears witness, stands as the great Unutterable in opposition to the word. And we know that it is the object of the word for the
reason that as transcending all antitheses of spiritual and of natural
existence, it signifies their fulfilment; and as participating in the
transcending of the last fundamental antithesis of knowing and being,
it signifies fulfilment as such, absolute completeness.

Should we desire to question further about the essence and nature
of this X? Are we allowed to? Is there any positive answer to be given?
Will our guide be able to do anything except to put his finger to his lip
and bid us be silent; because any word beyond the great negative is
here too much? What can be said of the unutterable and neutral except
that it is comparable to death?

If we expected such an answer, we would have misunderstood what
has been said hitherto. Schleiermacher himself continually invites us to
question further. Whoever wishes to claim him as a mystic must at least
recognize that he does not share the silence or the negative path (via
negativa) of the consistent mystic. He gave a positive answer, not only
when he was speaking concretely, historically, expressing himself
specifically as a Christian, but also when, in apparent detachment, he
was preaching the Universal which is the substance of the particular.
More exactly stated—he dared to speak concretely, historically, as a
Christian, because the universal, that unutterable and neutral, that fulfilment of which he wanted to speak, is completely the fulfilment of
concretion, the sum and the epitome and the strength of the particular;
because he knew of no negation outside the cosmos of the positives
which reflect and present the Universe; because for him religion meant
viewing and feeling the infinite in the finite.

[1] *Sämtl. Werke zur Philos.*, I, p. 447.

It is this last point, precisely this understanding of the nature of religion, which explains Schleiermacher's basic position, explains why he became, not a consistent, not a negative mystic, but a positive thinker with a vital philosophy. In viewing and feeling he possessed the Universe, he became one with that which he saw presenting itself in the whole spiritual-natural cosmos. In religion he saw God's presence established in men. Religion is the finite with capacity for the infinite (*capax infiniti*). Therefore the idea of death is excluded as a description of the essence and nature of the unutterable. That which is established in man is, indeed, present in him as the most immediate element of his selfconsciousness, established and present as the deepest continuum of his heart, is experienced as life in the same sense and with the same breath in which man feels himself to be alive.

Therefore Schleiermacher dared to comprehend the unutterable, the Universe in all its myriad reflections, the infinite in all finiteness, as life, as life-force, life-spirit, life-process. Under its positive sign all finite life stands—or rather, since life is growth, comes ever and again to stand. Therefore—and this is decisive—all possible affirmations about nature and history can be in no way separated from the central and fundamental statement 'Religion is Life'. They can enter only as variants of this equation. Schleiermacher had little desire to make a speculative use of the principle so established, either in relation to explaining the world or in relation to the concept of God. The whole remains in feeling. And it is only the main thesis, religion is life, which was important for Schleiermacher—not any kind of philosophy of nature or of history.

By *life* Schleiermacher understood the movement or activity which reason and nature possess in common, but which is at the same time above both. It is the movement and activity of the Universe, as in his early days he liked to put it. Therefore to call his view naturalism without qualification is gross oversimplification. Schleiermacher himself would have had it understood as 'higher realism'.[1] According to him, religion breathes wherever freedom itself has again become nature.[2]

Always *realism, nature*! Certainly Schleiermacher cannot be claimed as an idealist. By the emphasis he lays on religion as established and present, as the finite capacity for the infinite (*finitum capax infiniti*), the infinite life (*vita infinita*) is pushed into the sphere of the given, is localized as present. Its characteristics become—here the perfect balance seems disturbed—accommodated more to the natural than to the spiritual.

[1] *R.*, p. 54; *S*, p. 40.   [2] *R.*, p. 52.

We have already heard that the original basis 'is found established in us precisely as things are established in us in perception', not *as* a thing but similarly as things are established. That is Schleiermacher's positivism, and it is a decisive weight in the scale for answering the question on the nature and method of his teaching as a whole. Religion belongs to the nature of man, he said in the *Speeches*. It has its abode in a 'portion of the soul',[1] in its own 'peculiar province of the heart'.[2] It is a 'continuum in man'[3] which is propagated through the family,[4] which finds in Germany a more favourable 'climate' than in England or France.[5] The *Speeches* talk of product, tendency, drive, force, instinct; of processes, sometimes chemical, sometimes biological; of 'the marriage of the infinite with the finite'.[6]

We obviously find ourselves on the same ground in a sermon of 1835[7] when we read that the divine spirit 'in and for itself works as infinite force'; but in the Christian Church and in every individual soul as a 'force subordinated to the law of nature'. Schleiermacher the preacher saw religion budding, growing, increasing, progressing. Therefore the phrase 'more and more' is one of the most significant characteristics of his pulpit vocabulary. 'More and more' the divine life is to be made glorious in us; 'more and more' we are to live in communion with it. Keeping one's self within this upward movement and clinging tightly to it is commended again and again as the only requisite needed for further progress in Christian development.

Of decisive significance, in the next place, for our understanding of religion as life is the principle of *individuation*. We begin at the point at which in 1804 Schleiermacher dissociated himself from Schelling. In his influential review of Schelling's *Vorlesungen über die Methode des akad. Studiums* (Lectures on the Methods of Academic Study) he pointed out that Schelling had not understood 'the lofty arbitrariness' of Christianity. What is Schleiermacher's own position? Even as the great X is known because it is experienced as life, so, on the other hand, life is given always only in the form of experience, of a unique, particular movement of the feeling of an individual.

This movement of feeling can, however, be transmitted, and has by such transmission the power to establish community. And so there arises from the religion of the individual the genus religion, a type of religion. In the finite the infinite! According to the *Speeches*, religion

---

[1] R., p. 269; S, p. 229.   [2] R., p. 37; S, p. 32.   [3] R., p. 298.
[4] R., pp. 230 f.; S, p. 178. Cf. *Hausstandspredigte* and Gl.L., § 6.4; CF, p. 29.
[5] R., pp. 16 f.; S, p. 10.   [6] R., p. 267; S, p. 228.   [7] Pr., III, p. 179.

begins with an incomprehensible event, with a memorable occurrence, with a single isolated insight derived from nature, history, society, or one's own inner life. Only the man who surrenders himself to such a central insight has a 'fixed abode' and exercises valid citizenship in the religious world.[1] That world is certainly 'a complete republic',[2] in the sense that no one of the possible central insights excludes any of the others possible. Rather, innumerable views of the Universe have their right, opposite and beside one another, like the 'splendid branches into which the heavenly tree of the priestly art divides its crown'.[3]

If the Unity (which is never and nowhere given as such) has its actuality in the individual, so the individual, far from being an isolated entity, has its truth in the Unity. For example, Christianity, according to *The Christian Faith*, section 10 (*CF*, pp. 47, 44), receives its 'colour and tone', its historical extension and possibility of existence from 'the impulse which proceeded from Christ'; yet its content is the feeling of absolute dependence. (On the highest level this bears the seal of the consciousness of redemption.) The former (the impulse) is the individuation, the latter is the Oneness; the former is the actualizing, the latter is the truth.

An important statement on the subject of individuation is found in the Postscript to section 10 of *The Christian Faith*. There we are given a definitive statement of the correlative concepts of the 'positive' and the 'revealed' in religion. Schleiermacher's thought can be briefly summarized. The positive is the individual or individualized; the revelation, on the other hand, is the individualizing; in every religion it is the 'original fact' (*CF*, p. 49) which gives to this specific religion this specific form. Obviously the latter is the same element which in the *Speeches* was called the central insight. Schleiermacher laid stress on the designation 'original event'. Revelation does not teach; it acts. It produces a 'total impression' (*CF*, p. 50). It has nothing to do with the antithesis of true and false. All revelation is true—and none.

The complete truth of a revelation would presuppose a publication of information by God himself. But how could such a publication be possible or be subjectively comprehensible? What makes a revelation is not that it is true, but that it is effective; not that it presents God as he is in and for himself, but that it presents God in his relation to us, or rather that the revelation effects that relation. Revelation is the basis, the 'causality' (*CF*, p. 50) of a specific modification of our religious

[1] *R.*, p. 261; *S*, p. 224.   [2] *R.*, p. 184; *S*, p. 153.
[3] *R.*, p. 221.

consciousness. Wherever religion is, there is revelation—not to be explained psychologically, but easily explicable historically as the beginning of the life-process of this religion. On revelation so understood depends also the 'lofty arbitrariness' (*CF*, p. 557, 'divine caprice') of Christianity which Schleiermacher defended against Schelling. For Christianity is in this sense a positive religion, a religion of revelation.

The category of causality which here emerges leads us back again, still on the point of 'religion as life', to section 4 of *The Christian Faith*. This section, in antithesis to the theme just treated, deals not with the singleness of the One, but with the unity of all singles—that is, with the essentially identical nature of all religions. It offers the famous definition that in religion we are conscious of ourselves as absolutely dependent or (what means the same thing) of ourselves as in relation with God.

We cannot here enter into the numerous questions of the interpretation of this much-discussed section, nor into the critical, factual question of how far Schleiermacher succeeded or failed in making the concept of absolute dependence clear in itself or in grounding it in his presuppositions. We must content ourselves with determining his main intention and with seeing how, in general, he elaborated it.

As we have already noted, feeling is the centre, dominant over knowing and doing, because it is understood in its depth as *religious* feeling; because it is the feeling of absolute dependence. As the consciousness of absolute dependence, religion must be understood as life. It is life, the innermost life, of man in which he knows himself to be—neither absolutely free, since absolute freedom does not exist, nor merely relatively dependent and relatively free, that is as alternately free and unfree in relation to the world. But he knows himself to be absolutely dependent on an Other (Schleiermacher says on 'something') who accompanies all his self's activity, who therefore, since his activity is never zero, accompanies his whole existence.

In human selfconsciousness, the consciousness of this Other is included, is established, is revealed, so far as selfconsciousness is fundamentally consciousness of the Other that absolutely determines it, is conscious of a *Whence*, of a basis for absolute dependence, of the absolute necessity of the selfconsciousness being as it is. The actualization of the selfconsciousness in this form is religion, because this determining Other, the *Whence* of absolute dependence, is truly God. Therefore, actualizing the selfconsciousness in this way is really actualizing the God-consciousness. And one can even dare to say 'God is given to us in feeling in an original way'; [1] given obviously as the non-objective cause whose effect is everywhere objective, but is pure feeling in distinction to knowing and doing. So far as Schleiermacher sought in spite of this reservation (i.e. the cause, God, is not objective; the effect, the feeling, is objectless) to make the givenness of God in feeling comprehensible under the category of cause and effect, the preponderance of naturalism as an element in his description of the religious life appears to be substantiated.

As a last point in this connexion, I should call attention to the unique character of Schleiermacher's Systematics. In *The Christian Faith* chiefly in relation to dogmatics, but in the *Kurze Darstellung* in relation to theology as a whole, Schleiermacher has accomplished what was not achieved before him even by an Augustine or a Thomas Aquinas, a Melanchthon, a Zwingli or a Calvin in their corresponding works with their articulated Chapters, Articles or Loci. He has presented a single, astonishingly coherent view of the separate parts (*disjecta membra*) of the historical Christian faith.

For this reason Schleiermacher has often been praised as an artist. But without decrying that praise, I should like to raise the question of whether it is not more accurate to liken his systematic construction to a natural organism rather than to a work of art. Is it accidental that he himself in the *Kurze Darstellung* called philosophic theology the root, historical theology the trunk and practical theology the leafy branches of the tree? Do not the distinctions he made exhibit in the relativity in which they are all to be understood precisely the nature of cell divisions? In so many of the sections where he dealt first with the emergence from religious immediacy to reflection and then of the return from reflection to immediacy, do we not think involuntarily of a living animal breathing in and out, or of the systole and diastole of its heart-beat? If that impression is justified, it would be an indirect support for the naturalistic character of the life which Schleiermacher wanted to expound—a character which in this portrayal would achieve an artistically adequate expression.

Certainly—and here we bring together what has been said—Schleiermacher in the first letter to Lücke could not assert strongly enough that his analysis of the Christian selfconsciousness, was intended 'very simply and honestly, to be wholly empirical', that he wanted to present 'actual facts in accordance with experience' and not states of consciousness preceding experience.[2] This assertion was cer-

[1] *Gl.L.*, § 4.4; *CF*, p. 17.   [2] *S.L.*, p. 21.

tainly justified, since he had established in §§ 3–4 of *The Christian Faith* the basic nature of feeling. He had established this datum of religious life as really a *datum*, as something given and not any sort of not-given entity, not an a-priori, not an intellectual concept. And he dealt with it throughout both theoretically and practically as object of a positive science.

Did he think of it in the last analysis as a third entity above the antithesis of spirit and nature, above the Kantian antithesis of transcendental and empirical? On the basis of his assumptions as a whole, one must suppose so. Actually his positivism (as he himself affirmed) consisted in the preponderance of the presuppositions and methods of the natural sciences, with which he approached this object.

4. *The Historical Element in Religion*

Discussion of Schleiermacher's naturalism is undoubtedly of value. But to take naturalism as a comprehensive formula for his theological thinking would involve an unendurable mutilation of its content. Ritschl, with his strictly ethical and spiritual concepts, unavoidably misunderstood Schleiermacher at the point where he mounted the heights above in his knowledge of something beyond 'spirit' and 'nature'. We shall be careful not to follow Ritschl's road.

Although the attitude of the natural sciences may have predominated too much in Schleiermacher's thinking when he was dealing with religion as a given, present entity, yet we must remember that as soon as he turned to the question of the basis or rather the genesis of religion, the problem of history became acute for him. Even though it may be admitted that he treated the historical more or less as a natural science because of the strongly naturalistic trend of his thinking, it is no less easily proved that he himself was never satisfied with the result, but remained vitally concerned with the problem. He felt compelled to recognize that the historical was never completely integrated into the other elements of his thinking and never fully lost its enigmatic character. He had to admit both its existence and its importance. Moreover, in spite of the consequences to his system, he wanted it so to remain and function.

Schleiermacher's Christology—which we must now consider—might possibly be dismissed as an unsatisfactory concession. But if we are to be fair to Schleiermacher, we cannot deny that in this concession there is included a serious purpose which is in itself consistent—even though in the context of his theology it is perhaps inconsistent. He was determined to preach Christ as the Bearer of the great Peace, as the original source and bringer of life. He pursued this purpose with an inner passion which is unmistakably clear to everyone, in his writings, in his sermons especially. And the method by which he sought to achieve it made a deep impression on his contemporaries.

Did he really achieve that aim? Who shall be the judge? Let us try at least to make clear to ourselves the *way* in which he *tried*. How does Christ, Jesus of Nazareth, come into this theology of the ineffable, of the centre, of life? The answer of the sermons is very simple. Christ is the all in One; he is the authority to be cited for the verification of the truth presented, or rather of the reality. He is the source of the spirit, of power, of life, etc. He is the initiator of the kingdom of God—that is, of the complete relation with God which overcomes the law, the contradiction. He is the Redeemer. So runs Schleiermacher's stereotype and the formula is copiously demonstrated in *The Christian Faith*. 'Redemption' means according to § 11.2: passively, the 'passage' of man from the evil condition of 'obstructed vitality' (*CF*, p. 54) of the higher selfconsciousness to the better condition of its relative liberation. Actively, redemption is the help in that passage given to man by an Other. This Other is Christ, the Redeemer.

Christianity is distinguished [1] from other religions of the same type in the history of religions because in it everything 'is related to the *redemption* accomplished by *Jesus of Nazareth*' (both emphases are necessary). Or the difference may be expressed negatively: [2] 'there is no other way of obtaining participation in the Christian communion than through faith in Jesus as the Redeemer'. To this principle Schleiermacher the preacher consistently adhered.

In his Christocentric emphasis, he confronted the rationalists of his time with an astonishing novelty, he put the Supernaturalists deep in the shade, and he equalled even the 'Awakening' theologians of his day—if he did not, in fact, surpass them—at least in the systematic consistency with which he admitted Christ to be all in all.

Constantly, even though with many twists and turns, his homiletical scheme remains the same. Part I: Christ, his nature, will and action; Part II: Ourselves, our nature, will and action as these are determined by, are already taken possession of by him, and become more and more filled by him, penetrated and renewed by him. The two parts often approach surprisingly close together, even appear on occasion to melt

[1] *Gl.L.*, § 11.   [2] *Gl.L.*, § 14.

into each other. Often Christ seems to be almost an abstraction in his role as mover, giver, initiator of that which is in process of becoming in man. On the other hand, often he is surprisingly concrete as the bearer of the principle which was already existent in man—and surprisingly similar to the preacher himself. But Schleiermacher's purpose remains clear. This preaching has to move around two foci like an ellipse, not around a single point like a circle. The historical, with the tensions it necessitates between *ought* and *is*, between giving and receiving, beginning and continuing, once and always, pattern and copy, is 'somehow or other' in the diagram and it receives due recognition.

If we ask how this historical element really works, how Schleiermacher conceived the leap over the famed 'foul ditch' of 1800 years, the best answer is found in the idea of the 'corporate life' which dominates §§ 87–8 of *The Christian Faith*. This 'corporate life' goes back to the work of Jesus in redemption. By that redemption, Schleiermacher understands very concretely a definite 'impulse of historical life' given by Jesus of Nazareth. Those believing in him are as such moved by this impulse; by it they are bound together (whether or not they are separated in space and time); through it they build a living whole. The work of Jesus is immediately effective for this community as a whole—not for the individual. (The individual as such plays a smaller role in Schleiermacher's theology than one would expect on the basis of the impression given in the *Soliloquies*.) A man is touched, seized and carried along by this corporate life which flows like a river through continents and centuries or which circulates like blood through the veins of humanity. It is this which makes him a Christian, which puts him in relationship to the redemption consummated by Jesus of Nazareth.

The category therefore to which Jesus must be assigned is certainly revelation. This means, as has already been established, that in this particular religion, the Christian religion, the effective original event through which the divine life in the community is determined, 'the central view' or 'insight' (in the terminology of the *Speeches*) of this religion, is Christ.

Before we turn to the Christology finally developed by the later Schleiermacher, let us glance at the *Celebration of Christmas* of 1806, which is especially important in this connexion. There we become acquainted with the problems as Schleiermacher dealt with them in the stage of a running battle. 'What do we celebrate at Christmas?' is the theme of this dialogue, the core of which has been looked for, as we well know, in the opinions expressed by the three 'cultured' men and developed by them to a high point theologically and philosophically. Each one of them presents to us a specific side of Schleiermacher's own thinking.

But we must not ignore the fact that the answer was first given in the lyrical expression of the women's emotion which turns very simply and directly to the eternal relation of mother and child presented in Mary and Jesus. The perception of the women as expressed in religious songs and music is explicitly praised in the conclusion. In contrast to all answers given in words it is the 'better part'.

Therefore there is no genuine discussion; and no common conclusion is reached. We hear the various theories of the men. (1) Sheer humanity, joyous as it appears at the German Christmas, may be the primary element; and the supposed 'occasion' of the festival, Christ, may be the reflection which that joy casts backwards (Leonard). (2) Is not what we celebrate at Christmas much more the idea (in the second edition Schleiermacher added 'the experience') of the beginning, of the centre for the crystallization in humanity of the new untroubled life, free of contradictions (Ernest)? (3) Is it much more concerned with human nature as seen and known from the divine principle? That is, with human nature in its identity of becoming and being; as it exists not in any individual, but in the Church as the selfconsciousness of humanity, so that we are compelled to seek for the point from which this self-consciousness proceeded and was imparted. That point was found in Jesus Christ and celebrated at Christmas (Edward).

Schleiermacher is speaking in all three—not only in Ernest's middle position. Christ is essential as the basis for the actual completeness and universality of love among men. Christ is the highest manifestation of love, the greatest symbol of God's grace. Throughout the preaching of the later Schleiermacher ring the echoes of Leonard's speech and of Edward's. However, on the whole, the Christology of *The Christian Faith* follows in the direction of Ernest's speech, although the deviations of Leonard and Edward into historical scepticism and speculative mysticism still occupy the background and must not be lost to sight if we wish really to understand Schleiermacher's attitude to the historical.

In *The Christian Faith*, the main sections 'On Christ' (92–105), together with the others (106–17) which treat of the 'Order of Salvation' (*Ordo Salutis*) of the old Dogmatics, are set under the main heading 'The State of the Christian as Conscious of the Divine Grace'. But in spite of this title, the emphasis falls on the second, the opposite focus of the ellipse, on the historical. In the language of the *Speeches*: a corresponding view is not to be postulated from the feeling; on the contrary, this view is *given* in and with the feeling. Christ made a *beginning*; from him proceeded and still proceeds an impulse, a movement, an impartation. That is where the stress of the whole falls.

We can best begin with the statements on the work of Christ.[1] Schleiermacher indeed said in § 92 (*CF*, p. 374) that 'the peculiar activity and the exclusive dignity of the Redeemer . . . are inseparably one in the selfconsciousness of believers'. The context in which he said it and all his presuppositions show indubitably that his thinking on the person of Christ was based on his conception of the work of Christ (as this in turn was based on his description of the state of grace in itself) and not the converse. 'If the peculiar dignity of the Redeemer can be measured only by his total activity as resting upon that dignity, while this activity can be seen in its completeness only in the corporate life he founded . . . then the dignity of the Redeemer must be thought of in such a way that he is capable of achieving this.' [2]

We are vividly reminded of the Leonard and Edward speeches in the *Celebration of Christmas*. And following the pointer there given, we may state first (§ 100; *CF*, p. 425): 'The Redeemer admits believers into the power of his God-consciousness, and this is his redemptive activity.' That is, in the Christian's experience the activity of the Redeemer has become the Christian's own activity, the furtherance of his own higher life. Through Christ a divine infiltration into human nature is effected which, seen as a whole, is world creation; seen in the individual is person creation (*CF*, p. 427). For this infiltration Schleiermacher will aceept the term *mystical* so far as the term is understood to mean 'the true centre' between 'immediate, magical' and 'empirical' (*CF*, p. 429). (By 'empirical' he means an infiltration which is effected only by teaching and example.)   Then according to Schleiermacher there follows upon redemption, or rather there is included within it, like a small circle inside a larger,[3] reconciliation, the acceptance of the believers into the community of the Redeemer's untroubled blessedness; untroubled, that is, by the consciousness of evil and sin with the concomitant consciousness of guilt. Such consciousness has not vanished; but it no longer disturbs the inmost life of the new man.   This is the reconciling moment of the forgiveness of sin; upon it follows the second, the feeling of the corporate life of blessedness, for all believers as a whole and for each one individually. For this life in common with Christ,

---

[1] *Gl.L.*, §§ 100 ff.   [2] *Gl.L.*, beginning of § 93; *CF*, p. 377.   [3] *Gl.L.*, § 101.

Schleiermacher explicitly accepts the term *mystical*, making the same distinction as before against orthodoxy and rationalism.

When questioned about the meaning of the suffering and death of Christ in this connexion, Schleiermacher answered that these can only constitute an element of secondary importance. For redemption and reconciliation were necessarily completely 'intelligible' even before the death of Christ. The death of Christ marks the appearance of the redeeming and reconciling activity of Christ in its 'perfect fullness', in so much as Christ submitted to the suffering in obedience and in so much as he in that same obedience was not overcome by the suffering. Therefore Schleiermacher usually preached elliptically, even on Good Friday, on Christ's obedience and the victory of his obedience, the fruit of which is the imitative repetition of both the obedience and the victory in us and through us. Redemption and reconciliation are, according to Schleiermacher, a continuation of the same creative divine activity which began with the 'formation' of the person of Christ (*CF*, p. 427). With the new life which awakens in us through the work of Christ in us and becomes more and more intense and heightened, the originally intended destiny of man is achieved (*CF*, p. 437). Beyond that, there is for a nature like ours nothing further to be thought of or striven after.

From this point we turn back to Schleiermacher's view of the person (of the 'peculiar dignity') of the Redeemer. If his work is imparting to others the power of his God-consciousness, of his untroubled blessedness, then obviously the doctrine of his person must treat of the original implanting of both, that is of the original existence of God (*CF*, p. 384) in human nature and in Christ himself. The spontaneous activity of the new corporate life in the specifically Christian power of the God-consciousness must [1] have been *originally* in the Redeemer, that is not only as a prototye but as the archetype, completely and productively; for the incomplete could not complete itself from itself.

If humanity (so Schleiermacher himself answers on obvious criticism) had the power of itself to produce this archetype, then its actual condition of sinfulness would be incomprehensible. If in spite of its sinfulness, it has knowledge of this archetype, it follows that the possession of such knowledge can be explained only as the result of 'a creative divine act in which . . . the conception of man as the subject of the God-consciousness comes to completion'. Therefore, as an historical individual, he from whom this effect proceeded and proceeds is the Archetype and at the

---

[1] According to *Gl.L.*, § 93; *CF*, p. 378.

same time what is experienced in him is the experience of the true ideal of man. Because he is an object of experience, because as the perfect ideal, he is at the same time historical, there must be ascribed to him a becoming within time, a development, a national conditioning which includes even his God-consciousness. But this development is to be thought of as wholly free from all struggle, as 'a continuous transition from the condition of purest innocence to that of purely spiritual fullness of power' (*CF*, p. 383); to a purity which cannot be designated as *virtue* nor seen as the result of an external protection, but which derives only from the higher God-consciousness implanted in him. And the national conditioning of his person is not to be thought of as an opposing or exclusive principle. With this reservation, every historical occurrence of his advent carries at the same time in it the original perfect ideality.

Therefore, the sinlessness of Christ [1] is not the abrogation of human nature, since the possibility of a sinless development is not incompatible with the concept of human nature, and since temptation also existed for him. But this sinlessness distinguishes him from all men, even from Adam before the Fall. For we must think of Adam, Schleiermacher explained, as at least prepared for sin even before the Fall; and this is not to be said of Christ.

Christ's 'dignity' consists entirely in the strength of his God-consciousness which is implanted in his selfconsciousness. Now this God-consciousness of his is identical with the existence of God in him —and in us because he has imparted it to us. This identity could not be asserted of our disturbed and incomplete God-consciousness in and for itself apart from him. He is the single, original seat of it. Now, so far as first through Christ, the human God-consciousness becomes an existence of God in human nature, and so far as only through human nature, i.e. the totality of finite powers, there can come an existence of God in the world, it follows that all existence of God in the world is mediated through Christ and brings with it the wholly *new* creation, a creation which contains and develops the power of God-consciousness.

The beginning of Christ's life, in which this unity of God-consciousness and the existence of God began, is, as the first act of human nature not affected by sin, the 'completion' of the creation of human nature. For the appearance of the first man constitutes only the sensuous life of the human race (while the spirit remained on the whole 'sunk in sensuousness'): but the appearance of the second Adam constitutes the

---

[1] So continues *Gl.L.*, § 94.

new spiritual life. Behind both is the undivided divine plan, and both together constitute in the higher sense one and the same undivided whole, even though such wholeness is for us unattainable.

I shall content myself with presenting Schleiermacher's Christology in its positive character and in its own context. I pass over his attempt (§§ 95–9 and 102–5 in *The Christian Faith*) to deal with the biblical and orthodox tradition, partly by accommodating himself to it, and partly by critically juggling it out of the way. Schleiermacher's purpose should have become clear. He intended to give its rightful place to the moment of the establishment of the communion of God and man through the Other, Christ, as found in the theological tradition which he accepted. He neither could nor would evade in principle the necessity of that tradition. He presented the establishment of this communion as explicable in the form of a causal sequence. The concept of human nature served him as the higher order within which he could move from the sensuous to the spiritual, from the disturbed God-consciousness to the dynamic God-consciousness; and on the causal side, he arrives at the effect of Christ on us.

Schleiermacher's doctrine of the person and work of Christ preserves thus the form of the ellipse with two foci, but the figure tends to shift towards a circle with one centre. Consequently it is still doubtful whether the methodological point of departure, the exalted humanity of Christ, is not really the original, and whether Christ himself is not the derivative destined to vanish. Under redemption, Schleiermacher in the last analysis understood only an empowering, and under Redeemer only a strong helper or a helping power. Therefore there could not be any word of a *founding* of communion in the strict sense, but only of confirming it and of continuing the fulfilment of an already existing communion.

This relativism naturally has its consequences on all sides. It is reflected, for example, in Schleiermacher's treatment of history, where the moments of authority and of freedom do not preserve a mutual equilibrium; the second is regularly overweighted. In the *Kurze Darstellung* it is clear that the New Testament writings are for him essentially documents of church history; and the other fact, which Schleiermacher intended also to state, that they are canonical, that they are documents of the original Christianity (*Ur-Christentum*), is subordinate. The syllable *Ur* (original) acquires here as in the word *Urbild* (original pattern, ideality) a certain harmlessness, because it means only the beginning. It reflects the fact that Schleiermacher's concept of the Church is characterized more clearly and effectively by the definition of Christ-likeness as a subjective experience, weaker or stronger, than by the opposite view (to him the opposition was only apparent) that the community 'is the full revelation of the highest existence in the world'.[1] The same relativity is reflected also in the peculiar embarrassment revealed conspicuously by the way in which the preaching of the older Schleiermacher developed. To his congregation at Trinity Church he felt himself driven to expound again and again, from the most diverse points of view, the problem which he had apparently settled in certain forceful passages in *The Christian Faith*—the problem of the absoluteness or the non-absoluteness of Christianity.

Why just Christ as the incarnation of peace with God? Is that peace not possible perhaps without him? Or perhaps with another in his stead? Perhaps with such a one as is still to come? Is Christ not merely the best 'for now'? Schleiermacher called the notion of superseding Christianity a 'fantasy' and a 'fable'. He adjured those who so represent it not to lay the defects of the Church to the charge of Christ; he urged them to realize that the whole progress of the human spirit and life is bound up with Christ, to listen to the truth that 'through the experiences of the whole of world history, everything glorious in humanity can be only a refraction from the light of Christ'. He cited Novalis: 'If all become unfaithful. . . .' He challenged them:[2] 'This image of a soul always one with God—whence did we get it? The loftiest height of our consciousness would be lost if he had not existed. . . . No! Without this fullness of life and joy which the existence of the Redeemer gives us, I should not wish to live.'

But does there not remain as the background of these assurances, uncontradicted, and indeed affirmed by § 10 of *The Christian Faith*, the assertion of the *Speeches* [3] that the basic insight of every religion is in itself eternal, because it is a contributing part of the infinite whole in which all must be eternal? Therefore can the ultimate seriousness of the assertions in the sermons go any farther than to say that the affirming subject imputes an ultimate seriousness to himself or to the corporate life of the church community?

Whatever the answer, Schleiermacher achieved his purpose—we might better say he thought that he could honestly and piously achieve it. He dared to base validity on the sequence: substantiate an existent divine life; conclude from this divine life an activity witnessing to it; and from this activity deduce a correspondingly endowed active being.

[1] *Pr.*, III, p. 591.   [2] *Pr.*, III, p. 9.   [3] *R.*, pp. 307 f.

He persisted in thinking that the reality of the life and the peace which he wished to preach could be justified only in the form of this sequence, in the form of the historical Christian context, in the form of Christology. And he believed with equal pertinacity that the claim made by the traditional Christology, by the paradox of the historical in Christianity, could be defended only if given this content, this interpretation. Therefore he filled the form with that great X of which he was to say on his death-bed, struggling between consciousness and unconsciousness, 'how beautiful it all is to me; mediating, how splendid!'

Certainly he put himself between two fires. It is questionable whether the reality he had in mind was such that it could be fitted into the form of a Christology. His critics on the left have charged against him that such adaptation was precluded. And it is problematical whether the form of Christianity would allow itself to be filled with this content. Those on the right asserted that it did not. Both judgements have the same ground. The great X which Schleiermacher had in mind was not so much the Christian revelation as the modern pagan feeling for life. Therefore in relation to the Christological form it was a kind of foreign body which had been encysted in it.

The basis for the support of these objections is impressively strong. It can be found epitomized with symbolic force in the well-known account of the last fifteen minutes of Schleiermacher's life. He desired passionately to celebrate the Communion with his family, and the physician had expressly forbidden him wine. 'Then', according to his wife's account, 'he laid two fingers on his left eye, as he often did when he was thinking deeply, and began to speak. "I have never clung to the dead letter. We have the atoning death of Christ, his body and his blood. But I have always believed, and I still now believe, that the Lord Jesus gave the Lord's Supper with water and wine." When he had considered this, his features began to light up, his voice became clear and strong. He asked with priestly solemnity, "Are you all one with me in this belief that the Lord Jesus blessed the water also in the wine?" To which we answered simply "Yes". "Then let us partake of the Lord's Supper; for you the wine and for me the water," he said very solemnly.' [1]

The question is unavoidable: was the water in the wine blessed so that the water could serve *as substitute for* the wine without the service ceasing to be the Lord's Supper? What has the water to do with the

---

[1] Schleiermacher's last sermon, published by J. Bauer, Marburg, 1905, pp. 17 f.; cf. *Aus Schleiermachers Leben*, II, pp. 484 f.

Lord's Supper and what has the Lord's Supper to do with the water? Did the content of Schleiermacher's Christology correspond to this scene? Do we find there, in the place of the wine of the Christian revelation, the water of the modern feeling for life? What then? But perhaps the symbolism of that scene is too impressive. Perhaps we can do no more than to *ask* the question earnestly. And we can certainly be sure that even as Schleiermacher *wished* to celebrate a true Lord's Supper, so also in his Christology he *intended* really to preach Christ, however many considerations go to show that he failed to do so.

Yet it must be recognized that the problem which here confronts us is the problem of the whole century and that Schleiermacher appears pre-eminently the fit person to be discussed because his thinking ranged more widely and more persistently in both directions than that of others. The final decision upon his position—whether he was an outstanding fighter for a lost cause, or an equally outstanding betrayer of Christ—can be given neither on the one side nor the other by the judges of this world, by his fellow men.

5. *The Mystical and Cultural*

Our sketch of the basic ideas of Schleiermacher's theology would show an all too serious omission if we did not include at least one last question to which Schleiermacher's answer has been of decisive significance for the whole century. I mean the question of the ideal life. For Schleiermacher as preacher or speaker the vision of this ideal life hovered constantly over religion. What is Schleiermacher's human being like, when he possesses the living spirit somehow imparted to him by Jesus and desires to bring himself nearer to that centre? What does he do? In what direction does he move?

We begin with Schleiermacher's sermons dealing with prayer. In that context he especially distinguishes a double movement in which the Christian finds himself and ought to find himself. The two components are fundamentally of equal importance to Schleiermacher; but practically much more emphasis falls on the second. I have called them in the heading 'Mystical and Cultural'. I could equally well have said 'Prayer and Work,' or 'Religion and Life in the World', or 'Inner and Outer Activity'. Although both were important for Schleiermacher, he was clearly more concerned with the second. And perhaps the first was important to him only for the sake of the second. It is this fact which seems to me too much ignored in Emil Brunner's discussion of Schleiermacher. From Brunner we could not understand how truly the Protestant theology of the modern age, which received its character from Schleiermacher, can be called according to its major emphasis (*a parte potiori*) 'cultural Protestantism' and not 'mystical Protestantism'.

Religious life as human activity certainly meant for Schleiermacher primarily an activity wholly inwardly directed, a self-concentration upon God, or since through Christ God is in us, upon ourselves. It is prayer.[1] Prayer arises out of the antithesis of resignation and thankfulness; it is 'the inner combination of a wish for full success with the God-consciousness'. Prayer is the satisfaction 'of the continually renewed, daily need of the heart for receiving spiritual life.'[2] It is a withdrawal from participation in the things of this world and from being moved by them; an entrance into that deep inner stillness where (as we have heard) a union of man with God occurs and must continually recur. This union Schleiermacher himself, in distinction from orthodoxy and rationalism, called mysticism. He knew and approved examples of withdrawal by religious men, their search for the religious goal in isolation. In this context belongs his firm advocacy of the separation of Church and State, which appears early in the *Speeches*. And as an old man, he still declared 'the kingdom which the Saviour purposed to build ought to be wholly separated from the civil state'.[3]

But Schleiermacher cannot remain in such isolation. This solitary inward action can be no more than the lifted baton, the preparation for, the bridge to a wholly different position. 'If the word first received in the human heart blossoms only there . . . then our life also is nothing more than a voice in the wilderness like the witness of John. The life of Christ which is now in us must go out of the desert into the world.' And 'there should then be for us no difference between the desert and Jerusalem; no difference between the moments of self-renewing concentration in the silence of withdrawal . . . and our active life'.[4]

How does this shift from withdrawal to activity occur? The sermons on prayer and § 147 of *The Christian Faith* give a clear answer. When in prayer man seeks and finds God, he actually finds the true centre, above the antithesis of rest and motion, or of receptivity and self-activity. Prayer, according to the example of Jesus, can be directed only to the will of God. Therefore, prayer is not a separate, special activity alongside of communion with God; it is not to be distinguished from that communion nor from all other activity pleasing to God.[5]

[1] *Gl.L.*, § 146; *CF*, p. 669.   [2] *Pr.*, III, p. 59.   [3] *Pr.*, VI, p. 171.
[4] *Pr.*, III, p. 728.   [5] *Pr.*, III, pp. 682–7.

Prayer at its height necessarily becomes action; the particular becomes universal; the mystical becomes cultural activity; the religious man becomes the ideal man. Prayer is 'the living, secure feeling that however far in the depths human life may still be on man's gradual ascent towards ruling the world by his work, yet the great miracle of God can always reach fulfilment in all men'.[1]

It is interesting to note (as a sign that we are now within the sanctuary of Schleiermacher's theology) that just here the shift has its parallel in his teaching on marriage. Love, so he said in the first *Hausstandspredigt* of 1818, 'can only bless men who wholly fulfil the requirements of their calling, who evade none of its demands. Two human beings can mutually satisfy each other only when they are living an active life, when they must deal with temptations and trials and give each other mutual help in them. We can rejoice in the most beloved soul only when we see her busy in her normal tasks.'[2] Or as the Lucinde letters of 1800 had already put it (certainly not without an intended criticism of the gifted idler, Fr. Schlegel)—'So the frivolous need to obtain for themselves one quality of the knight. . . . If Hercules is to be the symbol of manhood which we adore, certainly the prowess with which he embraces women is not the whole; his labours are also a necessary part of his manhood. Anyone who cannot do his own work in the world is unfit for love; and love ought to hinder nobody from working, but should rather give double enjoyment and eagerness to work. Therefore, I think, in a description of love this influence should never be omitted. Such an omission is as repugnant to me as the naming of faith without works was to our Heavenly Father.'[3]

But to return to our main line! The sanctuary has one door through which a man enters and another through which he goes out. There 'in the peace of the Lord all good things are included'.[4] 'All which we do by virtue of the spiritual power with which God has equipped the human race becomes a work of God from whom the gift comes.'[5] 'All which pertains to the true welfare of men in all that happens to them, stands in close relationship to the kingdom of God.'[6] 'Of all that is great and good we must know that it proceeds from him.'[7] All the characteristic terms of the modern churchmen are already to be found in Schleiermacher. Religion is merely a matter of *ennobling* everything, of *carrying through*, of *applying*, the 'wise words' of the Lord to everything.

---

[1] *Pr.*, III, p. 424.   [2] *Pr.*, I, p. 578.   [3] *Zur Philos.*, I, p. 444.
[4] *Pr.*, III, p. 764.   [5] *Pr.*, III, p. 184.   [6] *Pr.*, III, p. 317.
[7] *Pr.*, III, p. 458.

In this context we should consider Schleiermacher's specific teaching on the significance of the biblical miracles. He found in the miracle an example of an astonishing victory of spirit over nature, and saw in it precisely a stimulating prediction of our own actions. The Bible says 'whoever believes on me, will do the same works and works even greater than these'. What does this mean? You are to 'rule the earth by the divine spirit of love. That spirit ought to enlighten and in fact will always more and more enlighten your spiritual eyes. It will teach you to penetrate deeper and ever deeper into all the secrets of nature. Through it new powers, which have been sleeping, will arise within you; and in the united life of spirit and nature, the power of the former will be increased from one generation to the next. To this increase you can see no end, until the whole world, which was given to men, will have become transparent for him and will serve the divine spirit in him. . . . And behold! All which the human reason led by the spirit will progressively accomplish is the continuation of the miracles of the Lord. And we are called not only to believe in them, not only to proclaim them, but to do them.'[1]

He saw a prediction in process of the most splendid fulfilment. 'Whether the mountains are removed can be a matter of indifference to us; we step over them as if they were not there.'[2] 'Where are more forces in operation to attain in greater measure the original purpose for man, that he have dominion over all which is on earth; where are more such forces in operation than in the Christian world?'[3]

Here is the explicit expression of Schleiermacher's belief. With other miracles, as with this great prediction of man's rule on earth and its fulfilment in the miracle of human *culture*, there is no further problem. 'The miraculous, the supernatural, has now vanished; with the departure of the Redeemer from the earth, it became necessary to enter by God's grace into the province of nature.'[4] Now there is 'no other miracle except God's great miracle which enables us to comprehend all as ordered by the great law of nature and determined by the guidance of God'.[5] There we see fixed order and divine decree combined together. Therefore the outer activity which proceeds from inner activity can only be an activity within the regular course of human affairs. Its teleology coincides absolutely with the teleology of the kingdom of Christ. For 'all things happen just as they happen for the purpose of advancing the kingdom of Christ'.[6]

[1] *Pr.*, III, pp. 457 f. [2] *Pr.*, III, p. 420. [3] *Pr.*, V, p. 348.
[4] *Pr.*, V, p. 58. [5] *Pr.*, III, p. 425. [6] *Pr.*, III, p. 147.

'What comes from God, can come from God only through men; what God needs to do in order to accomplish this or that, he does only through the service of those who hear his will.'[1] The meaning of 'Cast your care upon the Lord' is 'above all, trust the collective strength of those who are bound to the good; trust the religiously supported wisdom of those who, in accordance with the divine plan, are guiding the whole'.[2] 'Do not kick against the pricks', like Saul, means to move along with the hidden driving power; that is, to establish right, light, and order, to strive to make them prevail.[3] The faith which removes mountains is manifested when we proceed unwearied on the road which is marked for us to walk. And if you had faith, says Jesus to his disciples, then you would surmount all the difficulties of your calling and remove all obstacles from the way.[4]

Schleiermacher anticipated one of Ritschl's main ideas when he gave high value to the fulfilment of the duties of citizenship as an activity in the 'kingdom of God'. But since he was more broadly, liberally, and humanistically oriented than Ritschl, he has fertilized this idea with the demand for tireless progress in all areas of cultural life. On the one side, as a good Prussian who found cause again and again in his academic addresses to refer to Frederick the Great, he preached especially the virtue of political order in the form of the State. But on the other side, in a way truly prophetic for his time, he placed above all else the demand for social equality, the call for economic security, for social welfare (as a right, not as a charity), for shortening the hours of work. It must never be forgotten that in this area Schleiermacher saw and preached things[5] for which the great 'Awakening' preachers of his time (their later descendants will be Wichern and Stöcker) had neither eyes nor sympathy.

The principle lying behind this whole shift from mysticism to culture must be sought in § 9 of *The Christian Faith*. I say intentionally 'behind' not 'under', 'background' not 'foundation'. In the context of determining the position of Christianity in the history and philosophy of religion, after he had in § 6 set Christianity with Judaism and Islam on the highest level as monotheistic religions, he dealt with the way in which Christianity is to be differentiated from the two associated with it.

As the principle of division, Schleiermacher used the question whether the selfconsciousness is determined by the religious emotion

---

[1] *Pr.*, III, p. 637.   [2] *Pr.*, III, p. 19.   [3] *Pr.*, III, p. 348.
[4] *Pr.*, III, pp. 663, 656.
[5] For example, *Pr.*, III, pp. 52, 103, 348, 352-5, 390 f, 620, 745; V, pp. 127 f, 407. It would be rewarding to review and compare with these and similar passages the attitudes of his contemporaries.

more towards passivity or towards activity. If towards the first, he called the religion aesthetic; if towards the second, teleological. He sought to show that Islam belongs wholly to the aesthetic, Judaism predominantly and Christianity wholly to the teleological. For in Christianity, the 'God-consciousness' is wholly 'related to the totality of the active states' (*CF*, p. 43), in the idea of the kingdom of God.

The significant point in this section is that the proof for the high place of Christianity offered in the preceding sections, where he was dealing with the different kinds of religion, is not carried further. Instead, he offered without argument the assumption that Christianity belongs to the teleological class of religion. And if one justifiably wishes to understand the higher value of teleological religion, since Schleiermacher found it realized in Christianity, one is faced with the peculiar difficulty that, according to Schleiermacher's presupposition of the purely passive character of the feeling of absolute dependence, the teleological class of religion would have to be ranked second.

Schleiermacher therefore was confronted with the dilemma either of defining Christianity as aesthetic religion in order to give it first place; or if he really wished to ascribe a teleological character to it, then of setting Islam and Judaism above it. Neither of these choices could he or would he make. He was convinced of the highest value of Christianity, and equally convinced of its teleological, ethical character. And he was convinced of the necessity of turning from mysticism to culture—quite apart from any determination of religious superiority by the criterion of the feeling of absolute dependence.

Logic in itself would have turned here in another direction; just as in the frame of his doctrine of life, his Christology is, if strictly interpreted, a foreign body. But here as there, he has erected against the direction demanded by his basic approach an 'As I will, I judge' (*sic volo, sic jubeo*). He had a passionate need to establish a correlative and a corrective over against the mystical position, which as an ideal of life would have best corresponded to his basic doctrine. (Actually it would be the only possible ideal, excluding all others.) In the sermons, although not in *The Christian Faith*, the incomparably heavier emphasis is given to the ethical. In the sermons, that which is the centre of *The Christian Faith*, the feeling of absolute dependence, resting in itself and in peace, or the consciousness of salvation, plays, as has been said, more the role of the raised baton to focus attention on what the preacher really wants from the people. He will set them in the world, conscious of their salvation, so that they may work on the tasks of civilization and culture.

Finally, in so complicated a situation the question may be ventured whether Schleiermacher in view of his real purpose is not best labelled a theologian of Christian culture. Was he not heralding, on a religiously Christian foundation, the penetration of nature by reason ? As such a herald, did he not have to safeguard that religiously Christian foundation against modern apostasy by becoming an Apologist ? In opposition to the assumed unique validity of pure logic and ethics did he not have to put the question of the dominant and absolute nature of religion and of Christianity ? Did he not arrive, more with his head than with his heart, at that mystical, naturalistic-pietistic doctrine of religion as the means to achieve this ? And was this doctrine acceptable to him only because he wanted to be really a theologian of *culture*, but still a *theologian* ? Did he accept it because for him, in contrast to most of his great contemporaries, Christianity appeared indispensable for the mastery of the stupendous task imposed more imperatively than ever before by the new age (the task which he accepted joyfully); and Christianity in any other than the mystical guise would have been unacceptable to modern men ?

The often-noticed coldness of the *Speeches on Religion* (a coldness not to be denied in spite of or within the pathos) and the comfortable dryness of *The Christian Faith* would find an explanation here. In neither was Schleiermacher in his proper element.

The Christian character of his theology would then be manifest in his refusal to swim with the current and be a modern man with no Christian reservation, and even more in his determination to know modern humanity as a humanity based upon and guided by Christianity. On this assumption, the tragic guilt or apostasy of his theology consisted in the following:

1. He forced Christianity, solely for the sake of culture, into a position where the whole was already surrendered.

2. Consequently he allowed himself to be forced into the fundamentally unworthy position of the Apologists; and influenced by apologetic considerations he looked at Christianity and framed his statements about Christianity for the sake of Apologetics.

3. (But only as a third point—it did not really much matter, since the game was already lost.) He let himself be pushed into this mystical-naturalistic corner where the historical in Christianity could play only a questionable role.

If our assumption should be wrong, we could only conclude that in the co-existence of mysticism and cultural religion with Schleiermacher, in the continual shifting from the one to the other, the third motive, the apologetic, is supplementary. We should then have before us a final riddle, perhaps explicable only in the personality of this great, bold, and religious theologian.

Schleiermacher is a force with which one cannot expect to come to terms at a first or second or third attempt. I should like to have this summary of his thought accepted not as my 'settlement' with him; but in expectation of further attempts at understanding him, as an interim accounting of the present state of my debate with him. I believe that I am in agreement with my friend Emil Brunner when I consider our common controversy with this man as a running battle. I would continue it as such.

VI

THE WORD IN THEOLOGY FROM
SCHLEIERMACHER TO RITSCHL

A lecture given in the second Theological Week of the Reformed Association in Elberfeld, Wednesday, 19th October 1927. The theme of this
Theological Week was the problem of the Word in theology from the
Reformation to the present time. At the conclusion, a few addresses dealing with practical implications of doctrine were presented. The main
theme was divided among a great number of participants. It is perhaps
unnecessary to say as preface that what is said in this paper concerning
the individual theologians of the period assigned to me is not intended in
the least as an evaluation of their work and their personalities as a whole
but only as a brief presentation of their relation to this particular problem. The problem is certainly fundamental.

THE problem of the Word (that is, of course, the Word of God) in
theology I understand to be the question of whether and how far
theology recognizes its obligation of directing Christian preaching to the
repetition in human words of what is said to men through God himself
about God, in distinction to all which man can say to himself about God.
It is my task today to discuss briefly whether and how far this consciousness of obligation was present or not present in the German Protestant
theology of the first half of the nineteenth century.

Two considerations determine the answer to the question of whether
the concept of the Word governs or does not govern a theology, i.e.
whether a theology knows or does not know that Christian preaching is
a human iteration of that which man had let God say to him. The first
is concerned with the concept of contemporary Christian man. Does he,
precisely as a Christian man, stand confronted by the truth of God,
confronted by it continually as a truth which must really come to him
new every morning, as to one who does not know it and who therefore
listens to it, not as its master but as its obedient servant? Is his knowledge
of it therefore an acknowledgement of its authority? Or does he not
stand so confronted by it? Is it unnecessary that it come to him, since

he already knows and possesses it because it is or has become in some way his own? Does he merely have to remind himself of it? Can he dispose of it as he disposes of himself or at least thinks he can dispose of himself?

In the first case, he allows himself to be told by God whatever is needful. In the second case, he says to himself whatever is necessary. Theology must choose. That is the psychological side of the question.

But the decision depends simultaneously on a second consideration, on the conception of the relation between the truth of God and history. Does the truth of God confront man also in history? Does it stand there as a reality which is different from man himself and which can really confront him? Does it convey a knowledge which man can in no way create and establish for himself, the givenness of which is demonstrated every moment because it is given him not by his own knowing, although and while it is given *for* his knowing, but is given through his being known by it and in it? Is the revelation history because and while it pleases God to reveal himself in history? And is this divine 'pleasure' a problem which man could never for an instant be in a position to consider solved? Or is history revelation because and while it pleases man so to consider history, to set God firmly in the history and to have him there, firmly fixed? Has man access to the truth of God in history, as he has or thinks he has access to history in general, by interpreting history in the light of the truth which is within himself or which becomes his?

In the first case, he lets himself be told truth. In the second case, he tells himself what truth is while he takes a tour through history. Theology must give its decision here. This is the historical side of the question.

Obviously, I have here presented only the difference between the subjective and the objective side of the same question and answer. On both sides, the important point is whether there is an encounter between God and man, an encounter which could never conceivably be interrupted except by God; or whether man is conceived as possessing by nature or by acquisition the power himself to end this encounter.

The theology of the first half of the nineteenth century which I am to discuss is (to state my conclusion at the outset), in the characteristic line of its work, theology of the second kind. Against this position there was both an apparent and a real protest. We shall speak of both. But on the whole (the apparent and the real exceptions prove the rule), the decision significant for the historical picture of the period was to ascribe to man, more or less confidently, power over God—or it is better to say, over *a* god. Power over a 'god within man' himself who then turns out to be identical with a 'god in history'.

Therefore the theology of this period instructed the Christian preacher that man was in the position to seek, find and possess the truth of God in his own Christian consciousness or in history, that the preacher in the pulpit therefore had to say not what was said to him but what he himself could, might or ought to say. That is what in this period was called the Word of God.

I

We shall first present the position of this theology in one of its purest and most unambiguous manifestations. The preaching of the divine Word is, according to Schleiermacher, with whom we rightly begin, defined briefly and clearly as 'the selfcommunication' of the preacher.[1] The truth to which the sermon must bear witness is the empirically given reality of the life existing beyond knowing and action in the feeling of men incorporated in the Christian community. This ineffable life is expounded in the form of speech (most inadequately— music would be better) with the aim of instilling its own energizing force, which can then be turned outward to the necessary work of culture. That is the purpose of preaching; and preaching is to be done by those who by nature, education, and practice are or ought to be virtuosos in the art.

This life, the highest peak of our consciousness, streams as a 'corporate life' through the Christian Church of all ages and localities. But it has been only once fully individualized; the highest individualization of the higher human life was complete in the Christian revelation in Jesus of Nazareth. As the original fact and impulse, and as the continuing bringer, inspirer, mediator, and achiever of this highest life, which is potentially present in all men, he is called the Redeemer.

But what he had in astonishing measure, we also have. He awakens it in us, establishes it, and completes it. He receives us into the power of his God-consciousness and into his untroubled blessedness. This is his redeeming work for us; and in as much as he was fitted for this work, God was in him as in no other man. The divine is given in consciousness and given in history.

Any distinction other than the relative difference between the subjective and the objective moment of the same life, the life of which

[1] *Gl.L.*, § 133.

every man knows himself to be master, Schleiermacher does not admit. Holy Scripture, the witness to the Redeemer, is subject to the judgement of the 'corporate spirit' on the question of whether and how far it is Holy Scripture. Its witness is therefore not the basis but the result of faith.[1]

And Dogmatics can properly be nothing except 'doctrine of faith' (*Glaubenslehre*), that is, the branch of church knowledge in which the self-representation of the Christianity current at a given time is brought into a scientific system. Schleiermacher's man does not need to listen; and he has not listened. He stands under an influence; he experiences an excitation. Apart from that, there is nothing new for him to hear. And so as preacher he has nothing to say except what he himself can say to himself.

After hearing the voice of Schleiermacher, it is informative to listen to his younger contemporary, the rationalist Julius Augustus Ludwig Wegscheider, who at the time was much more read and had a much greater influence. What for Schleiermacher was the mysterious datum of life received through feeling, was for Wegscheider the pellucid datum of the right (*recta*) or sound reason (*sana ratio*), released by God's Providence from the ancient darkness of the Church through the higher culture (*aevum cultior*) of the new era that completes the Reformation.

This theoretical and practical reason in its unity is source, authority, and touchstone (*lapis Lydius*) for Christian truth. In the positive religions, it *can* speak distinctly. In Christianity it *does* so speak, since in the Bible, along with much that is recognizable as divine accommodation, or human misunderstanding, or even as simply myth-making, there is also a 'form of purer religion' (*typus purioris religionis*). Such portions, 'which are easily understood, are best suited to instruct and calm men's minds'.[2] And Christ, out of whom the foolishness of his adherents wanted to make more than man, has validated himself as the 'divine messenger' (*legatus divinus*) and the 'prototype of men who are to become imbued with true religion and virtue'.[3] Through 'his superlative genius, far removed from all fantasy', through his moral purity and through the goodness of his purpose, he has put the whole human race in his debt.[4]

Schleiermacher was very right when he warned against driving away from the Church 'the estimable men who are called rationalists'; for he himself would have had to leave! Although Wegscheider and his

[1] *Gl.L.*, §§ 128–9.
[2] *Instit. Dogm.*, 2nd ed., p. 105.
[3] Ibid., p. 277.
[4] Ibid., p. 122.

like were only pettifoggers and merely touched the surface (this one cannot say of Schleiermacher), yet the design they drew is unmistakably the same as his in principle. It was constructed on the same assumption that man is the measure of all things. Wegscheider merely says more frankly that he has no intention of allowing himself to be told anything because he already knows it all better.

I take as the second independent theologian to compare with Schleiermacher one of the many forgotten men of the period, Wilhelm Martin Leberecht De Wette. He is undeservedly forgotten, because, apart from his merit as a historian, he anticipated as a systematic theologian what came to deserved honour in the second half of the century through Lipsius, Auguste Sabatier, Herrmann, and Troeltsch. He called his theological project 'critical anthropology', connecting it with Jacobi and Fries. It could also be called 'theology of faith', since for him everything revolved around the concept of faith. He could express and affirm the ideas, images, and symbols of faith as such with the sympathetic art of a Herder.

De Wette, influenced by Kant, saw the theologian's difficulty more plainly than did Schleiermacher and Wegscheider. He realized that the theoretical and practical reason had no windows open towards God. He saw the boundary which was overstepped every time man undertook to speak of God. But in the end he did propose such a window, though a very modest one, in a particular power of the human reason which he called, in agreement with Fries, the power of 'divination' (*Ahnung*), on the basis of which man can have faith. Faith means, according to De Wette, to lose one's self in the eternal life of the spirit, which in enthusiasm, self-denial, and worship can reach God, who is unattainable by the reason and the will. Thus by faith (and for De Wette that meant faith 'in Christ') is achieved what is without faith impossible, the actualization or the fulfilment of the ideas of human reason. True humanity is attained.

By thus making both a distinction and a connexion between a religious a-priori and its concrete Christian actualization, De Wette thought he could give due place not only to philosophy and theology, but also to Rationalism and Supernaturalism, and even within theology itself to Pelagianism and Augustinianism. He could reconcile them mutually with one another and at the same time erect the bulwark of Apologetics. Theology demonstrates the possibility of salvation in the human situation, the necessity for it in human need, finally its actuality in human experience. Certainly De Wette stated the problem more clearly than Schleiermacher and expressed more plainly their common view that 'theology of faith' can only be a theology of the man who has nowhere to go outside of himself.

In this connexion, we should consider the most influential of Schleiermacher's pupils, Alexander Schweizer of Zürich. His significance for our problem lies in the fact that, more explicitly than his teacher, he made 'the Christian experience of the contemporary Church' a valid source of truth. Schweizer knew that faith arises from hearing and seeing; that is, according to him, from hearing and seeing the experiences of life which others have.[1] He was confident that in the Church's present consciousness of faith (which according to him, as to Wegscheider, is to be accepted from the hand of Providence as it now is) are included not only the truth of the Bible, of church creeds, of theological tradition, but also the elements of truth in the Enlightenment, in culture and in philosophy. We have there a corpus of objective material, the subjective appropriation of which is the business of individual faith.[2] Since we are good Protestants continually purifying ourselves more and more from all elements of Judaism and paganism, we are implicitly (*implicite*) also good Christians; and as such we are again implicitly good religious people in general.[3]

We shall not be able to discover, and Schleiermacher himself would certainly not find, any deviation from the line of his own teaching involved in this enriching of his point of view by the introduction of the objective content of this present objective moment. Almost no one who has chosen this path has been more certain of his position on the psychological as well as on the historical side than was Alexander Schweizer.

II

In this second section we shall consider the emergence of an apparent —but only apparent—protest against Schleiermacher's road. Three groups come into view: the 'Awakening' theologians, the theological Hegelians of the right and the so-called Biblicists. The significant fact is that not only the Hegelians, but also the Awakening theologians and the Biblicists were fundamentally in heart and soul one with Schleiermacher and his adherents, at least so far as concerns our topic, the Word.

The Awakening theology proclaimed itself with no little pathos as a renewal of the Reformation theology. I intend to show by examples

---

[1] *Gl.L.*, I, § 12.   [2] Ibid., I, § 17.   [3] Ibid., I, §§ 34 f.

taken from Tholuck and Richard Rothe that at least in relation to the problem of the Word this claim is not true.

Tholuck differs from Schleiermacher as a real flower from a painted. The 'excitement' of which Schleiermacher could say so much has with young Tholuck at least become personal. Speaking is to be *out of* feeling, *out of* experience, instead of *about* feeling and experience. Out of 'the heart', out of 'the mind', says Tholuck himself; or if, ascending to the choir loft, he cites Plato, out of the 'divine frenzy' *(μανία)*, out of the 'divine inspiration' *(θεῖος ἐνθουσιασμός)*. What is this? we ask in astonishment. Is there anything of that kind in Christianity? Does the author of that awesome book on Sin and the Saviour know anything of this kind? He himself answers, 'Yes'; and precisely in that book. 'The spirit as spirit has as the foundation of all its manifestations an immediate being, which is given forth from within, the life in God';[1] 'the aliveness of the original truth *(ἀλήθεια)* in man'.[2] Man is in the position to seek 'to penetrate ever father' into the Spirit of God, 'for that Spirit is akin to him; he can seek to take possession of it, to understand it. And this understanding becomes equivalent to the appropriation of the beloved object, to a passing over into it. What happens here is not really different from what occurs in every act of living understanding.'[3]

Is this position really essentially different, so far as content is concerned, from De Wette's, for example? What use is all the terrifying talk of sin, at least for theology, if it is still true for Tholuck even in his sermons that all revolves around 'the ability to experience', the human capacity for experiencing; if the miracle and the dialectic of this theology is simply the miracle and the dialectic of the human heart—of the inspired, the enthusiastic, the awakened heart but, for flesh is still flesh, still the human heart? What use is the rediscovery of Anselm's doctrine of the atonement and of Luther's doctrine of justification if the result is advice to concern one's self more than ever with one's self, with man?

It was certainly worth while for Tholuck to bring to the front again the great objectivity of the old Dogmatics. But strangely enough that did not interfere with the theme which chiefly occupied him throughout his life as theologian. Certainly the most influential concept which he offered to countless others was the religious subject, himself, August Tholuck. The 'victory of faith' which was celebrated at the Golden

---

[1] *Lehre von der Sünde und vom Versöhner*, 8th ed., p. 151.
[2] Ibid., p. 165.   [3] Ibid., p. 159.

Jubilee of his promotion at Halle was *his* victory, the victory of *his* faith (quite apart from the worldly aspect of this affair). Yet these words were once written to this much-admired theologian from among the circle of his own friends: 'Beloved Professor. . . . You ought to have drawn a sharp line between faith and the conclusions of reason. . . . You ought to have said that faith in Christ our Saviour is purely and wholly a gift of God. . . . If I am to speak out: in the doctrine of the Holy Spirit you are not entirely correct.'[1]

'Not entirely correct' is a mild expression for Tholuck's failure to draw that 'sharp line'. However much Genesis 3 and Romans 7 might be honoured, he did not draw that line. In fact, he saw it as little as did his 'unawakened' contemporaries.

Tholuck's companion on the left, Richard Rothe (along with others), exemplifies another position to which the Awakening theology could lead. Rothe is the more worth attention as an example of the purified Christian personality even more sensitively organized. Also, among the theologians of that century he was to an extraordinary degree loved and honoured by many men with differing points of view, not so much for his doctrine as for himself, for his own personality.

Rothe is interesting in our context because in his Christian consciousness of self and God, which for him also is 'the fountain of truth' (*fons veritatis*), the pietistic certainty of re-birth reveals at once and very radically its identity with the actual modern consciousness of culture. Without being forced to break with his pietistic youth, Rothe can accept Schleiermacher's programme and can subordinate Biblical Exegesis and Dogmatics to Ethics as the science central to Theology.

It is Ethics which can speak with certainty on God, world, and men. Rothe can with friendly understanding affirm the 'unconscious Christianity' of the modern cultivated man as holy. And to the Church he can preach the immanent, gentle dissolution of the Church in the State which is becoming more and more the Church. In this he saw no contradiction of the Awakening theology, but rather its honestly drawn consequence. If there is no encounter between God and man (and the Awakening theology developed the concept of that encounter as little as did Schleiermacher), then there seemed to be no reason why the relative contradiction between believing and non-believing, between Church and State should not cease, why the Pietist should not—as Rothe himself did—wake up one morning inside the Protestant Union.

The theology of the Awakening appears to be a departure from the

---

[1] Witte, *Das Leben Tholucks*, I, pp. 328 f.

classical theology of the century as represented by Schleiermacher and his adherents, at least in so far as the activity of the Christian subject seemed much more vital in it than was allowable for Schleiermacher and his like. Certainly in the form of a revival of Augustinian and Reformation thinking, the hold upon the Christian object (without which Schleiermacher neither could nor would proceed) was apparently much stronger with them. But the Awakening theology is only an *apparent* departure from Schleiermacher's line. It put the religious man in the centre of theology much more consistently and much more emphatically than Schleiermacher had done; and it added the weight of a real not just a painted enthusiasm. But then it was obliged to discover, if it was wholly honest, as it was in Rothe, that the religious man looked terribly like modern man in general.

The second group of apparent opponents consisted of the right-wing Hegelians. I shall take as an example Philip Konrad Marheineke, the somewhat belligerent Berlin colleague of Schleiermacher. In him also we find a more intense activity of the subject, in comparison with Schleiermacher, and consequently a bolder grasp on the object; but both occur in the sphere of the intellect rather than being expressed in emotional terms. The relation of this group to the first group can be seen in the fact that Tholuck, as a student in Berlin, could discover no point of contact either in Schleiermacher's lectures or his sermons; but with Marheineke's lectures of 1818 he found himself 'extremely moved'. With 'blessed certainty' he understood Marheineke's purpose as 'to be wholly in Jesus', and 'with infinite emotion, finally, finally' obtained a sight of 'the only shore where I could be saved'.[1]

Actually, just as something of the Augustinian, Lutheran religious experience could later be recognized in Tholuck; so with Marheineke, if the reader does not let himself be frightened by the heavy Hegelian phraseology, he can find something which might be a concept of revelation (as it could never be found in Schleiermacher). Marheineke knows that real faith is faith in authority;[2] that man cannot discover, cannot invent religion, but can only re-think it.[3] And even then he re-thinks it only 'as in a mirror', since by revelation alone is the possibility of God established in reason.[4]

'In the human spirit, God is not accessible through [any activity of] the human spirit; but through the act of God himself. Therefore God manifests himself to men. The human spirit as reason is abolished

[1] Ibid., I, pp. 103 f.   [2] *Dogm. als Wissenschaft*, §§ 30 f.
[3] Ibid., § 32.   [4] Ibid., §§ 24 f.

in him. This is the hardest demand which theological science makes on all who are engaged in it, that the pure substance is to show itself as subject; the theologian with his spirit is to submit himself and be passive.'[1] The thinking (*cogitare*) of the dogmatic theologian follows upon the compulsion (*cogere*) of the revelation.[2]

These are important and significant statements. However, the context in which they stand unfortunately leaves no doubt that the encounter of God and man, the 'let it be said' which for a moment seemed to have become visible, is only a phase of the dialectic process. And this phase is presently surmounted by another in which we find that the relation of God and man just depicted is a completely reversible relation. In the pure concept man in himself comprehends God, even as he knows himself to be comprehended by God. Because God became man in Jesus Christ, according to Luther's understanding, our thinking about God is throughout the thinking of God himself.

It is no accident, therefore, that for Marheineke also when theology concerns itself with the Bible and with the historic doctrine of the Church, such concern can have only supplementary and corroborating significance. It can be only a matter of repetition, or of analysis of the content of faith.[3]

The clearest conceptual knowledge concerning what revelation is now promotes not the triumph of the human heart as with Tholuck, but instead the triumph of the human head. (There is therefore no real difference from the pietistic grasp for the object.) The result carried to the extreme is to set the clever theologian on a chair high above God and himself. Seated there, after he has digested the correct concept of revelation as a giant snake digests a rabbit, he really cannot let anything further be said.

We turn now to the third group mentioned, the so-called Biblicists. The beginning is promising. Open the Bible again! (Who will not remember what was done by the Reformers three hundred years earlier?) The Bible and only the Bible must give theology its right content. Will this great revolution now attain to a 'letting it be said'? Will God now stand in his place and man in his without a possibility of the reversal of their relation which was accomplished in the rest of the theology of the day? (Marheineke let that secret slip out to us.) Who can doubt that the subject now makes a strong, bold, and quite promising grasp upon the object?

But there is still the question of whether in this attempt something

[1] Ibid., § 115.   [2] Ibid., § 26.   [3] Ibid., § 116.

new has happened in distinction to Schleiermacher and his group, to the Awakening theologians and the Hegelians, all of whom certainly intended to give honour to the Bible. Or did the Biblicists after all only venture to rely on the Bible after they had first satisfied themselves as to the grounds for such reliance and as to its feasibility ? The real question is whether the supposed object becomes visible as subject, as Marheineke correctly defined it; a subject in relation to which man can take no position of mastery, which he will respect as a real subject, and which therefore he will never in any way change back into an object which would be at his disposal. That question must be asked, but it is not answered by the fact that theologians now began to busy themselves systematically with the Bible.

It is noticeable that the three great representatives of the movement, G. Menken, J. T. Beck, and J. Chr. R. von Hofmann, were all highly gifted men, original thinkers who allowed little to be said to them by other men; and that the enthusiasm with which they threw themselves upon the Bible had certainly some structural likeness to the enthusiasm with which other men rushed upon all sorts of other things in that decade of intellectual excitement. It was said of the young Menken in significant phrasing, 'He was possessed to create his Christianity from the Bible alone.'[1]

But it is indicative that the category under which the Biblicists investigated the Bible was history. Whoever says history is not yet saying revelation, nor Word of God as the Reformers called the Bible, nor the subject to which man must submit himself with no possibility of becoming its master. He has not said it even if, like the Biblicists, he says salvation-history. The appeal to the objective in history can mean that the human subject has the idea of undertaking an excursion from which he returns to himself newly strengthened and supported, but without allowing the least word to be said to him. History can be observed, manipulated, interpreted (and all this also holds for salvation-history) as if one had power over it. The Word of God is the covenant of God with men in the actual process of fulfilment. To call it the history of salvation is to view this covenant as already fulfilled, as an event finished like other events.

Why were the Biblicists interested in the Bible as salvation-history ? Why did they take the road of Coccejus and not the road of Calvin, who sought in the Bible doctrine ('*doctrina*') and still more doctrine ? At this point our scrutiny inevitably becomes suspicion. How does it

[1] Gildemeister, *Leben und Wirken des Dr Gottfried Menken*, II, p. 7.

happen that the Biblicists, exactly like Schleiermacher and his group, vie with one another in fighting against the concept of doctrine? Why is their high evaluation of the Bible connected, by Menken and Beck most explicitly, with a delight in emphasizing Anti-confessionalism? Their depreciation of so-called orthodoxy as such is often expressed in terms surprisingly similar to those of their non-Biblicist contemporaries. The Biblicism of the Reformation when it appealed to the Bible never thought of setting itself up as sovereign over the authority of the Church. The authority of the Church, although relative, was nevertheless to be taken seriously. But for Menken and Beck, superiority over the Church plainly was almost the principal element in what they called obedience to the Bible.

Does such an attitude give any indication that here the human subject is really willing to let everything be said to him instead of saying everything himself? What does it really imply to want to begin ecclesiastical and dogmatic history on one's own, at a desk with the open Bible?

But suspicion becomes certainty, the whole situation is clarified, when we recognize that these men, in spite of and along with the biblical theology, and notwithstanding the many valuable insights we owe them, have all by-passed the doctrine of justification by faith alone. If man's situation in relation to God is really such (as Menken and Beck allegedly discovered in the Bible) that his justification is a communication of his own righteousness to him, there is nothing surprising in the certainty of these men that by means of the same Bible they can bring the truth of God into a system of knowledge, by reproducing what is given in the same way that natural science proceeds. (So Beck specifically said.) Thus they develop a history of God and man which includes heaven and earth, as Ranke's student, Hofmann, thought he could do in his 'Scriptural Proof'.

Such knowledge is not created out of the Word of God, even if it is introduced by thousands of biblical quotations. It is, exactly as with the non-Biblicists, the knowledge possessed by the Christian subject who makes himself master of the Bible. This is not a reproach which *I* make; it is the opinion of Hofmann himself. He says quite plainly: 'The essential knowledge of any matter is not attained by the historical method. We must ask whether the result of the historical investigation is consistent with what is attained on systematic grounds.' [1]

The scriptural proof serves as a supplementary corroboration. It

[1] *Enzyklopädie*, p. 26.

proves what the Christian already knows without it. 'Theology is an independent science only if that which makes a Christian to be a Christian, his independent relation to God, is also what makes the theologian to be a theologian in scientific self-knowledge and self-expression. It is an independent science only if I, the Christian, am the most basic material of my science for myself as a theologian. Of course, I am what I am as a Christian only because of the activity of the Church. . . . But what makes me a Christian is not merely the presence of Christ actively using the community and its activity. The relation to God, after I have become a partaker in it, has begun in me an independent existence, which does not depend on the Church or on the Scripture on which the Church itself rests. This relation to God therefore does not have the guarantee of its truth from the Church or from the Scripture; the guarantee rests in the relation itself and is immediate truth, carried and guaranteed by the spirit inherent in it.' [1]

Schleiermacher did not state more precisely the idea that Christianity lies at the disposal of the theologian in his own believing self than did Beck when he said 'the substance of Christian doctrine which becomes to man a spiritual possession and becomes dynamically immanent in him'.[2] If this is accepted, then even Biblicism is very far from 'letting it be said'. To do that, other and very different presuppositions must prevail among Christian men.

III

In this final section, we shall concern ourselves with a few theologians of whom it must be said that they really saw the ambiguity in the dominant theology and really protested against the road it was taking. None of them, however, was able to halt the steadily rolling wagon—it continued to roll even in the second half of the century.

The first two such men of whom I think are two publicans and sinners—indeed, both were unrepentant publicans and sinners—who are mentioned in the usual accounts of theology only with head-shaking and horror: Ludwig Feuerbach and D. F. Strauss. The contributions of both of them to our problem come, in fact, not from love but from hatred of Church and theology. But the good God has many times used such Assyrians and Babylonians for calling Jerusalem to order. And whoever is awake to such possibilities and looks at the matter fairly cannot deny that the contributions of these two men, however wrong they may have been otherwise, have been important and valuable contributions.

---

[1] *Schriftbeweis*, I, pp. 10 f.   [2] *Einleitung*, § 8.

Feuerbach attacked theology from the psychological side. He used against it the slogan *Anthropology*, which De Wette had purposely employed, and undertook to show that consistently with that label, religion had its origin really and unambiguously from men. He stripped its object, its God (about whom anyhow the theologians spoke only very softly and in secondary connexions) of all apparent transcendence and set him in the place where the theologians were accustomed (first and last) to seek and find him, in the human heart. That was the original and the only place where he is and has truth. All beyond that, all which is concerned with a transcendent reality of religion, he explained as illusion, as the product of the desires and fears, the ideals and abhorrences of the human heart. There can be no encounter. There is nothing to come to us. There is no question which we do not put to ourselves and no answer which we do not give to ourselves. There is nothing, nothing at all which we need to have said to us. All, all is in ourselves!

Had not the theologians really said exactly the same thing with their whole attitude towards divine truth? Of course, they had not so intended it. But from the approach of Schleiermacher *and* Wegscheider *and* De Wette *and* the Awakening theologians *and* the Hegelians *and* the Biblicists it was impossible to show how anything other than what Feuerbach asserted had been intended. Feuerbach 'did not believe in God', as we say. But at least he had an understanding of the truth that the God of his theological contemporaries, who was conjectured on the authority of the religious man, had better for honesty's sake be entirely stripped of all the superhuman predicates with which they wanted to furnish him. Man should come wholly to himself and remain with himself.

The question was asked by a godless man, but it was asked. And a truly penetrating Christian judgement on the nineteenth century, instead of crossing itself with horror at the idea, should regard the asking of just this question so pointedly as one of the few wholly satisfactory achievements of the period.

The attack by D. Strauss was directed against the historical aspect of theology and asked the question with equal definiteness. The theologians supposed that they could seek and find the road to the 'God in history' as easily as to the 'God in us'. So Strauss only took them at their word: man has the power to know God in history. If through the thinking ability which is given to him as man, man knows what is given in history, then, Strauss objected, man does not at all know *God* in history. For it will be necessary (this is only one important example) to reckon

the Gospel with its miracles as an unreliable source for the establishment of historical fact, and to recognize that any historical kernel in
the account is at least questionable. The historical Jesus is an entity
which cannot be discovered with any certainty in the fog of what historical
science must call myth. Finally, the whole picture of an historical individual who should at the same time be an Absolute must be seen to be
an inconceivable construction, viewed historically and scientifically.

This has a horrid sound, but Strauss has only taken seriously what
the theologians before him and after him continually claimed to be
doing. He has treated the Bible as history instead of as Word of God, and
has shown that then it is impossible to get any hold on God, on a real
God, in the Bible. The question was stated, and there was again
ground for hope that since the question was so asked, the theologians
might perceive that what they thought they had at their disposal is, even
on the objective side, not God but something human—all too human.

If we turn now from the Assyrians and Babylonians back to those
within Jerusalem itself, two names at least ought to be mentioned.
There were two men who, without departing on the whole very far from
the main highway, have at single points raised a strong and true protest
against the theological spirit of the time.

I think of Vilmar of Marburg, with his reminder that the Church is
not only and not primarily a community of believers, but is also and is
primarily an institution whose supporters have something to say not on
the basis of their religious subjectivity but as revelation empowers them
to speak. One cannot have Christ apart from his teaching Church. It is
perhaps of interest that the reproach brought by me against the
Biblicists was in its main points already raised against them by Vilmar.

And I think of Julius Müller of Halle, who in his well-known mono-
graph on sin, struck forcibly at the point where the distanceless Monism
of the dominant theology could not be carried through, or rather the
point where it identified itself as the attempt to climb on its own
shoulders in an effort to see over itself. If that effort ceases, if man can
no longer in his thought combine himself the sinner and God into one,
then the assumption becomes possible—or a new assumption may be
made—that man can let something be said to him by God. It is not
without reason that the 'sin-Müller' was one of the few German theologians of whom Kierkegaard spoke with respect.

Further, there was one man who saw the wounds of Israel in an
inclusive fashion and gave important directions for their healing,
although he attracted astonishingly little attention—Isaac Augustus

Dorner. (I shall omit all in which he paid tribute to his own time—who does not so pay?) But I think I am not mistaken when I say that Dorner saw far beyond his time and saw with full understanding precisely in the area of our problem. He knew that faith, the century's darling concept, is merely a point of mediation.[1] Faith is not the foundation, not the basis of truth. Faith is 'a subjective principle of knowing' (*principium cognoscendi subjectivum*) opposite to which stands an 'objective principle of knowing' (*principium cognoscendi objectivum*), the Bible. Not the Bible as history, but the Bible as authentic witness of Christ, as truly canon.[2]

Dorner knew that Christian truth is not dependent on experience, that its basis is in itself, as classically formulated in the doctrine of the Trinity; that this doctrine, contrary to the opinion not only of the modern age, but also to certain statements of the Reformers, could not possibly be surrendered. He knew of God in Christ and in the Holy Spirit as Christianity's sole 'principle of being' (*principium essendi*).He gave warning against the deification of faith, derived from Luther, of faith which could be a faith without an object; against the 'apotheosis of churched humanity', as we found it practised most typically by Alexander Schweizer; and against confusing the continuing work of the ascended Lord with a mere (historical!) after-effect. And again going back of the Reformation, he knew that theology must admit a wholly different eschatological orientation, if it did not want every supposed turn from subject to object to be a mere 'running in place'. The time is coming when men will be surprised—or perhaps will *not* be surprised—that Dorner could be ignored for Ritschl.

One more name remains to be mentioned, a name which to this day rings no bell in the Universities. I speak now of Hermann Franz Kohlbrügge, not as a gesture of respect for the *genius loci* of Elberfeld, but because he belongs here, because in the section of theological history which I have to discuss, he offers the brightest and best gleam of hope.

Why does he belong here? Because, wholly unlike his famous contemporaries, he knew and asserted a very simple truth. He said again and again with the greatest persistence, that God's grace which makes a Christian to be a Christian is free grace and always remains (on this everything rests) free grace. The Christian has no claim upon it, no certainty of it; he does not possess it. It is grace which, no matter how one may twist and turn, in every relation, as justification, as salvation, objectively and subjectively, is grace and remains grace.

[1] *Ges. Schr.*, p. 32.   [2] *Gl.L.*, I, §§ 157, 162.

Where this truth is understood, there the solution of the problem of the Word, so sought after by the dominant theology of that era, is basically achieved. The solution rests on the presupposition that the grace, which the theologians of the time could describe so beautifully as free, did not remain free for them. They claimed it as a right, a certainty, a possession of the Christian, the so-called believing Christian. If they were right, if the truth lies in the Semi-Pelagianism which entered Protestant theology in the eighteenth century by the double open door of Rationalism and Pietism, and which achieved in Schleiermacher a triumph such as it had scarcely won in the Middle Ages, then the unassailable solution of the problem is: the Christian is a man who has already heard God and can always hear him again. The problem of the Word is decided by the problem of grace.

If Kohlbrügge was right that there is no being a Christian except by being a lost sinner who can never stand before God otherwise than as one who has heard nothing and can hear nothing, then the possibility of a different solution could at least be visible, the possibility that God himself alone does God's work, that he alone speaks.

VII

LUDWIG FEUERBACH

An extract from lectures on the history of modern theology given at Münster in the summer of 1920.

W E might question what place there is for Feuerbach in a history of theology. In the annals of philosophy, Feuerbach is never once classed with the idealists, but is put regularly into the section with the sensualists, the positivists, and even the materialists—in the section apparently farthest removed from theology. Feuerbach was the man who urged anti-theology with a passion equalled by few of his contemporaries.

But I would begin by calling attention to three facts:

1. Among the philosophers of modern times there is perhaps no other who occupied himself so intensively and so exclusively with the problem of theology as did Feuerbach—although the love which motivated him was a frustrated love. He himself once said positively and bluntly, 'All my writings have, to speak accurately, only one purpose, one will, one theme; and this theme is truly religion and theology with all that depends thereon.' [1]

2. Feuerbach, in his work—especially in all which was concerned with the Bible, the Church Fathers and particularly with Luther—, showed himself to possess a theological knowledge which sets him far above the majority of modern philosophers.

3. None of the other philosophers in his time penetrated so far into the theological position; said so little that was extraneous to it and so much that was exactly pertinent to theology itself as did Feuerbach. And I will add that the position of Feuerbach the anti-theologian was more theological than that of many theologians, since in strict adherence to the old, accepted theological content, he wanted to say, not many things, but *one* thing with a tenacity which did not fear a thousand repetitions. And not so much *desired* to say it—rather by a kind of prophetic inspiration he felt himself forced to say it. He could not refrain from proclaiming the antithesis to all theology—an antithesis no

[1] R, p. 3. (See page 218, note 3.)

better grounded in philosophy than was theology itself; perhaps we might say an antithesis which could be grounded only theologically.

Feuerbach's teaching was essentially a summons, an appeal, a proclamation. If by his determination to give that summons, he did not forfeit his own skin, he did certainly sacrifice once and for all his academic career. If this tenacity and its penalty bring him humanly closer to us, it is equally true that the content of his anti-theology demonstrates the crucial importance of one possibility within the problem of the new theology. And that possibility so sharply illuminates all the other possibilities that we should miss something decisive for us theologically if we refused to let him speak to us here, on the ground that he did not outwardly belong to our guild and had done it so much harm. Who knows whether it ought not to be said that he belonged inwardly and truly to the guild of the new Protestant theology as legitimately as anyone else?

Ludwig Feuerbach (the uncle of the painter Anselm Feuerbach) was born at Landeshut in 1804. (He was an elder contemporary of J. T. Beck.) He studied under Daub in Heidelberg and after 1824 under Hegel in Berlin. He became instructor (*Privatdozent*) at Erlangen in 1828, but soon withdrew to private teaching and study. After 1860 he lived on the Rechenberg near Nuremberg. He died in 1872.

Here today we are concerned with three of his books: *Das Wesen des Christentums* (*The Essence of Christianity*),[1] 1841; *Philosophie der Zukunft* (*Philosophy of the Future*),[2] 1843; and *Das Wesen der Religion* (*The Essence of Religion*),[3] 1851, thirty lectures given in Heidelberg in 1848.

Feuerbach summarized his aim at the close of those Heidelberg lectures. (It was then that Gottfried Keller among others sat at his feet.)[4] That aim was 'to transform his hearers from friends of God to

---

[1] Critical edition by K. Quenzel, Reklams Universalbibliothek. Cited as C. English translation by Marian Evans (George Eliot), Harper Torchbooks, 1957. Cited as E.

[2] Edited with notes by H. Ehrenberg in *Frommanns philosophische Taschenbücher*, I, 2, Stuttgart, 1922. Cited as P.

[3] *Volksausgabe* (Popular edition), Leipzig, Alfred Kröner. Cited as R.

[4] In this context, 'Der gefrorener Christ' (The Frozen Christ) in the fourth volume of *Der Grüne Heinrich* is worth reading. Feuerbach is called there (he is even named), 'the philosopher who simply turns these questions around and around in classically monotonous but passionate phrases which are wholly understandable to the average intelligence. And like the magic bird in the lonely bush, he sings God away from the hearts of thousands . . . [He was] the great friend of God, if one may dare to so call him either ironically or in earnest, who throughout his whole life could never separate himself from his beloved.' Also 'Das verlorene Lachen' (The Lost Laugh) in the second volume of the *Leute von Seldwyla* can only be understood from Feuerbach.

friends of man, from believers to thinkers, from beggars to workers, from candidates for the next world into students of this world; to make them whole men instead of Christians who, according to their own confession, are half animals and half angels'.[1] An earlier passage adds the transformation 'from theologians to anthropologists, from religious and political lackeys of heavenly and earthly monarchies and aristocracies to free, responsible citizens of earth'.[2]

Feuerbach was sounding a trumpet-call. (The somewhat demogogic style belongs to the nature of the call itself and should not disturb any reader who really wants to understand him.) He summoned men to turn away from lies to truth, to turn from religious subjects to the religious predicates which alone are meaningful and real; to turn from God to the *world* and *man*, from faith to *love*, from heaven to *earth*, from Christ to *ourselves*, from the bodiless ghosts of supernaturalism to *real life*. 'Actually and truly, I am putting the blessing of real water in the place of the futile water of baptism.'[3]

Water is, in fact, 'the image of selfconsciousness, the image of the human eye . . . the natural mirror of man. In the water a man rids himself unashamed of all mystical wrappings; he trusts himself to the water in his own naked form. In the water all supernatural illusions vanish. So, long ago, the torch of pagan astro-theology was extinguished in the water of Ionian natural philosophy.' [4] Therefore Feuerbach could jestingly call his teaching 'directions for the spiritual water-cure'.[5]

What was Feuerbach's real meaning? The worst of free-thinking, Voltairean Enlightenment, seems to find expression in his words. But no! Feuerbach solemnly and justifiably repudiated the supposition that according to his teaching religion is 'nonsense, nothingness, pure illusion'.[6] That was not his meaning.

Is the healing water, then, perhaps reason's critical self-analysis in the manner of Kant? Or is it the insight into the identity of the infinite and the finite in pure concept according to Hegel? No, it is not that either. As far removed from Hegel as from Kant, Feuerbach belongs among those pupils of the master who scented the theological residuum in his teaching and cast it away. (Schelling's whole teaching was for him

---

[1] R, p. 170.   [2] R, p. 14.   [3] C, p. 45; E, p. xl.   [4] C, pp. 29, 395 f.
[5] C, p. 28. Compare with this, in the tale of Gottfried Keller mentioned above, the account of the habits of Herr Peter Gilgus. 'In spite of the cold season of the year, he plunged into pool or mill-stream to bathe, disregarding observers near or far who saw him naked as he went into or came out of the water. Then, with his face blue from cold and his hair wet, he presented himself as renewed and reborn.'
[6] C, p. 42; E, p. xxxviii.

'the philosophy of a bad conscience', 'the most absurd frivolity', 'this theosophical buffoonery of the philosophical Cagliostro of the nineteenth century.')[1] Feuerbach saw the Kantian and Hegelian philosophy as under exactly the same condemnation as theology. If, in thought, in reason, it abolished the divine essence separated from men, yet it abolished that essence in reason only and at the same time separated it all the more sharply from the world of the senses, from the known world, from man.[2]

And it was *man* whom Feuerbach was determined to help, help him finally to gain his right. Therefore Feuerbach's philosophy had to begin with the sentence: 'I am a sentient being; yes, the body in its totality is my self, my very being.' It will be 'openly a sensuous philosophy'.[3] For 'only where sensation begins, does all doubt and conflict cease. The secret of immediate knowing is sensation'.[4]

Therefore 'the new philosophy has as its first principle of knowledge, for its subject, not the *I* nor the absolute, that is the abstract spirit—in a word not reason in itself alone; but the actual and complete being of man'.[5] 'I hate idealism which rips men out of nature.'[6] 'I am separated by the width of heaven from the philosophers who tear their eyes out of their heads in order to be able to perceive better.'[7] 'The *man* thinks, not the *I*, not the reason. The true and the real is the *human*; only the human being is the reasonable being. Man is the measure of reason.'[8]

'From this follows the categorical imperative: Do not be a philosopher in distinction to a man. Be nothing other than a thinking man. Do not think as a thinker, that is do not think with some faculty torn out of the totality of real human nature, with a real existence of itself. Think as the living, real being that you are, exposed to the quickening waves of the world sea. Think within *existence*, in the world as a part of it; not in the vacuum of abstraction as a solitary monad, nor as an absolute monarch, as an unparticipating God apart from this world. Then you can be sure that your thoughts are unifications of being and thinking.'[9] 'Truth is only the totality of human life and being.'[10] 'Man, that is the human *being*, is the most real being (*ens realissimum*); and not the *I* of Kant and Fichte, nor the absolute identity of Schelling, nor the absolute Mind of Hegel.'[11]

This *being* of man 'is achieved only in community, in the union of man with man—a unity which depends on the reality of the difference

---

[1] C, pp. 50 f.   [2] P, p. 43.   [3] P, p. 72.   [4] P, p. 73.
[5] P, p. 85.   [6] R, p. 21.   [7] C, p. 36; E, p. xxxiv.
[8] P, p. 86.   [9] P, pp. 86 f.   [10] P, p. 91.   [11] C, p. 38; E, p. xxxv.

between *I* and *Thou*'. 'Man with man, the unity of *I* and *Thou*, is God.' 'The true dialectic is not the monologue of a solitary thinker talking to himself, it is a dialogue between *I* and *Thou*.'[1] Feuerbach really means 'Thou and I', as the following passages show. 'An object, a genuine object, is only given me where there is present an entity which has an effect upon me, where my own self-activity—if I start from the thinker's standpoint—finds its limit, meets opposition in the activity of another being. The concept of object is in origin nothing but the concept of another *I*. As a child ascribes a free-acting, voluntary nature to all things, so the concept of the object is mediated by the concept of the *Thou*, the objective *I*.'[2] It is 'the first stumbling-block on which the pride of *I*-ness breaks'; but precisely as such it is 'the bond between me and the world'. 'I become reconciled with, I become friendly to, the world only through other men.'

'A man existing entirely for himself alone would be lost in the ocean of nature without self and would be indistinguishable from the ocean. He would neither know himself as man nor nature as nature.' 'The consciousness of the world is mediated for the *I* through the consciousness of the *Thou*. Hence man is the God of man. That he is, man owes to nature; that he is a *man*, he owes to man.'[3] Also it must be noted that precisely *man* is the object of man's sense-perception.[4] Only as a sentient being am I *I* (for myself) and at the same time *Thou* (for the other man).[5] Sensuous perception includes both inner and outer, spirit and flesh, thing and *I*.[6] Therefore truth, reality, perception—and humanity—are identical.[7] But this identity is being, that is it is being as an object of being, being in actuality; not being in thought. It is a secret of perceiving, of feeling, of love.[8]

The real object of the *head* cannot but be the real object of the *heart*.[9] Therefore the right of the stomach to have its say in high, even in the highest, matters is not to be gainsaid.[10] And so Feuerbach, when forced to it, could resort to the paradox, 'Man is what he eats.' His words have become a byword, for which the brutal interpretation so often accepted is possible only if we overlook the fact (on which, of course, everything depends) that Feuerbach was talking specifically of the *human* stomach and of *human* eating.

This brief glance at Feuerbach's philosophy could not be omitted if we wish really to understand his 'water-cure prescription' with the help

[1] P, p. 41.   [2] P, p. 68.   [3] C, pp. 155 f.; E, p. 83.
[4] P, p. 76.   [5] P, p. 69.   [6] P, p. 76.   [7] P, p. 68.
[8] P, p. 69.   [9] P, p. 90.   [10] P, p. 89.

of which theology is according to him to be healed. Feuerbach's purpose (often ignored in theological accounts of his work) [1] was as positive as that of any other theologian. He was no mere sceptic and negativist. That was only the side he turned towards theologians—and it was not the only side he showed even to them! He said an enthusiastic and impassioned 'Yes'. 'I deny only to affirm; I deny the fantastic phantoms of theology and religion in order to affirm the real being of man.' [2] 'It is true that my writing does deny, but note that it denies only the reality of the non-human, and never denies the human reality in religion.' [3]

Feuerbach put forward a specific doctrine of salvation in which he believed that he was honouring the well-understood interests of theology. I am emphasizing this purpose of his because, in my judgement, this is the only point from which Feuerbach can be critically evaluated. Therefore in considering his proposal to transform theology into anthropology it is necessary for us to hear not only that there must be an end to theology—and this is it—but to hear also on the other side that it is *theology* which Feuerbach himself is determined to transfer to anthropology and so to transform it. 'Although I do bring down theology to anthropology, it is much more true that I am raising anthropology to theology. And the latter is true of Christianity; while it brought God down to man, it made man God.' [4]

Feuerbach was concerned with '*making God real*, with *making him human*', but he was always concerned with *God*.[5] The denial of God as an abstract being, separated from nature and from man 'is only a necessary corollary from the *knowledge of the being of God*'; from the knowledge 'that this being expresses nothing other than on the one side the being of nature and on the other side the being of man'.[6]

In the structure of the book on *The Essence of Christianity*, Feuerbach's thought proceeds very clearly from the *Yes* to the *No*. In Part I, the *true* meaning of theology is presented wholly without polemic as the identity of all predicates of the divine and of the human subject, and the consequent identity of the subjects themselves. Part II moves over to the attack and eliminates as non-existent and as meaning-

---

[1] Cf., for example, B. W. Elert, *Der Kampf um das Christentum*, 1921, pp. 171 f.
[2] R, p. 14.
[3] C, p. 40; E, p. xxxvi. 'It has no relation to atheism or the doctrines of the Free-thinkers, nor with the desire to doubt, nor with world-weariness, nor with any of the spiteful epithets which men have used to label unwholesome things. It is a matter of the right to remain at peace with one's self', asserts the typical Feuerbachian in Gottfried Keller's tale.
[4] C, p. 43; E, p. xxxviii.   [5] P, p. 14.   [6] R, p. 14.

less the distinction between theological and anthropological predicates, and therefore makes an end of theology in the false sense.[1] The passion and the force of the Feuerbachian negation is rooted in the Feuerbachian *positive* position. He who would honestly combat Feuerbach must attack his doctrine of salvation, his positive doctrine of the essence of man as the essence of God. If he is unassailable there, then all criticisms of his negations, of his anti-theology, dwindle to assumption and mere assertions.

Feuerbach himself epitomized his doctrine at the beginning of the third Heidelberg lecture. 'Theology is anthropology, that is to say in the object of religion, in what we call *Theos* in Greek and *Gott* in German, nothing is specified except the essence of man.' [2] But we misunderstand Feuerbach if we see in this 'nothing except' any derogatory implication. The essence of man is exactly what Feuerbach affirmed solemnly and enthusiastically against theology and against idealistic philosophy. When he identified God with the being of man, he paid God the highest honour which he could possibly bestow. It is truly Ludwig Feuerbach's strange *Magnificat* to the beloved God.

Man has the will to live. But in his existence he is dependent, limited, insecure. Hence he has needs and wishes; and on a somewhat higher level, he has ideals. He loves and fears. He covets and denies and rejects. He knows values and detriments. He seeks for means to possess the former and to be rid of the latter. Therefore his life is a struggle and a fight.

But note that Feuerbach was not finding fault with all that. He did not dream of valuing it cheaply; he approved it; he praised it. And he also found it praiseworthy that man hypostasizes, deifies, absolutizes the base, the source, the necessity, the law of this struggle of his, and therefore becomes religious in the most varied ways. 'God is for man the album of his highest feelings and thoughts, the record book where he has entered the names of the being dearest to him and most holy.' [3] Feuerbach respected such feelings, he respected man's nature; but he insisted on examining the contents of the book and on learning from it that there stands in the book only what first stood in the heart of man. He demanded only the honest admission of the fact that the assumed mystery of religion treats only of man. Man *dreams* if he supposes that a second entity standing over against him is that base, that source, that necessity, that law from which his wishes and ideals flow; is the sea of fulfilment towards which they rush—instead of recognizing that it is

[1] C, pp. 48 f.; E, pp. xxxvii f.　　[2] R, p. 10.　　[3] C, p. 132; E, p. 63.

his own being, his will to live and be as a man, which he as a religious man (*homo religiosus*) rightly sets up as an absolute, as a God.

Let us now listen to Feuerbach himself in some characteristic variations on this basic theme. Now then—who or what is 'God', actually ? We have already heard the brief formulation: 'Man and man, union between *I* and *Thou*, is God.' [1] In another passage Feuerbach gave a different and fuller definition. 'God as the totality of all realities or perfections is nothing other than the totality (presented in a compendium for the use of the limited individual) of the qualities of the species which are divided among men and come to realization in the course of the history of the world.' [2]

What is the sense of talking of the essence (*essentia*) of God in negatives only (*via negativa*)—it cannot be spoken of otherwise! 'The divine essence is the human essence illuminated by the death of abstraction. . . . In religion, man frees himself from the limitations of life; here he lets go of all which presses on him, which limits him or affects him adversely. God is man's own consciousness of self, freed from all actualities. Man feels himself free, happy and blessed only in his religion, because only in religion does he live in his genius; there he celebrates his holy day.' [3]

In the *personality* of God, it is self-evident that man celebrates the supernaturalness, the immortality, the independence and limitlessness of his own personality. [4]

What about the *existence* of God ? The desire that God exist is one with the desire that I myself exist, that I exist eternally—so I may be certain of my eternal bliss. God is my hidden, my assured existence. He is the subjectivity of subjects, the personality of persons. [5]

What does the *aseity*, the unoriginateness, of God mean ? What else than an exercise of human thinking in positing an absolute, an absolute beginning, by abstraction from all objects ? [6]

What does God's *unity* mean ? Unity and universality, the absolute universal validity, of the standards of reason. The human reason has the consciousness of this universal validity in itself; and this consciousness is simply the consciousness of absolute unity. [7]

God is *unending* ? Humanity as such has no end; that is, the human species is obviously unending. [8] Accordingly the endlessness of God is

---

[1] P, p. 91.   [2] P, p. 28; cf. C, pp. 242 f., 407; E, p. 145.
[3] C, pp. 173 f.; E, pp. 97 f.   [4] C, p. 175; E, p. 99.
[5] C, p. 268; E, pp. 173 f.   [6] P, p. 30.
[7] C, p. 103; E, p. 41.   [8] C, p. 63; E, p. 153.

identical with that of the human species in contrast to the end of the human individual.[1]

Similarly, the difference between God's original, immediate *knowledge* and man's derivative, mediated knowledge coincides with the difference which philosophy knows as that between a-priori or speculative knowledge and a-posteriori or empirical knowledge, both of which, however, are certainly human knowledge.[2]

God as a *morally perfect* being is the actualized idea, the personified law, of morality. He is moral being, established as absolute being.[3]

'God is the *love* which satisfies our desires, our heart's needs. He is himself the actualized wish of the heart, the heart's wish raised to its highest terms, to a certainty of fulfilment, of validity, of assured possession, before which no contradiction of reason, no protest of experience with the external world can stand. God is the objectified essence of the emotion; he is pure emotion without limit. "God is an unutterable sigh, deep in the depths of the soul"; these words (of Sebastian Frank) are the most significant, the most profound, the truest expression of the Christian mystic.' [4]

What is the meaning of the *incarnation*? 'A tear of divine pity, a manifestation of a being with the feeling of a man and therefore an essentially human being', the manifestation of man become God.[5] It is the confession of religion itself, a confession which theology denies that God is wholly human being.[6]

The meaning of *Christ*? 'The consciousness of the species. We are all to be one in Christ. Christ is the consciousness of our unity. Therefore whoever loves man for man's sake, whoever raises himself to the love of the species, to the universal love which corresponds to the nature of the species, he is a Christian, he is Christ himself.' [7]

Of *miracles*? 'The magical power of fantasy which fulfils all the wishes of the heart without contradiction.' [8]

Of the *resurrection of Christ*? 'The satisfied longing of man for an immediate certainty of his personal survival after death.' [9]

Of the *Word of God*? It signifies the divinity of the word. The word of a man contains also his being; 'it is his imparted self if only it is a true word'.[10]

Of *baptism*? A reasonable and admirable institution if in it the moral

---

[1] C, p. 61; E, p. 152.
[2] P, p. 26.
[3] C, p. 110; E, p. 46.
[4] C, pp. 202 f.; E, pp. 121 f.
[5] C, p. 115; E, p. 50.
[6] C, p. 123; E, p. 54.
[7] C, p. 388; E, p. 269.
[8] C, p. 219; E, p. 134.
[9] C, p. 220; E, p. 135.
[10] C, p. 153; E, p. 79.

and physical healing power of water, of nature in general, is made perceptible to the senses and celebrated.[1]

Of the *Lord's Supper*? The highest self-gratification of human subjectivity. 'In it even the Protestant, not according to his words but in truth, transforms God into an external object and subordinates him to himself as an object of sensuous enjoyment.' [2]

Of the *Holy Spirit*? It is 'the religious heart's representation of itself to itself, the representation of the effects of religion, of religious enthusiasm; it is the personification of religion in religion. The Holy Spirit is therefore the yearning of the creature, the longing of the creature for God.' [3]

And so on. Feuerbach always uses the same rule (not to call it a stereotype) to achieve these interpretations. 'The first true divine being is not the deity with attributes; the divinity or deity of the attribute is the first true divine being.' Therefore the only atheist is someone for whom these attributes would be nothing. But the attributes do not depend on the concept of God; the opposite is true and the latter depends on the former.

God the subject is determined; the predicates are determining. To them in reality, and not to the subject, belongs the rank of the first being, the rank of deity.[4] 'In the infinite being as the subject, as essential being, there is for me only what is predicate, a characteristic of myself.' [5]

It is this liberating knowledge—liberating because it brings clearly and simply into the greatest possible closeness to man what man was seeking in the distance under a thousand contradictions and violent antinomies—which Feuerbach wanted to express and make effective for the greatest possible number of people. So he was never weary of emphasizing that such knowledge has been evidenced in the actual course of the history of religion, of the Church and of theology. 'Not *I*, but religion, worships man, although it or rather theology denies this fact. Not my insignificant self, but religion says God is man. Not I, but religion itself repudiates and denies the God who is *not* man and who exists in thought only (*ens rationis*); while it accepts God become man and now makes *this* God in human form with human thoughts and emotions the object of its worship and honour.' [6] 'Theology became anthropology long ago';[7] after Protestantism, especially Luther, turned its attention from what God *is in himself* to what God *is for men*.[8]

[1] C, p. 392; E, p. 276.
[2] C, p. 354; E, p. 242 f. n.
[3] C, p. 132; E, pp, 67 f.
[4] C, pp. 79 f.; E, pp. 21 f.
[5] C, p. 401.
[6] C, p. 39; E, p. xxxvi.
[7] C, p. 38.
[8] P, p. 14.

As the development of religion steadily continues, man more and more repudiates God and more and more affirms himself. It is an open secret, which can no longer be concealed by silence, that Christianity in its theological aspect vanished long ago not only from theoretical thinking but also from human life; that it has become nothing more than 'a fixed idea which stands in the most startling contradiction to our fire and life insurance companies, our railroads and steam engines, our galleries of painting and sculpture, our military and technical schools, our theatres and our museums'.[1] Therefore 'man is the beginning of religion, man is the middle point of religion, man is the end of religion.'[2]

We have listened. For anyone who has listened intelligently, two impressions will obviously contend for priority. One is that we have heard something extremely, almost offensively trivial; the other that this triviality really propounds a question which could justifiably be directed to the theology with which Feuerbach was surrounded.

Let us ignore the first impression. Then the problem can be seen as a general attack on the methodology of the theology of Schleiermacher and of post-Schleiermacher theology. It is the question of whether and how far religion, revelation, the relation between God and man, can be made understandable as a predicate of man. Theology had let itself be driven by the upsurge of a self-glorifying and self-satisfied humanism from Pietism over the Enlightenment to Romanticism. It had been forced into an apologetic corner where it had ever lessening power of defence. In that embarrassing position Feuerbach's question was unavoidable.

But does setting the problem lead to any result other than what the upsurge of humanism sought to achieve without the wise advice of theologians—the apotheosis of man? That is Feuerbach's question to the modern theology. There is not one of those surrounding Schleiermacher for whom this question is not pertinent—and directed to him at his most vital point.

Let us consider Schleiermacher himself. Think of his doctrine of religion as a conditioning of the selfconsciousness of man in which he feels himself absolutely dependent in such a way that the Whence of this feeling, that is God, is 'given' in this feeling 'in an original way'. What does that mean? [3] Think of his teaching, too little noticed, of the

---

[1] C, p. 50; E, p. xliv.   [2] C, p. 282; E, p. 184.
[3] Does that mean anything better than what the *first* edition of *The Christian Faith* had explained more clearly: 'that in the religious emotions God is given only in the innermost way as the producing power'—§ 9.4 (second edition, § 4.4)?

'three dogmatic forms', the second and third of which, the statements about God and about the world, are really superfluous or reducible to statements of the first form, statements of the religious consciousness. What does that mean? Consider his Christology and his doctrine of redemption, explicitly projected backwards from his own experience of the human subject. What does it mean if man is in a position to be able to construct the whole content of Christian faith just as well, in fact better, by taking such a detour? I mention only these three points. (The third applies directly to the atonement doctrine of a man who ostensibly is an unmodern Biblicist, Gottfried Menken.)

We can think also of the audacious assurance of Wegscheider (he was more often read by his contemporaries than was Schleiermacher), who permitted God to be merely the nail on which the complete outfit of human reason is finally hung. We may think of De Wette, who with his keyword 'critical authority', with his correlation between Christian faith and the Kantian concept of reason, seems to run straight into the arms of Feuerbach. But we can also include Tholuck with his proclamation of the 'heart' as the seat of divine wisdom. And also Marheineke, who knew more accurately than Schleiermacher (and all his sort up to the present day) what revelation might mean, but who nevertheless with his magic key of the 'concept' put into the hand of man the instrument with which, according to Marheineke's presentation, man becomes wholly master even of the self-revealing God.

What is the significance of all this? Surely the whole was not motivated as frivolously as Feuerbach assumed when he took it as the full meaning of theological activity. But can it be denied that Feuerbach's conclusion defines the point at which all these lines appear to meet inevitably and precisely? Was Feuerbach himself really a very sharp-sighted but not too intelligent spy, when he reported to all the world (*urbi et orbi*) indiscriminately that the esoteric secret of this whole priesthood was 'theology long ago became anthropology'?

Do we assume this sentence to be a malicious, bungling slander on Schleiermacher and his generation? But if we do, we must still meet the question of how it happened that they were so wholly unprotected against, so vulnerable to, this suspicion. Why were they apparently so blind to the obviously existing possibility that their lines were extending too far in the direction of Feuerbach's trivial intersection point and to the necessity of guarding themselves against reaching it? Why did they not at some important point speak so decisively that Feuerbach's question would not apply to them, that such a slander would be impossible?

And if the eyes of that generation seem 'holden' on this point, will the same be true of the generation of their pupils who carry on their work, of an Alexander Schweizer, a Richard Rothe, a J. Ch. R. von Hofmann, etc.? (These are questions to which we must proceed from Feuerbach.) Or will the theological generation in the midst of which this spy lived at least notice the contemporary threatening danger and therefore find time to consider how theology can be so practised as not to be subject to that base suspicion? And if Feuerbach and his question were doomed to remain hidden and without infiuence on his contemporaries and to leave no impression upon them—as can well be—what will happen in the next generation whose leader or most important representative will be called Albrecht Ritschl? 'God is essentially only an object of religion, not of philosophy; of the emotion, not of the intellect; of the need of the heart, not of the freedom of thought. In brief, God is an object, a being which expresses the nature of the practical, not of the theoretical, viewpoint.' [1] On this line you would not meet the Ritschlian theology, would you?

In the year 1900, about a hundred years after Schleiermacher's *Speeches*, a book will appear bearing for the second time the title *Das Wesen des Christentums* (*The Essence of Christianity*). It will cause much more discussion than the first one. Will the author see nothing sinister in the choice of just this title? Evil tongues [2] will assert that he perhaps did not know Feuerbach's book; but that is impossible. Not only must his purpose be entirely different; he must also wish to deal fundamentally with the question posed by Feuerbach—still a serious question —of whether the theologians of the modern age really consciously bear as the coat of arms on their shields the apotheosis of man. He must intend to clear himself and his contemporaries from the shameful suspicion. Will theology now, sixty years after that book, have made certain that its rear is unthreatened on that side, that it has a good conscience?

There are three reasons, if I see clearly, why Feuerbach's question is pressing and crucial, whether or not it was heard and dealt with by the theologians of the last century.

1. The illumination it sheds is certainly not confined merely to modern theology nor merely to the mystic in the older theology. (But it must be said that the shadow of Feuerbachian suspicion expands most obviously in the area occupied by the depths of the mystic components

---

[1] C, p. 284; E, p. 186.
[2] Overbeck, *Christentum und Kultur*, pp. 210 f.

of all theologies.) [1] However, we Protestant theologians need especially to ponder the fact that Feuerbach could so often choose to cite Luther, and not without some apparent justification.

Two emphases in Luther seem especially to have impressed him. First, Luther's characteristic talk of *faith*, as almost a divine hypostasis, which moved and worked independently. Cannot and does not faith do everything ? Not only does faith justify, console, and alone produce love and good works; it also overcomes sin and death, it makes blessed. Faith and God belong together, 'in the same bundle'. Faith (the heart's trust!) makes both God and idol; faith can on occasion be called a 'creator of deity'—even though only 'in us'. This extravagant judgement is certainly in need of interpretation and proof. After Feuerbach, one cannot just repeat Luther's words without qualification.

The second point is more important, the doctrine of the incarnation and what relates to it. Feuerbach briefly paraphrased this Christian doctrine with the formula: 'God becomes man; man becomes God.' This interpretation, which is certainly crass, is neither impossible nor absurd under the presuppositions of the specifically Lutheran Christ-ology and doctrine of the Lord's Supper. The enthusiastic overemphasis with which Luther himself taught that the deity is to be sought not in heaven but on earth, in the *man*, the *man*, the man Jesus; and insisted also that the bread of the Lord's Supper must be fully the glorified body of the ascended Christ was the basis of the orthodox Lutheran doctrine of the 'idiomatic communion' in the 'majestic nature' (*genus majestaticum*),[2] according to which the communicant partakes of the nature of the risen Christ. According to this doctrine, the predicate of the divine glory belonged to the humanity of Jesus as such and in abstraction (*in abstracto*). The same enthusiasm overrode joyfully the Reformed *finitum non capax infiniti* (the finite is incapable of the infinite) —and still overrides it! All of that emphasis points plainly to the possibility of a reversal of above and below, of heaven and earth, of God and man, a possibility of forgetting the eschatological boundary. Hegel in exploiting this possibility perhaps simply demonstrated how good a Lutheran he was, how consistent to his professed adherence.

---

[1] Cf. the attitude of Gottfried Keller and others towards Angelus Silesius, *Cherubinischen Wandersmann* (The Cherubic Wanderer).

[2] *Communicatio majestatis*, βελτίωσις, προσθήκη μεγάλη, ὑπερύψωσις, μετάδοσις, δόξασις, μετάληψις θείας ἀξίας, μετοχὴ θείας δυνάμεως, θέωσις, ἀποθεοσία, θεοποιήσις (Communication of majesty, melioration, great increment, supreme exaltation, gift, glory, partaking in divine honour, sharing divine power, divinity, deification, being made God) the Old Lutheran dogmatists said (Schmid, *Dogm. d. ev. luth. Kirche*, §§ 33, 21).

It is certain that Luther and the Old Lutherans with their heaven-storming Christology have left their successors in a somewhat compromised position, without defence against the speculative anthropological consequences which may very unacceptably intrude.

To repulse Feuerbach's attack effectively one must be certain that man's relation with God is in every respect, in principle, an irreversible relation. And of that truth, German theology after a century of vigorous resistance to the Calvinist corrective was *not* certain. It took over, as Schleiermacher exemplifies, the most destructive elements of the Reformed School, the analytic method of Amesius and Keckermann and the historicism of Coccejus and his group; and then combined them all happily with the fatal inheritance of their own past. The omens under which the newer 'German evangelistic theology' originated were not good!

Therefore it is that the name of Feuerbach has been a thorn in the flesh of the newer theology and perhaps will continue so to be. So long as the irreversibility of the relation with God is not unconditioned and absolutely fixed under all circumstances, there will be no peace in this area. To win peace, it would be wise to understand Luther (even against Luther) as Kattenbusch praises Gogarten for doing, 'as if he had refreshed himself at the spring of Calvinism and then gone farther'.[1]

2. Feuerbach had and has one hidden but most effective advantage over the new theology (and again it is an advantage not only over the moderns). All his elucidations or reversals of Christian dogmas (however boring and uninspiring their effect in the long run) are developed from a starting-point where he had the old, in fact the oldest, Christian tradition on his side. I mean his determined anti-spiritualism, which did not spare even his teacher Hegel. To put it positively—it was his anthropological realism. (This rather surprisingly relates him most closely to Menken among his predecessors and to J. T. Beck and J. Chr. Blumhardt among his contemporaries.)

Feuerbach is concerned with the reality, the whole reality of man (heart and stomach!). There can be real talk of God only where the concern is with that reality of man. His interest lay (whether or not with complete consistency is another question) in man's actual existence and situation (*Dasein* and *Sosein*), in the apparently quite uninteresting and obvious life of human beings—in neither man's spiritual nor his physical life by itself, but both together in the unity in which alone the existence of man is possible. (Whether in his reaction against idealism

---

[1] *Die deutsche evangelische Theologie seit Schleiermacher*, 5th edition, p. 126.

he did not overemphasize the sensuous may again be queried.) He
wanted to be assured that this existence is affirmed as it comes to
consciousness of itself and of the world through the relation of *I* and
Thou. When religion concerns itself with that affirmation, religion is
sense and not nonsense.

Toward this end Feuerbach worked not only as an honest man, and
not only as a zealous opponent of all specifically academic theology
which begins with some kind of abstraction and runs out into some
kind of ideology, which stands in no sort of relation to the real life of
men in their cities and villages, their taverns and inns. He worked also
in *actuality* as a Christian in so far as he seems to have seen—even
though from afar off—Adam and Eve in their nakedness and the
resurrection of the body as 'somehow' the beginning and end of
theology.

That is not all there was to be seen! But that could be *so* seen that
implicitly all the rest would be seen with it. Feuerbach certainly did not
so see it. But why did not Christian theology see here, earlier and better
than Feuerbach, what it would have been forced to see had it kept the
Old and New Testament in its hands ?

Theology's neglect of the Christian hope—a neglect which goes back
to the Reformation—and its spirit of 'this worldliness' [1] have separated
it from real life, from the *real man*, and at the same time have made it
all too human. Its highest human idealism has fallen under the suspicion
that its 'God' or its 'other world' side might be human illusion; on
encountering it, one had better remain true to earth.

Because he gave this most true reminder, most necessary also for the
knowledge of the true God, Feuerbach was and is (however badly he
himself may have managed the business) literally and simply the stronger
in the contest with the *great* majority of modern theologians, including
the most recent. There will be no respite from Feuerbach's question in
this area until the witness of both Blumhardts (and through them
the heritage from the Würtemberger 'Fathers') is assimilated by
Protestant theology—one could also put it, until the radical Easter faith
of the Eastern Church (without vitiating our problem as defined by
Augustine) has become ours. He who is concerned only with the spirit,

---

[1] I. A. Dorner (unjustly disregarded and unfortunately overshadowed by
Ritschl) pointed this out accurately (*Gesammelte Schriften*, 1883, p. 16). For he
who denies 'this side' of men denies the 'other side' of God at least as much as the
usual and much less dangerous denier of the existence of the 'other side'. The
Christian hope first deserves its name when with *one* stroke it makes materialism
and idealism impossible.

the heart, the conscience, the inwardness of man, must face the question
of whether he is concerned really with God and not rather with the
apotheosis of man.

3. The third important and positive contribution of Feuerbach's
teaching is its unconscious but very obvious affinity with the ideology
of the workers' socialist movement. This affinity was first discovered
by Engels, and Feuerbach became *the* philosopher of religion for modern
socialism, called 'scientific' in contrast to the 'Utopian' socialism of the
beginning of the century.

Feuerbach was concerned with the unmasking and overthrowing of
the hypostases, powers and forces upon which the unenlightened man
mistakenly feels himself more or less dependent. He was concerned with
the 'negation of the negation', with the expropriation of the expro-
priators, wherever a God apart from the world or apart from man is
involved. Similarly in socialism the aim was to put an end to the
abstraction of the capitalist right of private ownership, to give back the
profit from work and therefore the tools of work to him to whom they
rightfully belong, to the worker. In the light of this connexion,
Feuerbach's anthropologizing of religion became an obvious part, and
not the least important part, of a struggle for emancipation, of a fight
for freedom which was initiated as well as limited by the Revolution.

Of the right and necessity of this struggle not only the bourgeoisie
glorifying itself with idealistic philosophy but also the Christian Church
knew nothing at all. In that struggle they intentionally or unintention-
ally even took the role of the inert, uncomprehending, and hostile
opposition.

Does the guilt of the Church also show itself here in its lack of
prophetic insight into the signs of the times ? How restricted was the
vision of even the few upright guardians in the theology of the nineteenth
century! (I am thinking, for example, of such as A. Fr. Chr. Vilmar and
H. Fr. Kohlbrügge, who did high service at other points.) Especial
credit must be given to Schleiermacher, who in this area was *not* blind
and was *not* dumb. What strenuous energy was then expended (already
too late) in rearguard action against the bourgeois Enlightenment;
while already wholly different real needs, questions and hopes were
moving up in front.

Was the whole compaign of modern theology only a tardy diversion,
an attempt to run after a train which had already left and which was
the wrong train anyway? Yet there would have been need of haste to
attend to the incoming train, and one could only vainly run after it. For

one was in no position to be able to leave off running, now to the bourgeoisie, now to the proletariat as one could do who knew himself how to
speak a timely word to the world better than the world knew, how to say
at the decisive moment what needed to be heard.

If only the Church had been compelled before Marx to show in
word and action, and had been able to show, that it is just the knowledge
of God which automatically and inevitably includes within itself
liberation from all hypostases and idols, which of itself can achieve
liberation! If the Church had had that insight and had proclaimed it
before the children of the world, would the Church have had the power
to show, in opposition to those errors of self-redemption, that self-
knowledge unaffected by knowledge of God can never achieve true
freedom, but can only create *new* ideologies, new idols ? Who can answer
that question ?

But it is certain that with the ideas of the bourgeois Enlightenment,
of bourgeois idealism, even the 'God' whom the Church proclaimed
came under the suspicion of being only a pleasant dream, not only for
the lonely thinker on the Rechenberg (who if I am not mistaken was
himself quite bourgeois), but also for the great and ever-increasing
masses of the people. And these masses suspected that the 'God' was
not just a pleasant dream, but that he was rather a false pretence
intentionally supported for use in stifling the struggle for freedom.
And religion became suspect as being maintained neither for the sake of
religion nor for the sake of people—and not for the sake of truth. And
with this premise, it could be held in the name of truth that only revolt,
repudiation of the Church and war against it, was truly right.

If the atheism of social democracy is a warning, a *mene tekel*, for the
Church, before which the Church should not be pharisaically outraged
but should rather do penance, then the convincing power of Feuerbach's
teaching in comparison with the theology of *this* Church is no riddle, even
though the core of his teaching is superlatively banal. The Church will
be free of Feuerbach's question only when its ethics have been radically
separated from both the ancient and the modern hypostases. Then the
Church will again win belief that its God is no illusion—but never until
then.

I come in conclusion to the criticism which ought justly to be applied
to Feuerbach's theology. Naturally his doctrine is extremely trite, and
not only nor indeed primarily his interpretation of religion in which
alone theology for the most part has been interested and against which

theologians have usually produced such weak arguments. Take, for example, Heinrich Scholz. According to him, there must be ('there is!'), along with various kinds of religion to which Feuerbach's interpretation does apply, a 'highly valuable', 'solid', 'weighty' religion 'at the peak of humanity' which is not explicable from the needs of men.[1] As if Feuerbach had not dealt specifically with the religion of Luther, which is still very 'weighty'!

Or consider Wobbermin, who gives Feuerbach some tardy advice. 'He owes his best insights to Schleiermacher' for whom Trinity Church in Berlin, on his own witness, remained his life long 'a hallowed city'. He would only need to judge the religious experience from the viewpoint of its objective content (as Luther did according to Wobbermin) to come presently on the right track—that is, of course, to the circle of religious psychology.[2] Is not the implication here that one can take the so-called 'objective content' of religion boldly into his hand and play it out triumphantly, as if it were wholly in his control? As if so he could turn a new and fresh stream of water on Feuerbach's mill?

So the fact is ignored that with Feuerbach there was firmly fixed, preceding all his correct or incorrect interpretations of religious experience, the conviction that man is not only the measure of all things, but is the sum total, the origin and goal of all values; the conviction of the legitimate validity and security of human existence with its needs, wishes, and ideals. (This conviction, of course, was in its way as unsupported as is revelation itself.) Banality is inherent in that conviction and out of it arises the banality of his interpretation of religion. But no one who is not in the position to laugh in his face will ever prevail with tearful or angry criticism of Feuerbach's interpretation.

Hans Ehrenberg [3] has excellently combined in a few phrases what can and must be said against Feuerbach. 'As a true child of his century', he was a man who 'did not know (*Nichtkenner*) death' and who 'misunderstood (*Verkenner*) evil'. Truly any man who knew that we human beings are evil from head to foot, and who bore in mind that we all die, would know that the illusion of all illusions is the notion that the being of God is the being of man. Even if he held the good God to be a dream he would certainly leave him free of any identification with such as we.

This double ignorance of Feuerbach's, moreover, is closely connected

[1] *Religionsphilosophie*, 3rd edition, pp. 68 f.
[2] *Das Wesen der Religion*, pp. 399 f.; *Wesen und Wahrheit des Christentums*, pp. 452 f.
[3] In his edition of the *Philosophie der Zukunft*, p. 94.

with a third. To have pointed out the third is the service of a Hegelian more left than Feuerbach, Max Stirner.[1] For Stirner, even the 'being of man' with which Feuerbach operated as with the one thing needful (*unum necessarium*) was still too much, was too abstract, too ideal, too far from the actual reality. The actually existing reality, according to Stirner, is rather the 'single individual', who rests his affairs on nothing but himself—𝕴𝕮𝕳! Stirner also was a man 'ignorant of death' and 'misunderstanding evil'; entirely too much 'a true child of his century'. Otherwise he would certainly not have written that little word *Ich* with those absurd ecclesiastical capitals. But it is not to be denied that with his discovery he had taken a decisive step nearer to 'existential thinking' than Feuerbach. But the posited 'single individual' is still only an individual *man*, and what that fact means in relation to the knowledge of evil and death remained hidden from Stirner. And so it happened that while in him, Feuerbach's original audacity came so much closer to the real matter, it also with Stirner reached and crossed the boundary of insolence.

But Stirner has put his finger precisely on Feuerbach's weak point, on the question of whether Feuerbach's man is *really* the *real* man. If Feuerbach's teaching on the 'being of man' is to be recognized as the final priestly illusion, if the real man is always *I* for whom no human *Thou* at all can remove the burden of existence as an individual; if I am rather one on whom this burden is laid just by the unavoidably present human *Thou*, then the road to Feuerbach's God—and also the road to Stirner's 'single individual'—is cut off. And then there is a possibility for the insight that the identification of God with man is impossible. More cannot be said.

If I really think as an individual, I ought to be on the road to un-learning the gay forgetfulness of evil and death and to leaving strictly alone any identification of God with myself. Whether or not I really do that is to be found in another book, not to be opened here.

We now see what we do if we take in our hand the only weapon which can touch Feuerbach. We cannot strike him without ourselves being struck by it. It is no argument with which one can do a job of apologetics. It is only a base where one can stand and with fear and trembling let it speak for itself. There is a test of whether or not we stand on this base, of whether we are able to admit to Feuerbach that he was right on the whole line of his religious interpretation so far as it related

---

[1] *Der Einzige und sein Eigentum*, 1845. In the same year appeared the first pseudonymous work of Kierkegaard.

to religion as an experience of men—even if it was related to the 'elevated' and the 'impressive' religion, even to the Christian religion of men. That test is the recognition that *we* are and remain liars in relation to God, but that we can lay claim to God's truth, his certainty and his salvation as grace—and *only* as grace.

Then a man knows what he is about when he offers the reminder of evil and death in opposition to Feuerbach. Then he speaks as an 'individual' and abandons the impudent identity theology. So long as this nail is not firmly fixed, so long as all talk 'of God being in man' is not cut off; we have no reason to disagree with Feuerbach. We are along with him 'true children of *his* century'.

VIII

THE PRINCIPLES OF DOGMATICS
ACCORDING TO WILHELM HERRMANN

A lecture given at the Ministers' Study Group in Hanover and at the
Conference of Free Protestantism for Anhalt, Braunschweig, and the
Province of Saxony at Halberstadt, 13th and 17th May 1925.

For this assembly, I can assume without further preamble an
interest in the theology of Wilhelm Herrmann. But permit me to state
in a few words what the choice of this theme means to me personally.
The immediate impulse was given by the publication of Herrmann's
Dogmatik.[1] But the duty to present to myself and others an accounting
both for what Herrmann has said to us and for what he has left unsaid
is an obligation which, apart from that publication, I should have felt
sooner or later.

Herrmann was *the* theological teacher of my student years. The day
twenty years ago in Berlin when I first read his *Ethik* (Ethics) I remember
as if it were today. If I had the temperament of Klaus Harms, I could
speak of Herrmann in the way he spoke of Schleiermacher, or I could
say as Stilling did of Herder, 'From this book I received the push into
perpetual motion.'[2] With more restraint, but with no less gratitude,
I can say that on that day I believe my own deep interest in theology
began.

I came to Marburg as a convinced 'Marburger'. And when on the
day I began my minstry the mail brought me, five minutes before I was
to go to the pulpit, the new, fourth edition of the *Ethik* as a gift from the
author, I accepted this coincidence as a dedication of my whole future.
Did I deceive myself? I cannot deny that through the years I have
become a somewhat surprising disciple of Herrmann. 'Much is altered

---

[1] Wilhelm Herrmann, *Dogmatik*, Gotha 1925 (English: *Systematic Theology*,
Macmillan, 1927). Cf. further F. W. Schmidt, *Wilhelm Herrmann, ein Bekenntnis
zu seiner Theologie*, Tübingen, 1922; and Wilhelm Herrmann, *Gesammelte
Aufsätze*, edited by F. W. Schmidt, Tübingen, 1923.

[2] Klaus Harms, *Lebensbeschreibung*, Kiel, 1851, p. 68.

here, the dishes differ and the wine is changed.' But I could never inwardly agree that I had really turned away from my teacher. Nor can I so agree today.

Scholars are not of one mind on what precisely is entailed in being a real pupil of a real master—neither in general nor in theology in particular. In my own case, I let Herrmann say to me one essential truth. This truth, followed out to its consequences, later forced me to say almost everything else quite differently and finally led me even to an interpretation of the fundamental truth itself which was entirely different from his. And yet it was *he* who showed me that truth. I cannot claim its discovery for myself and I must now openly and gratefully acknowledge my indebtedness.

The last direct word I received from Wilhelm Herrmann was an inscription, written in the year 1918. It bore the laconic words, 'None the less, with best regards from Wilhelm Hermann'. What I want to say to you today may be understood as a commentary on this 'none the less', from my own side. I shall first attempt to present Herrmann's teaching as lovingly and as exactly as if it were my own, and then show why and how far I think I must understand Herrmann wholly differently (*aliter*) than he understood himself. You should not expect from me today more than a slight indication of the position where I myself stand. Our theme is to be the theology of the master, even in the second part where the pupil, like and yet unlike Gregory Thaumaturgos in his panegyric on Origen, will explain why, because of the instruction he received, he had to walk in his own way.

A further introductory word is necessary on the limitation which I am imposing upon myself in the treatment of the theme. To speak of the fundamental basis of Herrmann's dogmatic teaching, and of that only, is appropriate to the nature of that teaching. More consistently and consciously than other modern dogmatic theologians, he has stated not only the decisive part but the whole of his doctrine in the first part of his book. What follows in the second part is analysis, variations, explanation, application and often simply repetition of the first part.

The content of this second part, often original and profound, cannot be disregarded—a very important section must be discussed later. But the 'pure or normative doctrine of evangelical Christianity' as the 'understanding of revelation of God and religion', as the experience 'of pure dependence in free surrender'[1] is the quintessence of Herrmann's

[1] 'Christliche-protestant. Dogmatik' in Hinneberg's *Kultur der Gegenwart*, I, 4, 2; 1st ed., p. 624.

Dogmatik I. With Herrmann as little as with Schleiermacher can there be any doubt that what is of real significance in the 'considerations of faith,' to the development of which *Dogmatik II* is devoted, is not the ideas themselves, but the wings from the first part on which they fly and the load also derived from the first part, which they carry. Really to hear Herrmann in the second part, one must have listened to him in the first part.

A similar relation holds in his *Ethik,*[1] except that there the basic principles are to be sought in the middle of the book, in the section on 'the source of the Christian life'. It is from this section that not only the second (Christian) part on 'the development of the Christian moral life' but also the whole first (philosophical) part of Herrmann's ethical system is evolved, and it is understandable from there alone. Also the relation is such that the centre of the ethics is actually identical in content with the principles of the dogmatics.

The question arises therefore whether an attempt to understand Herrmann should not as well or even better be tied to his ethics.[2] But this possibility is to be excluded. Certainly it can be no accident that Herrmann has left us an elaborately detailed ethics. And if it is true that he is completely oriented towards ethics, then that orientation must throw light on the character and the meaning of his dogmatics. But that should be no obstacle against considering what he *intended* as a theologian. 'The individual representatives of the theological disciplines are in every case theologians only so far as they are dogmatic theologians.'[3]

And also it must be recognized that the centre of Herrmann's *Ethik* presents a summary of the propositions from his *Dogmatik*—and not the reverse. The scientific justification for turning from ethical thinking to Christian living which is there presented obviously stands or falls with the existence of the science of the faith which lives from the Christian revelation.

As a dogmatic theologian, Herrmann was an ethicist who interpreted and corrected Kant in a very specific way. Even if it be granted that in practice he raised the problem of religion from the standpoint of ethics and found its solution in the framework of the ethical question so that Troeltsch [4] thought he could feel in agreement with him—nevertheless

---

[1] Compare on this point Kattenbusch, *Die deutsche evangelische Theologie seit Schleiermacher,* 5th ed., Giessen, 1926, p. 89.

[2] 'Herrmann as a scholar was more deeply interested in ethics than in dogmatics; that is generally recognized', Kattenbusch, ibid., p. 84.

[3] *Ges. Aufs.,* p. 2. [4] *Gesammelte Schriften,* II, p. 570.

for Herrmann the answer stood on its own feet even against ethics. The status of *Dogmatik II* and of *Ethik* can only be supplementary; both are subordinated to the really basic science of theology, the science of the origin of the Christian faith, of the 'Way to Religion'. But that means that the significance of action belongs under the principles of dogmatics.

I

First therefore I shall present a summary of the content of the first forty pages of the *Dogmatik-Diktate* just published, supplementing and interpreting it from Herrmann's other writings and occasionally from my university notes written in the 1908 summer semester.

1. The task of dogmatics [1] is to demonstrate what is universally valid in the religion professed by the community of Christians (§ 1); it is the 'production of a normative ("pure") doctrine'.[2] The community needs this presentation for its 'protection'; against the outside, because it must maintain itself in the midst of a developing culture (§§ 1 and 23); against the inside, to prevent deviation and also because each branch of the community needs to see the common spiritual possession in the other branches also (§ 23).[3]

The difficulty of this undertaking arises from the fact that religion is not, like a natural science or ethics, a body of generally recognized and accessible material, but is the especial, particular, vital possession of individual men (§ 2). In it an intransferable individual element is bound up with the universally valid.[4] But it is also true that a real understanding of the content of the science of history is attained only by the road of shared *experience*. The historian trained in Ranke's school knows 'that the essential character of history is only grasped by him to whom personalities become revelations which he himself experiences' (§ 3).[5]

Dogmatics shares in this conditioned universal validity of history. Dogmatics ought to and can: *1.* make every man conscious that the

---

[1] Herrmann's terms were not strictly defined. He used the expressions, *dogmatic theology, systematic theology, science of religion, philosophy of religion,* for the most part interchangeably. And these first sections of the *Dogmatik* in their final form offer other difficulties of interpretation also. My presentation, undertaken with the utmost conscientiousness and to the best of my knowledge, is a kind of cross-section cutting through Herrmann's intertwined definitions.

[2] 'Christliche-protestantische Dogmatik' (pp. 619, 624).

[3] *Ges. Aufs.*, p. 126. 'Christl-prot. Dog.' p. 619. In 1908 he said more briefly that it should be 'demonstrated how a man now living will advocate religion as his own concern'.

[4] *Ges. Aufs.*, p. 383.   [5] *Christliche Welt,* 1918, no. 31–2, esp. col. 291.

search for religion is an inevitable part of his own individual life, 2. make the Christian religion in itself understandable for every man who is in any way religious, 3. keep before the eyes of every Christian the way in which he himself gained his religion. To the origin of religion belongs that universally valid element which dogmatics has to present.

Besides this task proper to it, dogmatics has also still another function, which is, so to speak, not inherent. This is where *Dogmatik II* enters. The faith which arises from the revelation is the new life of the Christian. It is expressed in specific thought-forms.[1] To develop these ideas is the second and secondary task of dogmatics. But here dogmatics cannot claim and ought not to claim any universality, any normative authority. Not for those outside: 'the forms of this new life are made up of thoughts and motives which can be true and effective only in the man whom God has set free' (§ 23). 'It is not possible to demonstrate their truth to the unbeliever.'[2] And not for those within: 'the doctrine which springs from faith has necessarily an infinite variety of forms. Different men see different things and because they must be truthful, they ought to express differently what they see.'[3] 'For every living person has his own way.'[4]

It is clear that under these conditions, dogmatics in its own province cannot exist at all in the sense of a science of dogma and that in the supplementary function which is concerned with non-obligatory concepts of faith, dogmatics can exist only through the actual coincidence of such ideas among religious people (and such a coincidence is fundamentally accidental). 'The concept of dogma as a uniform doctrine to be learned is contrary to the working of the Holy Spirit.'[5] If the name *dogmatics* is to be retained, 'that is done only because we wish to present the Christian faith according to its basis and content, as was done in the older dogmatics; and there is no gain in dropping an old name unnecessarily' (§ 1).

---

[1] *Ges. Aufs.*, pp. 186 f.

[2] *Verkehr des Christen mit Gott*, p. 13 English: *Communion of the Christian with God*, 1913, p. 17.

[3] Ibid., p. 9; Eng., p. 11.

[4] 'Christl-prot. Dog.,' p. 614. Cf. *Ges. Aufs.*, p. 188. In § 23 of the *Dogmatik-Diktate* this particular point is no longer unambiguously stated. There it is said that the task consists in making clear and preserving free from distortion that which religion engenders among Christians and that whereby religion expresses itself in them all. . . . Does this mark a departure from the original independence so long firmly upheld in unconditional formulae? Is there here something of the tendency discussed by F. W. Schmidt in his memorial (pp. 55 f.)? Schmidt will certainly recognize that this is not merely a minor correction and that it would mean an undermining of the Herrmannic foundation!

[5] *Verk. des Ch.*, p. 10; Eng., p. 12.

2. Before the first, the real task of dogmatics can be undertaken, there is needed a polemic safeguard against a series of *misunderstandings*, which Herrmann has subsumed under the heading, 'The intellectualist conception of religion'.

Religion is (as we shall hear later) the ability—based in itself and experienced only as miraculous historical event—to see the working of God in the events of life (p. 20). Or, as he stated it differently: 'In relation to empirically demonstrable objects, the decision must be made whether the subject can hold his ground in a life which he has for himself alone, an "inner life". The awakening of the individual to a consciousness, based on itself alone, of such a life of his own is religion.' [1]

How man comes to this 'ability', to this 'awakening' is the problem of dogmatics (§§ 4–5).

It is *not* reached by the road, so often trodden in the well-known proof of God's existence, the road of scientific knowledge of the world. The thought underlying such proofs—God is Lord of all—has validity only as an idea of religion itself; not as a road to religion. Also the most important of such proofs, the cosmological, leads no further than to the idea that all reality in time and space conforms to law.

'The supernatural, traces of which the natural scientists of our day are willing to recognize, is to be classed with the discoveries of spiritualism which (if there are any such) can still excite the astonishment of savages, but can mean for the civilized man only an extension of the known world.' 'Theologians who ally themselves with such a metaphysics or natural science betray the cause for which they ought to stand.' [2] 'A proved God is world, and a God of the world is an idol.' [3]

Certainly faith has 'the full value of knowledge', but the reality with which it has to do must be experienced by every individual for himself. Faith, which is incontrovertible by science and rejoices[4] in true science, brings death to the false science which tries to prove it. The God of faith is neither 'demonstrable' reality nor is he merely a possibility. This is not a lack; it is a necessity because he is God and not world. 'He is not known as a dead thing is known. For in him is nothing which is not life. Therefore he is known only where he reveals his life; and where and to whom he will reveal it is his concern alone.' [5] (§ 6.)

---

[1] *Ges. Aufs.*, p. 400.   [2] Ibid. p. 132.
[3] 'Gottes Offenbarung an uns', *Vorträge der Aarauer Studenten-Conferenz*, 1908, p. 79. (This lecture is not included in Schmidt's Herrmann Bibliography.)
[4] 'Joy' with Herrmann often means benevolent neutrality. He rejoices, for instance, in the biblical miracles (§ 32).   [5] *Ges. Aufs.*, pp. 199–207.

The second impassable road to religion is the attempt to present it as the deepest *motive of man's spiritual life*; as Herrmann saw the attempt made by Julius Kaftan. That road is impassable, even if with Eucken one understands thereby the directive to a genuine and therefore an independent, personal life and thinks to recognize in it the actual working of a higher world. For as Kaftan's formulation of this conception exposes religion to Feuerbach's suspicion that its ideas might be beautiful but untrue, so it can be said against the view of the more cautious Eucken that he supports the religious conviction upon ideas which are themselves the expression of the religious conviction. That is exactly what philosophy of religion as such primarily undertakes to do, and thereby it shows its worthlessness.

What we know of philosophy of religion comes to this: the ideas of religion which were developed by theologians are worked over at such length and so artistically that they can be exhibited to simple men as demonstrations of science.[1] We cannot 'feel ourselves under any obligation to attempt the labour of draping the mantle of philosophy upon religion. Such adornment we must leave to the Church of Rome.'[2]

The same judgement holds also for the shift to an emphasis on the theory of knowledge which Troeltsch employed in the same undertaking. There is no scientific possibility for anchoring religion in reason, for the assertion of a validation of truth in the reality of religious experience,[3] for the transformation of the psychological occurrence of a 'feeling of presence' into a religious 'a-priori'; however 'interesting the philosophy of religion proclaimed by Troeltsch may be'. The religious insights which give rise to such an attempt can be fruitful only on their own ground [4] (§7).

A third barrier is needed against the conception of Kant that ethics, moral idealism or moral earnestness would be the path leading directly to religion. In support of this view, it may be said that truly, in an act of moral conviction, the power of the good as the power over all, therefore as the power of God, and also a self which accomplishes the good are both conceived as present. But on the other side it should be remembered, with Copen and Natorp, that the relation of men to this conception can never be anything except a continually self-renewed moral earnestness, so that religion would always be re-absorbed into morality

---

[1] Ibid., p. 97.   [2] Ibid., p. 377.
[3] In 1908 Herrmann flatly rejected the possibility of a psychology of religion, 'because religion does not belong to psychic facts'.
[4] *Ges. Aufs.*, pp. 135–9.

or would be understood as a vitality which accompanies morality but which is without object.

Against Kant as against the neo-Kantians, it should be observed that the presupposed basis of that 'thinking' is an experience, in the hidden depths of the individual, of what is thought. 'The morally struggling will of a man stands under a pressure which he himself could not overcome, from which he becomes free only through an experience of a specific kind. Unfortunately, Cohen and Natorp ignore too easily the evidence or this human situation.' [1] True religion carries in itself the energy of the moral purpose. It is inextricably bound to the moral will and it will itself be the moral will; but it is neither begotten by it (Kant), nor identical with it (Cohen), nor is it the objectless emotion which accompanies it (Natorp). It has also its own root and its own life [2] (§ 8).

The fourth opponent to be met is the Schleiermacher of *The Christian Faith* and the *Dialektik*. According to Schleiermacher, religion is to be defined as a given reality present in the purely subjective emotion of absolute dependence, differentiated from knowing and willing as the unity of self-consciousness. There are three things to be said against this 'great man's' teaching.[3]

1. Against the givenness of this emotion. In the Christian faith, certainly as Paul (Phil. 3.12) and as the prayer 'Thy kingdom come' describe it, there is truly no state of mind, already given and already present; but there is a continual seeking and being born anew, an ever fuller experiencing of that which gave faith birth.[4]

2. Against the objectlessness of this emotion, its pure existence in itself. The Christian faith lives from revelation. It needs the ever-renewed sojourning with the power which created it.[5]

3. Against the description of it as the feeling of absolute dependence. It is certainly true that we feel ourselves buried alive in the world of demonstrable reality, but such an emotion is certainly *not* a feeling of absolute dependence. The morally alive man is not dependent on the world which is crashing around him; *impavidum ferient ruinae* (Unterrified he on whom the ruins fall). But in religion man is wholly and really dependent in the experience of *free self-surrender*. What Schleiermacher calls God is really fate [6] (§ 9).

---

[1] Ibid., p. 393.   [2] Ibid., pp. 133, 140, 381 f.; *Ethik*, 4th ed., §§ 14, 15.
[3] When Herrmann calls anyone, for instance, Kant and Ritschl, as well as Schleiermacher, a 'great man', polemic always follows.
[4] *Ges. Aufs.*, pp. 113, 154; 'Christl-prot. Dog.' pp. 604, 606.
[5] *Ges. Aufs.*, pp. 88, 114.   [6] Ibid., pp. 154 f., 346.

The common elements in all these attempts, the metaphysical, that of philosophy of religion, the ethical-idealistic, and Schleier-macher's,[1] is that in all of them religion is carried back to something else and so is made explicable before the bar of reason. It can be justified there and given a basis. Thus all are intellectualizations and are to be rejected.

3. The self-based reality of religion as an 'historical fact' must now be considered. In contrast to the elderly Schleiermacher, we must listen to the young Schleiermacher of the *Speeches*,[2] with his conception of religion as *in form* an historical appearance (that is, occurring and visible only in individual men) of a hidden life in the soul. *In content*, it is man's existence attaining its true reality. The individual becomes alive in a special way, experiencing unity in the whole of reality, hearing from all the events which affect men a single living power speaking to his soul (§ 10).

There is, however, a definite *way* to this hidden reality. Its universal validity is easily overlooked, since it is obscured by the demonstrable conformity of nature to law and by the demonstrable goal of genuine willing. It consists in the necessity of *individual* thinking and at the same time the impossibility of carrying such thinking to completion. The man for whom that recognized universal has validity is an individual person. What does that mean? It requires that he *himself* must genuinely *will* and he *himself* must have the knowledge of a reality which at every moment demonstrates the negation of such a possibility. Therefore *he himself* must set himself within the paradox of his own situation without permitting himself to lose confidence in himself through either resignation or distractions (the 'real atheism'). Belonging equally and simultaneously to the kingdom of truth and to the kingdom of actuality, he must look towards the power of God, towards the good as the *power* in the strength of which he is to become for the first time his destined self, a true individual.

'Through this demand for genuineness, religion is tied to both ethics and logic. In so far, it is rationalism [*sic*]. It is reasonable, since it is

---

[1] The 'mystical', to use Emil Brunner's term.

[2] He enjoys, in Herrmann's view of history, a significance approaching that of Luther. The final statement in the *Diktate* runs: 'Here Schleiermacher has for the first time expressed the sense of religion derived from its own essence.' And the beginning of the exposition continues: 'If the last statement is correct, Schleiermacher marks a new stage in the history of religion as a whole.' Cf. 'Christl.-prot. Dog.,' p. 593. 'It was Schleiermacher who freed Herrmann from authoritarian faith, who enabled him to comprehend that no believer lives from that which another has experienced' (Kattenbusch, op. cit., p. 85).

obviously unreasonable to relinquish the affirmation of one's own life and to fail to put the critical question of what gives us the right to a real life and raises us above a life of mere appearance.' [1] The goal of this universally valid way, a road which must inevitably be recognized as such, the answer to this critical question, is the hidden individual life of *religion* [2] (§ 11).

But man cannot give that answer to himself. It must 'overwhelm him' as 'power' with 'incontestable reality'.[3] This is the act of God in religion, the act of him who *frees* us from the division within ourselves which we cannot by ourselves overcome. 'If we understand by God a power which so affects us that we through this experience gain strength to overcome the world, then it is self-evident that we can know this God only as he reveals himself to us by his work in us.' [4] And the experience of this revelation, if it is to be really the goal of that way, must be pure experience of dependence and of freedom simultaneously. Therefore the revelation itself must be an epiphany which humbles and exalts us, which awakens in us awe and trust, which is spiritual power *and* absolute good (§ 12).

According to the measure of the power of this vision and the measure of our honesty in accepting realities (that is accepting both our own situation and this vision) as we see them, the decision is made in the hidden depths of our individual life as to whether we will to treat the power which creates life in us as a living power;[5] that is, whether God becomes for us a reality, the Lord of our soul. If such a decision is made, then we shall seek him and find him in all which inwardly moves us. 'God, who brings us in the midst of our dependence on the unlimited to a true life, thereby gives us to understand that he is raising our life from the depths, hidden to us, of the world to which we belong, as a life which is to rule in that world. In the pure offering of trust lies the evidence of the reality of which the living becomes Lord.' [6] Such is the religious experience through which religion becomes real in us and our life becomes life in truth (§ 13).

Here we find ourselves at the pinnacle of Herrmann's thought. When I listened in Marburg, this pinnacle was supported by three sections of apologetic content. The first defended religion as truth against the charge of illusion, the second dealt with the possible relation between religion and ethics, the third with religion as the only possible unifying

---

[1] *Christliche Welt*, 1917, no. 44, col. 842.
[2] *Ges. Aufs.*, pp. 142–8, 346; *Ethik*, § 18.
[3] *Ges. Aufs.*, p. 148.   [4] 'Gottes Offenbarung an uns' (p. 76).
[5] *Ges. Aufs.*, pp. 348–9.   [6] Ibid., p. 161.

conception of reality. The complete elimination of these sections in Herrmann's later formulation of his thought is not accidental, but belongs to the authentic Herrmann. Apologetics is for him a subordinate and temporary activity destined inevitably to vanish. 'Knowledge of God is the expression of religious experience wholly without weapons.' [1]

The enemy front towards which Herrmann's concept of religion and revelation faced is not the anti-Christian position of modern philosophy and of natural and historical science. (That position is merely addressed occasionally and with ironical superiority.) The real enemy's position is on the right, within Christian theology itself. The present conclusion of the crucial three chapters of Herrmann's doctrine is aimed at demolishing this position and this only.

Revelation is the event which confronts us with the reality of God. In opposition to this 'pure' doctrine of revelation stand traditionalism, rationalism, mysticism. And Herrmann's chief and burning scorn is directed against the first of these three. Revelation cannot be a transmission of the ideas of other believers, and faith cannot be an assent to them. Certainly revelation is expressed in such records; but the primary essence of religion is its creating of religious conviction in *us*. There is scarcely any other idea which Herrmann presented so frequently and so passionately. On this point even the dullest hearer or reader could not fail to understand what Herrmann wanted and did not want. What he could cite against superintendent-generals, Consistories, 'positive' theologians, etc., is beyond telling. 'Roman Christianity' was for him embodied in the error 'revelation is doctrine'. 'Dishonesty', 'immorality', 'sin', 'seductive evil'—no terms were too severe for him to use as a label. It was for this cause that he knew himself to be finally separated from his honoured teacher, the 'great' theologian Ritschl.[2]

If he scented this enemy (and he was always on the watch for him), then he had no hesitations. He could say even of Troeltsch that he was 'just a bit too fastidious' to assume for himself the decoration of 'positive'.[3] And he could accuse even Bousset in blunt words of 'orthodox narrowness'.[4] It can be taken for granted that wherever Herrmann was speaking of the problem of revelation, he would stress the negative limitation: revelation is not doctrine. This was more important than all else.[5]

---

[1] *Christliche Welt*, 1917, loc. cit.
[2] *Ges. Aufs.*, pp. 115–19; 'Christl-prot. Dog.,' pp. 611–16.
[3] *Theol. Literaturzeitung*, 1912, no. 8, col. 247.   [4] *Ges. Aufs.*, p. 165.
[5] For example: *Verk. des Christen*, pp. 42 f. (Eng., p. 47); 'Gottes offenbarung an uns', pp. 82 f.; *Offenbarung und Wunder*, Giessen, 1908, pp. 6 f.

The two other opponents are rationalism and mysticism. Revelation is not identical with reason, for the event which rescues us cannot be understood as 'eternal truth' or as a product of our thinking. Nor, finally, can it be identical with mystical, emotional excitement; for religion itself is understood not as a turning away from but as a turning toward the reality different from ourselves which impresses itself upon us.[1] Obviously there is less emphasis on these negations; they are, in fact, not continued beyond the polemic of Chapter Two (§ 14).

4. The final step is the application of the concept of religion to Christianity. The freeing of man for absolute trust, the religious experience as such, is indescribable; it can be expressed only in the inexhaustibility of genuine life.[2] But its foundation and origin can be specified. If it is a question of this experience at all, it must lie within history; it must consist in the fact, which is experienced by us, of a wondrous man[3] in whom that releasing paradox of majesty and goodness becomes visible. Any man in our environment could be for us—and perhaps is for us—this 'wondrous' man. There is, in distinction to the written tradition, a living tradition embodied in persons who are in this sense witnesses to the reality of God.[4]

But we find many such men agreeing together and all equally certain that they have found this manifestation 'purer and stronger' than elsewhere, even uniquely, in the 'spiritual personality', the 'inner life' of Jesus. That agreement is a fact which is accessible to every man even though its significance is not obvious to every man. It is as much a part of the concrete reality of our own environment 'as the coat we put on or the house we live in'.[5]

The inner life of Jesus is the 'saving fact'.[6] The men for whom this statement is valid constitute the Christian community. Jesus becomes for them an element of their life's environment[7] (§ 15).

How does this come to pass? 'We are not required first to believe in Jesus; we must merely desire to see him.'[8] The *kingdom of God*, which Jesus according to the synoptic record brings, is the beneficent saving miracle of the rule of God within man's own heart, which establishes the practice of goodness in him. That is to say, man's independent will, triumphing in the conflict, is directed towards community[9] (§ 16). This 'kingdom of God' Jesus really *brings*. That is,

---

[1] *Verk des Ch.*, pp. 24 f. (Eng. pp. 30 f.); *Offenbarung und Wunder* pp. 14 f.
[2] *Ges. Aufs.*, p. 160.   [3] Ibid., p. 149.   [4] *Ethik*, p. 113.
[5] *Offenbarung und Wunder*, p. 15; *Verk. des ch.*, pp. 52 f. (Eng., p. 64).
[6] *Verk. des Ch.*, p. 68 (Eng., p. 83).   [7] *Offenbarung und Wunder*, p. 17.
[8] *Ethik*, p. 107.   [9] Ibid., pp. 98 ff.

he gives it to his own; by him the rule of God in their souls is given. He says to those who are 'shaken to the depths by his personality' that their sins are forgiven them. Therefore, to this extent, he claims for himself the title of Messiah (§ 17).

If now the person Jesus is to become the pure manifestation of God for *us* also, then he must become a reality of our own experience. The New Testament accounts of his life, even the accounts of his miracles, of his resurrection, etc., are in themselves powerless at just this point. 'That only can be a saving fact for a man which actually impresses itself upon him, which he does not need first to believe but which he simply sees as real.' [1] But 'historical research cannot confront us with the Saviour Jesus Christ. It cannot help us to find the historical Christ whom Christians assert to be their salvation.' [2] The 'inner' or 'spiritual' life of Jesus which it is necessary for us to see is 'never in any sense a minimum of the historically demonstrable'; [3] it is a fact 'in experiencing which one sees his own existence as bound up with the Omnipotent'. [4]

I think Herrmann's doctrine of Jesus as Saviour can be fairly presented with a metaphor. He is, seen from behind, an irresistible light shining through the tradition (whether the tradition is accepted critically or uncritically) as through a transparency; seen from in front, he is the object of an immediate experience which uses and penetrates the same medium. He is the object of an intuition [5] of such a kind that to over-emphasize the sovereignty of this double happening, in principle, over *every* historical judgement becomes impossible. Historians[6] who dream of being able to affect the life of our faith with their discoveries would therefore be for us 'absurd people' [7] (§ 18).

If faith is essentially obedience to the power upon which, from our own experience, we know ourselves to be inwardly dependent,[8] then we Christians are convinced that this power is revealed to us, beyond all

[1] Ibid., p. 109.

[2] Ibid., p. 95; *Verk. des Ch.*, pp. 62 f. (Eng., pp. 76 f.); *Ges. Aufs.*, p. 184.

[3] *Ges. Aufs.*, p. 189. Of Bousset's popular religio-historical book on Jesus, Herrmann remarked, 'That so much could be historically proved I have never believed possible.'

[4] *Ges. Aufs.*, p. 181.

[5] The term *intuition*, which Herrmann does not use, can hardly be avoided here. Cf. also Kattenbusch, op. cit., p. 82. In the fifth edition Kattenbusch adds: 'Here the influence which Tholuck (the preacher!) had on Hermann is to be recognized.'

[6] We can 'observe with equanimity' their work on the Bible (§ 22, p. 35).

[7] *Ethik*, p. 97.

[8] In his enthusiasm for Germany's allies in 1915, Herrmann thought he could find in the word *Islam* the translation of the biblical word *faith: Die Türken, die Engländer und wir deutschen Christen*, Marburg, 1915, p. 8 f. (*The Turks, the English and We German Christians*).

else, because we experience 'the power of the person, Jesus' over us. Faith is (not 'mere acceptance of doctrines'!) the strength for the inner conquest of relationships on which we are externally dependent. As such it is God's gift and yet at the same time it is a work of our obedience, of our integrity, so far as it is based on our own reflection upon the most important element of reality in our own life.

In what might be called his last will and testament Herrmann stated what he wanted to have understood by the 'communion of Christians with God'. In his debate with Emil Weber he said: 'I started from the thought that our communion with God can only proceed from the fact that he lets himself be found by us in the reality in which he places us. What others say to us about God helps us only if it leads us to understand what is given to us in our own experiences. That service other men can and must do for us. Without such help we remain imprisoned in externalities; we perceive nothing of the coming of God who is hidden in them. We all need to be educated by human goodness and truth. Just in the same way, I think, our capacity to appreciate the splendour of nature is first opened to us by seeing others impressed by it. If God's nearness to men is similarly mediated through men, yet it becomes completely ours in the experience which we ourselves undergo. God redeems us by allowing himself to be found by us.

'We Christians, however, believe that we ought to say that Jesus Christ is our Redeemer. When we so speak, we certainly do not intend to cease to say that God alone redeems us by his presence. The Christian community therefore unquestionably means that in the person of Jesus as nowhere else the reality of God becomes attainable to us. . . . This awareness which we therefore grasp through Jesus, we call our faith in him. Such faith is experienced by us as the certainty of overwhelming reality, the reality of a creative, spiritual power. It is unthinkable that we could achieve this certainty by our own effort. None the less such faith becomes a living faith in us as our personal decision. It is God's new creation and at the same time it is the change of mind or repentance demanded of us.' [1] (§ 19.)

We are coming to the close of the exposition of the principles of Herrmann's teaching. The next section presents only his characteristic, violent protest against the legalistic conception of revelation and faith as correct doctrine. A comparison of my old note-book with his published works shows that in his last decade he clearly became more violent. To judge from the criticism he made, Herrmann saw in the well-known

[1] *Christliche Welt*, 1918, no. 31–2, col. 293.

orthodox analysis of faith—knowledge, assent, trust (*notitia*, *assensus*, *fiducia*)—a psychological, genetic presentation and even a pastoral method of instruction as a preparation for faith. Therefore he cannot condemn strongly enough the putting of assent before trust. It is senseless to suppose that an act of the old unrenewed man, the intellectual assent to the teaching of the Holy Scripture or of the Church can be the origin of renewing faith, can be 'saving faith' (*fides salvifica*). It is equally absurd to suppose that a sin, the sin against honesty, can be the prerequisite for grace to the sinner, that an affirmation, made by forcing oneself contrary to sense and reason and therefore a *work*, can be called faith.

What remains of 'by faith alone' (*sola fide*)? [1] In the doctrine of assent, so understood, Herrmann saw orthodoxy's divergence from Luther.[2] And he continued (unmoved by the protest of Ihmel against such an interpretation) to see in it 'a veritable monster in our church' which was for him unquestionably the evil above all evils[3] (§ 20).

In close relation to the preceding, stands Herrmann's teaching on Holy Scripture. It is not accidental but rather consistent with the emphasis just noted that what is said positively concerning the authority of the Bible has diminished in the printed *Diktate* as compared with 1908. The final sentence in the earlier version reads: The more we become acquainted with the Holy Scriptures, the more we become convinced that here more than elsewhere the personal life of men, set free by God or faith, finds its expression.' What the present section when read carefully has to offer is found to consist almost wholly of reservations by which the force of that statement can be evaded. In the earlier version one sensed something of the correlation which Herrmann formulated in his *Ethik*. 'We cannot live without the support of authority, and yet we do not genuinely live if we are not independent.' [4] But now a strong overemphasis on the second half of this sentence is unmistakable. 'Out of what we *experience* in it, our faith in the Bible grows' presents the quintessence of Herrmann's positive view and there is no corresponding balance. The whole furthermore turns into a polemic against the doctrine of inspiration, arguing:

---

[1] *Verk. des Ch.*, pp. 178 f. (Eng., p. 158).
[2] Ibid., pp. 184 f. (Eng., pl 182).
[3] *Ges. Aufs.*, pp. 364 f. Later, in a writing which bears the apocalyptic date 1918 (*Der Sinn des Glaubens an Jesus Christus in Luthers Leben*, Göttingen), we find him wholly absorbed in this aspect of the problem.
[4] *Ethik*, p. 120.

(1) It originated when man no longer knew, as Luther did, how to base its character as revelation 'on one specific element of the Bible'.[1]

(2) And it has already become untenable because of the multiplicity of readings established by textual criticism.

We are therefore not prepared for finding included in § 23 an assertion that dogmatics has to discover the reality, which is hidden from the natural man and unveils itself only to faith, from the Holy Scriptures —and not as the Erlangen school would have it from the faith of important theologians. And this polemic sentence, so suddenly turned against the left, was inserted after 1908!

Was the former view of Herrmann's development as towards the left then wrong? Such a development can hardly be denied! Or did he move simultaneously towards the left and the right? A page farther on do we not read that 'Christian doctrine is actually to be understood *only* as an expression of new personal life'? I should like to hear a genuine, fully acknowledged pupil of Herrmann comment on these last paragraphs. My own view is that the true course of Herrmann's teaching is to be discerned through just these inconsistencies.

II

So far Origen-Herrmann. Now comes Gregory Thaumaturgos, the man who has received the teaching and must depart from it 'after the flesh' (κατὰ σάρκα) and yet 'after the spirit' (κατὰ πνεῦμα) *will* not wholly depart. I should now like to show in what direction we should look for the really consistent conclusions to be drawn from Herrmann's theology. These conclusions I do not find drawn by him—and not merely on the last point mentioned.

Let us begin with a short summary. The final statement in Herrmann's *Dogmatik* on the doctrine of the Trinity, § 58, reads:

Winter Semester 1907–1908	Winter Semester 1915–16
The religious knowledge of the Christian begins with the group of obvious facts establishing religion's power to affect conscience, but it ends with the confession that the God whose	By the doctrine of the Trinity we are reminded that we can find eternal life in communion with God only if he remains for us unsearchable and therefore an eternal mystery. The way to the

[1] Paul Althaus!

innermost nature has become revealed to us as love, still remains for us a God enthroned in unapproachable light (I Tim. 6.16).

The doctrine of the Trinity has therefore supreme significance because it reminds us that God who gives us eternal life through himself must be inexhaustible and therefore an unfathomable mystery.

Christian religion is the unconditioned will to truth or to submission to facts which we ourselves experience. But its *beginning* and its end is none the less man's humbling of himself before the unsearchable. 'God dwells in unapproachable light, whom no man has seen nor can see' (I Tim. 6.16).

The alteration consists primarily in quoting the biblical passage. The basic thought 'God is mystery' sounds more clearly. The 'it ends' has become 'its beginning and its end'. 'Confession' has become 'man's humbling himself'. And our finding of eternal life in the communion with God has been tied specifically to the acceptance of the whole content. The change may appear slight, but it illuminates the course taken by Herrmann's thought at this point. What is happening here ?

There is no word more significant for Herrmann's theology than the word 'self'. His theology stands or falls with the assertions that man must 'himself' will, yet cannot; and then must 'himself' experience or receive the revelation. But in this passage, just before the door shuts, we are told that not only at the end but also at the beginning of the 'submission' (as so understood) to facts, there must occur another wholly different 'submission', man's humbling himself before the 'eternal mystery' which God must remain to us; and even that there is danger of the loss of the eternal life which had before seemed secured to us in the communion with the same God depending on that first submission.

But then—the little word 'self' suddenly appears not to be the last word of this theology. And the doctrine of the 'way to religion' which is crystallized around this little word appears now to be put in question, not in relation to the world—in relation to the world it has legitimatized itself as universally valid so far as that world is concerned—but (and is this not much more dangerous ?) in relation to God.

The consummation of our life in communion with God depends on this second, wholly different 'submission' which has nothing to do with the first, the 'submission' to the 'self'-experienced. (The older version spoke here of conscience and God's love.) Herrmann knows that one does not 'experience' God the Father, Son and Holy Spirit, the mystery of God. 'Even where he reveals himself, God continues to dwell in darkness.' [1] And yet the acceptance of this mystery is not at all, as has

[1] *Ges. Aufs.*, p. 20.

been assumed from the thousand-and-one-times-cited passage of Melanchthon on the 'benefits of Christ' (*beneficia Christi*), a luxury which can be discarded; but (it is Herrmann who says it, not I) it is the *beginning* and *end* of the 'way to religion'. And the absoluteness of our will for 'self'-experience does not change at all the necessity of this last prerequisite so definitely proclaimed by the admission that it is the doctrine of the Trinity under which according to Herrmann himself his fundamental teaching of the way to religion comes to stand.

The objection can be raised that this remarkable statement is unique in Herrmann's work. That is true—at least I have looked in vain for parallels in his other writings. None the less, it does stand here and it confronts us with a question which affects the whole. How did Herrmann himself understand the relation of this concept to the rest of his teaching? Why is it not found in some form at the 'beginning', if it really belongs there? Would not a continuous relation be necessary between that significant, determinative second 'submission' and the well-known basic first principle? In consequence of the predominant and essentially primary character of the second 'submission' does not the whole of the teaching necessarily take on an entirely different aspect?

For example, would not something which was left unsaid have to be included on the significance of the person of Jesus or on the authority of the Bible? The way to faith in *the* God who is eternal mystery to us even in his revelation—yes! What would that now mean? Ought not dogmatics to have more to say about the way God comes to us?

But I go too fast. I shall be told that the doctrine of the Trinity with the signal conclusion which Herrmann derived from it is in fact according to him only one of those 'reflections of faith' belonging to the second, supplementary part of dogmatics. Therefore what is said here can be said in that context only and presents a truth in which man takes pleasure, but of which he can make no use. Again that is correct. So Herrmann himself thought or tried to think.

But we must *ask* the question whether what is said here, once it has been thought and said, *can* be rendered harmless in such a way. Actually in the theology of today we are no longer sure that there are any irrevocable ideas which are not liable to be neutralized and made harmless by reminding ourselves of their subjective conditioning. (With all due respect to the alleged 'Reformation correlation of faith and revelation' into which the 'moments of truth' of Schleiermacher and Ritschl are to be so prettily fitted,[1] along with the hither and thither

---

[1] F. W. Schmidt in the Preface to Herrmann's *Ges. Aufs.*, p. iv.

excursions of the 'religious-psychology circle'!) But the fact remains that if one has once had the idea that at the beginning and end of the pageant, where we theologians are amusing ourselves with such things, there stands the majesty of the Triune God, the Father whom none sees except in the Son who is One with him and through the Spirit who again is One with him; if one has once thought that God is eternally Subject and never object, that he determines himself and is knowable exclusively through himself in 'pure act' (*actus purissimus*) of his Triune Personality—then one has thought it and must continue to think it. The thought cannot afterwards be put in brackets as just a 'reflection of faith'.

But conversely—the lion breaks his cage; a wholly different 'Self' has stepped into the scene with *his* own validity. An a-priori of the so-called religion becomes visible *above* all that has been or can be experienced, above all circles and correlations. This is an a-priori of which Troeltsch at least never even dreamed, which certainly cannot be eliminated by the justified abolition of Troeltsch's a-priori.

Therefore it is not the truth of this 'religious idea' which is to be bracketed, but rather the truth of the teaching of 'the way to religion'. It becomes obligatory to ask whether dogmatics does not have to begin where Herrmann ends. Herrmann on paper naturally rebuts me. But there is also a Herrmann *in heaven*, who perhaps does *not* offer a rebuttal.

But enough on this concluding statement! I have much wider ground than this for understanding Herrmann differently than he understood himself. Let us now return to a sequence of five assumptions which were examined in the first part.

1. Herrmann claimed *universal validity* for his doctrine of the 'way to religion'. This point cannot be overstressed. For one reason because the whole of one very concrete side of his professional personality can be understood from this point only. A word must be said here regarding Herrmann's unforgettable fervour. The ordinary academic and scholarly fervour, which seldom appears without an admixture of Fichtean pride, can be observed on every street in German University cities. There has been and there will perhaps be again a philosophical fervour which is almost priestly, as was impressed on us at Marburg in Herrmann's time by the figures of a Cohen and a Natorp. But what confronted us in Herrmann was neither the latter nor the former. He showed us that theology, not merely as a participant in the Four Faculties, but theology as such, could have its *own* professional fervour.

There was a ring in Herrmann's voice—those who heard him lecture hear it today in his writings—the ring of prophetic utterance which pointed to a content, hidden indeed but to be evaded by no one without penalty, the recognition of which demanded a scientific *theology*.

This possibility, which gave the calling of the theologian its unique tempering, was what we felt we gained from Herrmann's teaching. That possibility! It is truly no small achievement that Herrmann really showed us such a possibility again. It was a promise—to which indeed succeeded a certain disappointment. For the insecurity of the grounds on which he based his claim presented a very great contrast to the deep fervour with which he made the claim.

Did it not appear as though he wanted to say something which at the critical moment he *failed* to say? What did Herrmann mean by 'universal validity'? We heard that dogmatics shares in the validity given an historical fact, for instance an historical personage, when one experiences it. That assertion is in itself somewhat questionable. But we also heard—and this is something very different and is in itself not indubitable—that dogmatics, because of its fundamental requirement for truthfulness, shares in the universal validity of logic and ethics. As a scientific discipline, then, would theology come somewhere midway between a romantic philosophy of immediateness and a Kantian science of law? Did Herrmann believe that?

Or did Herrmann not rather speak as though he *knew* apart from and above the two levels of reason and experience with which he appeared to reckon, still another relation of men to 'reality', a relation in which man does not 'stand' at all, but in which he knows himself wholly *set*? Just consider for a moment the decisive point in Herrmann's argument, the doctrine of the necessary, critical question of man's real self. For this question to be possible in the first place, there must be a standard of measurement, an original pattern of the human self, possessing unconditional validity for *every* man, a real 'principle of individuation' (*principium individuationis*). Secondly, for this question to be necessary, man would have to *know* of this pattern and its authority, he would have to see himself tested by it. Finally, for the question *actually* to be asked, for the man really to put this question to himself (and for Herrmann's argument everything hangs on this actual asking) there must exist a relation of knowledge between the man and that pattern, which rules out any refusal to put the question, a relation only comprehensible as a knowledge of the self, of the original pattern imparted to men.

From the Beyond, beyond reason and experience, in the context designated by the doctrine of the Trinity, in the context of the Word of the Father received through the Spirit, man must be put in question; he must be questioned through God's Self upon his own self. But this means that the revelation towards which, according to Herrmann, that question is to *lead* must be already understood as the presupposition for the question. And the claim of dogmatics to universal validity, if it is based upon this question, would be understood neither historically nor epistemologically, but strictly theologically as assertion of the universal validity of God's claim upon mankind. Hence it follows that man asks about his 'self' because and if God is pleased to give to him knowledge of himself, because and if God's Word is spoken to him.

The place to begin in dogmatics would therefore be with 'God said' (*Deus dixit*), repudiating the wholly futile attempt to attain to that beginning (if possible again) as a mere 'reflection of faith' on the summit of an alleged 'experience'. (As if there were any such experience!) Did not Herrmann speak *as if* he had that intention of beginning there? (Naturally I know that he had no idea of so doing.) If that could be said, then the claim to universal validity and his own great fervour arising from that claim would be no riddle.

2. Herrmann was certainly at his best when he was engaged in battle against apologetics, both the old and the new, the modest and the arrogant. This fact also illuminates one side of his theological personality. Not only was he a 'personally convinced Christian' (whatever that means), but also—what is very rare in the pulpit or behind the lecturer's desk—his theological science was definitely determined through his knowledge of what the ancients called '*autopistia*', that is by the conviction of Christian truth as based on itself. This knowledge is rat-poison to all intellectualizing subtleties in theology. What is already established can well be left without proof. Herrmann was *not* ashamed of the Gospel. His countenance wholly lacked that expression of worldly wisdom which too often makes the 'systematic' theologian recognizable afar off. His theology also lacked it. . . . Many therefore have found his theology naïve. Like the Marburg students who shrugged off his 'advanced confirmation instruction', they have ridiculed an *Ethik* which used a paragraph to say its final word on 'morally allowable recreation'—at a time when the star of Troeltsch with his world-wide programmes and perspectives was nearing its zenith!

Here belongs also Herrmann's notorious *monotony*. Did he not always say the same thing in all his writings and in his short series of three or four lectures? Certainly he did.[1] But his monotony and his simplicity are so closely bound with the impressive knowledge of the matter itself, that I should not dare today to speak a word against them. The theology of the redeemed has always been simple and monotonous. 'Follow in their path'.

But when this has been said, it still remains necessary to weigh the real significance of that anti-apologetic second chapter of the *Dogmatik*. To be really simple is not, in fact, so simple. Thus—neither an Aristotelian metaphysical foundation of religion, nor an integration of religion into the world-view of philosophical idealism, *nor* epistemological analysis of the psychological reality of religion. Good! All of that one has listened to and has learned to accept from youth on.

But from what summit does this torrent really come, sweeping all before it? And what happens next, when it has done its saving work? Somewhere the sphinx of religion must really belong, it must bear some kind of name; and to give correct information on such points must be the business of dogmatics. Herrmann has told us specifically of everything on which religion is *not* based. He opened a wide and empty gulf before which most of his contemporaries were wont to shake their heads and draw back. Who could endure to look with him into this abyss? Or rather how many were willing to abandon all safeguards and hurl themselves straight into the abyss? Even though Herrmann—unfortunately, one could almost say—had done his best to fill up the great gulf so that in his opinion it should be possible to stand there.

But it is precisely this attempt at filling in the hole which does not work! I repeat a quotation: 'Knowledge of God is the expression of individual experience and is without weapons.' 'Without weapons' is excellent! But 'expression of individual experience' is certainly not good. For before the Divine on which Herrmann obviously means here to make a claim, neither 'individual experience' nor its 'expression' is entitled to anything at all. Herrmann's 'weaponlessness' is not the weaponlessness of the *divine*. That which occurs as 'experience', as

---

[1] 'With a constant ability, which amounts to genius, always to be emotional without being wordy, he has basically only one topic on which to speak or write: what *faith* is. . . . The final form of his lectures plainly shows the monotony (the term should not be misunderstood) of Herrmann's method of teaching. It was precisely in this method, which was never tiresome for it struck on the heart and the will like a bell peal, that there can be found the secret of his power as a teacher over the minds of the young' (Kattenbusch, op. cit., p. 83). In a later passage (p. 84), the narrowness of his problem is indeed called a 'very obvious limitation'.

'historical fact', cannot be isolated from the world in the way Herrmann wished. It is like everything human, very much in need of apologetics of many kinds. To introduce in its behalf the great twilight of the gods would certainly be decidedly premature. It is *in* the world and *of* the world. Cohen and Natorp were right when together they shook their heads over a theology which refused to defend itself in *this* corner of the world.

Herrmann once asserted, against Natorp, that one could discover religion in *no object*, however sensitive, not even in the hidden nature of the soul.[1] Beautiful! Most excellent! But if true, then Herrmann himself would have been compelled at the very first to deal quite differently, to deal *dialectically*, with the concepts of 'experience' and 'historical fact'.

But perhaps the words just cited point to the truth that in this connexion also Herrmann wanted to say something wholly different from what he actually said. What if this last attempt to fill up the yawning gulf of religion's unprovability by means of the 'individual experience' should also be abandoned like the rest in the knowledge that to *this* entity, *autopistis*, no one can possibly assert a claim? What if faith can only be a sign pointing toward that basis, founded in itself, which is never in any sense 'object', but is always unchangeably subject? How would it be if the datum with which dogmatics has to begin were not man—in his experience as little as in his thinking—but again God himself in *his* Word?

Obviously this is no datum to be found in any sense on the level of our consciousness. It is not God as an assumption of our consciousness. It is God setting himself over against our consciousness and its assumptions and now become known in that height, fixed and unchangeable by any manipulation of the circle of human knowledge; known as above the knowledge which can be grasped as mere self knowledge; he is God giving himself to be known through his Word. If this is the truth, then Herrmann's repudiation of Thomas as of Eucken, of Kant as of Troeltsch, would be meaningful and so would the simplicity and monotony of his teaching in itself.

It would then be clear whence came his polemic and whither it led— not from poverty certainly but from riches, not into emptiness but into fullness. Perhaps it did not need to be so bitter and vehement. It could have found room both for the humour, which Herrmann did not understand but which classical theology still could use, and for a little

[1] *Ges. Aufs.*, p. 401.

apologetics not taken so seriously. Why should one not be allowed to offer proof of God when one is certain of him?

Now, of course, this was not what Herrmann consciously meant. But again I ask whether he did not speak *as if* this was his meaning? Does not Herrmann's cardinal question 'How do I attain faith?' become pointless if we take seriously the greater Herrmann answer of *autopistis*, of Christian truth to which I do not need to attain because it has first come to me? Is not that magnificent disdain of all rubbish, which we loved in Herrmann, incomprehensible if it is necessary always to understand him 'according to the flesh' *(κατὰ σάρκα)*?

3. We have seen on what a fabulously sharp edge the centre of Herrmann's theory of religion is balanced. The 'way to religion' is the road from the individually experienced problem of truth and actuality to the also individually experienced solution of the problem in transcendence of it through God or in free surrender to him. It was important to Herrmann that in tracing this 'way' in opposition to orthodoxy, he should be in the position to give 'a view of the prologue to the inner change', to show 'how the Holy Spirit is given' *(quomodo detur spiritus sanctus)*.[1] Apparently it was with this in mind that Troeltsch, answering spite with spite, called Herrmann 'one of the liveliest of our edifying writers'.[2]

It is the pietistic (in a good and a less good sense) element in Herrmann which we recognize here. Certainly it was not for nothing that in his youth he was amanuensis for that great virtuoso of the heart, Tholuck.[3] Herrmann's whole system is oriented towards the cure of souls, to the genesis of Christianity in the individual.[4] This is fundamentally the plane of Kierkegaard's middle period,[5] on which according to him theology had established its headquarters. In order to have a share of religion in Protestantism 'we must be certain of the eternal God who himself has communion with us. That happens to no one without a "great shaking of soul" *(sine magna concussione animae)*. Then we must meet the demand of the special situation in which we currently stand,

---

[1] *Ethik*, p. 94.
[2] 'Whose influence I can find no way to escape' (*Ges. Schriften* II, p. 768).
[3] *Dogmatik* p. x; cf. above p. 250[5].
[4] In his review of Herrmann's *Dogmatik* (*Christliche Welt*, 1925, no. 20–1, col. 467 f.) H. R. Mackintosh of Edinburgh wrote: 'Henry Drummond's gospel lectures thirty-five years ago and Herrmann's lectures in Marburg differ in the method used, but the atmosphere of both is the same. There would have been no incongruity if the lecturer on any suitable day had closed with the announcement of an after-meeting (i.e. for the converted). Conversions must often have followed from his instruction.'
[5] Herrmann seems scarcely to have known of him.

with seriousness and fidelity. If this is true, then theology must demonstrate that the fundamental concern in Christianity is the encounter with our present existence.' [1]

I do not need to lay particular emphasis on the incontrovertible truth of this conception, because it speaks for itself. The sense that in Herrmann's lectures each listener felt himself individually addressed belongs to the best of our Marburg memories. It must be said again and again that for Herrmann the problem of dogmatics was concerned with a situation, but a situation closely related to the revelation which depends on God speaking to mankind—and mankind *exists only as individual men*. A 'theology of the unregenerate' (*theologia irregenitorum*) in any form would be a crude and essentially a fraudulent and offensive construction.

But this does not imply that the problem of dogmatics is a genetic, psychological, and pastoral problem. Perhaps Herrmann's finest quality is shown in his *failure* to carry through *such* a programme.[2] Is his description of the 'way to religion' really clear ? Is it really a description of a *road* on which man actually walks ? I think the knife-edge along which he would lead us is much too sharp for walking. This way is *not* a *way* at all. A man does not 'experience' it, or 'pass through it'. What he does pass through and experience is certainly *not* that way. Consider, for example, the acute and deadly conflict between truth and actuality! When and how far does this battle involve us ? Do we actually experience it in perceptive moments of our inner development as specific stations on *our* road ? Surely not. We encounter it only when and only so far as we come into God's court of judgement. Only the pietists would say otherwise.

Further, what does the solution or the transcending of this conflict mean ? Who would really dare affirm that he had anything of the sort in his past as *his* experience ? If it were asserted that when God's grace is revealed to us, this solution is achieved, that assertion would be true.

And consider also the significant dialectic which Herrmann continually emphasized between dependence and freedom, opposition and surrender. The statements he made are neither clear nor edifying,

---

[1] *Verk. des Ch.*, pp. 196 f.
[2] F. W. Schmidt writes (*Ges. Aufs.*, p. iii) of 'Barth, Gogarten, and their friends': 'Perhaps even they might notice that the understanding of the Pauline "by faith alone" (*sola fide*) did not begin today to awaken for the first time after 400 years.' Certainly he never heard one of us assert any such thing; if for no other reason than because a renewed understanding of 'by faith alone' constitutes at most only one section of our position. Schmidt's understanding of 'by faith alone' differs somewhat from ours, as he proves by adding that he sees in Herrmann's theology an effective shield against all (!) the historicism and psychologism against which we are fighting. No! Surely not against *all*!

for they seem to imply—what is, in fact, Pietism's final word—that the real nature of life's deepest moment is a kind of see-saw game of 'Yes and No' (*Sic et Non*). If it is actually such a game, then ought not men to remain stuck in Pietism? But if Herrmann's formulation were a sign pointing to a summit *beyond* objective and subjective, to the 'kingdom of God' in the New Testament sense, to 'justification, peace and joy', not in the precariousness of our 'inner life' but 'in the Holy Spirit' through whom God becomes our God, then the whole would be clear and consistent.

Alas! Herrmann did not so mean it. On the contrary he boasted of presenting, in antithesis to orthodoxy, man's actual experience. This claim he could not make good, for the frankness and sincerity which were characteristic of him made it impossible for him to prevent the invisible reality of God from breaking out at every edge and corner of the shell of psychological pragmatism in which, in spite of his occasional better insight, he enclosed it. 'How the Holy Spirit is given' (*quo modo detur spiritus sanctus*) is precisely what man must not wish to show. (Melanchthon made the ill-judged attempt long ago). We must proclaim the *Word*, subordinate the cure of souls to the sermon and not the reverse. And through the Word of God, God himself will let himself be revealed. Is not *that* what Herrmann really meant? What he sought?

4. The theory of the significance of the 'inner life' of Jesus as revelation. This has become the shibboleth of Herrmann's theology because it seemed to define most clearly his position in the history of the new dogmatic, differentiating it from orthodoxy and liberalism, and showing his correction of Schleiermacher through Ritschl and of Ritschl through Schleiermacher. This historical application of the teaching we can ignore.

'From the theologian we expect that he shall not only know the history of the Christian community but also that he shall make the concerns of the Christian community his own. . . . We do not stand free, as neutral observers of our object. We will to be ourselves determined by it in our inmost depths.' [1] I see the true significance in principle of Herrmann's Christology in this acknowledgement (which, in fact, accepts the aims of Schleiermacher and Ritschl) of a constraining obligation of dogmatics to—should I say to the Church or to history? Obligation to history (alas!) would have seemed to Herrmann the better label. On the one hand, this was a constraint which confronted us in the unforgettably persistent tenacity with which Herrmann always

[1] *Ges. Aufs.*, pp. 1 ff.

came back to the 'person of Jesus'. But such persistence would have had no sense in relation to the merely historical. It therefore requires an interpretation different from that given by Herrmann himself.

What was his aim in his Christology? We have seen what role the word 'actuality' played in this part of his teaching. What reveals God to us must be 'actual' in the same sense as all else which in its existence and nature does not reveal God to us. This actuality does not apply to all the teachings about Jesus; it does not apply to the biblical accounts of his miracles, etc.; but it does apply to his 'inner life'. That such a man, presenting these spiritual characteristics, lived on earth is 'actuality', and this actuality *is* the Christian *revelation*.

'*Is*'? Yes. *Revelation* stands under the condition that this *is* becomes known in faith. But the '*is*' itself stands under no condition. One need only read in Herrmann's *Dogmatik* the significant (and to him obviously exceedingly important) historical § 55 on the Christological dogma to be convinced that he held as a certainty the statement in support of which he could call upon Luther, apparently not without justification: '*In the power of the man Jesus* we apprehend God himself working upon us.' That is monophysite [1] and it is impossible.[2] In the power of *the man Jesus as such* we never 'apprehend' God himself.[3] That power, if so isolated it existed at all as a conceivable entity (which it is not), would be an historical influence which would necessarily diminish as the square of the time-space-distance, like any other historical potency.

What is the revelation of God to us cannot be at all something 'actual' in the same sense as are all other objects. It must certainly be 'actual', but it must be wholly a '*divine*-actual'; it must be human, but it must be wholly divine-human.[4] Because Jesus is the Logos, the Word of God become flesh (*not* because of the man in himself), we apprehend God in the man Jesus. Certainly in the *man* Jesus, that is in the 'person of Jesus'. But that is just the point—the person Jesus is the Logos—there is no person Jesus existing apart from the Logos. In the power of Jesus we 'apprehend' God acting. But this statement cannot be established on the basis of preceding experiences, as according to Herrmann's Christology it ought to be established. His Christology

---

[1] It is certainly not accidental that in Herrmann's detailed account of the developments before and after Chalcedon, there is no mention of the fact that a man named Eutyches was condemned there.

[2] Here I think I stand in agreement with F. W. Schmidt (*Wilhelm Herrmann*, pp. 41, 53), except that in what Schmidt feels to be a doubtful point, I see an example of the one great error in Herrmann's teaching.

[3] I Tim. 2.5 can hardly be used in support of Herrmann's doctrine.

[4] εἰκὼν θεοῦ, says F. W. Schmidt, op. cit.

obviously belongs in the Class B, the unauthoritative, section of theologoumena.

But this truth is the beginning, the basis and the presupposition apart from which Christian preaching and dogmatics cannot say one meaningful word concerning Christ. Without that truth, they both remain undeniably stuck fast in history. Here no other 'way' whatever exists except the road from above downwards. Orthodox Christology is a glacial torrent rushing straight down from a height of three thousand metres; it makes accomplishment possible. Herrmann's Christology, as it stands, is the hopeless attempt to raise a stagnant pool to that same height by means of a hand pump; nothing can be accomplished with it.

But did Herrmann really intend this? Or did he not rather, here also, speak constantly of the 'inner life' of Jesus which was supposedly a bare actuality comparable to a house or an overcoat, *as if* it were already self-evident that this 'inner life' is the basis of faith? Not in itself, not by virtue of its qualities understood historically, psychologically or intuitively and so comparable to other historical phenomena, but because *it pleased God* to reveal himself in this life? For what was it that made Herrmann's words about Jesus worth believing in spite of everything? Certainly not what he consciously presented positively as a description of this 'actuality'. That was thin in relation to the fullness of the old Christological dogma and quite arbitrary in relation to the New Testament. It was rather the impression we received that when he presented the deity of Christ, he dealt with an a-priori.

In spite of all the preliminary anagogics, the case had been already decided (*causa judicata*). The datum with which he began—his own contrary protestation had to be determinedly ignored—was the *risen*, the *exalted Christ*. From that beginning all the enigmatic statements which he made about the relation between history and faith, between the 'life' of Jesus and our *experience* of his life would become understandable.

We heard of a twofold action in which the New Testament tradition becomes so to speak transparent through the inherent power of the human life of Jesus on the one side and on the other side through the inherent power of our (that is the believing Christian's) experiencing intuition. But how are these two powers related to each other? Are there really two actions here? And are they rightly attributed when they are ascribed respectively to the *man* Jesus and to us, to *men*? Has anything essential been said when the 'indissoluble correlation of revelation and faith' is asserted? As if the problem which demands an answer were not precisely this inseparability! And has anything important been achieved when, after attesting to the 'theocentric theology' within this correlation, the greatest possible emphasis in the conclusion is put on the *objective* moment of the revelation? As if then the next theological generation would not have to insist with equal right on underlining the *subjective* moment!

There could be clarity here only if the action is twofold merely apparently but not actually; if it is *human* action only in a secondary sense; if that 'light shining' (*lucere*) from behind and that 'penetrating insight' (*intueri*) from in front are to be understood as a *single* act of Christ the King ruling his *Church* in the *Word* through the Spirit. Once this 'first principle of theology' (*principium theologiae*) is acknowledged, the religious-psychological circle could always be put to use later.

But it is very plain that then a basis would no longer exist for singling out the 'inner life' of Jesus as the unique bearer of the revelation. Then such a view shows itself to be a fragment from the pietistic-rationalistic attempt to avoid the stumbling-block of the absolutely inexorable requirement for faith and obedience, as a final attempt to build a bridge across from what human truthfulness calls actuality to what is actuality only through divine truthfulness, through 'the truth of God' (*veracitas Dei*).

It would then have to be said that the apostolic proclamation, in which the miracle of the epiphany was not merely the content of faith but was also the basis of faith, and the aims of the orthodox Christology were essentially correct. Both come from the Beyond which Herrmann wants to reach with his words. But one cannot *will* to reach that Beyond! Yet is it not true that in spite of his own words, the Beyond is really the place from which he started? That he meant a *single* action when he spoke of a twofold? That he meant the rule of *Christ* in his *Church* when he referred us to history and experience? Was not this insight necessarily the hidden cause of that narrowness which his attitude made us so honour?

5. The problem of authoritative dogma. At the beginning of Part I our attention was directed to the peculiar schism in Herrmann's thought. On the one side there was an ever more one-sided and heavier emphasis on the idea that revelation was not a doctrine, and faith was not an acceptance as true; that the authority of the Bible rested on experience and on experience only. On the other side there was an equally forcible expression of the idea that the content of the Christian teaching was to be gained not from faith but from the Holy Scriptures. Which is valid?

If we ask first on which of the contradictory positions which he presented Herrmann himself, his heart, his professional character, is to be sought, there can be no doubt of the answer—on the first. He made very clear what he intended by his *No* to the Bible and tradition; what his *Yes* affirmed is not so clear. The emphatic warning not 'to accept anything as true' without previous experience of it drowns out the admonition to take first respectful cognizance of it.

How clear and convincing his explanations were when he was spinning his own thread! And on the other hand, how plainly forced and artificial [1] when on occasion he sought to find support in the Bible and church tradition. The dependence noted earlier held in principle, but it was not concretely available. Herrmann was no textual exegete, but rather an articulate independent thinker. That is not a reproach. There is need of such personalities in theology. It was precisely as such an independent thinker that we honoured Herrmann.

The air of freedom blew through his auditorium. It was certainly not by chance that for decades every semester a small caravan from Switzerland made the pilgrimage to Marburg and felt especially at home there. Our rebellious minds, repudiating all authority, there found satisfaction. We listened gladly when traditionalism on the right, rationalism on the left, mysticism in the rear were thrown to the refuse dump, and when finally 'positive and liberal dogmatics' were together hurled into the same pit. [2]

The students who listened to Herrmann could then present themselves to Johannes Müller. They would be fully convinced that intellectualism is nothing, that everything depends on 'experience'. Now that ought to be and must be fundamentally true. I still so assert today, although I now know that then it was the old Adam rather than the new who rejoiced in what I was hearing. Freedom *is*, in its place and in its proper context, an important and fundamental theological concept, belonging to that necessity for existential thinking which at least in Protestant theology can never be denied.

But today we must remind ourselves that as surely as it accorded with Herrmann's predisposition and as certainly as it was his special

[1] Who would not prefer to see the 'Communion of the Christian with God' without the 'Concord with Luther'? Cf. Kattenbusch (op. cit., p. 89): 'However carefully he read his Luther, he only felt himself debating with him and he took note of Luther's powerful statements only in order to make use of them for the strengthening or the clarifying of the ideas he himself was advocating'—a kind of Luther-reading in which Herrmann does not stand alone, it should be noted.

[2] 'Christl-prot. Dog.,' p. 630. If anyone doubts how gladly I myself listened, he should read in *Zeitschrift für Theologie und Kirche* 1909, Heft 4 and 6, the kind of astonishing ideas I joyfully set forth as a 23-year-old candidate for the ministry —to the horror of less consistent friends of Herrmann.

mission to affirm the validity of this concern for freedom (he preferred to say 'truthfulness') in theology; he was equally sure that this concern cannot be the *final* and the *only* concern. Wilhelm Herrmann cannot be put into the same file—not even properly in a classified authors' list—together with Otto Baumgarten.[1] He did not merely carry over with blind courage a primitive philosophical idea of autonomy and apply it to the one theological subject. He knew definite limits beyond which he made no use of that right of independent thinking, dear as it was to him. There were areas where he did not allow others to use it without rapping their knuckles.[2]

He knew, at least fundamentally, that in theology there is also an authority over against freedom. Persistently again and again he pointed to history, not only to the inner life of Jesus, but also to the Bible, and even to the church tradition,[3] as norms according to which one must be judged in dogmatics; exactly as he also saw the attainment of normative doctrine to be the goal of dogmatic effort. He did *not* stand here with his heart—that can be said with certainty. He was not so convincing when he said *this*. He could not here make what he intended so clear. But we maintain firmly that this he also knew and also said.

Now, in my judgement, the harmful error of Herrmann's theology was *not* in his obvious overweighting of one side of his boat. That could be remedied by a smaller or greater push to the right, by a more or less slight reaction, by an 'on the other hand' (the phrase he so especially loved in theology); that is, by a somewhat greater emphasis on the moment of objectivity, authority, etc. On the contrary, I should say that the zigzag course on which this boat streaks through the waves as if it were coming out from a naval battle, belongs to the best in Herrmann's theology. It is evidence that here there was conflict with a 'tremendous shaking of soul' (*magna concussione animae*). A theology worthy of respect is always one-sided.

It is not the overemphasis on truthfulness which is bad in Herrmann. On the contrary, that emphasis is good! And the remedy is not to emphasize it somewhat less and therefore at the same time to emphasize history somewhat more. The result would be an apothecary's theology

---

[1] Cf. Otto Baumgarten, *Die Gefährdung der Wahrhaftigkeit durch die Kirche*, Gotha, 1925. This is the classic document of uneducated vulgar liberalism.

[2] Cf. *Ges. Aufs.*, pp. 87 ff. For the historical justification of the preceding and of note 1, I may add that this passage was aimed (as far back as 1898)—at Baumgarten.

[3] It was truly no accident that, whether it went well or badly, he felt it necessary to present the 'communion of the Christian with God' as throughout in 'concord with Luther'.

which can come to no good end. (And it is to Herrmann's honour that he was no apothecary!)

But clarity must be achieved on the reason *why* it is that one must emphasize one *and* the other, and probably emphasize one *more* than the other, without in the least ceasing to hold fast to the less emphasized. It is the lack of this clarity which is Herrmann's error.

To begin with the second, the less-emphasized side . . . It is scarcely enlightening to say of the Bible and dogma (in specific relation to the impossible theory of the 'power of the man Jesus') that they are expressions of human faith, 'religious ideas of other men', and therefore they are not binding upon us (wholly without reference to the fact that these other men happen to have been Apostles, Counciliar Fathers, Reformers and the like). Although they are not in themselves binding, they could be for us an incentive to undergo ourselves the experiences of which they speak; and they would then become authoritative for us, normative and an obligatory source of Christian preaching and dogmatics. That statement does not hold. 'Religious ideas of other men' do *not* deserve the kind of respect which one has for a genuine authority. If Bible and dogma are in entirety nothing but the 'religious thoughts of others', then they have *no* authority; neither can they gain it.

For, and this is the second point, an authority is either there or not there. What is not authority from the beginning cannot become such. How could we on the basis of experience possibly establish authority? Authorities so established could be only idols. No wonder that the positive thing which Herrmann was impelled to say and said with the best intentions concerning Bible and dogma came out so thin and was drowned out ten times over by the warnings against idols—he himself so named them.

And yet he *wanted* to say something positive here. He called the Bible very emphatically *Holy* Scripture; and he clung to the name *dogmatics* for a reason which is really no reason, although there was nothing to prevent him from saying 'the teaching of faith'. It was as though he knew that there where his finger somewhat awkwardly pointed, he was not really dealing with 'history'. As if he really thought that the voice of an apostle is not at all merely the voice of some religious man, nor is Luther's voice nor the vote of the Councils of Nicea and Chalcedon. As if there were an a-priori before all the 'experience' in the course of which the individual takes a position in relation to these things; as if there were something like a Christian Church built on the foundation of the apostles and prophets—built, that is, on the authentically attested revelation; a Church which is commissioned and equipped to proclaim the revelation authentically on this foundation. Finally as if dogmatics were not concerned with setting up irrelevant 'reflections of faith' on the basis of irrelevant 'experiences', but was founded from the beginning on *Holy* Scripture and directed by a dogma which must be fully respected in the search for the norms of the right and authentic Christian message. If Herrmann had meant something like *that*, then there would be no question that he had full right to refuse to have anything to do with liberalism, however close to it he seemed to be.

And now the other side of the antithesis, the freedom, the truthfulness. First a question: Who is really free here ? Wholly sincere ? Who is the measure of all things, sovereign over all human words ? Whose interests are served by the tirelessly repeated assertion that revelation is not doctrine and faith is not the accepting as true ? Is what is so defended ultimately only the right of the romantic individuality ? If so, then the 'plaster' bust [1] of Schleiermacher which Herrmann as a child saw standing on his father's desk would have been a bad omen.

If *man* is really the sanctuary which Herrmann in a kind of panic thinks he must protect against the ghost of legalism which he sees threatening from Rome, from orthodoxy, from Ritschl—from where not ?—then one could only turn away alienated by his procedure. The proclamation of the revelation seems too closely bound in every way to human truthfulness and freedom. We must not forget that even in our truthfulness we are liars and in our freedom sinners. It seems to expect too much of man, and first of all, fortuitously, of man's head.

The Church should always present the revelation to men in 'doctrine'. (In what else ? Surely not in lyrical poetry nor in disconnected aphorisms nor in unauthoritative emotional outbursts.) And it should always present it with the claim that this doctrine 'is to be accepted as true'. (How else ? Should it be offered as a fairy tale ?) Would to God that our teaching were so worthy of belief that it could compel such acceptance as truth! For that purpose the Church is here; it is that which the Church can do in relation to the revelation; it can teach what man should accept as true.

The other revelation, the unmediated, that which is not merely doctrine, not something to be accepted as true but God's authentic Word to man, is spoken on a different plane. But that Word is not heard when the teaching and the accepting as true are discredited and

[1] *Dogmatik*, p. ix.

neglected; only when they are perseveringly preserved on the plane on which the Church can act. And on that plane there must be 'positive doctrine' as Herrmann himself demanded.

But Herrmann's real concern here could be even *deeper*. Here also he could have meant the sovereignty of the *Word*, of the divine Word himself over all human words. His fight against 'doctrinal legalism' could be understood positively as an appeal to pay attention to the Speaker *and* Hearer who is above all that we say and hear. It could be understood as a reminder of the meaning of the demand which the Church with its doctrine makes upon men by pointing to the immediate event on the higher plane which the Church can only serve. It could be understood as a warning against all forced conformity, as a protest against every divergence by which that event is *not* served, as a thundering summons to the matter itself, to the true theme, to him about whom everything centres in the Bible, in dogma, in preaching. Then his polemic would be aimed not against but *for* the authority of doctrine.

Does the Church not need this call? Could we be grateful enough to Herrmann if what he had wanted to say to us was something like this? And would it not then be understandable that dogmatics, that theology must be *wholly* free as well as *wholly* bound, free and bound through its object, through its task?

I have finished. Herrmann has spoken and we have listened. Take what I have told you of my own listening as an attempt to be faithful to what Herrmann so often told us: listen for yourselves.

IX

THE CONCEPT OF THE CHURCH

A lecture given at the University Association of the Centre Party in Münster i/W, 11th July 1927.

We should not deceive ourselves; our present meeting together is a very daring experiment. But for myself, I can affirm that I am happy to bear at least half of the responsibility for the venture by my acceptance of the friendly invitation extended to me.

Can Catholics and Protestants really carry on with each other a discussion which is specifically theological? One which deals not merely with an historical or practical question, but with a theme of the greatest seriousness, with a fundamental concept of Christian dogmatics? And especially can they discuss that concept, which, as every intelligent person knows, always emerges in every basic attempt at understanding between the two sides as the limit at which yes and no (*sic et non*) inevitably clash and all understanding ceases? A concept which makes suspect all understanding apparently reached previously—the concept of the *Church*?

I would answer that *if* such a discussion is ever to be risked (and the possibility seems near here in Münster), then it would be wise to assume beforehand that for a discussion upon such a fundamental theme (that is upon a question of dogma and particularly upon *this* question on which, if we are not mistaken, we are essentially divided in spirit), the aim ought to be defined simply as the gain of a better understanding of why and how far, under present circumstances (*rebus sic stantibus*), we cannot understand each other. Our undertaking today is therefore a real risk; for at best it can end with no more than that result. And such a result I should certainly consider success.

In the sixteenth and seventeenth centuries Catholics and Protestants still looked each other in the eye—angrily, but *in the eye*. They talked with each other, sharply and harshly; but they really talked. We today, however, weary of the long conflict, and perhaps also weary of this kind of Christian seriousness, look past each other all along the line, and talk past each other in unfruitful and ineffective fashion about the deep mystery which certainly concerns us equally on this side and on that. Still oftener we stand opposite each other in complete detachment.

I accepted the invitation to come here because I judged this coming together to be an attempt mutually to take each other seriously. Taking ourselves seriously as those who are not united in Christ (as we certainly are not) cannot mean meeting in human friendliness, listening to each other calmly and attentively, recognizing mutual agreement on various side issues, nor even ascribing to each other 'good faith' (*bona fides*) however mistaken, in the great, critical, main issue. So much certainly we are all willing to do. Rather we are required to take again upon ourselves the whole burden of the opposition between us as our burden and as a mutual burden of opposition on both sides. (Too often we excuse ourselves from recognizing that the burden of opposition is there.) Such taking of ourselves seriously means *seeing* the other man over there who also calls himself a Christian, really seeing him in his whole shocking diversity of belief, in his alien repudiation of that which to us is the most central and irrefragible Christian truth. It means making clear to ourselves that he on his side is just as shocked by us and in the same way.

The great, painful enigma of the divided Church, division precisely where there should be no division, where division is a 'contradiction in terms' (*contradictio in adjecto*), must be again allowed to manifest itself. Then we may leave here as better, more convinced, but also as somewhat more thoughtful, Catholics or Protestants who are homesick for the peace in Christ which we do not now know, who are seeking for that peace. In the hope that we may perhaps succeed in taking each other seriously in this sense, I can undertake to speak to you here.

I

The division in Western Christianity, which appears nowhere else so glaringly as in its disagreement on the concept of the Church, is so serious because neither side can possibly deny that it is really *the same object* on the right concept of which they cannot agree. Nor can they ignore all the serious results which follow from this fact. It is not true that Catholics and Protestants mean totally different realities when they speak of the Church (although it cannot be denied that we *also* in part see different realities). But the conflict over these differences can be important and necessary only because, previously and first of all, it is the *same* reality which we *see differently* here and there. Or ought we not rather to put it: because *the same reality*, according to God's mysterious plan, *appears* so wholly differently here and there? It appears so differently that we cannot understand each other on the right concept of it, that we are not united in Christ but disunited, that we cannot think of the Church without being forced to think of its irreparable rift.

Therefore, because we see so differently (*aliter*) we really in part see different things (*alia*). And there is added to the conflict over 'what kind' (*quale*) a secondary conflict over 'how much' (*quantum*), for example over the precedence of the functions of the Church, whether it is primarily a sacramental or a preaching Church; over the relation of the bearer of the Church authority to the rest of the Church members; over the scope of the Church authority; over the specific right of the Bishop of Rome to jurisdiction over Church doctrine and law for the whole Church; and the like. All these are burning and crucial questions certainly, but burning and crucial only because we are already fundamentally in a conflict which is wholly different.

In order to focus attention on this quite different conflict, I shall first demonstrate explicitly that we see substantially the same reality (I do not say that we see it alike) when we speak of the Church. Discussion is made much too easy for both sides if this identity is *not taken into account*; if each side, by ignoring the most important things which his opponent *also* knows and *also* says, assumes that his opponent is kneeling before some strange kind of idol. For by listening to him more closely, one is forced to admit that he indeed prays to the same God, although in such a different and divisive fashion that no common petition is offered. Both sides must recognize the presence of the true Church on the opposite side. And yet, in spite of all well-intentioned 'enlightenment', mutual tolerance must be refused and the bitter words 'differently believing' have valid force.

Let me then first clarify the assertion (it is not made with any irenic intent) that Catholics and Protestants see the same reality when they speak of the Church. I shall cite statements defining the concept which are recognized as authoritative. 'I believe the one, holy, catholic and apostolic Church' (*Credo unam sanctam catholicam et apostolicam ecclesiam*) is the wording of the symbol and creed common to us both.

1. 'The Church means a summons, a call' (*Significat ecclesiam evocationem*).[1] The Church is a summoning forth of God's people, the

---

[1] *Cat. Rom.*, I, 10, 2.

community of men of faith, created through Christ on the foundation of the Covenant between God and man, awakened by the Holy Spirit. It is as incorrect on the Protestant side to suppose that Catholicism understands by *evocatio* a calling forth in any sense which would make the Church an institution magically providing salvation, as it is on the Catholic side to think that Protestantism understands the Church not as a divine institution but only as a corporation of men who are religious or who want to be.

Listen to the two following definitions of the Church:

(*a*) 'What dost thou believe concerning the holy, universal Christian Church? That the Son of God assembles for himself out of the whole human race a chosen community for eternal life through his Spirit and Word, in the unity of true faith from the beginning to the end of the world; protects and preserves them; and that I am and ever shall be a living member of the same.'

(*b*) 'The Church is the congregation of the faithful who are called by faith to the light of truth and the knowledge of God, so that having rejected the shades of ignorance and death they may worship the true and living God in piety and holiness, and serve him with their whole heart.'

Who would not be compelled to say that the first formula emphasized more the character of the Church as a divine institution and the second the Church as a community? In the first, Christ is the subject; in the second, the faithful. But the first formulation is that of the Heidelberg Catechism, the second is that of the Roman Catechism (op. cit.).

I cite these statements only to show that Protestantism obviously recognizes the objective and Catholicism the subjective element in the concept of the Church. There would be little sense in elaborating on the point.

2. The Church is *one*, as surely as there is only one God. The Church is the body of Christ on earth—of that there can be only one. It is an absurdity to speak of several churches opposing one another. If this seems to actually happen, then one is the true Church, the others are false churches, non-churches. Hence we can only reiterate, remembering the divine institution of the Church, that the members of the others are mistaken, though without fraud on their side, and that they belong basically to the one true Church. (Something like this was declared valid by Pope Pius IX when he confronted Kaiser William I.) We must distinguish between the Church triumphant in heaven and the Church militant on earth, between the Church of the Old Covenant and the

Church of the New Covenant, between the visible and the invisible Church; but the unity of the Church we cannot question.

The distinction mentioned last is, in fact, crucial; and Protestantism, as is well known, emphasizes this distinction. But it must not be overlooked that also according to Protestant doctrine the invisible and the visible Church are one and the same, not two species of one genus, but two predicates of the same subject. The assembly (*coetus*) of the elect, the invisible Church of those who are not only called but also chosen, is not a Platonic state (*civitas Platonica*) somewhere above the visible; it is identical with the visible in its ambiguous existence. The Catholic Dogmatic emphasizes the visibility of the Church, but also recognizes that there exists for the Church something like the relation of body and soul and that the soul is discernible as real only spiritually and 'to a certain degree'.[1] And the Roman Catechism [2] explicitly teaches that in the Church, like the clean and unclean animals in Noah's ark, good and bad are together and outwardly indistinguishable. A differentiation of the Church within the Church, a differentiation invisible to men's eyes in which even a Pope, as is fully recognized, may be found standing on the left hand, seems to be fully accepted.

Also in regard to the unity of the Church it should be noted that even on the question of the necessity of the Church for salvation there does not appear to be any substantial contradiction. To the famous words of the Church Fathers which Catholic dogmatics is in the habit of introducing here—'Where the Church is, there is also the Spirit of God, and where the Spirit of God is, there is the Church' or 'Outside the Church, there is no salvation' or 'I should not believe the Gospel unless the authority of the Catholic Church compelled me' [3]—the Protestant dogmatics also confesses. According to Luther,[4] the Church is 'the mother who conceives and bears every Christian through the Word of God which he opens and practises; the Church enlightens and kindles hearts so that they grasp the Word, accept it, depend on it and abide with it'. According to Calvin,[5] 'separation from the Church' is nothing more nor less than 'denial of God and Christ'.

3. The Church is *holy*, singled out by its origin and institution as the place and tool of the divine act of revelation and reconciliation, distinct

---

[1] Bartmann, *Lehrbuch des Dogma*, II, 189 f.
[2] *Cat. Rom.*, I, 10, 6 f.
[3] *Ubi ecclesia ibi et spiritus Dei et ubi spiritus Dei illic ecclesia.*
Extra ecclesiam nulla salus.
Ego evangelio non crederem nisi ecclesiae catholicae me commoveret auctoritas.
[4] *Gr. Kat.*, 3.3.　　　　[5] *Institutes*, IV, 1, 10.

from every other organization and association. How far is it holy (*sancta*)? Listen again to two statements:

(*a*) It is holy 'among so many sinners . . . because like a body with a holy head it is joined to Christ the Lord'.

(*b*) 'Because whom God chooses, them he justifies and transforms into holiness and innocence of life, that his glory may shine in them.'

Who would not take the first objective formulation for the Protestant, probably Calvinistic, and the second with its emphasis on the sanctification of the members for the Catholic? Actually, the first is from the Roman Catechism,[1] and the second is Calvin's;[2] although there can be no doubt that the Protestant could gladly subscribe to the first and the Catholic to the second.

Here belongs also the assertion which is equally common to both that the Church as a whole cannot err in its fundamental faith (*fundamento fidei*), that the people of God, as such, whatever may be said by or of individuals, cannot mistake its goal. Therefore the essential infallibility and permanence of the Church is asserted.

Agreement seems to exist also on differentiating the holiness of the Church from the holiness of God. This distinction is emphasized not only by Calvin [3] but also by the Roman Catechism.[4] The Creed says 'I believe the Church' (*credo ecclesiam*), not 'in the Church' (*in ecclesia*) as is the wording with the three Persons of the Trinity. 'So by this different use of words, God the Maker of all things is differentiated from all created things and we designate all those glorious attributes which are combined in the Church as gifts received from the divine bounty.'

4. Also no fundamental disagreement appears possible in the acceptance of the predicate *catholic*; whether the term is understood as expressing the unconditional priority of the Church community above communities of race, speech, culture, state, and class; or whether stress is laid on the priority of the body united with its Head, as such, over the separate branches. We also clearly agree that this predicate is to be understood, not mechanically and quantitatively, but spiritually and qualitatively, as a divinely given, rightful claim of the Church which cannot be based on numbers but must be based only on the actual superiority of truth.[5] Catholicity means literally universality, not a numerical majority. A noteworthy and valuable clarification of this true position is presented on the Catholic side by the fact that the Pope in the

---

[1] *Cat. Rom.*, I, 10, 12.
[2] *Cat. Genev.*; Müller, p. 125. [L.C.C., XXII, p. 103].
[3] *Institutes*, IV, 1, 2.   [4] *Cat. Rom.*, I, 10, 19.   [5] Bartmann, II, 199.

validation required for a Council decree is not bound by the majority decision, but may agree with 'the lesser and wiser minority' (*pars minor et sanior*).[1]

5. Again the designation *apostolic*, indicative of the origin of the doctrine and succession in the Church, is evidently recognized by both sides. And the Catholic will not fail to note that Protestantism fully recognizes the authority not only of God but also of the Church so far as the Church is founded on the normative witness of the Apostles for the understanding and the proclamation of the divine revelation. But the Protestant who at first glance naturally assumes that he finds in Catholicism an authority of the Church which is considered to be like the authority of God will convince himself that according to Catholic doctrine, the authority of the Church is a matter of the *delegated*, *relative* power which Christ gave to the Apostles or to the Apostle Peter. Seen clearly and correctly this is the same authority which in Protestantism is understood under the authority of the word of the Bible, written and proclaimed. There is an apostolic authority in the Church (it is documented in Matthew 16) and there is no fundamental need to become excited over the well-known application of the 'Thou art Peter' (*tu es Petrus*) to Peter's Church in Rome. Over this we do not need to quarrel.

6. My last point is this: on both sides there is agreement that the 'I believe' (*credo*) which begins this section of our Creed requires acceptance of the truth that although the existence of the Church is visible and is in itself comprehensible to reason, yet *believing* the Church involves believing the mystery of its institution and preservation, believing all the signs by virtue of which it is nowhere *a* church, but is always *the* Church of God. Not in a Protestant creed, but again in the Roman Catechism [2] I read: 'Since therefore this article, no less than the others, is beyond the capacity and power of our reason, we most rightly confess that we do not know the origin, the gifts and the honour of the Church by human reason, but we see them with the eyes of faith. . . . And men were not the founders of this Church; the founder was the ever-living God himself. Nor is the power which the Church received human; it was assigned by divine gift. Therefore since it cannot be compared to any natural powers, it also is *by faith only* that we know that in the Church are the keys of heaven, and that to the Church was given the power to remit sins, to excommunicate, and to consecrate the body of Christ.'

---

[1] Ibid., II, 161.   [2] *Cat. Rom.*, I, 10, 17, 18.

II

Faced with this broad base of apparent agreement, on which it would be easy to enlarge further, one might well wonder for a moment how it was and still is possible for the adherents of the Reformation of the sixteenth century to repudiate unanimously and in the emphatic speech of that time the Roman Church as Anti-Christ; and for the revivified Roman Church of Trent on its side to have for the Church of the Reformation only a monotonous anathema. And possible for all sincere men on both sides today to be obliged to say a real Amen to this judgement of the fathers on both sides; although it is said with heavy hearts and in the muted expressions of our day. Only, *why*? Yes, why?

This question must be answered, answered to all kind and well-intentioned folk who would like to walk a middle way, stressing the recognition of this truly important common minimum and urging mutual conciliation. The answer must be: *because* everything, everything without exception, everything adduced or further adducible, is so differently meant on this side and on that; *because* the reality of the Church, undeniably seen as common to both, is seen so differently or is so differently visible on this side and on that, that neither of us can accommodate our position to the other even with the best will on both sides. We cannot recognize each other as one flock under one shepherd and we must leave in God's hand the question of whether and in how far we ought to be one.

Where do our paths separate? Of that we must now speak. It would be possible to state the contradiction on each point I have mentioned. The best starting-point is to be found in the words last quoted from the Roman Catechism, 'By faith only we know' (*fide solum intelligimus*), affirmed of the divine reality of the Church. It can be confidently asserted that if we were agreed on the meaning of these three words, there would then be no division of the Church, there would then be no need to add the cognomen 'Catholic' or 'Evangelical' to the name Christian. Then it would be possible—I speak advisedly—to discuss from that starting-point everything else, Papacy and sacrament, dogma and ritual.

If a Protestant understands these three words like a Catholic (here in their context) then he is basically a Catholic—even if he were a Professor of Protestant theology. And if a Catholic understands the same three words in the Protestant way, then he has in his heart become a Protestant, however he may stand outwardly. But a true Catholic and a true Protestant cannot unite on the meaning of these three words and therefore there can be no basic talk between them on the other points— or at most they can only discuss why they cannot discuss.

I shall now try to explain briefly and simply how we Protestants understand these three words, 'by faith only we know' (*fide solum intellegimus*), or how in the light of these three words we should understand the Church, if we did not know where and by whom they were written.

We Protestants understand by *faith* men's receiving of and laying hold on the grace of God, which is itself the effect of grace, and in which the grace, since it is *grace* is in both its aspects the inexpressible *mercy* of God. Both in what is received and in the act of receiving and laying hold, faith is and remains God's grace. The reality of the Logos and of the Spirit of God so holds mastery over the man that he perceives that reality (in Word and sacrament), knows it intelligibly in his mind, and experiences it in his heart. And yet—this is the decisive element—the man does not thereby possess the slightest mastery over the grace as he does over other realities which he perceives, knows, and experiences.

He does not possess it because in grace he has to do with the holy *God*, who while he is gracious to us yet dwells in a light inaccessible to any man; and because he, the man, is a sinner whose communion with God at any time is never possible and actual in any way except from God's side. That communion is without reciprocity, without any possibility that man can ever be in a position to lay his hand on God as God lays his hand on him. Therefore at every moment and in every relation man is supported by God and by God only; and not at all by himself. He cannot support himself by means of his perception, nor by means of his knowledge, nor by means of his experience, although his faith is a perceiving, a knowing, and an experiencing. For God is God, and man is a creature and truly a sinful creature. How could he with his perceiving, knowing, and experiencing keep himself in communion with God? To be so kept by himself would be equivalent to sin without grace, death without hope. That he is so kept in communion by God, that rescue and salvation are bound up with being so kept, that he is so kept by God alone, that is what faith affirms.

And such precisely is the meaning of the 'I believe the Church' (*credo ecclesiam*). The Church is the place and the instrument of the grace of God. There faith is, in the Church and through the Church. There the reality of the Word become flesh and of God's Holy Spirit speaks and is heard.

As the place and the instrument of grace, the Church has its part in the affirmation that it has authority over us. The reverse is not true. We do not possess the Church as we can possess all other objects. We have the Church as we have God if and in so far as he has us. Of course, there is the radical difference that in the Church we are dealing with a visible, historical entity, existing among men and included among other human conceptions, institutions, and undertakings; an entity which *per se*, as the earthly body of the heavenly Lord, is the place and instrument of grace. How otherwise could it be place and instrument, the *accessible* place and the *usable* instrument of grace?

But this visible actuality does not at all affect the truth that we have it only as we have God. We so have it that in it and through it the claim of God reaches us, but not so that any claim of ours on God arises from it or any claim on what is reserved for God alone. From every other claim on us, there may arise a corresponding claim of ours, a claim asserting ownership over what is promised us, validating the promise. But from God's claim arises no such counter-claim of ours. Our relation to God is, in distinction to all other relations, irreversible. Therefore the fact that the Church has the 'summons' (*evocatio*) and has the divine promise cannot mean that any claim is put in our hands, that there has been delivered to us human beings in that visible, historical place and instrument of grace some kind of tool with which we can gain control over grace, can make ourselves *secure* in relation to grace.

How would grace still be grace if there were in the Church a security other than that resting in God himself? Therefore, if grace is precious to us we must not desire to possess the Church differently from the way we have God; that means that we can not have it as wealthy, secure and powerful folk, but as beggars who live from hand to mouth. The Church is the medium between Christ and the begraced sinner. What Jesus Christ and the begraced sinner have in common is that in both there occurs an entrance of God into time, into the twilight, into the relativity and uncertainty of history and human life. God enters that obscurity in which he is never to be known as objectively manifest, never known directly, but is known always and only through his immediately present will, through the immediate act of his love.

In this sense, then, the Church is a divine institution; in this sense it is the communion of saints. It is of the essence of grace that it be objectively realized in the Word become flesh. And therefore, by the fact that Christ took his cross upon himself and became obedient unto death (and therefore, *therefore* God has exalted him), the Church has been shown its position and its nature. Also it is of the essence of grace that it be subjectively realized in and for the begraced sinner. And therefore, since the begraced sinner cannot live except under the judgement and the promise of God before whom he is dust and who alone can make any good out of him, so also the Church is told where it belongs and how it must stand before God.

The Church which constitutes the medium between Jesus Christ and the begraced sinner can stand under no other law than they. In the hiddenness of God, in the lowness of men, the Church is the place and instrument of grace or it is nothing at all. Because of the divine hiddenness, it is necessary that we have the Church as we have God and not otherwise. We perceive it, we know it, we experience it; however, we do not possess it, because we perceive, know and experience it, but because God takes possession of *us* in what we there perceive, know, and experience. There he deals with us as our Lord because he has chosen us in this way which is suited to us—not because we, even in the finest way, chose him.

If we were to reverse the relation, what then would we have left of the Church but the degradation of all things human? At best something a bit idealized and dressed up, but not elevated in the least, a poor servant who even in the most elaborate costume would no longer be the servant of Christ, but just a servant among other servants. For to have in the Church the servant and bride of Christ depends on our not making the Church the mistress—and thereby, since we ourselves are the Church, making ourselves masters, masters (be it noted) in our relation to God. The relation between us and God must not be reversed because of our desire to have a Church without degradation or with its degradation covered by a king's robe.

The splendour of the Church can consist only in its hearing in poverty the Word of the eternally rich God, and making that Word heard by men. The Church does not control that Word as earthly things can be controlled. Nor does the Church possess the Word as material or intellectual goods are normally possessed. Nor does the Church take the Word for granted as it would count on something which was not a gift. The splendour of the Church cannot and must not shine out except where the glory of the begraced sinner shines. But the place where that glory shines on earth is the cross. Whatever shines elsewhere is a glory of a different kind—the glory of this world which passes away—and to this the Church is not to be likened.

In the same way the Church is *one*. Truly the one beside which there is no other. But the Church does not have control of its unity; that is controlled by the one God—and the control is twofold. The Church is one, not because it differentiates itself unavoidably, but also in a very relative degree, from other institutions which call themselves Churches; but because by God himself it is and becomes differentiated from all false churches. It is the one, not because the Church itself makes visible its invisible reality; but because God is pleased to make visible in it and through it that which only he as Lord of the Church can make visible. It is the one, not as though it were in the position to prove itself necessary for salvation by its words and works; but because God himself in it and through it brings the proof of Spirit and power, serving not its honour but his.

In the same way the Church is *holy*. The Church does not control its holiness; the holy God controls it. The Church is not holy because it sets itself up as a second, Christian world over against the world. It must indeed so set itself, but even while it is doing so, it is naught else but world. It is more than world, not when it establishes itself in the world by the 'law of the Church', but when it is and becomes so established by the law of God, and so long as it never abandons that establishment given by God. The Church is holy so long as it obeys, not so far as it commands.

The Church is infallible, not because its pronouncements, which are of necessity humanly limited, possess as such inerrancy and perfection; but because by its pronouncements it bears witness to the infallible Word of God and gives evidence that it has heard that Word; because the Church,[1] 'abandoning all its own wisdom, lets itself be taught by the Word of God'. So far as it does not so act, it is certainly not the Church. But when it does so act, it will seek infallibility in what *is said* to it in antithesis to what it can itself say, to what is spoken not from heaven but on earth, to what is not *the* dogma but *a* dogma, to what is not the divine Word but is specifically the word of the Church— although the word of the Church *as such* has real authority and requires serious attention. The authority of the Church is genuine authority precisely because the Church is not for an instant unready to bow before the higher authority truly appointed over it.

The Church must will to be *pure*, pure in its doctrine above all else. For that purity it must struggle, and therefore when necessary the Church must suffer for that purity. But the Church cannot will to be

[1] Calvin, *Institutes*, IV, 8, 13.

holy. It can only have faith under the judgement and promise of God that it is holy.

In this sense the Church is *catholic*. Again it must be said that the Church does not control its catholicity; the eternal, omnipresent God controls it. Therefore the Church will not boast of its centuries and millennia. The idolatrous church of ancient Egypt could do that with a very different right! Nor will it boast of any geographical extent which it has in common with the Roman or the British empire. What has that to do with its real, its spiritually qualitative catholicity? Where two or three among you are gathered in *my* name, there am I in the midst of them. *I*! That is what establishes and preserves and validates the catholicity of the Church. Without that presence, it is not a Church at all. But the content of that promise is such that it can only *become* true; no one on earth can *make* it true by any means or guarantee whatever; for it men can only pray. *Faith*! Faith is required also for the great truth of the catholicity of the Church.

In this sense also the Church is *apostolic*. It is such because it serves the Logos and the Spirit of God in accordance with the witness and the example of the apostles. For that service the apostles were set apart, and Peter among the apostles. For that service Peter's genuine successors have been set apart. How else could the Church prove and manifest the apostolicity of its origin, of its doctrine, of its succession than through 'the ministry of the divine Word' (*ministerium verbi divini*) in which they were our predecessors?

Certainly with this 'ministry', the Church exercises a power, 'the ecclesiastical power' (*potestas ecclesiastica*), the power to bind and to loose, beside which all other powers are negligible. But if it exercises such power as the apostolic Church, then it knows that this power, just because of the apostolicity of the origin, doctrine, and succession of the Church, does not lie in the hand of the Church. The Church knows that while on earth it binds and looses, the power lies wholly in the hand of him who alone can forgive sins and impute sins.

This is the meaning of 'I believe one holy catholic and apostolic Church' (*Credo unam sanctam catholicam et apostolicam ecclesiam*). I believe the Church as the place where honour is given to God and where therefore divine honour for the Church is repudiated, and therefore I believe the Church as the instrument of grace. I believe the Church as the divine institution and therefore that it must be not so much God's palace as God's shanty among men until the world's end. I believe the church as the communion of saints, that is the communion of sinners set apart and called by God, which yet is the communion of saints. I believe the Church as the proclaimer and the hearer of the divine Word. I believe it also as the people of God on earth, who—precisely as the people of God—shall live from God's mercy (and that is not to be counted a small thing!) until the kingdom of glory where the transitory, even the transitoriness of this community, of the earthly body of the heavenly Lord, shall put on eternity, where here also what is sown in weakness shall be raised in strength.

It is thus that we Protestants understand the meaning of 'by faith only we know' (*fide solum intellegimus*) in relation to the Church. On the fact that this is in sharp contradiction to the Roman Catholic doctrine and on the ways it contradicts it, I have no wish to elaborate. You will have recognized the boundary of which I spoke in the beginning, and you will have heard the protest of Protestantism.

The writers of the *Catechismus Romanus* certainly understood these words quite differently. How? The clarification of the difference may be left to our discussion.

X

CHURCH AND THEOLOGY

An address given 7th October 1925 at the Göttingen Autumn Conference and 23rd October 1925 at the Theological Week at Eberfeld.

'What is theology?' In a little book with this title, which is equally brilliant, enigmatic, and lofty, Erich Peterson has recently presented his answer.[1] Theology is, in contrast to mythology and to a dialectical theology related to mythology, the obedient realization of the possibility of knowledge, truly unparadoxical knowledge of God, a possibility which is given in the form of concrete authority. Theology does not have to *speak* the Word of God; for only Christ can and does speak that Word. It has nothing to *say* about God; for that is the office of the Old Testament prophets in preparation for the revelation of the Logos. It also has nothing to *assert* about God; for that the Church does, with judicial power. The task of theology is to *argue* on the basis of concrete authority.

The concrete authority which is meant is not the Bible. The Bible, its spiritual exegesis, and the preaching based on it belong, strictly speaking, not in theology at all but in worship. Nor is the authority to be identified with the Church creed. But analogous to the institution of the sacraments, it is given in dogma as the exercise of the power bestowed upon the Church at the ascension of Christ. And in so far as it is a continuation of the Logos-revelation, dogma confronts men with a positive claim by divine right (*jure divino*), positive and effective even to the burning of heretics.

Through its relation to dogma, theology itself becomes a making concrete of the Logos. Through dogma, theology is first released from a

---

[1] *What is Theology?* by Erich Peterson, Professor of Theology at the University of Bonn (1925, Friedrich Cohen, Bonn).

The first printing of this lecture (in *Zwischen den Zeiten*, 1926) included a series of observations, with which I was currently occupied, upon some other writers prominent at the time. I have omitted them here only because the content was of merely temporary interest, and today would be simply tiresome.

fatal attachment to the so-called sciences; it is elevated to a sphere in which man can truly live; it becomes obedience to Christ, becomes the concern of wide circles of men, becomes possible as a definite position and a branch of knowledge.

What I wish to present to you today is in the form of a debate with these ideas. And I ought to make clear beforehand that I am forced to oppose Peterson on the main points. But it is possible to say *no* in many different ways; and I hope that my *no* will not be confused with other negations of a different kind.

Permit me, then, a brief foreword. I should not consider it right nor wise to give the all too obvious answer to Peterson's thesis that it is Roman Catholic in its presuppositions and conclusions and can therefore be met with silence as deserving to be ignored rather than discussed. That it is Roman Catholic and in more than one section super-Catholic, I certainly agree. But I think that this easily made assertion has no polemic value and that it is not good, for such a reason, to refuse beforehand to discuss the content of these and similar propositions.

This holds true for the following reasons. If any theology had in itself the inherent right to react to an attack like that of Peterson with a flat repudiation and no discussion, it would be the *old* Protestant theology. That theology would have known exactly what its aim was and what it was doing. The old Protestant intolerance was not the result of accident; it was created by the logic of the subject-matter. It was directed as sharply against visionaries and spiritists, against Carlstadt and Servetus, against Socinus and Arminius as against Rome. It saw the same opponent on both sides, merely differently garbed. On both the right and the left it contended for the glory of God and the purity of faith against the presumptuousness and wilfulness of religious men. In the singlemindedness of this defensive struggle the warfare of the Reformers and their successors against the Papacy was legitimate and reasonable, a war fought with a good conscience and a protected rear. The same can be said only in part of the conflict of present-day Protestantism with the opponent on the right.

Present-day Protestantism has approached inwardly close to its former opponent on the left, much too closely for its expressions of anger against the right not to sound hollow and insincere when measured by those of Calvin and Luther. The suspicion must arise that for the most part things are today defended in which the Reformers would have recognized (in Erasmian or Anabaptist dress) the old evil enemy whom they fought in the Papacy. Until our religion is better purified from the contamination of the left, that is from the Rationalism and the Pietism which have so successfully infiltrated us, we need to be cautious and chary in grasping too quickly the final reason (*ultima ratio*) for Protestant anger at the loud speaking of 'catholicizing' voices on the right—as if we were there encountering something alien to us.

To speak specifically: the evolutionary historicity, moralism, and idealism which rule our present-day theology have run up too heavy an account against it when measured by the Reformation to leave it the right to throw stones at a catholicizing phenomenology such as Peterson presents. If one accepts Schleiermacher without blushing, then Thomas Aquinas is equally acceptable. Both are equally far from Luther and Calvin. There is no sense today in labelling a confessional difference instead of examining the grounds for it. Certainly not where we are confronted 'within the walls' (*intra muros*) by the mediaeval deviation rather than some kind of modernistic variety.

And really why, when we are confronted by Peterson's propositions, should we refuse (however little sympathy we have for the place from which they come) to judge the questions which they bring to our attention on their own merits apart from their confessional import? Our forefathers did not fail to oppose the Catholic tempter with serious arguments as well as with angry repudiation. Perhaps we are more hesitant than they because as Protestant theologians we are less certain of our position—it has shifted so far from theirs. But if so, we have need to accept Peterson's attack as a challenge and to consider where we really ought and where we wish to stand. A burst of 'Protestant zeal' (*furor protestanticus*) in any form, either in silence or ridicule, would only be a subterfuge and will avenge itself. I hope to serve better what is called 'the evangelical cause' if I do *not* give my evaluation the character of a confessional antithesis, but follow Peterson into the area of fundamental theological thinking which he himself chose and held to.

I have called my lecture 'Church and Theology'. I did so in the belief that in the area so ably handled by Peterson the definition of the concepts 'church' and 'theology' and their mutual relation constitute the decisive question for which we must seek clarification.

I

I hope I understand Peterson's meaning correctly when I begin with the statement that theology consists essentially *in the concrete obedience to concrete authority* (p. 9). This sentence does not indeed (and this is also Peterson's judgement) say everything which is to be said. But it is in itself correct, for the following reasons.

Theology is the continuing service to God's revelation, performed by specific men, in the form of conceptual thinking in a specific here and now.[1] Between God's revelation, given at a specific place and moment, and theology there stands, however, the separation of *time*. In order to become the object of theology, the revelation must become contemporary with the theology. This 'contemporizing' of the revelation is accomplished not only directly through God's immediate speaking at a all times; but also—although not without the witness and seal of that immediacy—it is mediated. The biblical canon and text, the credal affirmations, more or less commonly received and achieved by the Church as established truth, the correct lines marked by the work of certain teachers recognized by the Church as normative; finally the specific way in which the revelation presents itself as so and not otherwise in every specific here and now—all these together constitute the *form* of the object of theology. This form is only approximately knowable; but it is, none the less, truly *given*, and in it alone theology finds its content. This form is the concrete authority to which concrete obedience is to be paid.

Revelation is the content of theology—that is of an ectypal ($ἔκτυπος$) theology, a 'theology of wayfarers' (*theologia viatorum*) as the ancients called it in contrast to the archetypal ($ἀρχέτυπος$) theology of God himself and to the comprehending theology (*theologia comprehensorum*) of the angels and saints in heaven—it is the content of the theology of men on earth at a specific point in time. And the revelation is the gift of God's grace. To the specific position on earth corresponds the specific form of both the revelation and the theology which serves it, the form of both the authority and the obedience.

There is then no theology (because there is no mediated *presence* of revelation) without the immediacy of the eternal omnipresent Word and Spirit of God, in which its *freedom* is based, the freedom of faith bound to God. But this does not alter the fact that theology is *also* concrete obedience to concrete authority. A theology which was not in fact such obedience would necessarily be without a content; it would not be theology at all.

[1] Cf. the definition of Gogarten: Theology is 'the critical, methodological thinking of the theologian which he does when he speaks on the basis of the revelation of God' (*Z.d.Z.*, 9, p. 78), and that of Bultmann: Theology is 'the conceptual presentation of the existence of man as an existence determined by God' (*Z.d.Z.* 12, p. 353).

II

We shall next clarify the question of how much is included in what is to be understood as the 'concrete authority'. Strangely enough, Peterson speaks only of dogma. He certainly does not mean the idea or essence of dogma but (the emphasis lies on the concreteness of the designated entity) specific dogmas formulated and approved at specific times. One could, of course, press Peterson as Harnack [1] pressed the High Church party to answer the question of actually *which* dogma. Which dogma, measured by the *norm* of *which* century, has *the* Church made *the* dogma?

But here I must strike a blow on Peterson's side. To that question today a single theologian unfortunately can give only a personal, contingent, unauthoritative answer. He can say, this and that confession of faith of the branch of the Church to which I am bound, established at the time of the Reformation and since then neither revoked nor substantially modified, together with this and that presupposed affirmation of the Ancient Church, on which the confession rests, constitute what I call dogma, when I am pursuing dogmatics. But this answer is *his*; and however well it is grounded, it is not the answer that should be given here, precisely because it is *only* his answer. Here the church must bear the responsibility for a considered answer—even if it be only a small regional church or a general synod which would be the legitimate representative of such a church.

A fundamental cause of the weakness of our present-day theology is the fact that when we pursue theology we have no church behind us which has the courage to say to us unambiguously that, so far as we talk together, this and this is dogma in the highest concreteness (*concretissimo*). If the churches do not say this to us and yet demand that we learn and teach 'Dogmatics', they are truly like King Nebuchadnezzar, who demanded that his wise men tell not only what his dream meant but also what he had dreamed.

The embarrassment which one could cause Peterson with the question 'which dogma?' only reflects the embarrassment in which our evangelical church finds itself. It does not at all affect the truth of his statement that there is no theology without concrete authority, without dogma.

Therefore it seems to me more important and of greater significance to establish that the real dogma, which not without a certain wry humour

[1] *Christliche Welt*, 1925, 7/8, esp. pp. 166 f.

we assume to be known in the concrete (*concretissimo*), has never any-where had for real theology the *isolated* meaning which Peterson wants to ascribe to it. For example, the newer Catholic dogmatics is founded, so far as I see, on the following authorities: (1) biblical passages, (2) the Church Fathers, (3) dogma, (4) wherever possible, new papal decisions. Peterson could have maliciously noted that with us, in place of (4), there is substituted the point of view of the individual theological professor. But he ought not to have ignored the multiplicity of the authorities to which theology actually takes its appeal when he calls it 'the expression of an actuality'. It should have been evident to him that within the con-cept of the concrete authority of dogma there still remains one element after another.

Behind dogma stand the decisions of the Church on the canon and text of the Bible, beside dogma stand the opinions of the normative Fathers, the 'Doctors of the Church' (*doctores ecclesiae*). (Do not forget the peculiar weight of a citation from Luther in the theological discus-sions of us Protestants today. The highly respected particular traditions of the Lutheran and the Reformed Schools could also be mentioned.) Finally, after dogma and the Fathers stands, not indeed the point of view of an individual professor, but just the arbitrariness of an authority theo-retically deliberative but really active in the real present. In the Catholic Church this authority is enviably (not really to be envied) available, designated by the concept of the teaching office of the Church embodied in the Pope. We Protestants must be content to recognize the objective givenness of a 'Kairos' (to use Tillich's word) as necessary for all theo-logical work; that is, we must recognize the definite command of each moment. This command is written in no document, but its authority is binding; although the theologian cannot by reason or rule differentiate it from the equally indispensable illumination of the individual worker which is immediate through Word and Spirit.

We must therefore recognize in the concrete authority: the decisions of the Church on the canon and on the canonical text of the Scripture revelation; certain assertions in the Church's message, more or less clearly accepted as fundamental, based on the former and explained by the words of the Fathers; and lastly also that command of the hour (which likewise is to be understood as given to the Church). These three or four elements lie obviously on very different levels and are significant in very different ways. But all these components together—and not dogma alone—constitute the concrete authority to which theology must render concrete obedience.

III

Theology lives from dogma, Peterson affirms. We have shown that the statement which must be accepted is that theology lives *also* from dogma. We now ask further how does theology meet the necessity of dependence on dogma in relation to the other components named above? Whose authority is it which theology here recognizes? The answer to this question is again in decided agreement with Peterson: the authority which theology here recognizes is indubitably the authority of the Church—although certainly obedience is not *piety*.

It would not be correct to speak here of an authority of *history*, although the fusing of the components of the authority presents unmistakable historical dates. But history, or a fragment of history, canon and text, the Fathers and dogma, the command of the hour, when understood as historical events and eventualities, do not mean authority for the view-point of Christian theology. They are not authority because the cardinal assertion of a certain theologizing philosophy that history and God, history and revelation, are 'at home' [1] together is false. History can indeed become a predicate of revelation, but never *possibly* can revelation become the predicate of history. History means in theology exactly what Pontius Pilate means in the creed. For history as subject stands like man himself in direct relation to God's creation, but also in direct relation to Adam's fall and expulsion from Paradise; it does not stand in direct relation to Christ and the reconciliation which came in him. History is 'the whole incomprehensible interim between creation and redemption in which we find ourselves'. [2] It is darkness (σκοτία) which has not comprehended the light.

But as the pollution and misery of human nature is taken up in the Word become flesh merged and elevated in the holiness and sinlessness of the eternal God, as man without ceasing to be in himself a sinner is in Christ forgiven, justified and made holy; so and in the same sense it can be said of a history qualified by revelation that, without ceasing to be in itself what all history is, yet when qualified by revelation it is not *merely* interim.

Certainly the realm, in which 'chosen sinners' (*peccatores electi*) unified and reconciled by the Word become flesh, await their redemption in the midst of history, is itself in all its aspects history and stands in the same dark shadows with all other historical realities. But that is

[1] So Schmidt-Japing, *Zeitschrift für systematische Theologie*, I, pp. 69 f.
[2] So Thurneysen, *Z.d.Z.*, 9, p. 27.

not all which must be said about it. There is the other and the extravagant statement which must be made: this realm even in the midst of the realm of shadows is the kingdom of light, ruled by the heavenly Lord and believed by miserable men who yet are his chosen and called—the one holy, universal, apostolic Church.

That Church, in all the dubiousness of its manifestation, is through all ages the road, hidden yet not hidden, on which the revelation comes to nations and races. It is on this road that the revelation ever and again becomes the content of theology. While theology recognizes that the revelation is given to it mediated and in the form of concrete authority, theology without forgetting for an instant the historical limitations of the form also knows that theology does not depend on history. For history has no theological authority; the *Church* has.

IV

But even when recognized as the authority of the Church, the concrete authority which theology must concretely obey needs closer definition. Peterson determines the relation between Christ and his Church by applying the biblical metaphor of head and body; and he asserts that the authority of dogma is the authority derived from Christ and granted to the Church by him at his ascension. Fundamentally that statement is to be accepted. If the authority of the Church were not the authority of Christ transferred in some way to the Church, it could not be an authority for theology any more than is history.

But for exactness, greater emphasis should be laid on the fact that we are confronted here with an authority of Christ which is (in Peterson's own words) a 'conferred' or, less happily, a 'derivative' authority. The body is here on earth; the Head is in heaven. The body functions in the complete ambiguity of the fleshly human world, awaiting its redemption; the Head abides in the glory of the Father. Therefore the body can claim the presence of the Head only in a way which is consistent with the complete majesty and omnipresence of the Head. But that means to claim it only as the Word and through the Spirit of the Father and the Son. Peterson's statement, 'But when he had ascended to heaven, then neither the others nor he himself spoke of his authority; for he had granted his power to the Church' (p. 22) is not a good statement. For Christ's bestowal of his power on his Church cannot be reasonably understood to mean that he had partially relinquished his own power, that in relation to the Church he had ceased to be wholly God.

The ascension means not only, as Peterson states it, the transfer of a delegated, secondary power to the Church, but also the departure of the actual, primary holder of that power. It means that the eschatological limit set for the Church becomes visible. The exaltation of the Head really means for the body a lowering, its demotion to a position of humility and waiting, and a definite limitation of the miracle of Pentecost. The conditional character of the gift of Pentecost must never be forgotten; the gift is never to be taken for granted when one speaks of its power. Therefore Peterson's often-repeated formula 'there is', ('there is given', *es gibt*) this and that dogma, sacrament, theology, etc., requires at least a very cautious or (if you will pardon the term) a 'dialectical' use. What 'is there' in this context of which it is not essentially true that it 'is there' only as God's gift? And that God gives it not once for all, but keeps giving it repeatedly?

To avoid a naturalistic confusion between heaven and earth, it would be better not to talk of the prolongation and the continuation of the revelation or of the derived authority and the like. And if one wants to say positively that dogma 'from the body of Christ' prescribes to us 'by divine right' (*jure divino*) (p. 20), then it will be necessary to define in what exact sense one can here speak of 'divine right' (*jus divinum*). The authority with which the Church sets the canon, proclaims dogma, etc., is clearly Christ's authority in a secondary sense; it is temporal, relative, formal authority.

It is (1) temporal authority, that is it is such authority as there can be on the earthly side, on *this* side of the second coming of Christ. It is, in fact, authority which (different from the authority of its Head) has its limit set in its very beginning, which can make no claim to infallibility and immutability in its decisions. The Church is the Church of forgiven thieves, who wait for their redemption. This fact does not destroy the authority of the Church, but it does mark its limit.

It is (2) relative authority, that is it only 'represents', as Peterson says, the divine authority. The custom of 'physically punishing' heretics which Peterson mentioned, not without a certain Spanish warmth, is to be judged discreetly as abuse (*abusus*) and not as use (*usus*) of the Church's authority, since it obviously rests upon a disastrous deviation at precisely this point. The authority of the Church is not authority in itself but in relation to the real authority of the Lord in his glory. Under this presupposition, it would be judged better *not* to burn one another.

Lastly, it is (3) formal authority, that is it does not in any way supersede revelation. It does not even limit and alter revelation, neither in content nor in force. It only provides a channel for it; the question of the water itself and the question of its flow stand in a different book. In this limited sense and not otherwise, dogma and the other components of concrete authority prescribe for us 'by divine right'. The 'divine right' is restricted to the mediated presentation of the revelation.

The right is not such that the Church could ever, in any way, either *before* or *after* its decisions, be exempted from seeking after the Word and asking for the Holy Spirit which alone leads it to all truth. It can in no way be identified with that 'divine right' with which Christ through Word and Spirit decides immediately, inerrantly, and unappealably as the Lord of the Church. But Christ's immediate authority, in which the freedom of faith and of faith's obedience is based, is for theology as constitutive as is the mediated authority of the Church.

V

If, then, a distinction is to be made between the direct authority of Christ and his mediated authority which he granted to the Church, there must be a cardinal point at which the subordination of the Church under its Lord comes to view.[1] There must be in the giving and receiving of the revelation a differentiation, valid for all time, between the Lord and the Church; there must be a concrete rule and criterion, a concrete antithesis between the mediated action of Christ *in* his Church and his immediate action *upon* it. The naturalistic fashion in which Peterson, by forcing the metaphor of head and limbs, presents the relation between Christ and the Church has prevented him from asking himself any question on this critical point. And in addition it has led him to force the Bible, its exegesis and the preaching based on it into that astonishing (more than Catholic!) deviation in which the question, What is theology? is finally decided wholly in favour of dogma.

In reality, however, the transference of power to the Church is accomplished simply by the primary exercise of its concrete authority as it undertakes the unique, inimitable, and unsurpassable office of witnessing to the revelation—and that witness is in the form of confirming the Old Testament prophetic message and energizing the New Testament apostolic word. This spoken and written word, into which the Logos-revelation has entered in order to go out into all the world,

[1] Cf. on this point 'Das Schriftprinzip der ref. Kirche', *Z.d.Z.*, 11, esp. pp. 228 ff. = Dogmatik I, pp. 346 ff.

is in itself (as the principle of all concrete representation of the revelation) the origin and the limit of all such representations. It is the standard against which all that the Church 'speaks' in the name of its Lord is measured and must always be re-measured.

We must add further—only so far as God the Holy Spirit now and again acknowledges this word of witness as his own Word, so far does he make it ever and again incomparably true and powerful; and so far does he initiate and complete his decisions in the hearts of believers by means of this word. For, as the Word of the Spirit, it is established by Christ as the foundation of his community.

Therefore the same condition is required also on the other side. The transference of power to the Church is accomplished by the Pentecostal gift of the Holy *Spirit*, through whom the old prophetic and the new apostolic word became the effective witness to Christ for peoples and generations. This Spirit, through whom the Logos-revelation goes out in the spoken and written word of witness to all the world, is as such the principle of all representation and revelation, is the infallible and unchanging Lord and Judge over all which the Church 'speaks'. But then we must add: so far as it is indeed the Spirit of the Son, that is of the divine Word become flesh, which is also the Spirit of the divine Word written and spoken; so far that Word, as the Spirit speaking in the hearts of believers, is no other than the Spirit of the prophets and apostles. The Spirit of the Word—and no other spirit—leads the Church into all truth.

Therefore Word and Spirit together (and neither of the two is the greater or the lesser) constitute the critical point where the immediate authority of Christ, on which is based the mediated authority of the Church, meets and limits that authority. Related to that point stand those things the presence of which we must recognize, for example the established canon, the proclaimed dogma, the validity of the normative teaching of the Church, etc. In looking at the form-principle of all representation of the revelation, that is in looking at the immediate authority of Christ, theology, obedient in *faith* to God himself and therefore in *freedom*, exercises its concrete obedience to concrete authorities because and in so far as they conform to the authority of Christ.

VI

From this point of view the seat of the recognized concrete authority needs to be defined more closely.[1] Peterson suppresses half of the actual

---

[1] Cf. 'The Desirability and Possibility of a Universal Reformed Creed,' pp. 112 ff.

reality when he asserts that dogma does not depend on any expression of the human act of faith, that it has essentially nothing to do with the creed. Certainly dogma does not consist in the result of the sinful, creaturely ratification of faith (such as a creed), however deep and pure that expression may be. 'An expression of faith' in Schleiermacher's sense, that is as the outcome of human experience and conviction, is certainly not to be understood as dogma, as authority. Equally it should be said of the canon that its authority is obviously not to be based on its historical origin. And in the same sense, it should be said that Augustine and Luther, when regarded as heroes of religion, are not theological authorities; and that every command of the present hour, however difficult its validation may then be for us Protestants, stands always under a Zinzendorfian 'it is so for me'.

But the legitimate and necessary delimitation against theological psychologizing is one thing; an entirely different thing is the wholly impossible complete exclusion of faith and creed from the concrete authority which Peterson requires. To fall out of subjectivism into an equally naïve objectivism, out of psychology into ontology—that I call exchanging the devil for Beelzebub.

If there is, as Peterson elsewhere does not deny,[1] a distinction between faith as resultant and faith as *act*, then faith as *act* is specifically the work of the Holy Spirit in the hearts of sinners in direct correlation with God's revelation. Faith as act is, finally, the Church as the community of saints, that is as the community of those claimed in God's revelation. The Church therefore is completely the community of the faith established and given by God. Therefore no objection holds against the assertion that the authoritative 'speaking' of the Church in dogma, etc., is to be understood as an act of faith, as a confession of faith. We must, of course, emphasize and underline that it is an act of faith and a confession of faith by *men*, by *sinners*; but also it is an act of *faith*, a confession of *faith*.

But this is not to say that Church and dogma belong to men as an actual possession, as Peterson claims (p. 32). As if it were not inherent in the concepts, revelation, Church, faith, that between the eternal truth of God, which is the exclusive predicate of his Word and Spirit, and the religious opinions thrown out by the human subject there were not set a third element! It is in this intermedium that the Church knows God and confesses him through God's full grace, but does both with human limitations according to the measure of faith given to it, to the Church

[1] He asserts it and defends it against Paul Althaus (*Z.d.Z.*, 11, esp. pp. 228 f.).

of sinners. There the Church receives and proclaims God's Word, but does both in weak, human words. There it makes its decisions by the *divine law*, but then sets up a *human law*. There the infallibility of the God-given and the fallibility of the human acceptance of God's gift make an exclusive antithesis as little as the covenant of grace into which the individual is taken is an absolute antithesis to the daily penitence of which, precisely as begraced, he is in need. In this intermedium 'there is' concrete authority; 'there is', along with whatever else comes under the concept of such authority, also dogma. That it is there as the gift bestowed on the Church by Christ cannot exclude the fact that the confession of faith is also actually the outgrowth of the human act of faith.

What does *concrete* authority mean, except that such localization in this intermedium belongs to its existence? If its validation lies in the mercy of God in Christ, in the essential sovereignty of the Lord over the community, yet it is also true that in this intermedium the holy Church has its existence in the unholiness of everything human, but under the saving crisis of the divine Word and Spirit. In this intermedium the Church has its authority, which is concrete but also temporal, relative, and formal.

VII

If theology is really concrete obedience to this concrete authority, then it is certainly, whatever may be the nature of its determination by its authority, a real relationship and action of real men—what else can concrete obedience mean? It is, then, not an item to be abstractly conceived in the inventory of an unrelated spiritual world which hovers above our vale of tears. But along with the truth that theology lives from God's revelation which it wills to serve, we must also recognize what is performed with more or less ability, industry, and effectiveness by professors, pastors, and scholars at their desks.

For theology as for the Church, it must be granted and recognized actually as essential that it is always an earthly activity in a definite 'here and now' (*hic et nunc*). It is an activity carried on by man, as man is defined by Adam, a wayfarer (*viator*) journeying towards his country, but not possessing (*comprehensor*) any country. And it is then presumptuous to deny. as Peterson does, that theology is essentially tied to the manifold intellectual activity of men who talk, write, proclaim, etc., and is therefore essentially limited by the possibilities of such activity. To deny that is obviously to deny the concreteness of its obedience.

'The author of theology is not the theological professor but primarily Christ and secondarily the Church', so Peterson writes (p. 30). Well and truly said! The service of the doctor of theology is, in fact, like the service of the pastor, meaningful only as the 'ministry of the Church' (*ministerium ecclesiasticum*); and this ministry is Christ's representative. But the 'Church militant' (*ecclesia militans*), within which there is concrete authority and concrete obedience, is the body of Christ in the dust and warfare of this world which is the world of this age, after man's fall. The proximate author of theology, the theological professor, may not be erased by any definition of the nature of theology, however disastrous it may be to remember him or however great a desire to get out of his own skin may often beset the theologian himself.

And it is also presumptuous to say that revelation itself can alone finally determine the real nature of theology (p. 19). Judged by that on which theology lives, that is certainly true! But it is none the less true that this very living, although it may be said to lie, if one wishes so to phrase it, 'in the prolongation of the Logos-revelation', is carried on in the forms of human sinful thinking, speaking and writing. If one wishes to think of theology consistently as a 'concretion of the Logos', then it must certainly be remembered that the road of the Logos on *earth* was the road from Bethlehem to Golgotha.

As the 'concrete authority' to which theology bows stands under the prerequisite of the real, primary, immediate authority of Christ of which it is the surrogate, so the 'concrete obedience' which theology offers stands in the shadow of the human, all too human, sphere in the obscurity of which it has pleased God now graciously to reveal himself. Theology is not only ectypal (*ἔκτυπος*) and the theology of wayfarers (*viatorum*); it is also, according to the further analysis of our elders, theology after the fall (*theologia post lapsum*). And that means that it is conditioned in its basic assumptions by human misery. And such conditioning involves the impossibility (in spite of all the energy which Peterson expends) of rejecting with a gesture of irritation the dialectical character of theology. The fragmentariness, the paradox, the continual need of radical completion, the essential inconclusiveness of all its assertions are not to be denied.

The revelation of which theology speaks is not dialectical, is not paradox (p. 11). That hardly needs to be said. But when theology begins, when we men think, speak, or write, or (if Peterson thinks it more accurate) 'argue' on the basis of the revelation, then there is dialectic (*διαλέγεσθαι*) Then there is a stating of essentially incomplete ideas and propositions among which every answer is also again a question. All such statements together reach out beyond themselves towards the fulfilment in the inexpressible reality of the divine speaking. (Whether or not we consciously know this and will it, we can do nothing to alter it.) The actual form of our doing and acting has a limit beyond which even the concrete authority we obey (for example the word of the Bible read as canon, the creed reverenced as dogma) does not carry us, because, as has already been shown, the concrete authority itself stands under the antithesis of the divine giving and the human receiving.

If Peterson now says to us that theology under such conditions does not with its statements attain to 'the seriousness of God' (p. 7), then we must answer that it can never have been intended to reach the seriousness of the knowledge with which God himself speaks. 'It did not please God to save his people by dialectic',[1] Peterson quotes from Ambrose. Certainly! But it must be said that what God does and what the theologians do ought to be quite different things. Their more modest part—I do not see why this has to be said as disparagement—is in fact 'taking' the *revelation* 'seriously' (p. 7).

To take the revelation seriously in the sphere of conceptual thinking means to walk with entire definiteness and determination on the double path marked out for us by the necessity we are under to speak as *men*, but about *God*. We must, for example, in order to recognize realistically the essential relation between God and man which is made known in revelation, speak of God's judgement and God's grace. In order to define God's relation to all which is not himself, we must speak of creation and Providence; to state fully what the Church is, of its visibility and invisibility. To speak rightly of grace, we must talk of justification and salvation, of faith and obedience on man's side. To make comprehensible the principle of Scripture, we must speak of Word and Spirit; to grasp the nature of sacraments, talk of 'things celestial and terrestrial' (*res coelestis et terrestris*), of 'eating with the mouth' and 'eating spiritually' (*manducatio oralis et spiritualis*). And if it is necessary to describe the position of the theologian, we must speak of the 'ought'and the 'cannot' rooted in the subject itself, under which he stands.

In all these and similar antitheses, there is no possibility of accepting both together. Such antitheses stand opposed to each other, not quantitively, not in a 'relation of tension', not to be comprehended in any *one* word; but unsubsumed by any word which we can speak, mutually exclusive. They are irreconcilable because in different ways they all

---

[1] *Non in dialectica complacuit Deo salvum facere populum suum.*

express the infinite qualitative difference between God and man with which a theology of sinners (and that is *all* theology), however theocentric or Christocentric it may be or may wish to appear, has to deal in presenting the communion of God and man.

In the 'and' with which theology combines in words what it cannot combine in thought because that combination can be made only in the act of the divine Word and Spirit, in this 'and' lies the theological 'taking' of the revelation 'seriously'. Only one who could say Jesus Christ, that is could say God become flesh, God and man, in *one* word, and that word a true word, could pride himself on *not* being a 'dialectical theologian'.

But the history of dogma teaches us and the Christological dogma, especially that of Chalcedon, requires of us not to will what man cannot will in reason. And what holds here holds for the whole of theology. The statement still stands (and universal repudiation will not soon make me doubt it): theology is in its whole course at best *Prolegomenon*, preface. Theology speaks the preamble for that which ultimately God himself must say—and will say. Just so far can theology 'take' revelation 'seriously'. May it so do!

But the 'seriousness of God', the synthesis without conflict beyond statement and counter-statement, question and counter-question, the Yea and Amen spoken in heaven upon our 'arguing', by 'the law' of revelation (*quo jure*), which actually decides the meaning of our 'arguing' (p. 19), cannot be anything but pure gift, given to theology as it is to the Church. It can be claimed only and in so far as God through his Word and Spirit makes himself to be known and confessed, as he must continually reveal himself to be confessed by their concrete authority. No concrete obedience to any concrete authority can achieve this or supply a substitute for or supplement or guarantee or continue this component which distinguishes theology from the empty, godless dialectic of mythology and differentiates it with complete, unambiguous clarity from that most dubious of all disciplines, the so-called faculty of 'the liberal arts and sciences'; which eventually makes theology the science of all sciences (p. 24).

It is intrinsic to the concept of revelation that it is the sovereign act of God alone which makes the Church truly the Church in the midst of the great ambiguity of the history of religion and in spite of its own role as servant; which makes the Christian, in the midst of the 'mass of corruption' (*massa perditionis*) into which he is also sunk, truly the *chosen* and *sanctified*. Theology stands under the same rule. This rule does not permit the moving of the fixed 'point of faith' (p. 8) so that it might entrench upon the righteousness of God by assuming beforehand what must be given to it new every morning by God. What it does require is that theology, in concrete obedience to concrete authority, hoping for grace, seeking for the Word, and praying for the Holy Spirit, dare afresh every morning to take the revelation seriously for itself in its special sphere, the sphere of conceptual thinking—but that means to take it 'dialectically'.

I cannot help it if this word *dialectic*, once it is thrown into a discussion, immediately becomes a bogy with which one frightens children, as if some kind of horror of sub-Christian philosophy lurked behind it. It means really only the simple recognition that the Scriptural word, 'Except the Lord build the house, they labour in vain that build it', applies to theology at every moment. Our talking, speaking, or arguing in theology can only be an appeal to God's speaking to men which happened and is continually happening in Christ. To complete that speaking does not in any sense lie within our competence and capacity. What we have to do is to conform ourselves to it.

There are religious communities where the place of honour in the refectory is fully prepared at every meal and then left unoccupied. So to leave empty the place where the decisive Word would be spoken is the meaning of dialectic in theology. Yes, Adam *is* dead (p. 25); but truly he is not yet redeemed with all his race. God *has* spoken in his Son, we *are* now God's children; but 'it does not yet appear what we shall be' (I John 3.2). The time of wholly human inquiry concerning God, of wholly human talk about God has not yet passed. The Church still has good cause to be content with the promise, to be conscious of its own limit, to wait for its Master and not seek to play the master itself. Just how far this limit extends for theology is not wholly clear; 'but we have this treasure in earthen vessels, that the excellency of the power may be of God and not of us.'

VIII

Theology is concrete obedience. Let us conclude with a consideration of what this obedience must mean. Obedience exists only in the action of a will which submits itself to a higher will. But Peterson says rightly that here we are concerned with obedience rendered to the Christian faith (p. 8). However, as obedience to faith, it obviously stands in relation to the will of God manifested in his revelation; and the will of God so manifested is the reconciliation of man with himself while he speaks to him, and the leading of man to his redemption. As the God who has spoken in his Son and still speaks through the witness of his servants and messengers, he will also speak today—*today*.

Obedience to faith must mean service to this manifest will. That is to say, service to this speaking by which God acts means giving and making opportunity so that this speaking today, even today, is not heard in vain. Such 'service to the Word' is pre-eminently the purpose of the Church and it is also the purpose of theology in its specific place in the Church.

Giving opportunity and making opportunity because God is speaking his saving Word—the whole community does that service by listening to the sermon, by celebrating the sacraments, by its penitence and thanksgiving, by its prayer. As the instrument of the community the ministry of the Church does it especially when, confronted by the inevitable waverings in the presentation of the message, it keeps guard over the preservation or restoration of pure *doctrine*, acting in conformity with the concrete authority of the Church and *also* in the liberty of faith, which means in the light of the primary authority of the Lord.

Pure doctrine is doctrine conforming to the Scripture and to the Spirit. Such doctrine leaves the divine Word free, above the claims of all human speaking of and about God. And so the sermon as the place at which the will of God will be done today is the place at which theology is geared into the Church. And to be geared into the Church means to be actually and methodologically subordinated. The freedom of faith in which theology functions can *not* mean, as freedom of *faith*, that theology denies its nature as service. 'So far as dogmatics departs from the domain of the Church', writes Vilmar,[1] 'it no longer serves beatitude but the intellectual vanity of the individual. Dogmatics must understand that, as a part of the preparation for the spiritual office, it stands in the relation of the school to real life, and that to it also are addressed the words "we learn not for school but for life" (*non scholae sed vitae discimus*). The life of the Church is above dogmatics.'

It is not that theology itself has to preach; but theology is not, as it seems to be for Peterson, merely dogmatics. Apart from the supplementary historical discipline, theology must, as exegesis, continually raise the fundamental question of the genuine prophetic and apostolic witness to the revelation given in the canonical sources. As dogmatics, it must continually work out afresh the fundamental affirmations of the Christian message in accordance with the prevailing background and the norm of that witness in the creeds and the Fathers. As homiletics,

---

[1] A. F. C. Vilmar, *Dogmatik*, Part I, Gütersloh, 1874, p. 59; cf. pp. 5, 89.

safeguarded through the principles so won and taught by the unwritten command of the present hour, it must consider the *What* ? and the *How* ? of the Christian message to the immediate present. But all of these things must be done expressly as service, as guard duty over the guards, as the place where the Church itself answers for its action. Theology must be understood as the place where, beyond the ambiguous needs of the time, of practice, of society, there must be considered the un-ambiguous needs of the Church, the very centre of its business, the 'ministry of the divine Word' (*ministerium verbi divini*). And this ministry will not allow itself to be bargained for or mislaid by the spirit of the times, even if it be a Churchly spirit of the times. This is how theology serves the revelation when it serves the preaching.

Such service involves an especial burden which in itself is laid fundamentally upon the *whole* Church; but it also involves a special grace (*charisma*) which is in itself conferred fundamentally on the whole community. The assertion that 'as all believers are priests, so also all are theologians' must be upheld as true in the reasonable sense in which alone it can be seriously made, in spite of the (not always honest) scorn with which it is viewed by Peterson (p. 32). For the particular wrong which makes theology a necessity, for the success with which heathen cleverness, heathen profundity, heathen (genuinely *heathen*) religion, introduced in ever new forms, gain control of the very place where God's honour should dwell, the whole Church is to blame and from it the whole Church suffers. The whole Church in all its branches shares the responsibility for and the effects of the lack of discipline and the laziness of human thinking and speaking left to itself, of which even the Christian mission must continually be accused. So likewise the reaction against it, the carefully considered call to the real centre, to discipline, to Christian strictness—and all this is in fact theology—must be given and carried fundamentally by the whole Church.

The existence of theology as a specific position, as a particular science, may be and must be understood as a special grace and, thus far, as a part of good Christian order. But it can be such only when it is practised in great humility and when full consideration is given to a certain jealous attitude with which this particular position as such is confronted on all sides in the Church, to a general mistrust of it, as if under the cloak of service it was establishing an unendurable dominance, a gnostic aristocracy, a 'papal authority of the scribes' (Schlatter). What theology is able to simply remove itself above the presence of this mistrust of all theology ?

And further there is the sceptical question for which the uniqueness of theology as position and as science necessarily gives opportunity to those outside. We shall silence it neither by force nor by clever talking; we must *listen* to it, as in its place a justified question. For to the unique way in which (in contrast to the way all other things which 'are' are given) God and God only gives his revelation, there corresponds the especial kind of vulnerability and offence in which theology stands in relation to all other positions and sciences.

But however that may be, theology cannot possibly be exalted (as Peterson has exalted it) for its own advantage, by any appeal to its uniqueness as a position and a science; nor exalted even for the sake of justifying its special character. Theology becomes possible as position and science only if it carries that special burden, that special eager fidelity of the Church to its Lord, that anxious guardianship of and zeal for the purity of the Church's preaching. 'The knowledge of theology and of dogmatics especially does not serve asceticism exclusively, nor wholly the theoretical speculation pursued in the quiet of monastic life. It serves the Church's leadership ordained by God, the spiritual office ordained by God; and it can be fully evaluated only from that starting-point. The knowledge which belongs to the spiritual office is *active*, outgoing, ruling the community and leading it to its goal, overseeing the whole progress and programme of the Church, backwards and forwards. It is a knowledge belonging to the "grace of government" (χάρισμα κυβερνήσεως) and serves to support this grace.' [1]

It is not well done to tear this complex apart, to cut out preaching, along with the Bible and its exegesis, from theology's sphere of interest, to allow its whole nature to be exhausted in the illustrious purposelessness of attaining by means of dogma to a knowledge of God—or rather to a knowledge of a world of spiritual entities, and making such knowledge comprehensible by 'arguing' in a 'metaphysical-ontological' context.

It is not accidental that the questions which I have to ask Peterson are directed to just this point. They must be really only questions. But for the sake of clarity and completeness, I cannot suppress them here.

Should there be inherently in the activity which Peterson describes to us as theology something of the 'seriousness of God' which he misses among the rest of us, the seriousness with which God 'is present' 'somewhat in the fashion of the Last Judgement' ? If theology inherently possesses this character, what has it to do with concrete *obedience*, with

[1] Vilmar, op. cit., p. 60.

honouring Christ? What differentiates it from an intellectual game or from the anthroposophic knowledge of higher worlds?

Is not a theology which rests upon itself or exists as self-sufficient, regardless of whether it appears in worldly modern dress or in the archaic ecclesiastical garb of Peterson's propositions, really in its emptiness an undertaking possible only in the air of heathenism? Is not its content, that pleroma of entities and relationships directly knowable in dogma, whose ultimate relation must not be investigated, whose fundamental subordination under Christ remains dark and unreal, astonishingly like the world of gods and demi-gods whose influence in Christian preaching a Christian theology ought definitely to repudiate?

How far is this sphere, which is the sphere of the twilight of a dogmatically based metaphysics, a sphere in which 'a man can live' (p. 23)?

Should not the passion of Luther (which Peterson sees as journalistic and nominalistic) and also the despondency, however much may be said against it, with which Kierkegaard as an 'individual' felt that he had to take upon himself the situation of the Church in the form of an 'attack on Christianity' (p. 12) always be preferable to the ostentatious seriousness of *this* theology?

The characteristic of the journalist is that he writes as an observer. As a man in close relation to the real need of the real Church, faced with this theology which is so free of all anxiety on that and on other accounts and sports in empty space, I assert in conclusion that the truly Christian theology, bearing the whole burden of faith, dare not throw away the burden of concrete *service*, but must carry it. For while it carries that burden, it is carried by God and by man as the 'theology of the cross' (*theologia crucis*), to use the words of the 'nominalist' Luther.

XI

ROMAN CATHOLICISM: A QUESTION
TO THE PROTESTANT CHURCH

A lecture delivered in Bremen on 9th March, in Osnabrück on 15th
March, and at the Lower Rhine Pastors' Conference in Düsseldorf on
10th April 1928.

I T is a well-known phenomenon of human life—a phenomenon which,
I think, appears even more conspicuously among the educated than
among the uneducated—that in a discussion with those who have a
different point of view, different modes of thinking or different aims,
we are much more concerned with saying something ourselves and
with using the concessions of our opponents or their manifest errors in
support of what we have said than we are with listening seriously to what
they have to say. And this attitude persists even when the subject of a
conference happens to be man's duty to his neighbour or the like.

In other words, we are much more anxious to assume and maintain
for ourselves the position of the examiner, questioning others—the
position commonly described since the time of Socrates as that of the
expert midwife of knowledge. We prefer, that is, to take a position
recognized as superior rather than to allow ourselves to be questioned
and cross-questioned by the other side and so to stand in the less
honourable position of pupil.

What is the real purpose of listening to a lecture? Of entering a
discussion? Of reading specific books? Or of writing specific reviews?
Why will a man debate with another man? In almost every case the
chief effect is the reinforcement of his own consciousness of being a
little Socrates. He has now become more fully conscious of his superiority; and it is a question whether the real, though hidden, purpose of
our activity was not to achieve this result. This attitude seems related to
the great law of the struggle for existence, to which obviously we as the
higher or the highest form of life are subject, along with lower forms.

But a relative rightness in this attitude even at higher levels cannot be denied for that reason. Wherever two men meet each other, with no exceptions, each of them is both the questioner and the questioned, both the expert and the ignorant. No human 'Thou' can legitimately claim that we ought to let him with his questions devour us with our questions. Actually we cannot let ourselves be questioned and cross-questioned without also putting questions ourselves.

Furthermore, who knows in a concrete case whether I am not fully justified in taking the position of expert and midwife in relation to the other man? Just *who does know*? Who has the authority to decide in such a situation? If that position is really ours, then it becomes so in the impact of the event itself, so that we ourselves can only be astonished at it, and can claim for ourselves no more than this relative right to it. And precisely when for the moment the possibility of our superiority does appear justified, even with this relative right on our side, we must in every case move cautiously. We must put our questions without misinterpreting the incidental and momentary nature of our superiority (which does not lie within our own power), and therefore *not* without conceding a similar possibility to the other man; not without recognizing that we are also questioned by him; not without 'fear and trembling'; finally, not without granting precedence to the questions of the other.

For to us has been said, 'But it shall not be *so* among you' (Matt. 20.26). '*So*', as it obviously is in the struggle for existence, where one's own question inevitably takes precedence over the question of the other. Needless to say, this happens continually; but we can neither desire it nor deem it good. For to us has been said, 'Be ye not called Rabbi . . . nor father . . . nor master' (Matt. 23.8–10). It might well happen that the moment of superiority would clothe us in that dignity to our astonishment and embarrassment.

But if we assume such dignity of ourselves, the consequence is certain to be an experience of the opposite. Therefore, 'When thou art bidden of any man to a wedding, sit not down in the highest room; lest a more honourable man than thou be bidden of him; and he that bade thee and him come and say to thee, Give this man place; and thou begin with shame to take the lowest room. But when thou art bidden, go and sit down in the lowest room; that when he that bade thee cometh, he may say unto thee, Friend, go up higher: then shalt thou have worship in the presence of them that sit at meat with thee' (Luke 14.8–10). He who is assured of the absolute justification of his position in relation to another, at once allows himself to be questioned and cross-questioned without being less certain of his own stand.

We cannot take for granted either the knowledge of such a possibility or the readiness to be genuinely questioned. We are speaking here of the knowledge and the readiness of the Christian Church. For the Church, the parable of the wedding feast is basic. That 'Not so' was spoken to the Church. In the Christian Church there is truly a Master and Lord, and every discussion carried on in the Church stands under notice that there is here a Master, and therefore no man can here be master. Therefore every man must be fundamentally much more ready to let himself be questioned than to question. Therefore we are to speak today of Roman Catholicism as a question put to the Protestant *Church*.

If we understood by Protestantism the aggregation of those who held a certain world-view in common, or an association of like-minded or like-thinking people, or an organization for achieving a common purpose, then it would not be self-evident that Roman Catholicism must be regarded as a question directed to us. Then, without the reminder that we have a Master, it would seem more fitting—very much more fitting—and properly within the natural framework of our own better knowledge, to proceed from and be content with the assumption that we have in our hearts plenty of questions for Catholicism. If in a discussion with its Catholic opponent there is usually on the Protestant side the will to speak but not to listen, this very attitude is evidence that Protestantism is really commonly understood as a unity of world-view, and that Catholicism is consequently regarded as simply an opposition party.

But if we say *Protestant Church*, those words make such an attitude untenable for us. For when we say not merely *Church*, but *Protestant Church*, we accept and affirm as the one Christian Church the Church which for the past four hundred years has been protesting against a great part of its past. But at the same time we admit that we, however hidden from us the actual connexion may be, are in the same room with the Church which calls itself, differentiating itself from and connecting itself with us, the Roman Catholic Church. We find ourselves in the church-room, in the room where the parable of the wedding feast and the 'Not so' are a part of the house rules. We should have to cease taking ourselves seriously as a *church*, we should have to really consider ourselves an Evangelical Association—which is something quite different—if we wanted to act toward Catholicism as one party usually acts towards the opposing party.

When we remember that we have a Master, we must give precedence to the question of Catholicism and let ourselves be questioned and cross-questioned. The question comes to us—however disagreeable we may find the admission—with the full, specific force of the question of a Christian brother, unweakened by any question we put to him. It relates directly to that moment of superiority over which we have no control; it comes with imperative claim to be heard, and then to be answered in 'fear and trembling'. Our right to seek and to find the one Christian Church in the Protestant Church of the last four hundred years can be allowed to defend itself only when we allow ourselves to be questioned and cross-questioned by the opposition as if we were in the wrong. Therefore today we are to consider the meaning of the statement that Roman Catholicism is a question to the Protestant Church and how far this statement holds.

Objection to this proposal ought not to be made on the ground that Catholicism does not actually present a question so far as most Protestants are concerned, even in confessionally mixed districts and not even among theologians. Roman Catholicism pursues its own peculiar existence and is much too remote, alien and unrelated to our actual thinking and experience for us to suppose it either rewarding or obligatory to listen to any question we might be asked from that quarter. There is no doubt that such is the fact. But in all seriousness I would ask whether Protestantism can be a real answer for anyone to whom Catholicism is not a real question. Whether we can have any real relation to the Church of the Reformation if we have indeed lost our grip on the opponent whom they fought. And I would give warning of the unhappy awakening which might some day follow such detachment. He who knows Catholicism, if only a little, knows how superficial are the remoteness and strangeness; how uncannily close to us all it is in reality; how urgent and vital are the questions it puts to us; how essentially impossible it is not to attend to them seriously when one has once heard them; and how necessary it is to leave this objection against our theme to the ostrich—and for an ostrich success is impossible.

Equally invalid is the objection that good, sincere, convinced Protestantism obviously involves the consciousness that the question of Catholicism has been settled successfully, decisively, and once for all. Apart from the possibility that any such complete settling may have its foundation in that fatal and dangerous ignorance which is the result of never having known anything, it should be said that, even at its best, 'settling the question' can only mean, as always for men on earth, that for a day they have disposed of serious problems which will always recur.

Do you suppose that Luther and Calvin would have laboured so hard to the end of their lives in the struggle against the Papacy if they had not all their lives recognized the urgency of the question put to them through the Papacy ? And do you think it really is proper for us their successors to take it more lightly than they ? Are we to consider ourselves good Protestants because we have happily and definitely and once for all taken possession—we speak very ambiguously of the Reformation heritage—of the result of their struggle ? As if the most convinced and vehement negation of the Roman possibility and, on the positive side, the most industrious building of our own house as the proper activity of the Protestant Church were not here in jeopardy unless, like the activity of the Reformers, our activity gives a serious answer to a serious question. A complete and final disposal of Catholicism must be called all too Catholic for us to let ourselves be deterred by an objection raised on that ground.

A third objection is also without weight. Certainly, Catholicism on its side never thinks of accepting our counter-right, of recognizing any occupation of a common room with us; and therefore on its side never takes Protestantism seriously as a question directed to the Catholic Church. So it might easily happen that what we here purpose would result only in a tactically rather unwise discrediting and weakening of our own position before a triumphing opponent. Actually, I do not for a moment suppose that Erich Przywara, Karl Adam, Hugo Lang or Romano Guardini (not to mention the older spokesmen of German and still less those of French, Spanish, and Italian Catholicism) will have any inclination to pursue today's theme with the title reversed. And I assume throughout that statements like those I intend to make can be entered as assets by the other side and be further elaborated, at least in the arena of professional polemics, as welcome concessions. In spite of this conviction, indeed because of it, I count this objection as the least of all. What concern is it of ours, if Catholicism in its opposition to us be determined to stand boastfully on the number of its centuries, on the basis of its better knowledge,[1] to take the attitude of an opposing party ?

[1] 'The Catholic Church, as the old (!), as the mother Church is still in possession (*in possessione*). . . . Protestantism is accountable to her, stands before her tribunal and her seat of judgement; let us say rather, before her motherly, cherishing and demanding eye, to be tested, to justify itself' (Hugo Lang on the problem of reunion in Germany, *Der katholische Gedanke*, vol. 1, 1928, Nr. 2, p. 182). Catholicism is 'still the final home for which the wildest Gypsy really longs, therefore it can wait as a mother waits. She knows that no child can wholly forget that it once lay on her bosom. It will surely find its way home . . .' (Erich Przywara, 'Die dialektische Theologie' in *Schweizerische Rundschau*, vol, 22, Nr. 12, March 1928). In my judgement, this attitude typifies, however elegantly and kindly it may be expressed, the fatal 'setting one's self above' others; the opposite of 'on bended knee' (*flectamus genua*) (Lang; loc. cit., p. 181) from which alone we could expect some gain for both sides.

Truly, so far as the Catholic does exactly that, he transforms the Church into an association holding a definite world-view or into something similar. But his action does not justify our doing the same.

The Catholic attitude would not annul the insight that we are required to act differently, not for the sake of Catholicism, but for the sake of the truth, and because it is dangerous to do anything or leave anything undone, contrary to one's conscience, on tactical grounds. Here there can be no waiting for a concession of counter-right, no partisanship, no considerations of prestige. Here there is no place for party interest.[1]

If it is true that questions are presented to us through Roman Catholicism, then it *is* true. And regardless of how Catholicism may relate itself to us and our counter-questions, we are not released from the responsibility of listening to the questions it directs to us. I should like to make the claim that such listening is really Protestantism's strongest defence; for so we meet Catholicism without considering the demands of higher or of lower strategy, absolutely differently from the way Catholicism meets us.

I

First, the Protestant Church is asked by Roman Catholicism whether and how far it is a church.

Catholicism is a forcible and sharp reminder that in the Reformation of the sixteenth century out of which the Protestant Church came into being the purpose was *reformation*, as the name implies; it was the rebuilding of the Church, and therefore was neither its destruction nor its transformation into a wholly different structure. The Reformation did not proclaim a new, a second beginning, but the rediscovery of the old, the only, origin of the Church. Protestantism protested not *against* but *for* the Church. Reformation does not mean revolution. Protestant Church means not less a church but more; means a church not weaker but stronger than the Catholic; means precisely the *Church*. Protestantism means the Church as the human instrument of revelation in the hand of God, the Church as the locale among men where God's Word speaks and is received, the Church as the community of men in which, on the basis of the divine call, God's Word is served through men, the Church as the community of men in which, again on the basis of the divine call, God's Word becomes an event for men.

---

[1] The way that in Düsseldorf, I was met with contradiction at this point from those in a responsible position, only made me question whether it might not be necessary to proceed much more ruthlessly against the profane unchurchliness of our usual confessional defence.

Whether the Reformation be considered in the light of its historical development or in its ideological content, there is no possibility of doubting that the meaning of Protestantism (both Lutheran and Reformed) was in the beginning not a lessening but a heightening of the force of all the claims which Catholicism makes for the Church. And this beginning has never been officially repudiated. A preference for a different interpretation of Protestantism assumes that in the meantime, in the eighteenth century or at the turn from the eighteenth to the nineteenth, a kind of second reformation occurred for which the way had fortunately been prepared by the Humanists and the visionaries of the sixteenth century itself. Thus a second 'new Protestantism' has appeared on the scene as the true Protestantism. Its character would consist not in the re-establishment, but in a relinquishment of the substance of the Church.

The course of the Christian Church through history has from the beginning been determined by both 'the confusion of men and the Providence of God' (*hominum confusione et Dei providentia*). Because of the confusion of men, the Reformation was necessary; by the Providence of God, it really came to pass. *Really*? Here our questions to the Catholic Church would begin—questions to which we today can give only a passing glance.

Certainly the history of the Church after the Reformation proceeded under this dual control. By the confusion of men, out of the Reformation might come revolution. The emergence, expansion, and consolidation of a second, new Protestantism which had in common with that of the sixteenth century only the name, the protesting, might become a fact. The situation even now is such that when we speak today of the Protestant Church we are never anywhere certain (the differences among its so-called trends are not very great) that we are not dealing with that second, new Protestantism, a Protestantism which wished to forget and has, in fact, forgotten that the Reformation was a reconstruction; which no longer knows and does not wish to know what the Church is, to know that the Church is not the house of individual or of community experience or convictions, but is the house of God.

Confronting precisely this confusion of thought on our side, Catholicism directs to us the question, What constitutes the substance of the Church? For it is the substance of the Church to be the house of God. Catholicism becomes the question of what has happened to this substance among us. It becomes the reminder that if we have really thrown away this substance and lost it, if we are unambiguously new

Protestants, it would be meaningless to call ourselves any longer by the name of Protestant Church.

Catholicism becomes this question to us because it has kept at least the claim to the knowledge of this substance and has guarded it, even though by opposition to its restoration it has made its claim highly doubtful as judged from our side. It becomes this question to us because its dogma, its ritual of worship, its general attitude, in spite of all to which we may object, does hold before men's eyes something of that which the Reformation reformed, restored, brought into clear light and improved, rebuilt and made valid—that *without* which the whole Reformation would have been purposeless, and *without* which the Church founded on the Reformation would be equally purposeless. Catholicism becomes this question to us because in its presuppositions for the Church, in spite of all contradictions, it is closer to the Reformers than is the Church of the Reformation so far as that has actually and finally become the new Protestantism. It becomes this question to us because, if any of the concern of the Reformation is still ours in spite of the new Protestantism, we cannot deny that we feel more at home in the world of Catholicism and among its believers than in a world and among believers where the reality about which the Reformation centred has become an unknown or almost unknown entity.[1]

I shall attempt to clarify the foregoing by stating a few main points.

1. Catholicism testifies and affirms a sure knowledge that he who really and primarily acts in the Church is absolutely and primarily God himself in Jesus Christ. Continually through its liturgy and its dogma, Catholicism attests: *God's* presence makes the Church to be the Church, *he* preaches, *he* is the sacrificer and the sacrifice, *he* prays, *he* believes, *he* is 'the real *I* of the Church'.[2] This insight leads straight to dangerous and worse than dangerous consequences, since this 'divine I' of the Church has earthly, human surrogates in the office of his representative on the Roman bishop's seat, in the sacrificing priest and the sacrificed host, finally in the collective visibility of the Church as such. And between God and these surrogates exist identities, very difficult to make

[1] It perhaps will make for clarity if I state explicitly one implication of this sentence. If I today became convinced that the interpretation of the Reformation on the line taken by Schleiermacher-Ritschl-Troeltsch (or even by Seeberg or Holl) was correct; that Luther and Calvin really intended such an outcome of their labours; I could not indeed become a Catholic tomorrow, but I should have to withdraw from the evangelical Church. And if I were forced to make a choice between the two evils, I should, in fact, prefer the Catholic.

[2] Karl Adam, *Das Wesen des Katholizismus*, 8th ed., p. 24. English translation by Justin McCann, *The Spirit of Catholicism*, p. 15. (References to both are given here. The original references were to the 4th German edition.)

logically clear, but certainly understood to be not indirect but exceedingly direct.

Perhaps the insight which Catholicism presents should be more important to us than the inacceptabilities bound up with it. Here is churchly *substance*. Here is imbedded the knowledge that the Church is the house of God. The substance may perhaps be distorted and perverted, but is not lost! Even the Catholic Mass confesses in its *Gloria*: 'Thou who sittest at the right hand of the Father, have mercy upon us. For thou alone art holy, thou alone art Lord, thou alone art highly exalted, Jesus Christ!'[1]

Also the Catholic Christian still believes 'if rightly understood, not in the Church but in the living God who shows himself to him in the Church'.[2] And the praying Christian of the Middle Ages pleads for the grace [3] 'to rest in thee above every creature, above all health and beauty, above all glory and honour . . . above all sweetness and consolation, above all hope and promise, above all merit and desire, above all gifts and rewards which thou canst give and pour forth, above all joy and jubilation which the mind is able to receive and feel; in a word, above Angels and Archangels and all the army of heaven, above all things visible and invisible, and above everything which thou, O my God, art not. For thou, O Lord my God, art best above all things.'

Now if the Reformation was the restoration of the Church, it was such because it accepted and underscored that 'Thou alone' (*Tu solus!*) and made it specifically concrete (as in the Catholic Church it never had been and never will be) by consistently fighting against all direct identifications with God in the visible Church. The Reformation applied the 'Thou alone!' (*Tu solus!*) to Jesus Christ as the Lord in his immutable unlikeness to all his servants, as the Word in ineluctable antithesis to all which we ourselves say, as the Spirit in unalterable contrast to all material things. The Reformation restored the reality of this 'Thou alone!' with the contrapuntal accompaniment of the 'by

---

[1] Qui sedes ad dexteram patris, miserere nobis. Quoniam tu solus Sanctus, tu solus Dominus, tu solus altissimus Jesu Christe!

[2] Adam, p. 76; Eng., p. 58.

[3] *De Imitatione Christi*, III, 21, 1 f.: in te super omnem creaturam requiescere, supra omnem salutem et pulchritudinem, super omnem gloriam et honorem . . . super omnem suavitatem et consolationem, super omnem spem et promissionem, super omne meritum et desiderium, super omnia dona et munera, quae potes dare et infundere, super omne gaudium et jubilationem quam potest mens humana capere ac sentire. Denique super omnes angelos et archangelos et super omnem exercitum coeli, super omnia visibilia et invisibilia et super omne quod tu, Deus meus non es, quia tu, Domine meus es super omnia optimus. (The English translation is Benham's.)

faith alone' (*sola fide*), by which it consciously willed to recognize and proclaim the presence of God in the Church.

Therefore the purpose of the Reformation was to make this *Thou* greater not smaller, not dissipating him into symbolism but fixing him solidly as the centre of the Church. And therefore the Reformation was determined to affirm the trinitarian and christological dogma of the old Church more strongly, not less; and with deeper meaning and greater consistency. Such affirmation was a strengthened and sharpened witness to the unalterable truth that God who is present in his Church is subject not object. It was a more precise witness to the essential *deity* of Christ and of the Holy Spirit. The Reformation protest against the Roman pontiff, the priests, and the sacraments must not be understood as if it were intended to cast doubt on the real and primary presence and action of God in his Church rather than to assert both in a purer, more compelling form. When the sacramental hymn of Thomas Aquinas[1] begins with the words:

Adoro te devote latens Deitas	In humility I pray thee, hidden
Quae sub his figuris vere latitas	Godhead
	Who art truly here, veiled in the
	symbol's sign

what change can Protestantism desire except the underlining of *hidden*, *veiled*, so that the *Godhead* and the *truly* have their proper force, differentiated from all that is not hidden, and therefore from all that is not God?

Or ought Protestantism really to want something else? Something different from a new and better comprehension of the old, the one substance of the Church? Should Protestantism be understood as a dilution of the Catholic idea of God's presence? Is Protestantism to mean an exchange of roles—God the object and Christians the subject of the Church? Does God in the end hold his truth in fee to us and our piety? We have cause to know ourselves questioned by the Roman Church with its 'Christ present' (*Christus praesens*) in spite of all the ambiguity of the forms in which the sense of that presence is expressed. We have cause to know ourselves faced with the fundamental question of whether we are the Church, the reformed Church, but still—or again—the Church; of whether we stand on the foundation of the Reformation or on that of some intervening revolution.

[1] Schott-Bihlmeyer, *Das vollständige röm. Messbuch*, 2nd ed., Appendix, pp. 258 f.

2. On the basis of this assumption that there exists in the Church a mediation of the divine revelation and reconciliation to men on earth, Catholicism dares to believe in the existence of an actual, earthly, human service of God in the Church. Just because God is subject there, men and things are there at his disposal, they can there be predicate. 'The Word became flesh.' Therefore and therein, in the reality of this divine condescension, the Church is the House of God. From this fact, the Catholic understands the sacraments as 'visible evidence that Jesus is at work in our midst';[1] from that fact especially he understands the Mass as the re-presentation (repraesentatio) of the unique sacrifice on the cross;[2] from there, the priesthood as 'the visible proclamation and mediation of the unique grace of the one High Priest';[3] and the Pope as the embodiment of the unity of the Church.[4] We gladly recognize how indirectly all this can be meant when Thomas Aquinas continues in the hymn already quoted:

Visus tactus gustus in te fallitur	Sight, feeling, taste delude themselves about thee.
Sed audito solo tuto creditur:	By hearing alone is sure faith given.
Credo quidquid dixit Dei filius	Only what God's Son has said do I believe.
Nil hoc verbo Veritas verius	The Word is truth, and what can be more true?

And another sacramental hymn[5] can declare, one would think in the phrases of the Reformation:

Et, si sensus deficit	When the senses fail to discern,
Ad firmandum cor sincerum	Certainty for the pure heart
Sola fides sufficit	Is given by faith alone.

Of course, we hear also quite different voices in which the supposed predicates appear all at once to possess the character of subject. The sacrifice of the Mass takes the place of the memorial of the Lord's death (*memoriale mortis Domini*);[6] and, with dependence on accompanying

---

[1] Adam, p. 28; Eng., p. 18.   [2] Schott, p. 4.
[3] Adam, p. 157; Eng., p. 124.   [4] Adam, p. 52; Eng., p. 38.
[5] *Pange lingua gloriosi*, Schott, Appendix, p. 249. Compare also in the sequence for Corpus Christi, *Laude Sion*, (Schott, pp. 593 f.), the strophe *Quod non capis, quod non vides animosa firmat fides* (What you do not touch, what you do not see, ardent faith confirms). The idea in almost the same words is found in Cyril of Jerusalem (*Catechetical Lectures*, 22.6; NPNF, p. 152).
[6] Thomas Aquinas, loc. cit.

faith expressly excluded, it becomes as a work accomplished (*opus operatum*), a work of Christ himself,[1] effecting reconciliation and conferring grace.[2] It is a 'shattering experience of reality, a re-living of the reality of Golgotha';[3] where the celebrating priest, surpassing the Virgin Mary and all the angels and saints, can make Christ present and bring him to the altar as sacrifice.[4] And the Roman pontiff (*pontifex Romanus*) is neither more nor less than Christ on earth (*in terris*).[5]

Here again the Reformation was clearly restoration, restoration of the knowledge of the absolute uniqueness of the person of the Lord and of the absolute unrepeatability of his work; restoration of the immutable relation of Word and flesh, of subject and predicate; restoration of the interrelation between the divine reality of revelation and the equally divine reality of faith. But in this restoration, the Reformation was affirmation not denial, strengthening and sharpening not weakening; least of all was it obliteration of the idea of mediation, of the concept of the church service, of the insight that the Church is the House of God.

The Reformers were certainly not 'consistent' with the kind of consistency which was afterwards so often desired, and which was often achieved by adding supplements, allegedly in their meaning and spirit. The Reformers desired to make more important, not less, the truth of the incarnation of the Word when they taught that the reality of the mediation must again be understood as *act*, as the act of God himself, instead of as an institution under the control of men. When they taught that Word and sacraments are instruments which are used and which are effective 'where and when God pleases' (*ubi et quando visum est Deo*)[6] because they are in God's hand and remain in his hand; when they saw the Church as the place where God is Master of men, not where men are masters of God. But they taught mediation, and in their restoring they taught the understanding and the honouring of Church, Word, and sacrament.

They took without scruple the step to the visible Church. Indeed, they warned against such scrupulosity in all its forms as blasphemy, a temptation of the Devil. In the same breath with which they discarded the mass as a 'cursed idol', they did not fail to repulse the 'heavenly prophets' who wished to bypass Church, Word, and sacrament, and to fly at once to the Unmediated and Absolute in pure spirituality and

---

[1] Adam, p. 35; Eng., p. 25.   [2] Schott, p. 4.   [3] Adam, p. 231; Eng., p. 186.
[4] Archbishop Katschthaler. Mirbt, *Quellen zur Geschichte des Papsttums und des römishcen Katholizismus*, 4th ed., p. 499.
[5] Arnold of Villanova. Ibid., p. 211.   [6] *Augustana*, Art. 5.

inwardness—as if that did not involve the same outraging of the majesty of the Lord who will not give his honour to another.

Is the final consummation of Protestant truth today to be sought in the certainly incontrovertible truth that God's gracious presence 'cannot be shut up in any sacrament box', but 'in every place, in the shoemaker's shop, in the factory, in the stone-cutter's yard, in the laboratory, everywhere, time flows into eternity'?[1] In the truth that a pastor has no religious authority which every other member of the community could not have?[2] And that, to talk like Luther, the water at baptism is no better than the water 'the cow drinks'?[3] Are we to accept the total loss of the insight that the problem of Church, Word, and sacrament as earthly-human service of the Word of God really begins on the other side of all these obviously true assertions? Do we not see that such assertions leave untouched the possibility and necessity of a *relative* mediation, of a *relative* service of God, which though relative must be taken seriously? Have we all had to become secretly a kind of Orlamünde?

Even if the Catholic concept of mediation were much more unambiguously wrong, it is certainly time that Catholicism should become a question for us. The question is whether and how far we are making a serious affirmation, when apart from what is done in factory and laboratory we affirm also the visible act of a visible Church. Do we believe that God has a special purpose for the Church or do we not? If we do not so believe, then in what real sense do we affirm it? This is the question of the *substance* of the Church. We cannot deny that Catholicism has in its own way protected this substance. And we can be certain that it is our own Reformers, especially Luther and Calvin, who ask us concomitantly with Catholicism and most penetratingly, what we would really be wanting if we should become Orlamündes.

3. On the basis of this same presupposition that Jesus Christ is the subject of the Church, Catholicism dares to claim *authority* for the Church. While the Church means to be only a surrogate subject, to be

---

[1] Karl Heim, *Das Wesen des evangelischen Christentums*, 3rd ed., p. 109. I use this particular example from Protestant polemic, because it was written by one of our most authoritative theologians and because another authoritative theologian has said that in this book there 'is given to us a spiritual weapon which it is to be hoped will be used in the urgent debate against the claims of the papal Church' and that 'currently we have nothing else of the same kind to put beside it' (*Theol. Literaturzeitung*, 1925, Nr. 22, p. 522). Also I quote from it because 'if this be done in the green tree . . .' But in so using it, I do not forget the other services of the Tübingen Professor and the wide area of my own agreement with him.

[2] Heim, p. 114.   [3] Idem.   [3] Ibid., p. 115.

the body for the Head, yet the full authority becomes visible in the Church itself. The Church acquires and keeps a consciousness of itself as able to execute a commission which can be subordinated to no other. And to execute this commission, it claims attention and obedience. God's binding of men becomes concrete in his binding them through the Church. We Protestants easily overlook the fact that there is involved here no question of a binding of the individual conscience by the authority of the Church. At least according to Catholic theory, obedience is owed to the conscience even when that involves disobedience to the Church.[1] We have, of course, the right to ask how the practice is related to the theory. We may indeed prove that the interest of the Catholic Church has never been directed towards this limitation on the pastoral office, but has always been wholly concentrated on the determination to make the authority of the Church effective.

The Reformation meant the restoration of the authority of God in antithesis to the authority of the Church, and so involved automatically the restoration of the freedom of conscience—not merely as permissible in the pastoral relation with individuals, but as necessarily basic in every way for the Church. But again there can be no doubt that the consciousness of its own authority, based on the commission held by the Church, belongs to the Church in the Reformation understanding of it not less but more strongly than to the Roman Church unless the Protestant Church is ready to surrender its own existence as a church.

Authority is by no means merely one of the requisites for the 'magic of the Catholic Church',[2] but belongs really to the essential nature of the Church as the House of God. The claim to authority is the courage to dare, never forgetting the supreme power of God and therefore always mindful of the freedom of conscience, to speak to men in the name of God, with the prophetic 'Thus saith the Lord'. It must not be overlooked that Luther and Calvin made the strongest possible claim upon this 'Thus saith the Lord'—not for themselves personally but for their work. Nor is the claim differently understood in the Catholic Church. If the Reformers reversed the metaphor of the early Church, 'the Church is the Spirit himself (*Ecclesia ipse est spiritus*)[3] for the sake of the authority of God and with that authority the freedom of conscience, nevertheless in their judgement, the Protestant man is not abandoned any more than is the Catholic to the guidance of his subjective conscience. He is a man bound, with the freedom of his conscience

---

[1] Adam, p. 242; Eng., 195.   [2] Heim, pp. 5 f.
[3] Tertullian, *Against Praxeas*, 21.

concretely bound and bound by the authority of the Church. He is more bound than the Catholic because Protestantism fully accepts the truth that the Church can in binding only act vicariously for God, and it makes this truth concrete by locating the binding by the Church in the freedom of conscience.

And the Protestant Church knows as well as the Catholic that it has a high commission to execute. It knows this better than the Catholic just so far as, in fulfilling this commission, the Protestant Church respects the limits set to its authority in the freedom of conscience. In this limitation, however, it is the supreme authority of God which is respected. Where the Church is, there is also the power of the Church. Today we often forget (I make use of Max Weber's words) [1] 'that the Reformers intended not the relinquishment of the rule of the Church over life, but rather the substitution of a new form of rule for the old form'. We cannot intelligently condemn the Papacy for exercising power. If that power had remained only churchly, spiritual power, and therefore a God-serving power, and had not become instead a power which displaces and replaces God, we, like Luther, should have no objection to kissing the Pope's feet. [2]

The anti-authoritarian thinking and attitude of modern man, which ignores all restraints, has nothing to do with the Protestant Church. It is untrue that we recognize even the slightest tincture of our spirit in the development which began with the Renaissance and has produced such men. [3] It is untrue that we find the cause of the division in the Church and therefore the reason for the foundation of the Protestant Church in the 'anger of the disappointed German man' Luther, and in our own resentment against the 'cold hand from the other side of the mountains'. [4] It is untrue that if we were driven into a corner and

---

[1] Max Weber, *Gesammelte Aufsätze zur Religionssoziologie*, I, p. 20.

[2] *Si igitur papa nobis concesserit, quod solus Deus ex mera gratia per Christum justificet peccatores, non solum volumus eum in manibus portare, sed etiam ei osculari pedes.* (If therefore the Pope admits to us that God alone by his mere grace through Christ justifies sinners, we are not only willing to support him in our hands, but willing also to kiss his feet.) Luther, *Commentary on Galatians*, 2.6. And compare with this Melanchthon's individual attestation in signing the Schmalcald Articles in 1537: *Ego Philippus Melanchthon supra positos articulos approbo ut pios et christianos. De pontifice autem statuo, si evangelium admitteret, posse ei propter pacem et communem tranquillitatem christianorum, qui jam sub ipso sunt et in posterum sub ipso erunt, superioritatem in episcopos, quam alioqui habet, jure humano etiam a nobis permitti.* (I, Philip Melanchthon, approve the above articles as pious and Christian. But concerning the Pope, I affirm that if he would accept the Gospel, it would be possible for the sake of the peace and common tranquillity of the Christians who are now under him and in future will be under him, even for us to allow him by human right his superiority over bishops, which he now holds.)　　　[3] Heim, pp. 102 f.　　　[4] Ibid., pp. 21, 27.

forced to choose between the Court of the Inquisition and Jacob
Boehme, we should of necessity vote for Jacob Boehme—and perhaps
at the same time for Frederick the Great.[1] Briefly, it is untrue that our
protest against the Roman concept of authority is in general about the
same as that of the modern 'educated man'.[2]

But—is it untrue? Really not true? There is no lack of powerful
voices in Protestantism (and they are not the voices of liberals only)
who say that precisely this is the truth! The Protestant Church is asked
through Roman Catholicism, whatever may be the Catholic errors, what
the situation actually is. The Protestant Church is asked to *whom* it is
actually speaking the Word of God in the conflict of the 'final solitariness'
of the spirit.[3] We are asked what is left of the commission of the Church
if the only task remaining for the Church is, as Richard Rothe says,[4]
'to make itself almost superfluous'? And what is left of the Church itself
without a commission?

We are questioned here concerning the *substance* of the Church.
Catholicism asks us—and has the right to ask us—why, after all has
been said which can be said against the concept of Church authority,
why at the point where it is most offensive to modern men, the claim for
authority for the Church, we do not join solidly with Catholicism in
feeling and argument? Do we not see that this is a real concern of the
Church and therefore our own concern?

II

Through Roman Catholicism the Protestant Church is confronted
with a second question—whether and in how far it is a *Protestant*
Church.

The Protestant Church is the Church, re-established, reconstituted,
regenerated in a very special sense. We have allowed ourselves to be
questioned on the regenerated *substance*. But there is also a second
question: How has it fared with the *regeneration* of this substance?
What is the state of the *Protestantism* of the Protestant Church?

We have already had to define somewhat the direction in which the
reformation of the Church proceeded, and thereby obviously the
direction in which a reformed Church (if it is really such) must continue
to proceed. It is determined simply by the insight that God, in the
house which is his house, is and remains the *Lord* of the house. The

---

[1] Ibid., pp. 108, 112.   [2] P. 105.   [3] P. 89.   [4] P. 117.

Reformers never contended, and we also cannot contend, that this insight is hidden from the Catholic Church.

But the Reformers asked, and we ask with them, whether in the Catholic Church this insight illumined and prevailed as it must illumine and prevail, independent and unconditioned, above the Church whose subject is God, above the Church's own service of mediation, the truth of which is again God; above the Church's authority, the reality of which is again still God. Because the Church was resolved to let this insight shine purer and clearer and prevail more consistently (only comparatives exist when we are speaking of the will of men), the Church was established in contrast to Roman Catholicism as the *Protestant* Church. Because it would not and could not be anything but a Protestant *Church,* a restoration of the substance of the Church; the Roman Church became and is now in our eyes an heretical Church.

We have seen reason to let ourselves be questioned by the Roman Church on whether the whole may not be merely a diagram; whether the *substance* of the Church may not have been lost to us in the rebuilding. But we have also reason to let ourselves be questioned by the Roman Church on how that restoration fares among us, whether we really have grounds to maintain our rejection of the Mother Church because the Reformation repudiated it. We need to let ourselves be asked whether the contradiction involved in the four-hundred-year-old schism is really still dangerous. Or whether it has not been blunted by a long, slow but genuine regression on our part, so that to keep our conscience clear we are beginning to think of an external return. Especially so thinking, if at the same time it becomes clear to us, on the first point, that the substance of the Church common to us both may, all things considered, be found in better hands there than here.

The Protestant answer to this second question is no more self-evident than the answer to the first. We have already noted that the history of the Church has progressed 'by the confusion of men and the Providence of God' (*hominum confusione et Dei providentia*). And because that is true, there is both the possibility and the actuality of such an inner turning back of Protestantism to the road to Rome.

Of the same new Protestantism of which we were already compelled to say that it has lost the substance of the Church, we must now say that it has also thrown away the restoration. It has ceased to be Church and it has ceased to be Protestant—the former more in its rational, the latter more in its pietistic form. But the boundaries separating these two aspects and their development are fluid; and in the greatest and most popular new Protestant, Friedrich Schleiermacher, the two have flowed together until they are indistinguishable. Here also it is true that when the Protestant Church is the topic of discussion, no one is sure that we are not dealing with this new Protestantism which because of its pietistic components has long been un-Protestant, and now finds itself again close to the Roman Church, both inwardly and outwardly. It would already have been wholly there externally except that, because of its rationalistic components, it had at the same time also ceased to be a church. It therefore objected to the Roman Church at the very point where no objection ought to be found! Accordingly Catholicism again becomes a question to the Protestant Church, the question of its Protestantism; and reminds us that if our Protestantism should really prove to have been lost, stubborn resistance against Rome would be a very great mistake.

Catholicism becomes this question to us because for its own part it has in these four centuries remained astonishingly true to itself; has, in fact, become more self-consistent. Roman Catholicism stands opposite us today more firm and explicit, but also more subtle and attractive, than it was in the sixteenth century. It has become Jesuit; and in this aspect has told us much more clearly what it desires and what it rejects, in opposition to the Reformation. Also it has revived Thomism and is therefore in a position to state its opposition more surely and incontrovertibly. The Catholic Church now speaks more boldly and speaks better. It asks us more urgently and at the same time more intelligently what we really find in it to condemn.

Let us try to be clear on our differences by considering a few main points:

1. Why were the Reformers not satisfied, and why can we not be satisfied with the insight that God is Lord in the house, as we see that insight alive and effective in the Catholic Church? Why in spite of every assurance are we continually in doubt whether there is a real recognition that God is the subject of the Church, that the means of grace are in *his* hands, that the authority is *his*? The Reformers answered and we must answer with them: because we are not able to see that those entitities which are there viewed and honoured as God's revelation and self-mediation have really the character of his Lordship—even though no word appears more often in the Roman Mass than the word *Dominus*, Lord—and are not merely a means of domineering over men.

The Reformation restored the Church as the Church of the Word. Word is the revelation and self-mediation of another person, a person who meets us. And if this person is the person of God, his Word is the expression of his authority; not of his domineering over us, but of his Lordship over us. God encounters me in his Word, and this means that he directs me through his commands and through his promise; that I am to believe him and obey him. These categories differ fundamentally from other categories. By them is declared and established—so far as is possible by the categories of human thinking—the immutable subjectivity of God, the freedom of God above all instruments, the uniqueness of God's authority. To declare and establish this truth is the business of Protestantism. We cannot see that this is really done in the Catholic teaching.

The characteristic concept which modern Catholic usage employs where we speak of the Word of God is the *supernatural*.[1] The goal set before men is not to hear the Word of God in faith and obedience, but to become partakers in the supernatural, in the divine nature. Nature! The secret of Christ is there described as an 'inflowing stream of life';[2] his Church is a living organism.[3] 'Affirmation of the whole, full life of men, of the totality of all the relationships and roots of man's life' is the distinguishing characteristic of the Catholic idea of revelation.[4] 'Vitality' is the great advantage of the living Catholic tradition over the 'dead (!) word' of the Bible.[5] The Catholic way to Jesus is 'immediate' in contrast to our Protestant Biblicism.[6] Grace is a 'life force' which irradiates man with a new Eros.[7] God himself is the 'primal creative force of all our being', the 'original ground in which the kernel of our being is ontologically rooted' and from which grace 'the new fountain of life' springs up.[8] Therefore finally, 'limitless freedom of religious self-expression' is the rule and law of the religious-ethical life of the Catholic.[9]

Where are we?[10] Apparently in a place very different from the one where we listened to Thomas Aquinas's 'By hearing alone is faith sure' (*auditu solo tuto creditur*); very far removed from the beautiful 'By the

---

[1] Adam, pp. 221 f.; Eng., p. 177 f.   [2] Adam, pp. 73, 76; Eng., pp. 55, 58.
[3] Adam, pp. 11, 25, 76; Eng., pp. 3, 15, 58.   [4] Adam, p. 19; Eng., p. 10.
[5] Adam, pp. 185, 189; Eng., pp. 148, 151.   [6] Adam, p. 59; Eng., p. 49.
[7] Adam, p. 224; cf. p. 20; Eng., pp. 179 f. and 10.
[8] Adam, p. 225; Eng., p. 181.   [9] Adam, pp. 186 f.; Eng., p. 149.
[10] Adam asserts (p. 197; Eng. 158) that since the days of St Cyprian, Catholic theology has claimed its good right to carry 'the gold of Egypt' to the Holy Land. Even Irenaeus, we might add, rejoiced in this scriptural precedent: *quaecunque illi cum labore comparant, his nos, in fide quum simus, sine labore utimur.* ('whatever they have with great labour prepared, we although we are within the faith, use without labour') *Against all Heresies*, IV, 30.1. But what was it that Israel made in the desert, presumably from this Egyptian gold and certainly according to the Egyptian pattern?

words of the Gospel let our sins be destroyed' (*per evangelica dicta deleantur nostra delicta*) which the priest must say in the Mass when he kisses the Gospels directly before the Creed. Certainly a place very different from that where the concept of the Word rules. Where the concepts of Life, Eros, Being, Nature (even Super-Nature, divine nature!) rule, there the neuter rules. How can one speak there of faith and obedience? Or how can there be a real encounter between a man and that great, allegedly divine something? Or how can there be talk of authority? Or talk in earnest about God?

However, it is not our purpose to consider here the validity of our questions to Catholicism, but of Catholicism's questions to us. How do we ourselves stand where those neuter categories rule? What is the situation among ourselves? Is that not the position of Schleiermacher, of Troeltsch, of Johannes Müller? And of Rittelmeyer? Is not the supernatural or life precisely what an ever-growing opposition in Protestantism has wanted to put in place of the 'dead word'? What it has to a great extent already substituted? Is not an understanding between that group and Catholicism necessarily an easy matter? 'The Word! the Word! Listen, thou lying spirit, the Word does it,' [1] Luther once shouted to a man who knew very well how to speak passionately in the language of that day about the 'streaming life'. Do we still understand such anger? Or has it become meaningless to us because we ourselves have long been interpreting the *Word* as something similar to 'streaming life'? Are we still Protestants? Or is it merely the law of historical inertia and a superficial after-effect which prevent us from getting up and going where the cult of the supernatural and of life, of the original source with its upsurging springs of life, has its dwelling, where in contast to our meagre, weak and shoddy counterfeit it has its classical abode?

2. Since the Word of God creates the relation between him and us, since God meets us in the Word as Lord and is as Lord truly God, we know ourselves, according to Reformation doctrine, as sinners before God. The *Word* of God means the judgement of God. If God is Lord, man is his servant; and in actual fact, in the concrete (the two are identical) his delinquent, untrue, disobedient, rebellious servant—rebellious in the very centre of his being.

The Word of God tells him, as the upsurging spring of life would certainly not tell him, that he remains guilty before his Lord—not only in this or that, but for his whole self, wickedly and inexcusably guilty. The Word never tells man anything different from that about himself. The

[1] Luther, *EA*, 1st ed., 29, p. 294.

Reformation is the restoration of the Church as the Church of sinners. Man even in the Church, especially indeed man under grace, stands before God as a sinner not only at the beginning, but at the beginning and the end, not only from fall to fall, but intrinsically. God loves him as a sinner, and as a sinner he is to trust and obey God. This is the insight which we find to be partly obscured in strange fashion and partly directly denied in the Catholic Church. Just here, in their understanding of the pervasive effects of man's fall, Thomas Aquinas and Calvin, who perhaps may be cited as the greatest theologians of the two churches, are absolutely irreconcilable.

Such a judgement does not ignore the incessant references to sin in the Catholic Church. The *Miserere nobis* (have mercy upon us) resounds with it—would that it resounded as regularly in the Protestant sermon! Nor do we forget the shattering peal of the Roman liturgy (to mention only two examples) in the lament for the Saviour (the Reproaches) of Good Friday or the well-known *Dies irae, dies illa* (Day of wrath that dreadful day) in the sequence of All Souls' Day and the Mass for the Dead. We honour the grim consistency with which man is led into the depths of his desperation before God, and the *mea culpa, mea maxima culpa* (by my fault, my most grievous fault) which is never omitted even in the Papal Mass.

But we fail to find evidence that all this is seriously meant. For, according to the doctrine of Trent, the fall of man from God does not affect the centre of his nature, his real being, but produces only a weakening and warping of his free, originally good will. And the Church meets him at once with the offer to take even this burden completely away in baptism, and is ready, after any recurring relapses, to make him sinless again through the sacramental restoration of the baptismal grace. We marvel at the even balance of the Catholic. It is merely shaken a bit by all that he hears about his sinfulness, but it cannot be upset, because of the relativism with which all is said; and it is immediately restored because he is told simultaneously that compensation for the evil which has intruded is always and completely within his power if only he genuinely desires it. We marvel and we ask how the Word of God can have validity and force unless such balance is really and completely destroyed.

But we are not now concerned with what we find astonishing in Catholicism. We must ask the question of ourselves: Are we really much *astonished* by all this? Certainly Pietism, which is in this connexion the most noticeable aspect of the new, second Protestantism has developed a great, often a shattering sense of sin. But is it essentially so different from the Catholic sense of sin, which itself ought not to be under-estimated? Does Pietism really attain to the knowledge that fallen man exists as a rebel, and therefore cannot possibly achieve the position of finding himself judged as something other than a rebel on the basis of an intervening conversion? He cannot be in a position to move from Romans 7 to Romans 8, as a man moves from one house to another—as he likes to phrase it. Has Pietism attained to the realization of that actual and final destruction of balance to which the only answer can be forgiveness of sin and faith? Is the Pietistic insistence on the necessity of grace more significant than the corresponding insistence which Catholicism also does not fail to reiterate emphatically? Is it any more important in relation to the whole picture which displays throughout man's attempt to be done with sin?

We should prefer not to discuss the teaching of Schleiermacher and Ritschl on sin. But what other leadership of the new Protestantism, except the one Kohlbrügge, can be cited as unquestioned and reliable? Where has there not been a hankering for the fleshpots of Egypt? Where has there been preserved the insight that there is no other grace except the free pardon of criminals, grace in judgement? Is it not shameful that we needed to have this truth retold to us by the Russian Dostoyevski? If we have refused to hear it from our Reformers who really understood it better than Dostoyevski, are we then still Protestants? If the homesick yearning for synthesis, for balance, for harmony, which found its theological fulfilment in the system of Schleiermacher, and its philosophical fulfilment in the system of Hegel, is to be the yearning of the Protestant Church of today, why does Protestantism not return to the Church which, as we have just heard, awaits us with open arms? We should not be given too heavy a penance to perform. 'We cannot' (*Non possumus*). The real question is can we *not*?

3. The Word of God which creates the relationship between God and us is in content essentially the Word of grace. It is the Word of grace, so the Reformers taught, not although but *because*, precisely because, the Word judges us and sets us in our place as sinners. This place is the place of reconciliation. Jesus accepts the sinners. He calls them his and so he tells us that we belong legitimately, justly to him. This is our justification. He claims us, our faith and obedience. This is our sanctification. Both justification and sanctification are without contribution from us, without a preceding or subsequent 'merit', as the catchword of the Middle Ages called it. We always find ourselves

known as sinners from head to toe. For us, as sinners, divine reconciliation is valid. And through this divine reconciliation we live as children of God by faith and not by sight; 'and it doth not yet appear what we shall be'.

This is the content of what occurs when God speaks his Word to us and we hear it. This is the content of our faith, of our love and our hope. There is no other Christian content than the mercy of God. The Reformation was the restoration of the Church as the Church of God's mercy. The third essential which we miss in the Roman Church is therefore the insight that precisely in the Church we live from the mercy of God; and not at all, not in any way whatever, from any other source.

We are not deaf to the words spoken daily in the Roman Mass [1] that God is 'not the reckoner of merit but the bestower of favour'. Nor are we deaf to the assurance that the forgiveness of men is 'the act of God alone' [2] and that all human deserving, all human preparation for it, is itself based on the prevenient grace of God. But again the earnestness of this assertion in the mouth of the Catholic Church is not convincing.

We hear the words of the question: 'Whereupon then can we hope, or wherein may I trust save only in the great mercy of God and the hope of heavenly grace?' [3] Yes, the Catholic Church also can ask the question.

[1] In the prayer, *Nobis quoque peccatoribus* (also to us sinners), according to the version in Schott, p. 483: *non aestimator meriti sed veniae largitor.*

[2] Adam, p. 222; Eng., p. 178.

[3] In quo igitur sperare possumus aut in quo confidere debeo nisi in sola misericordia Dei et in sola spe gratiae coelestis ? (*Imitation of Christ*, II, 9, 6). Compare III, 46, 5: *melior est enim mihi tua copiosa misericordia ad consecutionem indulgentiae, quam mea opinata justitia pro defensione latentis conscientiae. Etsi nihil mihi conscius sum, tamen in hoc justificare me non possum, quia remota misericordia tua non justificabitur in conspectu tuo omnis vivens.* (For better unto me is thine abundant pity for the attainment of thy pardon, than the righteousness which I believe myself to have, for defence against my conscience which lieth in wait against me. Although I know nothing against myself, yet am I not hereby justified, because if thy mercy were removed away, in thy sight should no man living be justified.—Benham's translation.) And also Council of Trent, Session VI, the final words on the doctrine of justification (chap. 16 end): *Absit tamen, ut christianus homo in se ipso vel confidat vel glorietur et non in Domino, cuius tanta est ergo omnes homines bonitas, ut eorum velit esse merita quae sunt ipsius dona. Et quia in multis offendimus omnes, unusquisque sicut misericordiam et bonitatem, ita severitatem et judicium ante oculos habere debet, neque se ipsum aliquis, etiam nihil sibi conscius fuerit, judicare, quoniam omnis hominum vita non humano judicio examinanda et judicanda est sed Dei.* (Far be it from any Christian man that he trust or glory in himself and not in the Lord, whose goodness is so great towards all men that he wishes those things which are his gifts to be accounted merits. And because we all offend in many things, each one ought to keep before his eyes severity and judgement as well as mercy and kindness, nor ought anyone to judge himself, even if he knows nothing against himself, since the whole life of men must be examined and judged by the judgement not of men but of God.)

But it can only ask the question *also*, and the character of the Church is not determined by such occasional asking, but by the fact that constantly in the rule and tenor of teaching and practice a wholly different question is asked. If the 'only by mercy, only by hope' (*sola misericordia, sola spe*) is valid, why then should there be talk of merit and preparation? If the latter are valid, how can the *only* be seriously meant?

What are we to think when—and significantly in connexion with Luke 15—we hear that 'the religiously and morally indifferent, the egoist, the man absorbed in sensuality' is emphatically excluded from the knowledge of the deity of Christ? [1] I should have thought that, in the sight of God, all of us belong with those poor creatures. I should have thought that it is as just such creatures that we are accepted by God—if grace exists.

What are we to think when, on the opposite side, Mary the mother of the Lord is glorified as the paradigm of the knowledge that we human beings are called 'to a kind of creative co-operation in the work of God, to take a redemptive initiative in the establishment of God's kingdom'? [2] In Mary 'shines out the wonderful fact that not God alone, but also the powers of the creatures—according to the limits of their creatureliness—have a causal share in the work of redemption'.[3] 'The Mother of God walks among Catholic humanity as an intercessory power; and we have clear knowledge that there is no pulse-beat of love in the heart of the Redeemer which his Mother would not feel, that she as the Mother of the Redeemer is also the Mother of all his acts of grace.' [4]

How is that to be taken? What does it really say? In plain words it affirms that prevenient grace (the Council of Trent says it explicitly) [5] puts man in the position to so apply himself to his own justification that it becomes effectual for him (*ad convertendum se ad suam ipsorum justificationem*), that humanity is 'also the subject of divine salvation',[6] partaking of 'a new kind of super-humanity', an elevation of human

---

And Canon 33: *Si quis dixerit, per hanc doctrinam catholicam de justificatione, a sancta Synodo hoc praesenti decreto expressam, aliqua ex parte gloriae Dei vel meritis Jesu Christi Domini nostri derogari, et non potius veritatem fidei nostrae, Dei denique ac Christi gloriam illustrari: A.S.* (If anyone should say that by this catholic doctrine of justification presented by this holy Synod in this decree, there is any derogation of the glory of God and the merit of Jesus Christ our Lord, and not rather that the truth of our faith and the glory of God and Christ is made plain, let him be anathema.)

[1] Adam, p. 66; Eng., p. 50.　　　　　[2] Adam, p. 138; Eng., p. 107.
[3] Adam, p. 143; Eng., p. 112.　　　　[4] Adam, p. 151; Eng., p. 119.
[5] Council of Trent, Session VI, chap. 5.　[6] Adam, p. 138; Eng., p. 108.

existence 'which in essence surpasses all creaturely powers and is
elevated to a truly new sphere of being and life in the fullness of the life
of God',[1] to the fullness of Christ (*plenitudo Christi*) operating in the
Church, which then embodied in one or another of the saints immediately 'bursts forth' 'into illuminating streams of light', into
'wonders of selflessness and love, of purity, humility, and sacrifice'; 'as
Nature is pleased sometimes in a unique perfect example to give so to
speak her best, to expend her surplus strength.'[2]

'Only mercy?' 'Only hope?' (*Sola misericordia? Sola spe?*) we ask.
But we do not ask Karl Adam; we ask Karl Heim. We ask about the
status of these things in the *Protestant* Church. Is it so very different
from what we have just heard, when the Protestant apologetic thinks it
can describe as 'susceptible' and 'ripe' for Christ a 'certain kind of men',
those for whom the quest for power, good fortune and comfort 'wholly'
(!) ceases, who 'have their soul's centre of gravity in the inner world
where Jesus is king';[3] when Protestantism thinks it knows as the
principle of evangelical morality a new 'basic attitude', an upsurging
emotion of self-surrender to God without compulsion (!), and a 'self-
forgetting labour with no thought (!) of reward and fame';[4] when
Protestantism is not ashamed to chant, under the heading 'Thanksgiving', a short litany of all saints with the names of J. S. Bach,
Zinzendorf, P. Gerhardt, Terseegen, Bodelschwingh, and Sundar
Singh [5]—we can of course be thankful that we are spared the name of
Bismarck in this context.[6]

And finally, what are we to think when Protestantism can so exactly
calculate the world's gain that the acts of mercy (Social Service) of the
Evangelical Church become 'considered economically, a most advan-
tageous business' for the State?[7] 'In America the Young Men's
Christian Association brings together the key forces of youth and
promotes their physical and intellectual training. Almost all the large
business firms make gigantic donations for this purpose because they
know very well that they themselves would not be successful with their
employees if it were not for this Christian organization and its social

[1] Adam, p. 221; Eng., p. 177.   [2] Adam, p. 27; Eng., p. 17.
[3] Heim, pp. 44 f.   [4] Heim, pp. 100 f.   [5] Heim, p. 102.
[6] In Düsseldorf, this remark raised a small tempest of indignation, as if I
had attacked the sanctuary with a 'These are thy gods, O Israel!' Therefore, it
could not be omitted here, although in my judgement, the content is quite
unimportant. I intended merely to point out the tendency of others besides
Heim to enrich the Protestant All Saints' litany; and to show how questionable
the undertaking is.
[7] Heim, pp. 120 ff.

service. For all this love asks no thanks.' [1] But obviously love does ask thanks—else it would remain modestly silent.

Catholicism may well ask us what fault we can find with it, so long as we ourselves continually repeat such sentiments. Do we really intend to cross the boundary of the Catholic doctrine of grace? Can we help seeing that if such statements really hold, Catholicism is in a position to make them more grandly?

Are we still Protestants if we are convinced that it is obviously right to replace God's Word of grace with the work and exaltation of men, either in the inner regions of the soul or in cultural and social activity? If we approve the substitution of a Protestant cult of saints and a Protestant cultivation of sainthood for the Catholic? We could get all that so much more simply and beautifully! If Christianity is to be for us the ultimate and highest art of living instead of service to God and hope, then we ought rather to seek the truly concrete and fundamental instruction for it in those famous four books of the *Imitation of Christ* or in the *Spiritual Exercises* of Ignatius. The new Protestantism in its youth in the seventeenth and eighteenth centuries sought it there with no inhibitions and found it.

If we have really become weary of the teaching of Luther and Calvin, according to which our justification and our sanctification are determined by and remain in the mercy of God; if we feel that their teaching needs to be improved upon and supplemented with a religious-ethical virtuosity, with a defence of the good life on which a man can put his hand; then the doctrine of grace of Thomas Aquinas and Trent certainly has the advantage, both in depth and clarity, over the dilettantism available to us. Anyone who knows Catholicism even a little, must know that it has a better knowledge of all the guarantees and reservations which modern Protestantism is in the habit of using to cover itself before the supreme majesty of God. It has a better knowledge also of the path to the Christian super-man; and if that ought to be the goal of our journey, Catholicism is certainly in a much better position to guide us than is the new Protestantism.

The question is not whether we continue to oppose certain crass degenerations, careless errors, and ambiguities in Catholicism. We are asked whether today even more sharply and irreconcilably than four hundred years ago we stand against the purest and finest core of this teaching; against the doctrine of justification by works, even although it has for a long time become inconceivably modest as presented by all

[1] Heim, p. 122.

serious Catholic thinkers. We are asked whether in the face of their irritating 'as well as . . . so also' we know how to draw the line definitely. Or is it true of us that, if only we correctly understood the Catholic teaching, we should find there nothing objectionable because for a long time we ourselves have not meant anything fundamentally different from what is meant there?

By their doctrine of the grace of God, free and remaining free, the Reformers thought to defend before all the religions of the world the right of the Christian Church as the right of the first-born. It was with a heavy heart, not light-heartedly, that under such a necessity they gave up the outer unity with the Church of the Pope. If this necessity no longer exists, if the 'mess of pottage', the value and well-being of pious and moral men, has become dearer to us than that right of the first-born, now would be the time to consider very seriously whether it would not be well to re-establish external unity at the price of abandoning those small, superficial differences which are of little real value to us and which might keep us separate from Rome.

*   *   *

I have finished. I have given no answer. I have only shown that we are being questioned. We agreed to let ourselves be questioned. Who here was ready to answer? The answer will be the future history of the Protestant Church. On reliable authority, the 'Century of the Church' is now dawning. True; but it remains to be seen which church! A young Catholic theologian, a lecturer at the University of Münster, recently declared somewhat rashly that he would give Protestantism another fifty years' existence. He could be wrong. 'The confusion of men and the Providence of God' will still act in the future. But the end of Protestantism is absolutely certain if it fails ultimately to give the right answers to both the questions directed to it by Roman Catholicism.

XII

CHURCH AND CULTURE

Lecture delivered at the Congress of the Continental Association for
Home Missions, at Amsterdam, 1st June 1926.

I

*The Church is the community instituted by God himself, the community
of faith and obedience living from the Word of God, the community of the
faith and obedience of sinful men.*

LET me begin by pointing out that the definition of the Church given
as my first thesis is intended as a theological definition, a repetition of
the definition which the Church gives of itself. The theological components of this definition are three: the Church is called (*1*) a community
instituted by God himself, (*2*) a community of faith and obedience, (*3*)
a community of the faith and obedience which live from God's Word.

The problem of the Church has a historical-sociological aspect as
well as a theological. If we wished to define the Church in that aspect,
we should have to omit mention of God and his Word, of faith and
obedience. We should then have to speak of 'that sociological group
which is concerned with religion',[1] or more specifically of a community
or a number of communities which share more or less the same religio-
ethical convictions; or (although this shows a slight tinge of metaphysics) of the total effect of the organically existing and spiritually
active force of the historical integration of life which proceeds from
Jesus.[2] But such definitions, even when advocated with the greatest
religious fervour, are unsatisfactory because they include only half and
that not the essential half of the Church. On the specific historical and
social level of observation and judgement, they are certainly necessary,
permissible and correct; and they are also informative theologically.

[1] So Paul Tillich, *Kirche und Kultur*, 1924, p. 3 (trs. in *The Interpretation of
History*, 1936).
[2] Cf. Troeltsch, 'Kirche' III, dogmatisch in *R.G.G.*, first edition.

I have tried to include the truth which is theologically valid in them by the addition which I made to the third point: the faith and obedience living from God's Word in this community instituted by God are (4) the faith and obedience of *sinful men*. Those words state fully the theological obverse of the external aspect of the Church viewed historically; they express the essential of what can be said theologically about 'religion', about religio-ethical 'convictions', about the historical effect of spiritual power and integration of life. We shall come back to the significance of this theological obverse of the historical-sociological external aspect of the Church under thesis 7. Because and so far as it concerns only the *external aspect*, we shall not now discuss it. In itself it is subordinate and secondary; and it is to be explained from the theological inner aspect, and not conversely.

This relation holds not only because by chance (but can it happen by chance and not rather by determining necessity?) we are here as Christians, united and claimed as members of the Church. It is true, quite apart from this circumstance, because the Church, which is obviously the expert on the subject, marked out this path in explaining itself; and therefore even if we were non-Christians we should have to take this road methodologically.

The inner essential of what the Church has to say of itself lies in the concepts: 'God's Word', 'faith and obedience', 'sinful men', 'community instituted by God'. The Church itself means to say that in distinction to all concepts acquired from historical-sociological observation, these concepts, separately and together, relate to a decisive event occurring between God and man, both protagonists understood in their qualitative uniqueness and difference, but both understood as *person*. Apart from the actuality of this event, these concepts would be empty. They can be misunderstood only when they are taken as designations of objects and possible interrelations of objects; when they are not understood of God and man, of the crisis which occurs at their encounter.

'God's Word' is his, the truth of the unknown, inscrutable, holy God, graciously revealed to us so far as God speaks it to us and by his speaking grants us hearing, so creating communion between himself and us, between us and himself. We do not possess knowledge of the Word of God. We do not have the Word except when God speaks it to us; the decisive event occurs in the *act* of his speaking. Or we can put it: Jesus Christ, fulfilling his office, as prophet witnessing to us, as priest interceding for us, as king ruling over us, always as person—he is the Logos, the Word of God.

Faith and obedience are bound to this Word of God, are born from it and live from it. I judge it essential to name faith and obedience together, neither one without the other. Faith perceives, hears, has the Word of God—faith only. But only an obedient faith, only the faith which acts upon the hearing, faith in the act of decision which abandons all considering and weighing, all combining of yes and no, an act in which faith is so fully conditioned by God's speaking that it cannot for an instant cease the agonized cry 'Dear Lord, help my unbelief!'

Now (and this is the essential in the third concept), the believing and obeying men are sinful men, not only before but also while they believe and obey—although only then do they know what they are. 'Believe and obey' means that a man sets his whole activity under the light of truth, he no longer tries to defend himself but admits and recognizes that we are not fit for God, that we have compromised ourselves before him and continue to compromise ourselves daily, but that *such as we are* we now are made worthy to be called his children. When the divine Word speaks to us, when the decision of faith and obedience occurs, then occurs also the verdict upon us that we must surrender ourselves naked to the mercy of God.

And so the Church is 'the community instituted by God' and is composed of such sinful men, of believing and obedient sinners whose faith and obedience live from the Word of God. Under *institution* or founding, we understand the divine regulation and organization, not for its own sake but, because of man's fall, necessary for the sake of the reconciliation which overcomes that fall, by which within the relativity of the historical life of man a corresponding human institution and organization is set. In this sense, the Church was instituted from eternity by the decree of the divine reconciliation, it was made actually existent in time by the incarnation of the Word, and established as a human organization and institution by the outpouring of the Holy Spirit at Pentecost.

This organization and institution consists in the summoning of sinners to faith and obedience in the building of this community which is visible in its human activity and invisible in its divine truth, in its life from the Word. Through it—certainly not through history in general but through the Church—God acts for the reconciliation of fallen men. Through it, God allows his glory to be proclaimed in the valley of death; God *acts*. Once again I would emphasize this moment of action, this event. The Church exists through the Holy Spirit and not otherwise. But the Holy Spirit is divine person. His instituting is decisive, divine act. And the institution's truth stands or falls with the continuous renewal and preservation of the foundation. How else would it continue to be instituted in the outpouring of the Holy Spirit?

Therefore the inclusion of every individual in the Church and his preservation therein is also decisive act. 'Preserve us Lord with thy Word!' This prayer is no rhetorical flourish. Man is not in the Church except as, on the basis of his baptism, he today confesses in the Holy Spirit (*in Spirito Sancto*) 'I believe the Church' (*Credo ecclesiam*). Not 'the Church is believed' (*creditur ecclesia*), but 'I believe the Church' (*credo ecclesiam*). *I* believe—dear Lord, help my unbelief!—as one among the number of the churched (ἐκκληθέντες) who have accepted the summons to the Church (ἐκκλησία) and now report themselves in their places.

II

Culture is the task set through the Word of God for achieving the destined condition of man in unity of soul and body.

My second thesis is an attempt to define theologically the concept of culture. Our first step necessarily entailed the second. Since we decided to give primacy methodologically to the theological inner aspect of the Church, and since the small but very significant word *and* in our title assumes a relationship between Church and culture, we are required to consider culture also in its theological inner aspect.

Culture can also be defined untheologically. For example (in approximation to the concept '*civilization*' which in French represents the idea of culture), as 'the sum of the aims proceeding from human activity and in turn stimulating human activity';[1] or, more in accordance with idealism, more in the sense of the German word *Kultur*, as 'the idea of the final goal and the totality of norms by which human activity should be guided'. If such formulations were to be accepted as determinative and all-inclusive, then the Church could speak only negatively and polemically on the significance of culture. The two entities would not only exist on different levels, but on mutually exclusive levels, as truth and error. Then the only reasonable possibility would be to speak first of the Church, and then independently of the so-called culture. And furthermore it would be necessary, from the presuppositions of

[1] S.Eck, 'Kulturwissenschaft und Religion' in *R.G.G.*, first edition.

the Church, to view this so-called culture with horror, as an impossible fantasy and an idol.

For when the Church states what the Church itself is, it also declares that ultimately neither aims nor values, nor goods, neither the idea of a goal, nor the concept of norms, determine or ought to determine human action. The Church sets the Word of God at the beginning and the end, above all empirical or transcendental principles, as the sole, supreme event which gives law. The Church accordingly knows nothing of human activity in general or in the abstract; but only the activity of a concrete man—who is first sinful and secondly believing and obedient, who lives from the Word of God. Here also, therefore, the Church cannot permit itself to be limited to the external aspect as such. Here also it remains on its own ground and seeks for the inner aspect. Instead of allowing itself to be forced into involvement with an alien concept with which it would have to come to terms, the Church is determined always itself to speak the first, the proper, the essential word to culture. Accordingly we now make the attempt to survey the inner aspect of culture.

The speaking and hearing of God's Word would not be the kind of act which we described under the first thesis if we could even for an instant forget that while we are in the Church we are also in the world and in time; and that we as Christians are neither animals nor angels but men. To say that we believe and obey the Word does not in the least imply that we are setting ourselves above our humanity. He who says 'I believe the Church' (credo ecclesiam) is a sinner, and a sinner is a man who knows himself and is convinced that he cannot get out of his own skin.

Because—and only because—I believe, I see the problem of my humanity. As unbelieving, as unjudged, as a sinner undisturbed in the dream of my likeness to God, I could deceive myself about myself. But the Word of God fixes the limit for man as such and thereby defines him. That is, the Word places man over against God who (1) as Creator, (2) as Holy and Merciful, (3) as in himself the Eternal, is absolutely and wholly not man nor like man. The Word confronts man with the problem of his existence. And that problem is precisely the problem of culture. Culture means humanity. But men exist as soul *and* body, spirit *and* nature, subject *and* object, inwardly *and* outwardly, *judged* on the synthesis of both these elements. But also it is just this synthesis which man *lacks*. With the 'I believe the Church' (credo ecclesiam), he has ceased to dream; he is driven in terror out of both pure externality and withdrawn inwardness. He can no longer endure life in the swampy region of a purely natural existence, but neither can he endure it above in the clouds of a purely spiritual existence. Least of all can he continue in the illusion that he is already living on the other side of the contradiction, as a spiritual nature, as a corporeal soul, as a man who lives in and for himself.

Exactly this dualism, the annihilating incongruity, the deadly conflict of his existence, which is manifest in the mortality of the body in contrast to the (not very consoling) immortality of the soul, is the punishment of his sinfulness. In his sinfulness, he is known by God, in it he cannot endure before God. It is the mirror of his enmity against his Lord. This mirror I hold before myself when I confess 'I believe the Church' (*credo ecclesiam*). Because man knows God, he knows his own destined character, he knows what it would mean to find himself, he knows that he can find himself only in wholeness. He would not seek himself, if he were not already found by God. As one found by God's Word, he knows that spirit must mould nature, that nature must fulfil and actualize spirit. The subject must become object, and the object become subject. The inward must appear in the outward, the outward find its true nature in the inward.

But he also knows—in the act of encounter with God, it is really all he knows—that he certainly does not at any point whatever live in wholeness. When, set before God, he comes to himself, he faces the rift which goes through his whole existence; and he is confronted with the problem of synthesis. Whatever deserves the name culture has in some fashion originated from this rift and this problem. Culture implies lack and consciousness of lack. It means seeking through men and failing to find the unity of God.

Inexorably the mirror of our dual existence which the Word of God holds before us shows us both the urgency and the frightfulness of the problem of culture. Its urgency makes problem and task unavoidable. Christian preaching in the old days and the new has always legitimately been simultaneously a summons to cultural activity. Its frightfulness makes the problem and the task insoluble and unachievable. Again it is legitimate that the same Christian preaching, unless it became untrue to itself, has met every culture, however supposedly rich and mature, with ultimate, sharp scepticism. Both attitudes are grounded in the logic of God's Word, received by the sinner who hears and obeys. More significant than either attitude is the truth that the problem of culture is in all circumstances set before us through God's Word.

III

The theme 'Church and Culture' therefore specifies the question of the meaning of the cultural task for every man as a question answerable only by hearing the Word of God.

I can deal very briefly with this thesis. It needs only the combining and emphasizing of the methodological presuppositions of theses 1 and 2. When we take up the theme 'Church and Culture' we do not find ourselves sitting in empty space as superior observers and wise judges of these two entities. It is not as if we knew a third scale of measurement which we were taught by philosophy or revelation and could with it master the problem of Church and culture and unravel it. Fundamentally, it is not a world-view which provides the proper basis for treating our theme (as if it were a problem of the world or of things). The only congruous basis is in hearing the Word of God.[1]

I offer three explanatory comments:

1. There is Church and there is culture only because of the decisive event of the speaking and the hearing of the divine Word through which we are called to the Church and confronted with the problem of culture. If this event ceases to occur, if God looks away from us and his Word is silent, if it is not an actuality that we are called to the Church and confronted by the problem of culture, then all thinking and discussing on this theme, even the most far-reaching and the most profound, is froth and foam.

2. I offer an analogy to emphasize the difference between a view of the world and hearing God. It is possible to turn our eyes in different directions or shut them, but not our ears. It is the ears which are here involved. When we hear God we are not free, but are completely chained and bound in our thoughts and in our words. Chained and bound *because* we ourselves when we hear God are already within the Church. But we are also within culture. From inside both we must question and from inside both we must answer. If we retreat from this position to a cleverly chosen observation post, then our thinking and speaking become a game played with empty abstractions.

3. When we hear God, we are not in a position to determine our relation to Church and culture as if we had not been claimed by both in a very definite way; as if we were not committed to and involved in

---

[1] The largest part, by far the largest part, of what is today called theology is really 'world-view'. I am thinking, especially in relation to the content of this statement, but not for the last time, of the work of Paul Tillich cited above.

both; as if a specific way of regarding both were not inevitable for us. We have called this way theological. Our *locus* is the Church; from there we understand and we represent culture, not conversely.

God, as we know, speaks from a higher, freer place. But from that place we, within our own capability, have absolutely nothing to say. Our position is that of the servant (and he is a servant precisely because he obeys) and it is intrinsically different from the position of the Lord. God is not bound; we are. Therefore not commitment but precisely non-commitment, not partisanship but neutrality and superior disinterestedness would here be for us the sign of an unrealistic bias.

And also the remembrance that God is in heaven and we are on earth must never serve as excuse for burying in a napkin the one talent we have received. The knowledge that God alone is absolute must not keep us from making relative decisions and judgements. God makes his demands on us as earthly and erring men. 'He knoweth our frame . . .' but he makes demands on us.

IV

Seen from the point of view of creation, the kingdom of nature (regnum naturae), *culture is the promise originally given to man of what he is to become.*[1]

The Word of God is in its content a word of grace, a word of reconciliation. It is directed to the fallen Adam, to lost men. The Church of Christ is a Church of sinners; it therefore has no knowledge of the original relationships between God and man except as broken relationships, broken in the cleavage between God and man.

But the Church knows that such broken bonds can persist, not in themselves but by virtue of the new unbroken tie of reconciliation through which the former relation can be restored. First, the Church does not forget that man, lost and damned, but rescued by grace, is God's creature. And second, it does not forget that the kingdom of the Word, the kingdom of Christ, did not have its beginning with the incarnation and is not limited by it. It does not forget that the divine Logos (here I depend on the important statement of the Reformed

[1] Readers of my earlier writings will be reminded of theses 4–6 in sections 3–5 of my Tambach lecture, 'The Christian in Society' (*Das Wort Gottes und die Theologie*, pp. 50–69). I said then: 'It will always be possible to speak differently from these points of view; but I am absolutely convinced that the points of view from which I wish to speak are the essential ones and that there are no others valid beside them' (p. 39). Today, seven years later, I do, in fact, speak somewhat differently from these points of view. But I have not yet been persuaded to adopt any others.

Confession, the so-called *Extra Calvinisticum*) while he is wholly man in Jesus of Nazareth none the less fills *heaven and earth*; that the Church's own invisible truth is truth also beyond the visible reality of the Church.[1]

I repeat: no independent, actual relation between God and nature, God and history, God and human reason, can be asserted except that the Word is spoken and received in the world of sinners. And therefore in the world of nature, of history, of reason, relation to God depends on the one possibility which sinners have not destroyed. It does not depend on a presumptive right—right sinners have destroyed; it does not depend on any claim of man on God; it depends wholly on God's claim on man and the claim becomes effective essentially through the reconciliation. Man is not his own, but God's. So runs the rightful claim of the Creator which the Fall could only conceal from men and could not make invalid or ineffective.

On the contrary, the validity and effectiveness of God's claim prevails the more—this is the rule of Christ in the kingdom of nature (*regnum naturae*). The kingdom of the Logos is above the contradiction of Fall and reconciliation. It is a kingdom of which in itself we can know nothing and say nothing, but it is an indispensable presupposition of his kingdom among sinners. In the incarnation of the Word, in the reconciliation through Christ, this presupposition subsists. Natural theology (*theologia naturalis*) is included and brought into clear light in the theology of revelation (*theologia revelata*); in the reality of divine grace is included the truth of the divine creation. In this sense it is true that 'Grace does not destroy nature but completes it' (*Gratia non tollit naturam sed perficit*). The meaning of the Word of God becomes manifest as it brings into full light the buried and forgotten truth of the creation.

To this truth of creation belongs not only the claim which God originally asserted over men, but also the promise which he originally gave to men. The nature and destiny of man is determined not only by law (as we must state in the fifth thesis), and not only by his limits (as we must state in the sixth). There persists also a promise of divine friendship, essentially approving man. God's affirmation of man as his creature and his image still stands; God's affirmation of man's life in communion with himself, a life to which the desperately sought unity of existence is not denied; for which such unity is not unattainable.

[1] In the discussion in Amsterdam the attempt was made to relate this section of my lecture to the teaching of Friedrich Brunstöd. I should like to ask the harmonizers to consider whether even here, where I approach Brunstöd's theme, we are not saying, thinking, and especially intending wholly different things.

Sin has not so wholly destroyed God's image in man that God's friendship for man is now without an object, that man has ceased to be man, created and loved by God. Man has not become 'a stick or a stone' (*lapis aut truncus*); he is still a human being (*homo*), although a human sinner (*homo peccator*). As such, God speaks to him in Jesus Christ; and humanity is therefore promise. Man is capable of partaking of this promise which is renewed with the assertion of the divine claim on man in Christ. The term *culture* connotes exactly that promise to man: fulfilment, unity, wholeness within his sphere as creature, as man, exactly as God in his sphere is fullness, wholeness, Lord over nature and spirit, Creator of heaven *and* earth.

Does not this promise appear to shimmer ahead of men everywhere where they are engaged in the struggle for form and realization, with labour and confusion enough, but with unappeasable restlessness and inexhaustible productivity? This promise (this is our fourth thesis) is not denied but confirmed by the Gospel. Is the struggle an insane activity, filling the bottomless casks of the Danaids? In itself, Yes. For man has fallen and in forgetting God's rightful claim on him, he forfeits his part in the promise. In Christ, No. For, as in Christ the separation between God and man is not a final reality, so also its consequence and punishment, the separation in man himself, the rift which splits his whole being, is not final. The struggle to overcome this division, the work of culture, *can* therefore be a reflection from the light of the eternal Logos who became flesh, and yet was, is and is to be also king in the whole domain of nature. Culture *can* be a witness to the promise which was given man in the beginning. 'It *can*', I say. In Christ, it *is*. Reconciliation in Christ is the restoration of the lost promise. It renews the status of the creation with its great 'Yes' to man, with its reasonableness of reason. It gives man again insight into the meaning of his activity. It gives him the courage to understand even the broken relation in which he stands and acts towards God as still a relation and to take it seriously. Because this *giving* actually occurs, because God effects this for man in Christ, the problem and the task with which man is confronted is for him the promise of joy. But the promise and joy are not a generality, and do not exist apart from this Divine act nor apart from man's faith and obedience. They exist not in themselves, not in addition to the forgiveness of sin, but *through* and *in* that forgiveness.

That is the first line which connects culture with the Church. The Church cannot detach itself as unconcerned with the problem and the task which confronts men as men. In practice the Church can abandon it to society or to 'experts'; but not in principle. The Church can also agree in practice to a separation of areas, for example between itself and the State, but only in practice, never in principle. The Church knows man only as a sinner: but the Church always hopes for man, sees him and his activity in the relation made possible in Christ, in the relation to the Father, Creator of heaven and earth. The Church knows the promise of which man can in Christ have his part.

All depends on the Word, on faith and obedience, on the act between God and men. In proportion as the Church hears the Word, believes and obeys, the problem and the task of culture become clear. The work of culture takes its place among the earthly signs by which the Church must make God's goodness, his friendship for men, visible to itself and to the world.

There can be no thought of a general sanctifying of cultural achievement, such as Schleiermacher accomplished with his idealism, but there is even less place for a basic blindness to the possibility that culture may be revelatory, that it can be filled with the promise. The Church will need to consider carefully whether it knows what it is doing when in a concrete case it affirms the presence of the promise. But it would be astounding if no cases for such recognition were to be found by the Church; and the Church would certainly be badly off if it refused to recognize any. The Church will not see the coming of the kingdom of God in any human cultural achievement, but it will be alert for the signs which, perhaps in many cultural achievements, announce that the kingdom approaches.

V

From the point of view of reconciliation, the kingdom of grace (regnum gratiae), *culture is the law in reference to which the sinner, sanctified by God, has to practise his faith and obedience.*

The Word of God to men is, according to its content, the word of the reconciliation of sinners to God. (I might say, to make the distinction clear, that according to its *meaning*, as we have just seen, it is the word of the original creation, manifest again in the reconciliation; and according to its *form*, as we shall see later, it is the word of redemption, eschatology.) We must now speak of the meaning of culture from the point of view of reconciliation.

The kingdom of Christ stands as the kingdom of grace 'in the midst of enemies' (*in medio inimicorum*). Therefore we are here wholly and entirely concerned with man as sinner (*homo peccator*); concerned with believing and obeying sinners certainly, but concerned with what faith and obedience mean to sinners. Clearly, if man lives from the Word of God and if the Word of God as the word of reconciliation is Jesus Christ himself, crucified and risen, it necessarily follows that he, the sinner, has died with Christ and also he, the sinner, has risen and lives with Christ. This communion with the Reconciler is the basis and the cogency of his calling, confirmed by the sacrament of baptism; of his rebirth and conversion through the Holy Spirit. He, the sinner, has died with Christ; this means that he who is and remains a sinner (not only in himself but in his communion with Christ) stands before God in purity and as a child. That is the miracle of grace as *justification*. He, the sinner, has risen and lives with Christ; this means that he who is and remains a sinner (not only in himself but in his communion with Christ) again does God's will in a new life. That is the miracle of the same grace as *sanctification*. As obedience is needed for faith in justification, so also faith is needed for obedience in sanctification. We are now to consider this latter.

There is no visible sanctification of men; no sanctification which can be seen, proved or measured; none which does not have to be *believed*. Sanctification is the act of divine mercy. It is not and it will not be a possession and ornament of men. The sanctified are also and remain also sinners. In Christ they do the will of God, not otherwise. Their life, their new life, is hidden with him in God. If it were not so, the sanctification would not be grace and therefore would not be true sanctification. Obedience in sanctification exists wholly and entirely in faith not in sight. There is no admixture of deification, not even as a 'tiny seed' or the like. There is no sanctification which is not wholly shrouded in the unsanctified.

But there is an obedience in the sanctification, the obedience of a sinner. All of it is spotted and distorted, like everything which is done by sinners; but in Christ, in the power of his resurrection, it is recognized and accepted as obedience. This obedience we who are called in Christ must practise. Faith is not in opposition to it; faith requires it. In faith, man *is* obedient. In faith, we *do* God's will, we *live* the new life—we, the unrighteous, the hypocrites, enemies of God as we are. But we do it, not as a promising beginning of our own righteousness, but as the proclamation of the righteousness of God in the valley of death. It is only practice, an exercise—what can our obeying be except an exercise in obedience? But it is an exercise which is *done*. It is only a gesture, but it is a necessary gesture which must not be omitted. It is only an offering, and the offering is holy only because the altar is holy; but it is an offering which is required and is joyfully brought, for the altar *is* holy.

Therefore, when the question is raised of the norm of this earthly, sinful obedience, which in Christ is nevertheless holy obedience, the truth holds that the Word of reconciliation does not abolish, but establishes the law. What must be done in the kingdom of grace (*regnum gratiae*) in the midst of its enemies (*in media inimicorum*), what lost sinners must *do* in their obedience, in their sanctification, is not left to their own volition—how could it then be obedience?—but is predetermined by God himself. Where and how? Obviously in the task set before man through the Word which speaks to him, and nowhere else.

That which, viewed from the standpoint of the creation, is the promise given to man, is, when viewed from the standpoint of reconciliation, the law under which he stands. What God demands from men is called humanity. The command of positive revelation coincides here in content with the command of the law of nature. That command is merely taken and lifted out of the sphere of wishing, of choice, and is made the actual, the divine command. The command revives the promise which from the creation lies dormant in the law of nature; and the law of nature is given, just because of the promise, necessity. The divine command requires that the spirit be not idle, that nature be not left to itself. It demands performance and actualization. It establishes an above and a below, a better and a worse, even for action which as a whole has lapsed into sin. The standard for such distinctions is always unity, the destined character of man, that man find himself as a whole. The content of the law is always simply human culture. Therefore sanctification, election for God, doing the will of God, is always in content being human. Men are to become men, not more than men; but also not less.

The law does *not* say that this goal is attainable, that a kingdom of God as a kingdom of peace, justice and truth is to be achieved by men, or that there is to be true humanity on the earth. The law says only that the exercise in obedience *has to do with* all these things. To say that men who obey will never know themselves to be anything but sinners, that they can only have faith that they are sanctified, is to say that the goal is actually unattainable, that we do *not* have to build the kingdom of God, that there is no true humanity in the world. True humanity in Christ, Yes! But not in the world. Obedience will not ask whether the goal set for it is attainable or not—it would not be obedience if it asked that.

This is the second line which connects the Church with culture. Through it the Church affirms the law which is given men in the Word. The Church cannot cease to represent the law, with society, without society, against society; in season and out of season. The Church knows sooner than society and better what is at stake in the human activity in which it sees society engaged, sometimes stupefied, sometimes cautious, sometimes violent. The Church understands sooner and better, because the Church knows *nothing* of any possibility of deification, because it proclaims, not a goal which is attainable, but the goal which is the real goal; because it is content to demand obedience, but only obedience in faith, an obedience which runs wisely and boldly inside the limits set for man. Woe to the Church if it does *not* proclaim this obedience! Such a Church would betray together law, gospel, culture—and itself!

VI

From the point of view of redemption, the kingdom of glory (regnum gloriae), *culture is the limit set for men, on the other side of which God himself, in fulfilment of his promise, makes all things new.*

The Word of God is the word of redemption. That is our third standpoint. Not ultimately, but continuously, the Word has eschatological form. That means that at all points it is related to what for men is never the given, never the possible, never the attainable. At every point it speaks of what is true only and exclusively in God and through God, of what comes from God, of what is given form and made actual by God. At every point it speaks 'in the light of eternity' (*sub specie aeternitatis*), which means it speaks with reference only to a fulfilment in God himself and in his truth. At every point it requires—and this requirement characterizes the decision which accompanies the speaking and accepting of the Word—'a lifting up of heart' (*sursum corda!*), a seeking of that which is above. Above not only in degree but in principle, the kingdom of glory (*regnum gloriae*), the final and eternal self-revelation of the glory of God in a *newly* created world.

Redemption is more than creation, more also even than (as Schleiermacher thought) the completion and crown of creation. God's creation needs no completion. It was and is complete. But we can lose that completeness of creation, and we *have* lost it. It must be restored to us inalienably, by forgiveness and renewal. Redemption means the resurrection of the dead to eternal life, the radical change of all the predicates of being, the obliteration of every possibility and dimension which is not

God's, to make way for the unconditioned and unconditionally manifested power of God himself, of God alone and all in all. Redemption is creation, but without the possibility of sin and death. Thus far, it is more than creation.

Redemption is also more than reconciliation. Reconciliation as the restoration of the communion of sinful men with God in Christ is certainly complete. Unquestionably, grace *suffices*. Grace has already in itself redemption, the life eternal. Whoever is in Christ, *is* a new creature: the old has gone; behold, it *is* become new! God *is* already, now and here, all in all to the sinner. But all in *faith*. In faith, the full consummation of our communion with Christ exists here and now. Yet there is no faith which is not also unfaith.

Trusting and staking our life upon the invisible *is* here and now full certainty, whether it be called assurance of Christian truth or assurance of salvation. But its basis and anchor remain in God, not in us. What is in us is always uncertainty. The truest human word is only a reflection of the truth, a witness to the truth, a pointing towards the truth. The most obedient doing of the will of God is only an exercise, a gesture and an offering. Here and now our portion is the sacramental presence of God, not his immediate presence—so we might state it.

But redemption is reconciliation without qualification, without the 'not yet' which we must here and now combine with the 'in Christ', to indicate faith and sacrament. Thus far, redemption is more than reconciliation. For redemption in its true, strict sense we *wait*. And Redeemer in this true, strict sense is Jesus Christ in his second coming —not before and not otherwise. To desire to receive redemption prematurely, to possess it, to feel it, to give it form and actuality in our own experience, leads not merely to unprofitable illusions but to disobedience and rebellion. The form under which God's Word comes to us now is inevitably the eschatological form, by which its meaning and content are set under the restrictive anticipation of the divine still-awaited fulfilment. '*Thy* kingdom come!' and 'Thy kingdom *come*!'

If now redemption is, viewed positively, the actualization of the destined nature of man (which has been not forfeited but frustrated by sin) in a new creation, in a manifest consummation of the reconciliation; then clearly humanity becomes, from this third point of view, a critical concept, a concept of limit. And culture is seen not only as promise, not only as law, but as event, as *formed* reality and *real* form, which is not already here but is in process of becoming. Its abode is not with us but with God; not on this side of, but beyond, the resurrection of the dead.

It is coming, it does exist, it abides with God; so God's Word as the word of redemption tells us. *Limit* is not a merely negative concept, it is also very positive. Our limit informs us of our situation. *God* is our limit. Is there anything better we could know about our situation? God who created men and reconciled them with himself in order to draw them to him for ever, God who is faithful, is over our faithlessness.

But it is clear that this third line which connects the Church with culture must be a critical line. The Church hopes in God and his fulfilling Yea and Amen. In the building of the tower of Babel whose top is to touch heaven, the Church can have no part. The hope of the Church rests *on* God *for* men; it does not rest *on* men, not even on religious men—and not even on the belief that men *with the help of God* will finally build that tower. The Church believes in the divinity of neither spirit nor nature, and certainly not in a supposedly completed synthesis of the two. The Church simply takes death too seriously for true humanity possibly to be anything more or anything other than a hope of the resurrection of the dead. The Church stands fast by the belief that the Redeemer will first speak his 'Behold, I make all things new!'

With this eschatological anticipation, the Church confronts society. Not with an undervaluation of cultural achievement, but with the highest possibly evaluation of the goal for which it sees all cultural activity striving. Not in pessimism, but in boundless hope. Not as a spoilsport, but in the knowledge that art and science, business and politics, techniques and education are really a game—a serious game, but a game, and *game* means an imitative and ultimately ineffective activity—the significance of which lies not in its attainable goals but in what it signifies. And the game might actually be played better and more successfully, the more it was recognized as a game. *Our* earnestness could not be impaired by making clear to ourselves that the game can never be ultimately serious, and never is; that the right and the possibility of being wholly in earnest is God's alone.

The Church does not serve society if for fear of being subversive or becoming unpopular, it fails to make this qualification effective, if it fails to express in its behaviour and its teaching the comfort and warning of eternity. Society is *waiting* for exactly *this* service. And society will have respect for a church which dares to be subversive and to make itself unpopular; and *no* respect for a church which refuses such a service—and necessarily other services with it. For society knows better than it will admit to itself that without this comfort and warning cultural achievement is ultimately impossible.

VII

From all these points of view, the Church, as a community of human and sinful willing and acting, must judge and must determine the direction not only for society but before all else for itself.

As theses 4–6 aimed to survey the attitude of the Church to the problem of culture as a problem of society, thesis 7 will stress the truth that the problem of culture is also a problem of the Church itself, and as such must be evaluated on all sides. This truth is self-evident on the assumptions presented in theses 1–3; but it will not be superfluous to present it explicitly.

We come back to the statement that the Church in its visible reality is a human organization and institution, a community of the faith and obedience of sinful men. That means it is a community of human and sinful willing and acting. The untheological, external aspect of the Church must now be given its due. Christians are men who know better than all others the kind of condemnation which hangs over men in all situations, who know themselves (not other men) to be without good. Christians are men who are less inclined than any others to deny by any vain hidden reservations the deep human solidarity, the solidarity of guilt and punishment which weighs upon us all.

The idea that the Church as the communion of saints confronts society from a superior position and under different laws and conditions must be farthest from the Church's own opinion. The Church knows thoroughly its profane outer aspect. It knows very well that as seen on the plane of history and human life it is, in fact, only an association (or in other words a 'life-club') along with others. The Church understands very well about the relativity of Christianity. It knows that its behaviour, its will and deed, its thought, its speech, is not fundamentally different from that of men in general; that its special concern, 'religion' so-called, is liable to the same doubts and suspicions as is all human existence, and that its special activity is under the same exigencies as all human activity. The Church knows therefore that all its work from the very first move cannot be in any way different from cultural activity, must be a striving for form and actuality, a seeking after true humanity— certainly on a very conspicuous, very exposed sector of human society, but none the less cultural activity within the frame of human society.

No Christian community, however deeply rooted, will be able to free itself even partially from the universal sociological laws. There is no good work of the individual Christian which will not have its less good psychological exterior. No Christian theologian (alas!) with his preaching and scholarship will ever visibly walk this earth as 'Angelic Doctor' (*doctor angelicus*) free, for example, of *all* human philosophy. There is no Christian love which cannot be justly labelled as sublimated, highly refined eroticism. No Christian temporal prophecy can keep itself from measuring by the actual political and economic standards of its own age. Throughout its whole course, the Church swims along in the stream of culture.

The *Above* and *Against* is in truth the hidden foundation of the Church's existence. But this hidden foundation can only be believed; and even as believed, since faith also is a human act and conceals its origin and object, it remains a *hidden* foundation. The existence of the Church and the existence of the Christian in the Church never for one moment ceases to be a hazardous venture, which like every human venture needs support and assurance. Therefore the position which the Church must take towards its own activity is analogous to the position taken by it towards human activity in general. The Church must judge itself and determine its direction according to all the points of view which I have already mentioned.

The Church will therefore first remember—and this is its consolation as a Church of sinners—that because of the reconciliation in Christ, human willing and doing *can* be a symbol which is transparent and meaningful and which partakes of the promise originally given to man; that therefore it would be senseless, and even more, it would be godless, to let our hands drop because of our all too deep recognition of human sinfulness and so to leave the willing and doing to others, to the devil. Even the activities peculiar to the Church, such as the preaching and hearing of the Sunday sermon, or the services of a nursing sister, or something as questionable as a theological debate, *can* be blessed. Not of course because it is a Church activity, but because it also is, though sinful, still human activity; because even what occurs on this exposed border of society where 'the business is religion' can, under the shadow of all cultural achievement, be blessed in Christ, can carry within itself a spark of the seminal logos (*λόγος σπερματικός*).

Why should there not be conscious and definite Church activity, not in the corner of the Pharisees but of the publicans? Why should its relativity prevent us from accepting the Church with no arrogance but deliberately, as a human possibility, and with the same seriousness with which the artist takes his art and the scientist his science? Even the Church *can* be the symbol of what is to be. Between the 'can' and 'is' stands God's free grace; the sigh of our heart's deep need is wafted by the Spirit and 'the Spirit bloweth where he listeth'. But the Spirit is a certain not an uncertain factor.

Second, the Church will consider that with the reconciliation God's right over all which is called flesh is established, and the Church, submitting itself to God's claim, not only may but *must* act. Even of the Church it is true that faith, faith in the grace that works alone and of itself, is not against the Church but for it. Consequently (under the shadow of all cultural achievement! in the midst of all human iniquity!) the attempt to proclaim the glory of God is not to be abandoned even on the narrow and dangerous line where the Church can act as Church. Even here the spirit may not be sluggish nor the flesh be unrestrained. Even here the course may be *run* with wisdom and boldness within the *limits* set for man; without fancying that after we have done all that is commanded us, we should be anything but 'unprofitable servants'. Run also without resisting God when his glory, perhaps oftener than we think, is *better* proclaimed where 'the business' is definitely *not* 'religion'. But run also without false shame, without the affectation which prefers at any cost to be secular and unreligious rather than churchly; with no refusal to do the work of the Church in *this* place as we are commissioned to do it. If the offering is commanded and is brought in obedience for consecration, why shall it not be accepted by God?

And third, the Church will apply the comfort and warning of eternity, the remembrance of God as the limit, most of all and especially to itself. It will do this service first of all for itself (not in spite of, but because of, the seriousness of the need to remain convinced of its ultimate non-seriousness), remembering that God leaves ultimately to none other his honour and the proclaiming of his glory. The Church will not erect a religious and devout church tower beside the tower of Babel; it will prudently abstain from all experiments in deification in its own domain. But it will humbly, conscious of its distance from him, yet joyfully and confidently, hold to the Christ who stands at the door and knocks, as the Redeemer of even the misery and weakness of the Church.

The hope, '*Thy* kingdom come! Thy kingdom *come*!' is valid also for the Church. So far as the Church gives judgement against itself—if it is true that the word of judgement which must begin in the house of God is first and most of all a judgement against the Church—the Church will at the end escape it, because the judgement is the judgement of hope.

VIII

The last, the eschatological, point of view is that under which the Church of our time must begin to again learn to ask God's will and way.

My final thesis is no more than a postscript to the whole.

In the discussion of theses 5–7, I have dealt with the three points of view under which the relation between Church and culture must be considered, and I have so far as possible kept the emphasis equal. But I believe I ought to ask in conclusion how far such an equal emphasis is correct. If the statement of the actual character of all Christian knowledge with which this lecture began is accepted, we ought not to be too strict and too wise about such an equality of all moments of truth. The same truth when it is actually spoken and heard cannot be spoken and heard in the same way in all times; it cannot always, perhaps it can never, be presented in its separate moments with a textbook equality, as we have today striven to do. There is an inevitable time determination of truth, even of Christian truth, the observance of which may perhaps be called prophetic objectivity rather than methodological objectivity. And I hope you have not failed to notice a certain inequality in the equality of my presentation, a certain heavier emphasis at one moment in my exposition. Now I want to bring this special emphasis explicitly to your attention.[1]

What the Church of our time needs most of all to relearn in relation to the problem of culture is, in my judgement, what I have called the form, the *eschatological form*, of the Word of God. Not as if we already had sufficient knowledge of the great truths of creation and reconciliation —quite the contrary! But if we wish to regain a better insight into the relation between promise and law, then, if I am right, we shall have to set our lever at the question of the *limit*.

The significance of the culture-promise under the point of view of the 'realm of nature' (*regnum naturae*), the truth of the identity of the fallen man with the man originally created by God, has been recognized

---

[1] As an illustration of the terrifying inability to hear with which even well-intentioned modern churchmen like ourselves are in the habit of listening, I may cite the report of this lecture by René H. Wallace in *Theolog. Blättern*, 1926, number 7, col. 184: 'Among the German contributions [at the Amsterdam Congress], the address of Prof. D. Karl Barth, Münster, on Culture and Church [*sic*] offered an impressive presentation of the relative value of culture as faith's act of obedience; even though in conclusion, in his well-known fashion, "the limit on the other side of which God makes all things new" was emphasized. There was at least offered a background of Christian thought against which the social action of the Church could be validated as meaningful and willed by God.'

since the eighteenth century impressed it on the consciousness of the Church. For this we will be grateful, whatever the need of caution against eighteenth-century ideas. Also for the second point of view, the meaning of culture as law in the 'kingdom of grace' (*regnum gratiae*), it must be said that the modern Church on the whole, however questionable one may find its attitude on single points, has seen and dealt with the problem of faith which is dead without works.

But we suffer from the neglect, almost the loss, of the comfort and warning of eternity. (The present neglect is not the first since the eighteenth century; Pietism, Enlightenment, and Schleiermacher nurtured rather than checked it.) We no longer have the knowledge, in every way so pregnant for doctrine and life, of God as the limit, of Christ who is to come again with his 'I make all things new'.

This is not a matter of a neglect of dogmatic subtleties. It is not a matter of a harmless doctrine of last things which ought to be somewhat more assiduously emphasized in pulpit and class-room. What has been left out is the insight that all Christendom and its relation to culture depends entirely on hope; that the difference between reconciliation and redemption is a fundamental difference, and so also is that between reconciliation and creation. Upon the knowledge of the limit depends also the knowledge of the promise and the law.

In opposition to the disregard of this point, that is in opposition to 'liberal', 'positive' cultural Protestantism, it is necessary to take one's stand on the other side and seek to rediscover this third point of view. One-sided? No—not one-sided, not ceasing to see also the first and second viewpoints without which the third cannot be seen. But today to seek and to see the *third*, and not least for the sake of the first and second.

There have been other times than ours, and there will again be others. Our time directs us, if we are not wholly deceived, in *this* direction. The Christian Church of all confessions and countries—I mention only two symptomatic examples—would have preserved a different attitude in 1914–18, and would have found a different word to speak at Stockholm in 1925, if it had not been sick. The Church will not regain health until it again dares to depend wholly, to build wholly, on the hope upon which it was founded.

Or we can say better: May the Lord lift up the light of his countenance upon us and be gracious unto us, that his Word may again reach us in full power as the Word of the Eternal God.

INDEX OF NAMES

INDEX OF SUBJECTS